Mario Colombo

MOTO GUZZI

GIORGIO NADA EDITORE

Giorgio Nada Editore s.r.l.

Editorial coordination
Daniele Antonietti

English translation
Alasdair McEwen

Editing
Claudia Converso

Cover
Barbara Bazzigaluppi

Acknowledgements
First and foremost the author and the publisher wish to thank the Moto Guzzi company of Mandello del Lario for their valuable cooperation and for all the assistance they supplied. A special thanks to Nicola Monti, Roberto Segoni and Pierlorenzo Vantini for the all-important contribution they made to the creation of this book. Finally thanks also to: Carlo Agostini, Luigi Agostini, Domenico Banalotti, Luigi Baroncelli, Renzo Berzi, Michele Bianchi, Jan Bianchetti, Roberto Bussinello, Renato Canessa, Giulio Cesare Carcano, Ettore Casadio, Romolo De Stefani, Piero and Giandomenico Fagioli, Libero Galanti, Enrico Lorenzetti, Giuseppe Massaro, Enzo Manili, Stefano Panciroli, Carlo Perelli, Umberto Todero and Gianmarco Torchi.

N.B.
Most of the photographs and documents reproduced or quoted in this book and, in particular, virtually all of the documentation published in the "catalogue" section, were made available by GBM S.p.A. of Mandello del Lario, the company which currently owns the Moto Guzzi marque. Other photographs were supplied by kind permission of *Motociclismo* magazine, or belong to the personal archives of Enrico Lorenzetti and Mario Colombo, while others again come from the following archives: Galbifoto, Grazia Neri, Publifoto and Franco Zagari (photographers Gandolfi, Scipi and Testi). The colour plates making up the colour section are by Giorgio Boschetti.

3rd edition revised and enlarged
© 1990 Giorgio Nada Editore, Vimodrone (Milan)

1st English language edition
© 1990 Giorgio Nada Editore, Vimodrone (Milan)

Moto Guzzi - ISBN: 88-7911-039-X

CONTENTS

PREFACE TO THE FIRST EDITION

Anyone picking up this book after having read the others in the same series would probably wonder "but what's so special about Moto Guzzi?". It would be all too easy to reply that it is certainly the most famous of the Italian marques, but this would be to beg the question. Are Guzzis famous because they won races, or because people liked them or because they sold better than the others? And if these are all concomitant factors, which of them is responsible for the current interest in the history of Moto Guzzi, and in the final analysis which is the most important?

It is not easy to supply a logical answer, given that the three criteria are neither homogeneous nor a fair basis for comparison. To ask yourself whether Brigitte Bardot was more beautiful than Golda Meir was intelligent is a nonsense. Functionality, beauty and pragmatism do not always go hand in hand: a bike can win a hundred races and still be ugly, while another model may achieve lasting fame simply because of its beauty. Neither beautiful nor ugly, the Model T Ford remains a milestone in the history of transportation because more of them were produced for longer than any other car, at least until the Volkswagen "Beetle" came along. It is extremely difficult to score a hat trick as far as our three criteria are concerned; about as hard as finding a woman who is extremely beautiful, very intelligent and gifted with a perfect personality. If such a creature existed, who could fail to fail in love with her? At the end of his monumental Critique of Pure Reason *Immanuel Kant states with lapidary precision, "beauty is that which pleases universally, without a concept" (ohne Begriffe); in other words, beauty is self evident and not something you need to rack your brains over. If we consider the unanimity with which both professionals and amateurs have acclaimed Moto Guzzi products for over fifty years (in Italy and abroad) we can only conclude that these bikes, like Ettore Bugatti's cars, constitute a rare example of a product possessing a balanced range of fine qualities.*

The real reasons for Moto Guzzi's currently high critical standing, reflected by the growing tendency to seek out and restore the marque's older models, have been obscured by the somewhat tiresome fashion for "revivals" which has recently substituted the fetishistic worship of liberty objects with the adoration of various manifestations of Art Déco: I refer in particular to the so-called "1925 style" which has spread rapidly from Paris to New York, aided and abetted substantially by serious film directors like Bertolucci.

If a critic makes a positive evaluation of the technical creations of the Twenties, he runs the risk of appearing like a species of cultural parasite who has battened on to the latest "revival". In other words, attempts to relate Guzzi, Isotta Fraschini or Hispano-Suiza products with Josephine Baker's banana skirt, seem to confer a certain order and logical consistency upon our little déco universe and this is tantamount to playing into the hands of fanatical collectors of period "icons". And given that most of these fads must soon pass, this means that tomorrow the spotlight will be fixed upon other frivolities, with the concomitant risk that, when it eventually falls out of favour, the "1925 style" will possibly take other creations worthy of lasting appreciation along with it.

The "1925" movement, of which Moto Guzzi has always been a part, was by no means a homogeneous affair. Perhaps it is precisely because of the enormous amounts of conflicting creative energies which characterized the period that the Twenties are still considered to be a crucial moment in the history of modern art and technology: but the roar of the "Roaring Twenties" was the sum of the most disparate noises: the despairing shout of the German expressionists, the forlorn echoes of the vanished Austro-Hungarian Empire, the dissipated folly of the victors of the Great War and the patriotic rantings of the Fascist blackshirts.

The relatively uniform technical and artistic universe of the belle époque *was shattered by the Great War and the Russian Revolution. Everything was suddenly topsy turvy and it seemed clear to all that the modern world, burdened by all the horrible social con-*

sequences of industrialization, was well on the road to a very sad end. There were some who wished to combat the enemy on his own ground: Le Corbusier, for example ("If the world belongs to the machine, then let the house be the perfect machine à habiter"). In point of fact the Soviet constructivists and the German functionalists tried to follow his lead – but they were too quick off the mark. The English garden cities and the entire Art Déco movement in general represent a desire to justify a refusal of the industrialized world with a prideful attempt to prolong the belle époque and the dominion of the precious, craft object, under the illusion that this comfortable model of society would be able to survive for some time to come.

However, these two ways of fighting the dictatorship of the machine did not develop along separate lines to emerge as easily distinguishable units, like the Swiss Guard and the troops of the SS. The threads are so closely woven together that it is often hard to see that they are not the work of the same hand. Adolf Loos, who preached that "ornamentation is a crime", was a refined dandy, and as big a snob as his Parisian client of 1925: Tristan Tzara. Still in 1925, Frank Lloyd Wright, the undisputed leader of the decorative liberty movement in American architecture, was experimenting with surprisingly modern prefabricated houses made of reinforced concrete. The Presidentielle railcar designed by Ettore Bugatti in 1931, had an interior which was a masterpiece of decoration, with walnut panelling just like the most luxurious English limousines, but the four Bugatti Royale engines which were so cleverly coupled to one another (the vehicle could run on one, two, three or four engines, to speeds of up to 180 km/h) represented a perfect example of automotive technology; in fact they ran for millions of kilometres, up to 1960, without – it is said – ever having been subjected to a major overhaul.

The German school of "neo-objectivism" or, more simply, "functionalism", influenced furnishings even more than architecture. The most outstanding examples are Marcel Breuer's seats and armchairs in chromed steel tubing. When Breuer saw this 20 mm tubing, which could be cold formed and produced at low cost for bicycle handlebars, he had an idea for a completely different application: and so the cycle frame (so closely related to the motorcycle frame) entered into that most private of areas, the home. It was no chance that all this happened in the Weimar republic, in Weimar itself in fact, in the Bauhaus founded by Walter Gropius, which was at the cutting edge of the rationalist movement. The BMW motorcycle was also pure Bauhaus in conception with its boxer engine and the frame devoid of the cycle-style double triangle, which had been replaced by a single straight line running from the steering head to the rear wheel. BMW has kept faith with this layout ever since and could not now do away with it and keep its identity at the same time.

Italy has nothing much to offer from this period. A combination of the worst kind of styling in the manner of D'Annunzio with a noisy brand of futurism, a movement which had lost its leading lights in the trenches, was unable to produce either artefacts or architecture of any value. Despite the apparent defiance of the Fascist slogan "me ne frego!" (I don't give a damn!), the average Italian remained attached to small, basically vulgar artefacts while the diffusion of "rational" furniture did not come about until after 1933, just when Germany was on the point of retracing its steps. From 1922 onwards Italian vehicle designers made a sudden, surprising leap forward. This trend began with the Scheider Trophy seaplanes: from Castoldi's Macchis to Rosatelli's Fiats, from Marchetti's Savoia to Pegan's Piaggio: perhaps the most beautiful aeroplanes in the history of aviation. Thoroughbred racehorses without any hidden military ambitions, the fact they were produced when the Italian airforce was being remodelled along fascist lines was mere coincidence, even though they were used to glorify the Fascist regime. The British, much more intelligently, used Mitchell's research on the Supermarine to produce the Spitfire, and the Germans played the same game by camouflaging their future bombers as fast transport planes.

In the motoring field the Lancia Lambda was an exceptional design event, since its original lines were the fruit of various technical innovations, like the bearing body, independent front suspension and the closely angled V engine. Compared to other production cars of the day, the Lambda offered something which was unmistakably new. The motorcycling equivalent of the racing aeroplanes and the Lambda, and linked to them by the motto "velocity equals victory" (a touch of post-war rhetoric was inevitable), was the first model created by Carlo Guzzi in 1921. In this case it was not as if motorcycles with flat cylinders did not already exist, or oversquare engines, or external flywheels (or hairpin valve springs either for that matter). Guzzi's achievement, which ranks along with that of Brunelleschi and Alberti in architecture, lies in having chosen precisely those components, which he then assembled in a simple and highly personal manner, in accordance with the rules of an adamantine logic. Since the horizontal cylinder with the characteristic longitudinal finning took up very little height – like the BMW – it was necessary to reduce the gap between the engine and the petrol tank, which up to that time had been connected to the horizontal strut of the frame. By angling this tube backwards and giving the tank a quasi-triangular shape as well as more width than was normal, Carlo Guzzi had taken a major step towards separating the motorcycle from its hitherto predominant image as a motorized bicycle. The typical large-diameter external flywheel, made with all the precision of a Berkel bacon slicer, also has its own aesthetic significance: it was a visible reminder of the machine's slowly beating heart (the engine's particularly regular performance was also due to the astute use of the flywheel masses). The rhythmic thump of the Guzzi was also an easily recognizable sound which we children of the Thirties learned to associate with the local bobbies on patrol. It was a sound for which we developed an acute sensitivity, as we had to be ever ready to hide the football we used for our illicit games in the city squares, still relatively free of traffic in those days.

Guzzi's merit also lies in having modified the initial design to create dozens of variants, for having experimented with two, three, four and

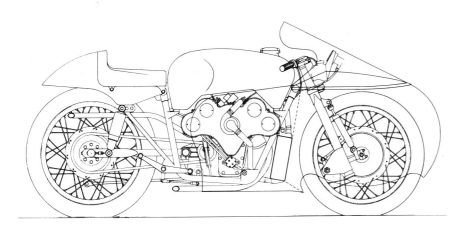

eight cylinders, and for remaining substantially faithful to his original vision; or rather, for preserving the integrity of the characteristic relationship between form and function. This relationship was immediate and simple, like the equally perfect British steam engines.

This is not a frequently occurring characteristic: the present day VWs and Porsches have nothing in common with the image of the rear-engined "Beetle" created by the great Ferdinand Porsche, and for a certain time VW was in the grip of what can only be called an identity crisis. The Japanese motorcycles, which have no claims to noble lineage, are imitations (albeit splendid ones) of other designs, the sources being British, (vertical singles and twins), German (boxers), Italian and American. Guzzi on the other hand, until a few years ago or so, remained faithful to its typical layout: the large flat single and the V-twin (if we can make an obvious exception for the racing bikes). The precise relationship, which we have

already mentioned, between form and function can be found in all the various designs, from economical and luxury models to touring bikes and military machines: but the archetypal Guzzi, which represents a pinnacle of technical and aesthetic perfection, still remains the Falcone and its descendants, many of which are still in harness today, and which are well on the way to beating Ford's so far unbeaten record for longevity.

But this peak was scaled in the Fifties, unfortunately, in a period when the success of the scooter and compacts like the Fiat 500 made it seem as if the motorcycle was doomed to become an unusual and even slightly snobbish item like the bicycle.

This was a disastrous moment for the major motorcycle manufacturers, all of whom took a severe beating (the British industry went to the wall definitively). But it was perhaps this momentary lapse of public attention which prevented Guzzi from giving in to the dictates of consumer society fads and the American taste for the bizarre.

The Fifties, that most unhappy moment for motor car design (especially in the United States where cars bore extravagant and unforgettable fins and bumper guards like the rostra on Roman war galleys), barely touched Guzzi, largely because motorcycle design, unlike motor car design, shuns the trite restyling exercises which still plague four-wheeled production to this day.

The reader, as he moves through the various stages of this honest and definitive technical history of Moto Guzzi and its sporting feats, will find it easy to follow the thread of the marque's development. But, if he wishes, he may also compare this story to the oeuvres of painters like Mondrian or Morandi, who seem to have painted the same picture three hundred times (with none of the freedom of expression displayed by a Picasso, for example). In reality the value of such artists lies in the fact that they have carried out a minute exploration of an artistic territory which is their own exclusive preserve, with an efficiency whose depth – and therefore value – is inversely proportional to the apparently limited nature of their subject matter.

I should not like this to sound blasphemous as far as pure art is concerned, but it is very probable that – if our civilization should resist for another two centuries or so – a Guzzi motorcycle conserved in a museum somewhere will be looked after with greater care and will attract a more enthusiastic public than the currently hosannaed works of many's the great contemporary artist.

November, 1977

Giovanni Klaus Koenig

THE ORIGINS

"We take pleasure in informing our numerous and deserving readership that next spring will see the launch on our market of a new Italian motorcycle. This new machine will be produced by a vigorous new limited company that has been established in recent months with the aim of creating a standardized motorcycle which will compete worthily against the best products in the world."

From the drawing board to the first success

This was the announcement which appeared in a December 1920 issue of a motorcycling magazine heralding the forthcoming appearance of the Moto Guzzi, a motorcycle developed upon the basis of new and exclusive technical, stylistic and functional criteria. At the beginning of 1921 the motorcycle was already quite a popular means of transport which had been around for at least a quarter of a century. A dispute has long raged – as happens with many seminal inventions – as to who was the inventor of the motorcycle. The first reliably documented effort was built in 1869 by an American called Silvester Roper who attached a 2-cylinder steam engine complete with boiler, firebox and chimney to a Hanlon bicycle. He was followed by the Frenchman Perreaux who, still in 1869, attached a steam engine to a Michaux bicycle, then the Englishmen Meek and Bateman, the Frenchman Vallée and many others. But all these vehicles remained at the prototype stage, in as far as the steam engine could not offer either lightness and manoeuverability, qualities which were typical of the new internal combustion engines and indispensable as far as motorcycles are concerned. Invented by Barsanti and Matteuci in 1853, the internal combustion engine was gradually improved by Lenoir, Otto and Langen, till Gottlieb Daimler, manager of the Otto and Langen works, managed to build one which was sufficiently light and powerful to be mounted on a vehicle (1885): with its swept volume of 246 cc it was able to supply 1/2 hp at 700 rpm. Daimler installed it on a wooden bicycle, which although rather rudimentary, already boasted some modern features, like twist-grip controls, and it worked fairly well. But its builder was thinking about the motor car, which in fact he was to build shortly afterwards, when he managed to construct an engine which was still light but more powerful, after which he no longer paid attention to motorcycles. Motorcycle innovations followed thick and fast, from the work of the Frenchman Millet to the American Copeland, the Italian Bernardi, up to the Germans Henry Hildebrand and Alois Wolfmüller who were the first to produce an industrial product (1894), which was launched with the aid of a heavyweight advertising campaign. Then came the famous De Dion with his tricycles, and the Werner brothers, two Russian emigré journalists living in Paris who appear to be responsible for coining the word *motocyclette* (up to then people talked of motor-powered bicycles), and the Czechs Lamrin and Klement, one a mechanic and the other a librarian. Then, little by little, in the early years of the new century, we come to those great names that in many cases have survived to this day: the British marques Norton, AJS, Ariel, Triumph, BSA, Sunbeam, the German NSU and Fafnir, the American Indian and Harley-Davidson, the French Peugeot, the Belgian FN, the Italian Lazzati, Rosselli, Stucchi, Edoardo Bianchi, Frera, Della Ferrera, Gilera, and many others.

Lombardy was at the forefront of the Italian motorcycling industry in those pioneer days and in 1989 a certain marquis Michele Carcano founded an engine and motorcycle factory at Anzano del Parco, a location in the Brianza area not too far from Mandello del Lario. Around the time of the Great War the motorcycle was already an established product and a profitable industrial enterprise, not to mention a relatively efficient vehicle. This was demonstrated by its widespread use throughout the conflict. However it was always a highly particular vehicle, that demanded enthusi-

By 1925 Guzzi was already a leading marque, even outside Italy. Number 1 is Guido Corti from Lecco, an athletic racing star and pioneer of alpine motorcycling. Number 2 is Pietro Ghersi, who was to make a valiant assault on the TT course the following year; number 3 is Carlo Guzzi, wearing his usual cap; number 4 is Amedeo Ruggeri, from Bologna, the winner of the Lario event that year and father of Luigi and Jader, also excellent riders; number 5 is Giorgio Parodi, Guzzi's partner and last of all, number 6 is Ugo Prini, Milanese, a veteran of the Circuito del Lario and eight-time winner. On the extreme left is Carlo Agostini, alias "il Moretto", one of the very first Guzzi employees and later the famous foreman mechanic in the Guzzi race shop.

Giuseppe Guzzi, nicknamed "Naco", was Carlo's elder brother. Busy with other professional activities, he took only an occasional interest in the motorcycle company. But he made a major contribution to the invention of the sprung frame, developed in conjunction with Carlo Guzzi during 1927. Here we see him among pupils of the motorcycling riding school, organized by Guzzi for the employees, with the dual aim of teaching them how to ride and creating a "nursery" of works riders at the same time.

asm, competence and a spirit of sacrifice before it could be used. Let's skip the issue of danger: this is an undeserved stigma which has dogged the motorcycle since its inception. We say undeserved because it is not the motorcycle which causes problems but the rider: but there is no doubt that certain technical features from that period appeared to have been made on purpose to discourage the honest and right-thinking customer.

Starting required ability, and luck into the bargain, while the hand-pumped lubrication systems did more to oil the rider's clothes than the engine. The primary drive chain running from the engine to the gearbox, almost always exposed, was the kiss of death for trousers (because of this the rider was obliged to wear puttees like some of his less fortunate countrymen at the Front). Suspension systems and brakes were for the most part merely symbolic. As if this were not enough, the makers almost always sought to obtain maximum speed, while the idea of making mechanical units able to withstand the stress and vibration involved was yet to gain currency. Unsurprisingly, breakdowns were the order of the day. It was clear that if the motorcycle were to become the truly widespread and popular vehicle which its cheapness and practicality merited then many things would have to change, both in terms of design and construction.

These were Carlo Guzzi's beliefs when he designed his motorcycle, a machine which by today's standards could not be deemed revolutionary, since nearly all the features it embodied had already been tried and tested even though they had never been assembled in one single invention. Guzzi's great merit lay in the fact that he created a synthesis of the most rational and advanced technology of the day and, more importantly, also of the years to come.

Being ahead of its time was to become a characteristic peculiar to Moto Guzzi, which in a few years was able to win a position of pre-eminence and supremacy long envied by the whole world. Furthermore, Carlo Guzzi intended to establish production upon solid industrial principles, in order to obtain the economies of construction that only volume production can provide, so as to offer the user a robust, long-lasting and efficient product which would also resist depreciation.

Originally from Milan, the Guzzi family owned a couple of houses at the turn of the century in Mandello-Tonzanico (later the name was to change to Mandello del Lario), then a small fishing village ten kilometres or so north of Lecco on the eastern bank of lake Como. The children Giuseppe, the oldest, Carlo and their two sisters therefore grew up breathing the healthy air of the lake, which became their definitive home when the mother, of English origin, moved to Mandello during the First World War.

A born engineer, with a great spirit of observation and sense of practicality, the young Carlo Guzzi conceived a passion for the engines (the mysteries of which were revealed to him by Giorgio Ripamonti, the Mandello blacksmith, the greatest expert in the area at the time) and the motorcycles of that period, which he was soon happily dismantling in his home workshop. But the motorcycles of those days, so defect-ridden, could not satisfy a man like Guzzi, who decided to solve the problem in his own way, i.e. by designing a machine the way he thought it should be done.

The bike he had in mind when he had to leave for the war had a four-stroke 500 cc engine, a capacity considered medium- small at the time, but which was able to provide sufficient performance for the great mass of potential customers. The cylinder was laid flat and faced forwards so that the head would be cooled by the air stream. The bore measured 88 mm against a stroke of only 82: an undersquare engine therefore, as normally used today, but an absolute novelty in the motorcycling field at the time. The short stroke tended to slow down the connecting rod, thus reducing the stress on that member, while the considerable bore made it possible to fit larger diameter valves which meant the engine could "breathe" easier. The engine was to have a large external flywheel, which would drastically reduce vibration and enable the design of the crank gear and crankcase to be more robust and compact. The latter, made of aluminium, would accomodate both the drive shaft and the gearbox, so as to have only one lubrication circuit thus eliminating the primary drive chain and all its inconveniences. In its place there was to be a helical gear pair, a rather sophisticated idea for those days, but nonetheless elegant and rational.

Since the gearbox (the three speed variety with *train balladeur*, i.e. sliding gears) was in constant mesh, the result was that the engine turned in the opposite direction to the wheels, something considered to be highly original at the time. Design considerations apart, this inverted rotation made for better lubrication, since the oil that flowed out of the big end lubricated the upper wall of the cylinder by splash, before gravity drew it down to the bottom end. Normal rotation, on the other hand, would have carried the oil directly to the bottom, thus leaving the top end dry. It is noteworthy, since we are on the subject, that one of the secrets of the extraordinary longevity and resistance to fatigue of the old Guzzi singles lay in this abundant and intelligent lubrication system, which was complemented by an oil reservoir mounted in an ideal place for cooling. And in an air-cooled engine with no fan, as is the case with the overwhelming majority of motorcycles, a generous supply of oil is essential for a long and trouble-free working life.

In order to house this rather low engine, Guzzi thought of a very low slung chassis so as to improve stability and comfort; as a result the rider could assume a position almost as if he were sitting in an arm chair. The frame was a tubular duplex cradle (unsprung at the rear), formed by two elements which descended from the handlebars and diverged to cradle the cylinder, before passing below the crankcase and coming together at the rear triangle, thus ensuring a notable resistance to torsional stress. But war was soon to interrupt Carlo Guzzi's motorcycling dreams and aspirations and he found himself wearing the uniform of Italy's fledgling Air Force, whose glamorous appeal had attracted the flower of the country's youth. At this point Fate threw him in with two young pilot officers who were as mad about motorbikes as he was: Giorgio Parodi and Giovanni Ravelli.

Giorgio Parodi belonged to an old and well-known family of Genoan shipowners with business acumen in their blood; Giovanni Ravelli, on the other hand, was already a famous name in the world of motorcycling. Originally from Brescia, he had been one of the best racers of the pre-war period with numerous important victories to his credit.

Emanuele Vittorio Parodi in a photograph dating from 1940. Giorgio's father and Angelo's uncle, he put up the initial capital for his son's and Carlo Guzzi's business with a letter – shown on the following page – which has become part of the Mandello legend. Parodi later took over the chairmanship of the company, which he retained until his death. He was a typical Genoan entrepreneur, active in the naval armaments sector and in industry. Prudent and parsimonious, he was the first to inspire that reputation for straight dealing, which along with product reliability and sporting success, is the pillar upon which the company's image has rested for sixty years.

Carlo Guzzi stimulated his friends' lively interest when he told them that he was planning a motorcycle with an unorthodox frame and engine configuration. The three of them talked at length about the project, and decided that when the war was over they would set up a joint venture aimed at producing the bike. Each partner had his appointed task in this regard: Guzzi, the engineer, would be in charge of construction; Ravelli, the rider, would be the standard bearer of the new vehicle, publicizing it on the race-track while Parodi would guarantee the financial backing needed to get the venture off the ground.

The letter written to his son Giorgio by Emanuele Vittorio Parodi, head of the dynasty, dated 3 January 1919 has since become legendary: "…the answer you should therefore communicate to your partners is that, by and large, I'm in favour, and that the 1,500 or 2,000 lire needed for the first tests is at your disposal, on the condition that this sum is in no way exceeded. I also reserve the right to examine the project personally, before lending my definitive support to a serious launch of the product. Furthermore, if by good fortune I should like what I see, I am willing to invest much more without further limits."

Emanuele Vittorio Parodi, like a true Genoan, wanted to have a particularly good look at the project before releasing the purse

GENOVA 3/I/1919

EMANUELE V. PARODI

Caro Giorgio ,

La tua del 30 mi è giun-
ta stamane .Parte fra poco per Roma e ti
devo quindi scrivere affrettatamente .

Già sapeva per notizie avute non da me
ma da altra persona aRoma che vi era colà la
proposta per una terza medaglia d'argento .:non
te ne ho parlato perchè non avendolo io appre-
so personalmente non sapeva se la cosa fosse po
sitiva . Mentre ciò è conferma a quanto tu pure
hai sentito , mi spiego ora perchè mai da tanto
tempo la pratica non sia andata avanti .Certo
tu fai più che bene a non protestare e a non
sollecitare ,ed a mantenerti piuttosto scettico
sulla sostanza di queste attestazioni se esse
debbono subordinarsi a quanto mi dici .E' ben
vero che ciò torna poi a discapito a chi le ha
seriamente ed effettivamente meritate !
Sull'altro argomento ho poco da dirti .Propen-
so per natura ad incoraggiare ogni iniziativa,

non sarò certo io che mi opporrò all'esperimento di cui mi parli . Però non posso neanche con
te spogliarmi della mia qualità,di industriale
e di uomo che deve valutare la cosa anche sotto
l'aspetto pratico .
Per conseguenza tu d vresti non dire che hai
un capitale proprio , bensì dichiarare che
ricorri a me per fornirlo , dandomi così il
diritto di intervenire per discutere, vagliare
e sindacare , prima che la cosa sia definitiva-
mente stabilita .
Anche se tecnicamente sono poco più di un asi-
no , tuttavia mi sento in grado di pote-r dare
un giudizio abbastanza competente e pratico
sulla convenienza e sulla probabilità di sucess
in una simile impresa .
La risposta che dovresti quindi dare ai tuoi
compagni è che io sono favorevole in massima ,
che le 1500 o 2000 lire pel I° esperimento sono
a tua disposizione ,a condizione che la cifra
non sia assolutamente sorpassata , ma che mi ri-
servo di esaminare personalmente il progetto , e

prima di assicurare il mio appoggio definitivo
per lanciare seriamente il prodotto .
Chè se per fortunata ipotesi esso mi piacesse
sono disposto ad andare molto avanti senza
limitazione di cifre .
Ed a proposito già che mi parli di Ravelli ,
desidererei sapere se egli ti ha più fatta la
restituzione di quella somma o se almeno ti
ha mostrato il desiderio di farlo o se ha invee
ce dimenticato .
Domani mi occuperò del tuo congedo o licenza
e ti scriverò .
Appena ritornato qui (non prima del 9 perchèil
giorno 8 devo essere a Milano) scriverò anche
a Canepa .

strings definitively and he even went to the Manufacturers' Association in order to inform himself regarding the number of motorcycles in circulation, national production levels, and imports; in other words he carried out a fairly thorough piece of market research. Having received a favourable impression, he supplied the 2,000 lire which his son and Guzzi needed. There were only two of them by that time, since Giovanni Ravelli had died in a tragic flying accident a few days after the end of the War. It was in his memory that the Air Force spread eagle was chosen to adorn the Moto Guzzi nameplate.

During 1920 the prototype of the new motorcycle began to take shape, first in the basement of the Guzzi's house in Mandello and then in Ripamonti's smithy.

The machine was initialled "G.P." (Guzzi and Parodi). At a later stage Giorgio Parodi, in order to make sure – or so it was said – that such initials would not be confused with his own, an example of the reserve typical of the well-to-do from his part of the country, insisted on the name "Moto Guzzi", which became the registered trade mark. The machine showed traces of its designer's aeronautical experience. The timing gear consisted of four parallel overhead valves controlled by an overhead camshaft which took its power from the engine via a shaft and two bevel

Genoa 3/1/1919
Dear Giorgio,
Your letter of the 30th has reached me this morning. I shall leave for Rome in a short while and so I shall be brief.
Thanks to information received not from me but from a third party in Rome, I already knew that there had been talk of a third silver medal, but I did not tell you about it because not having access to first-hand information I was unsure as to the accuracy of my information. This confirms what you have heard, and I now understand why the whole affair has made no progress for such a long time. You are quite right in refusing to protest and solicit a response and you do well to persist in your rather sceptical stance regarding the worth of such tokens if they are really subordinated to the things you mention. It is so true that such things end up by damaging the people who effectively and genuinely deserve (to receive) them. As far as the other matter is concerned I have little to say. I am inclined by nature to encourage every initiative, and would be the last one to oppose the experiment of which you speak. But at the same time, I cannot forget the fact of my industrial training and my consequent need to evaluate the practical aspects of the business. It therefore follows that you should not mention the fact that you possess capital of your own, but rather you should say that you have turned to me for financial backing. In this way you give me the right to take a hand and have things thoroughly checked out before anything is finalized.
Even if technically I am little more than an ignoramus, I nonetheless feel able to give a reasonably competent opinion on the suitability and on the probability of success which such a venture might hold. The answer you should therefore communicate to your partners is that, by and large, I'm in favour, and that the 1,500 or 2,000 Lire needed for the first tests is at your disposal, on the condition that this sum is in no way exceeded. I also reserve the right to personally examine the project, before lending my definitive support to a serious launch of the product. Furthermore, if by good fortune I should like what I see, I am willing to invest much more without further limits.
And since you mention Ravelli, I shuld like to know if he ever paid you back that sum, or if he has evinced any desire to do so, or whether he has merely forgotten about it.
I shall see about your discharge tomorrow and I shall let you know.
As soon as I return (no sooner than the 9th because I have to be in Milan on the 8th) I shall also write to Canepa.
Affectionately yours,

gear pairs. Other aviation characteristics included the four valves closed by hairpin springs and the dual ignition circuit (with two spark plugs fired by a shielded Bosch magneto), which guaranteed perfect results even with the relatively large combustion chambers typical of undersquare engines. With a very modest compression ratio of 3,5:1 (which after all was about the best you could get from the fuel sold in those days) this engine provided a dozen horses, enough to propel the bike to almost 100 km/h. It was a little too complex however, expensive and futuristic. When the time came for it to be mass-produced, Guzzi preferred to shelve the overhead camshaft and the four valves for a while, because these were still delicate parts and prone to breaking. However Guzzi was not content with orthodox engineering and so when the definitive model, known as the *Normale* (Standard), was put on sale in early 1921 it had an opposed valve engine with nickel-steel valve gear: the inlet valve at the side was closed by a coil spring while the overhead exhaust valve was actuated by a push-rod and rocker arm and closed by a hairpin spring.

The opposed valve engine was not new in itself, but the idea of positioning the exhaust valve in the head instead of the inlet definitely was. The advantage of this was that the valve most prone to overheating was exposed directly to the airflow: but this was not all, the route taken by the exhaust tract was much improved and this led to faster, more efficient evacuation of the exhaust gases. The cylinder was made of cast iron with radial finning, given its horizontal disposition, as was the head, which was attached to the block by three long studs. The aluminium piston sported four rings, grouped two by two, and two oil scrapers. The tubular section nickel-steel con-rod ran on special bronze bearings, with an etched effect for lubrication purposes.

The crankshaft, also in nickel-steel, was a one-piece fitting with screwed-in circular counterweights; there were internal ducts for big-end lubrication. The shaft itself ran on large diameter bearings. It was rounded off by the enormous pressed steel external flywheel (280 mm in diameter), which soon became a Guzzi trademark and a source of ironic comments (it was nicknamed the "bacon slicer"). The vertically split crankcase was composed of two aluminium castings. On the left hand side there was a cover behind which were fitted the gear pair with the primary drive transmission shock absorber and the multiplate clutch. On the right there was a vertical casting which enclosed the drives for the valve gear, the Bosch magneto with manual advance and the oil pump. The first models had semi-automatic lubrication systems: a hand-operated pump sent the oil from the main reservoir, mounted at the front under the petrol tank, to a small sump under the crankcase from where a gear pump driven by the crankshaft sent it under pressure to the gooseneck. As yet there was no scavenge pump, this was to come along in 1922, and therefore this was still a total-loss system, but the quantity of lubricant held by the sump was sufficient for about 70 kilometres, and so it was not necessary to pump continuously when on the road.

Fuel feed was handled by an English Amac semi-automatic slide carburettor, with twin hand levers for the throttle and the choke. Still on the right hand side, the crankcase was rounded off by a curious convex cover which hid the kick start mechanism, the Renold chain final drive pinion and the two concentric clutch springs; these held the plates together by means of a rod which ran the length of the mainshaft.

The frame was the same one as had been fitted to the prototype, a full tubular duplex cradle. However it was a one-piece unit (on the G.P. the rear triangle was bolted together) braced in the middle by a box-like structure made of sheet metal which ran down from the saddle to cradle the lower part of the engine. The front fork was a tubular parallelogram fitting with two central springs operating in traction. There were no dampers.

The spoked wheels were shod with Dunlop 26" × 2 1/2 beaded

The original prototype, built by Carlo Guzzi in the basement of his house with the help of a blacksmith from Mandello and a few other occasional collaborators. The ohc engine had four valves, a solution later discarded for economic reasons. The machine, known as the G.P., can still be admired today at the Guzzi works in Mandello del Lario, on the Lecco branch of lake Como, an area with a strong metalworking tradition.

The Guzzi plant in its first years of operation. Next to the office block the first workshops can be seen, built between the railway embankment and the slopes of mount Grigna. The scant available space had a strong influence on the way the factory was organized.

edge tyres. The rear hub was mounted on ball bearings with a spindle which could be removed from the right hand side. There was no front brake, but the rear wheel was fitted with a lateral drum brake with twin shoes and twin cams, of which one was actuated by a lever on the right handlebar and the other by a pedal fitted on the left hand side.

The presence of this super-brake on the backwheel may appear strange, especially when we know that during deceleration the weight shifts forwards and it is therefore the front brake which has the greatest effect. But one must not forget that on the awful roads of the Twenties wheels could lock in a trice, and it was therefore a better idea to brake hard with the back wheel, which handles better than the front wheel in the event of a skid.

Available power was around 8 hp, enough to take the intrepid motorcyclist to beyond 80 km/h; consumption was around 30 km/litre of petrol and 350 km/litre of oil. Pulling power was exceptional at low speeds and this made the bike virtually unbeatable on steep gradients, while at idling speed the engine was more reliable than a pacemaker.

The 10 litre petrol tank had a semi-circular metal tool box mounted on top and other fitments included a very low-slung Brooks saddle (only 62 cm above the ground), handlebars made of 25 mm tubing (complete with Bowden levers), and a capacious luggage rack. There were no lights: those valiant souls who felt like braving the roads at night had to put their faith in an acetylene lamp, supplied as an optional.

All that remained was to launch the product and hope that it would overcome that certain diffidence with which the public tended to greet novelties of this kind.

The most striking thing about a new Moto Guzzi was its appearance, which was markedly different to most motorcycles then on sale. It had a rather spartan profile, in which every detail was dictated not by chance, tradition or aesthetic considerations but by strictly functional criteria: it was a fundamentally utilitarian object, built in accordance with certain canons of industrial design which are common currency today but which were virtually unknown at the time.

The Guzzis go racing

The classic way to advertise a motorcycle, which was after all a sporting vehicle, was racing. In those days this consisted predominantly of long distance road races, partly because the Autodromes had yet to make their appearance (Monza dates from 1922, for example), and partly because such events were seen as better showcases for the durability and the resistance of the bikes. Some particularly demanding events included the so-called North-South Raid from Milan to Naples, the Circuito del Piave which took in the Falzarego, Pordoi and Rolle passes, the extremely fast Circuito di Cremona, the Sicilian Targa Florio, and the Circuito del Lario, which was run over the roads of Valbrona and Vallassina, held for the first time in 1921.

Guzzi made its sporting debut in the 1921 Milano-Napoli event, with riders Mario Cavedini, already a well known star, and Aldo Finzi, an outstanding sportsman and Member of Parliament, who lost his life in the tragic Fosse Ardeatine massacre. Finzi had been particularly impressed by the motorcycle after a short trial, and he later insisted that Carlo Guzzi let him ride one in the long-distance race. It was only after considerable pressure from Finzi that Guzzi agreed to enter the only two motorcycles which he had built so far.

The race left Milan in the late evening. Cavedini reached Bologna at 22.06. Two minutes after that Finzi arrived to be greeted, as a newspaper of the time reports, "...by a real ovation just like the one which accompanied his departure. A fall in the outskirts of Modena has put his headlight out of commission, and he will therefore race through the night aided by nothing more than the light of the moon. His Guzzi, the new original Italian machine, has sparked off keen interest and favourable comment." At the finish line in Napoli Cavedini was to come twenty-first and Finzi twenty-second. The average speed was about 44 km/h.

A month later, Aldo Finzi's brother Gino was to give the fledgling marque from Mandello its first taste of victory with a win in the famous Targa Florio, a very tough event raced over some truly atrocious roads. This was the first of a long series of victories, that developed into a continuous *crescendo* over the following years: there were two in 1922 (the Circuito del Piave and the Ravelli Cup with Mario Cavedini), four in 1923, twenty-one in 1924, thirty-two in 1925, forty-two in 1926, sixty-two in 1927....By now the motorcycle was known, demand was growing and this required production on an industrial scale. The *Società Anonima Moto Guzzi* – officially founded on 15 March 1921 by Chairman Emanuele Vittorio Parodi with registered offices in Genoa – built its first plant on a 300 square metre site which overlooked the workshop where the early experiments had taken place. Ten or so workers were hired, some of whom are still alive and deserve to be remembered here, men such as Carlo Agostini, nicknamed "il Moretto", who was later to become the master tuner in charge of the race shop, and Giovanni Gaddi, for many years the head of the assembly division. Angelo Parodi, an engineer and cousin to Giorgio, entered the business and responsibilities were assigned on a definitive basis. Carlo Guzzi – who soon after was joined by his engineer brother Giuseppe – was to head the technical side, Parodi was to look after administration.

Different men in many ways, Carlo Guzzi and Giorgio Parodi nonetheless shared what might be called a certain mutual interest in thrift, which doubtless helped the company over the leaner times. Giorgio Parodi was also brash and impulsive, he loved racing and did not hesitate to try the machines on the most demanding circuits, even after sustaining several spectacular falls. But this was nothing to a man who had left several of his own components on various fronts during the war, for which sacrifice a grateful government had awarded him an imposing series of silver and bronze medals.

Carlo Guzzi, instead was reserved and calm (and also a little stubborn) and, even though he had a passion for every conceivable type of experiment, he did not like racing. According to him everything was worth a try, but preferably on a test bench. He had built a "dummy" engine, a large box which could accept pistons and cylinders of every size, in order to be able to test everything that went through his head, even the most absurd and

The 1923 Circuito del Lario witnessed the victorious debut of the C 2V, the first Guzzi racer. Standing round the bike are; from the left, Cavedini, Guzzi, Parodi, Mentasti, winner Gatti and Ghersi. "il Moretto" can be seen peering out between Gatti and Ghersi.

The *C 2V* made another appearance that same year, this time at the Circuito di Cremona. Younger readers will notice with some astonishment the heterogeneous riding gear affected by the riders, who virtually never used boots.

17

The 1921 North-South event launched the fledgling Guzzi concern on the road to fame as the Mandello concern entered the first (and only) two motorcycles built up to then. The picture shows the usual assembly on the outskirts of Milan shortly before the start.
The *Quattro valvole* model with the prototype G.P. valve gear soon notched up a string of wins. On the straights of the Circuito di Cremona, on June 1924, it established the world record for the flying ten kilometres at 135.542 km/h. Below, from the right, Guido Mentasti, Pietro Ghersi, Carlo Guzzi, Valentino Gatti.

exaggerated notions. "I know that this is daft – he used to say to his assistants – but let's give it a try all the same" and in fact he called his gadget, the "mad machine". He appreciated beautiful women (whereas Giorgio Parodi was more of an ascetic), but even *amore* was a matter for calm and moderation. He was down to earth to a fault and very often he would dismiss those ideas which he found too bold (read "expensive"), inviting his colleagues to be more prosaic and less poetic (read "less expensive"). Convinced of the validity of his original idea, he continued developing it until neither he nor his cheque book could be persuaded to go any further. But let's get back to the bikes.

The first engine modifications date from 1922 and were dictated by racing experience and the demands of the first users. Just for a start, the bike received an automatic lubrication system in which a gear pump drew the oil up directly from the tank and sent it under pressure to the crankshaft. Oil which had collected at the bottom of the crankcase was picked up by a vane-type pump, coaxial with the pressure pump, and sent back to the tank. The total flow rate was 60 litres an hour, which ensured abundant lubrication and rapid heat exchange. Then the dual ignition circuit, rendered somewhat superfluous by the excellent functioning of the engine, was relegated to the optionals list. In place of the second spark plug they began fitting a special stay inside the combustion chamber which would catch a broken exhaust valve before it "dropped in". Other minor tuning modifications and an uprated compression ratio of 4.7:1 brought output up to 8.5 hp at 3400 rpm. The next year (1923), witnessed the birth of a new model, which can rightly be called the first Guzzi racer.

Up to then in fact, race participation had been limited to a slightly souped-up version of the *Normale*, but in order to have greater chances of success Guzzi decided that something more powerful was required. He plumped for an engine with two overhead valves, a layout which did not require major alterations. The two parallel valves were actuated by exposed push-rod and rocker assemblies and closed by two hairpin springs; the rocker assemblies were both fitted with Stauffer lubricators. This engine too had dual ignition, with two 18 mm spark plugs fitted to the sides of the combustion chamber. When the engine went into production the dual ignition circuit became an optional.

The piston was redesigned by mounting three simple compression rings and an oil-scraper. The carburettor, with its intake manifold facing the rear instead of the side, was a 25 mm Amac Race type. The internal gear ratios were slightly modified.

The frame too underwent some alteration: the wheelbase was increased in order to improve roadholding on the straights while

MOTO GUZZI

the box-type structure at the rear was substituted by a tubular element, which meant some increase in weight.

The new machine, named the *Corsa 2V* (the *C2V* for short), made its debut at the Circuito del Lario in 1923 where it notched up a good win at over 61 km/h. It was ridden by Carlo Guzzi's brother-in-law Valentino Gatti, a factory test rider who became one of the best racing riders of those years. Among the other noteworthy exploits of the *C 2V* in its first year of life there was a first place in the "Giro Motociclistico d'Italia", with Guido Mentasti, and a Monza lap record at an average speed of 128 km/h. Towards the end of 1923 it was decided that the new frame would also be used for the opposed valve engine. The *Normale* model was therefore deleted (a total of 2,065 units had been built, a few of which were sold in 1924) and substituted by the *Sport* type which remained in production until 1928. This bike was also available with a sidecar (and in this case it was fitted with a front brake), not to mention a complete set of electrics fed by a Bosch dynamo-magneto, an assembly wherein the two devices were enclosed within a single aluminium body, which was fitted instead of the normal magneto: these are signs that motorcycles had become roadworthy and safe enough to tackle the heaviest and most demanding working conditions.

Guido Corti astride the *Quattro valvole* in the paddock at the Circuito del Lario. Corti rarely missed entering the classic Italian event, but he never managed to win it. Below, Mentasti with the *Quattro valvole*. Looking on from the pits are Giorgio Parodi and Carlo Guzzi. For the speed events the motorcycle was made as light as possible and even the mudguards were sacrificed. Mentasti won the first European championship in 1924.

The first Grand Prix: the four-valvers make a comeback

The *C 2V* was a good machine but, even though it gave some excellent performances in long-distance races, it was not able to keep pace with its rivals on the track at a time when special Grand Prix racers were beginning to supplant the modified production models which had been used up to then. If the Mandello concern's reputation was to be maintained, something more powerful than the *C 2V* had to be produced. In 1924 Carlo Guzzi began thinking about dusting off his old prototype. Updated where necessary, a sohc four-valve engine was just what the doctor ordered as far as racing was concerned.

The modifications made to what had become the classic Guzzi engine layout concerned the timing chest, widened in order to contain the bevel gear pair which supplied the power for the camshaft drive; the cylinder, the cylinder-head and the crankcase.

The aluminium timing cover, which enclosed the driven bevel gear pair and the camshaft, was lubricated under pressure. The four valves, at a tilt relative to the cylinder axis but in two parallel pairs, were closed by hairpin springs and there was a valve lifter for easier starting. The 28.5 mm Amac carburettor was unique,

The cylinder head of the *Quattro valvole*, that is the competition model known as the *C 4V*, with the aluminium rocker box. The valves were closed by hairpin springs while the small lever with the coil spring inserted on the Bowden cable actuated the valve-lifter. Various oil pipes are also clearly visible. The model in the photograph has recently been restored.

with a dog-leg intake manifold which split into two branches just before it joined the head. There were two exhaust pipes, one on each side. In those years the anti-knock qualities of petrol had been greatly improved, thanks to the employment of the first additives. But that was not all, racing regulations permitted the use of special fuels containing benzole and other ingredients. It was therefore possible to run on a compression ratio of 6:1, which gave 22 hp at 5500 rpm. The frame was basically as before, with a few differences due to the new engine dimensions, whilst the front fork was fitted with a large centrally mounted Hartford-type adjustable damper. A rim brake was fitted to the front wheel (and to the rear wheel too, for certain races), while the usual drum brake was mounted at the rear. The capacity of the oil tank was considerably enlarged. Overall weight was around 130 kg.

Success greeted the debut apparance of this bike (officially baptized the *C 4V* at the Circuito del Lario event, which was won by Pietro Ghersi at an average of 67.630 km/h with two other *C 4Vs* taking second and fourth position. It went on to win many other races and September found it on the starting grid at the Monza Autodrome, which was hosting the first ever Championship of Europe one day event (the World Championship did not come along until 1949). For this occasion, the triangular rear frame element was braced by an additional horizontal strut, the front brake was eliminated and the oil tank was fitted on top of the petrol tank, a feature typical of Guzzi racing models for many years afterwards. Another noteworthy feature was the oil return tube at the front of the frame, which ran up to the tank in a series of wide serpentine curves to form a species of rudimentary oil cooler. This race was another successful outing for the Mandello firm, which virtually swept the board with Guido Mentasti in first place (he was an ex-works rider for the Frera team who had been notching up win after win aboard Guzzis for the previous two years), Erminio Visioli second and Pietro Ghersi fifth. For the overall distance of 400 km, Mentasti averaged 130 km/h and had a best lap of 136.200 km/h, therefore top speed can safely be estimated at something like 150 km/h.

This win caused a considerable furore, because it was the first time an Italian machine had carved out a place for itself among the great 500s, until then a capacity class which had been virtually monopolized by foreign makes, the British ones in particular. The Secretary of the International Federation, T.W. Loughborough, normally a dispassionate, reserved person who seemed almost a stereotype of the phlegmatic Englishman, let himself get carried away just for once: "I am pleased to congratulate Messrs Guzzi and Mentasti", he wrote at the end of the race, "on their magnificent victory. The three Guzzis, so unorthodox in comparison with most of today's machines, dominated the event virtually from beginning to end, thus proving the importance of the Italian motorcycle industry." This elogy amounted to a very important form of recognition, especially since it was pronounced by an influential representative of a nation with a great motorcycling tradition, which had emerged soundly beaten after a most demanding test. Some weeks later Pietro Ghersi won the German Grand Prix at the famous Berlin Autodrome, the Avus, and before the advent of winter the *C 4V* also broke various long and middle-distance world records at speeds varying from 130 km/h over a distance of 800 km, to 149 km/h for the 100 kilometres. The *C 4V* remained one of the fastest half-litre models in the world for some while and it continued to win numerous events, both in Italy and abroad. A series of intelligent modifications brought power up 30 hp and top speed to beyond 160 km/h, and this enabled the bike to break some of its own records. But the competition was hot on its heels and it was eventually sidelined as thoughts of a new machine began to take concrete shape, the *250*. The *C 4V* was still produced on a small scale for non-works riders, in versions which were the fruit of Guzzi's steadily growing stock of racing experience.

So it was that the *C 4V*, which was sold from 1924 till 1927 for 12,300 lire, gave way to the *4V TT* (built between 1927 and 1929) and to the quicker version, the *4V SS*, produced between 1928 and 1933. These were direct descendants of the works bike that had won the 1926 Circuito del Lario with Ghersi riding what was the first machine to be fitted with a Binks-type hand operated throttle control and a steering damper, as well as peculiar German-made Gazda handlebars made up of a nine-leaf spring. The *4 V TT* had a nickel-steel crankshaft and – for the first time on a Guzzi 500 – the con-rod big-end ran on needle bearings instead of bushes. The valves were made of chrome-steel wolfram, while there was a Bosch magneto, an Amac or Binks carburettor, and a bronze cylinder-head, which offered better heat conduction than cast iron. The frame was a rebuild, with two upper struts (from the steering to the saddle), a fully triangulated rear section and a rhombus-shaped front fork with a large spring in compression, two countersprings in traction and adjustable friction dampers at each side.

The gradually decreasing section of the frame elements was obtained by fitting tubes of a different diameter inside one other. Both wheels carried drum brakes, while the oil was contained in a compartment at the front of the petrol tank. The footrests had been shifted aft, compared to the *C 4V*, to a point directly below

The Guzzi factory team at the beginning of the Thirties, posing behind the *Quattro valvole* model. From the left, Amilcare Moretti, Alfredo Panella, Terzo Bandini (with his hands in his pockets) winner of the Italian 500 championship in 1930, 1931 and 1932; Riccardo Brusi, Ugo Prini (wearing gloves) and Carlo Fumagalli (who had apparently run out of hair-oil). Below, Primo Moretti from Macerata (another Guzzi stalwart, as was his son Giovanni): he too is astride the *Quattro valvole*.

the seat. On top of the tank there was a tool-box. The *4V TT* pumped out 27 hp, cost 8,900 lire and was shod with 27" × 3.00 tyres. The *4V SS* had a more powerful engine that produced twenty or so horse-power and a distinctive large oil tank positioned above the petrol tank. The tools were kept in a leather saddle-bag on the right hand side of the frame, next to the final drive chain. This bike was also equipped with a bronze head, which was replaced with a cast iron component in 1930. The last models had an Amal carburettor. The *4V SS* cost 9,600 lire (before the price fell to 7,950) and could be fitted with Bosch electrics and magneto-dynamo in exchange for an extra thousand lire.

The "Quattro valvole" made another official appearance in 1932. The engine was fed by a twin carb with a single float chamber, and power and speed had been upped to 32 hp and 170 km/h respectively, but the gearbox was still the hand-operated three-speed unit from eight years before. This machine notched up its last victory in the Milano-Napoli event (with Carlo Fumagalli) at an average of over 93 km/h before it was packed off to the museum forever.

In 1925 Carlo Guzzi reckoned it was about time to get involved in the 250 class, but he was only interested in the competition aspect at first. He consequently designed a "quarter litre" machine which, even though it went through some changes as time went by, was to enjoy a thirty-year reign during which it became one of the most famous and successful racing motorcycles ever made. It was used as a works machine and was also sold to private riders; it was the first competition motorcycle (along with the 500 twin) to have rear suspension, and the first single to be fitted with a blower; even a fuel injection system was tried out on it. Its engine served to establish new records on land and on the water, thanks to the efforts of Giovannino Lurani and Gino Alquati. It won three World Championships, 16 first division Italian Championships, the Grand Prix of Nations 16 times, the Circuito del Lario nine times, the English "Tourist Trophy" seven times and many more events too numerous to mention. All in all, this was probably the most successful power unit ever made in Italy.

Basically, the new bike was a "Quattro valvole" clone. The "square" engine still had the bevel-driven overhead camshaft but the number of valves had been reduced to two, given the smaller engine. These (exposed) valves were tilted at an angle of 54 degrees and closed by hairpin springs.

The cylinder-head and barrel were both made of cast iron, the crankcase was still composed of two aluminium alloy castings with covers at the side for the primary drive gears and the timing gear. The three-speed gearbox was operated by the usual lever on the right hand side, but the multiplate clutch was pressed together by six springs disposed in a hexagonal arrangement on the left, in place of the two concentric springs which had usually been positioned on the right hand side in previous designs. The frame was very solid and rigid, with two upper struts running from the steering to the back wheel, sturdy sheet metal pressings for the lower section and triple rear forks. The width of the cradle was 40 cm. It was first seen during practice at Monza in the spring of 1926 where it immediately obliged with an impressive performance. It was very light (around 105 kg.) and could develop 15 hp at 6000 rpm, with a power per litre figure which only the best racing cars of that time – with a greater number of cylinders at their disposal – were able to attain. A short while after the first trials, the new 250 was entered for the legendary Isle of Man TT, one of the oldest races in the world (the first event dates from 1907) and conceived at a time when England had no purpose-built racing circuits (racing was not allowed on public roads since the authorities deemed it unjust to forbid their use to the many for the gratification of a few).

Thus British sportsmen had been deprived of an outlet for their enthusiasm, when the Governor of the Isle of Man came to their aid. For historical reasons, the home of the famous tailless Manx cats, which lies half way between Great Britain and Ireland, enjoys a large degree of administrative autonomy. The Governor willingly gave permission to organize a motorcycling event (which grew over the years into a week-long affair, what with the major races and subsidiary events), largely because tourism was the island's biggest industry and it was calculated that the influx of racing fans would generate considerable income for local business people. This was the birth of the "Tourist Trophy", which is run over a course – still the same to this day – measuring sixty or so kilometres which cuts through villages with gardens full of geraniums, and passes by medieval ruins and Victorian inns, before skirting seaside towns and villages with mysterious names in the ancient tongue of the island: Greeba Castle, Creg-Ny-Baa, Cronk-Ny-Mona. It climbs up the peak of the island's only mountain, Snaefell, and crosses barren moors and green, quasi-alpine valleys (there is a stretch that Italian riders call the Valganna), in a continuous succession of innumerable bends and short straights, steep gradients and dizzy descents, between low dry-stone dykes and humpback bridges. A picturesque and fascinating route, but unforgivingly hard and dangerous, especially with today's motorcycles, so much so that in recent years many riders have protested. But the TT is still alive and kicking. The

longevity of this event is a complex matter to explain, but it has something to do with a particularly British view of life (and its only known alternative), which finds its expression in a cheerful disregard for personal danger allied to the kind of drive which propelled this small nation to a position of world dominance a relatively short time ago. At any rate the TT has served for many years as a peerless test bench for both men and machines and the British still consider it more important than the entire World Championship. British riders and motorcycles dominated this event for decades, even though this supremacy was partly due to the fact that the long and difficult course requires riders to possess what London cabbies would call "the knowledge"; an intimate familiarity with the route which springs from continuous training and, obviously, continental riders were rarely prepared to meet the expense of long and expensive visits to the Isle of Man. Armed with the hope of putting up a good show if nothing else, Italian riders were prepared to face the British Lion in its den, as it was put at the time, but despite their undoubted courage, they had not met with outstanding success. Worthy of mention in this respect are the deeds of Achille Varzi aboard the

A souvenir of the ill-fated expedition to the 1926 "Tourist Trophy": Pietro Ghersi (on the right) and Achille Varzi (on the left) fraternizing with the English rider Handley. The clothes worn by Italian motorcyclists, thanks partly to the influence of contacts with British sportsmen, had become pretty much standard: boots, helmets and leathers had arrived. The preceding page shows a picture taken by Testi at the Monza autodrome, officially opened on 24 August 1922. On the 10th of September it hosted the first Grand Prix of Nations. The photo shows the start of the up to 500 class race, which was to be won by Ernesto Gnesa on the Garelli 350. A few Guzzis were in the race: one of these (no. 36) can be seen bringing up the rear.

D.O.T. (an acronym for Devoid of Trouble) in 1924, and with the Sunbeam the following year.

In 1926 Guzzi set out on the great TT adventure with a new sohc 250 earmarked for Pietro Ghersi, a chunkily built twenty seven year old from Genoa with a brilliant career behind him. Ghersi had been part of the Guzzi factory team since 1923: a restless type, he had ridden for many other marques. In 1928 he was to give up two wheels in favour of four and he began racing Alfa Romeos in 1930. After having won the Spa 24 Hours and loads of hillclimb events for the famous Milan marque, he joined Bugatti and then Maserati before going back to Alfa Romeo in 1938. In no way intimidated by the presence of the most aggressive riders of the day, and armed with only an approximate knowledge of the course, Ghersi launched himself for the first time onto the roads of the Isle of Man, where he achieved the truly extraordinary feat of coming second a few moments behind the winner, after having recorded the fastest lap, under the admiring if somewhat bemused gaze of the locals, many of whom could not believe their eyes.

Unfortunately the Italian "victory" was merely a moral one, since during the race Ghersi had had to replace a plug with another of a different make from the one declared (the sporting regulations of yore were extremely severe and teams were obliged to declare the precise make of a great deal of accessories) and so an inflexible stewards' committee promptly disqualified him. But the memory of that outstanding feat lingered and revenge was to come along a decade later.

In comparison with the prototype seen at Monza, the TT bike had gained a front rim brake, the Binks throttle control and the Andre steering damper (the last two items being considered quite revolutionary at that time), but above all it had a big end which ran on roller bearings, a feature later adopted on the *Quattro valvole* and later still (1931) on production tourers.

The Circuito del Lario event of that year was a source of much satisfaction, with Ugo Prini taking first place at an average speed of nearly 66 km/h, leaving runner-up Saetti a good 11 minutes behind. For this occasion the sohc model "Monoalbero" had been fitted with a drum brake at the front plus a supplementary 350 mm rim brake at the back which operated in unison with a 160 mm drum. There was also an additional oil tank (which had previously been housed at the front of the petrol tank): one of these two tanks was fitted below the saddle and the other on top of the fuel tank. In the following years the same bike underwent a series of modifications, which included bigger brakes and a pedal-operated gear change (1930), a most important innovation since it made a big difference in terms of manoeuverability. It was then put on sale, as the *Quattro valvole*, in two versions known as the *TT* and *SS*. More specifically, the *TT* was built from 1926 to 1929 with a 3-spring fork (the original design had a fork with one big spring in the centre), lateral dampers, a Binks carburettor with a lever-operated throttle control, a kick starter on the right, and the oil tank in the front of the fuel tank, which also carried a small metal toolbox. A speed of 118 km/h was guaranteed. The *SS* (1928-1933) had no kickstarter. It had a bronze cylinder head (cast iron was chosen for the later models) while the oil tank was mounted above the petrol tank. Top speed was 125 km/h.

In 1934 the works bikes were to receive major modifications to the engine room, which was to acquire a four-speed gearbox, and to the frame; but this is dealt with in another chapter of the history of the glorious "quarter litre", which we shall come to later.

The sprung frame

By the turn of the Thirties the motorcycle had become a safe and trustworthy product, and a good deal of the credit for this must go to Carlo Guzzi's ideas and working methods. A trip by motorcycle was no longer a perilous journey from one breakdown to another which required prodigious athletic skills just to stay in the saddle. Even mere mortals could easily use the motorcycle in order to go about their daily business. Nonetheless, a very important accessory still had to be invented before the motorcycle could be defined as complete: rear wheel suspension. A fully sprung suspension system is indispensable not only for maximum comfort, but also for good roadholding, which is only possible when the wheels can get a firm grip on the road surface, no matter how bumpy it may be. At the same time these lumps and bumps must be filtered out so that the rider may survive the experience without being shaken to pieces. An unsprung vehicle just jounces from one bump to the next, with the result that the wheels spend a good deal of time spinning freely in the air. This does little for traction and consequently even less for stability, not to mention the wellbeing of the transmission.

It was not as if this problem had gone unrecognized: right from the stone age of the motorcycle attempts had been made to build a machine with rear suspension. For example, there was the Belgian Minerva (1903) with telescopic suspension, the American Indian (1913), which was fitted with two horizontal quarter-elliptical springs at the sides of the wheel (the same bike even had an electric starter!), as well as the Della Ferrara from the same

The Guzzi 250 very soon became a decidedly superior machine which dominated its class. This rare picture (the technology of those times did not make it easy to photograph objects streaking along the straights at high speeds) gives us a precise idea of the riding styles in vogue at the end of the Thirties. Note the footrests mounted well aft on the Guzzis, a feature which the rider on number 15 would have benefitted from. As it is, his position is far less comfortable.

Terzo Bandini with the *Quattro valvole*. Towards 1930 designers took to shielding the rear wheel (still with spokes) with aluminium discs in order to improve the drag coefficient at the high speeds which could be reached on the faster circuits. Any wind from the side played havoc with stability however.

period, also fitted with horizontal quarter-elliptical springs. All these attempts however, foundered on the practical impossibility (partly due to the quality of the available materials) of obtaining the necessary torsional rigidity for the frame, with the result that a motorcycle with no rear suspension guaranteed better stability and handling.

Carlo Guzzi (we are now in 1927) thought the time had come to solve this problem once and for all so that motorcyclists, especially those who enjoyed long journeys, could have a true Grand Tourer which was both fast and comfortable. With the aid of brother Giuseppe, he began by modifying the frame of the 500. He replaced the cradle below the engine with a pressed steel element which took the form of a rectangular box-like housing at the front, while at the rear there were two plates running alongside the downtube which supported the saddle. Pivoted on these two plates was a triangular swinging arm consisting of tubes and metal pressings (made as wide as possible to ensure the necessary degree of transverse rigidity). This structure supported the wheel and was attached to two rods which compressed a pack of four coil springs contained in the rectangular box. Another two tubular triangular elements were connected to the saddle downtube, one for each side of the wheel; these supported the rear mudguard and a couple of adjustable friction dampers attached to the free end of the swinging arm arrangement.

This design offered a good amount of travel (around 11 cm) allied to smooth, progressive suspension and Guzzi remained faithful to it for around four decades. Few other designs turned out to be as comfortable, so much so that the swinging arm system, even though the springs are now arranged in different configurations, has ended up by replacing every other type, right up to the present day. The new motorcycle with the sprung frame was launched in January 1928 bearing the initials *G.T.*. It had the *Sport*-type opposed valve engine and therefore offered almost the same performance, the slight reduction being due to the increased weight. The 3-spring front fork was a direct descendant of the design tried out on the racing machines of the previous year, whilst the wheels, both fitted with drum brakes, were shod with fat, balloon type tyres. Later on, the *G.T.* received the engine from the new *Sport 14*, of which more anon. Nonetheless, public diffidence was deeply ingrained as far as the "springer" was concerned and would disappear only several years later. Indeed so profound was this suspicion that this motorcycle – whose excellent qualities were demonstrated by Giuseppe Guzzi himself when he took it for a spin to the Arctic circle no less (a feat which led to the bike being nicknamed the "Norge") – was only built in 78 units, all highly desirable collectors' items. Better luck was to attend the new version produced in 1931 and baptized the *G.T. 16*, which had a rather different frame and a new *Sport 15* type engine. Fully sprung suspension systems did not really take off until 1935, when Guzzi was the first to adopt it for its Grand Prix machines, which swept to victory in the 250 and 500 classes of the TT. For some time to come, the unsprung *Sport* remained Guzzi's number one production warhorse. Logically enough, it received more than its due share of loving care, which led to the creation of the new *Sport 14* at the end of 1928. The changeover from one machine to the other took place gradually, the slowly ripening fruit of a steady process of improvement which lasted for the whole of 1928 and 1929, to the despair of both the historians and collectors of classic motorcycles, because it is now difficult to say with any degree of precision whether a given motorcycle belongs to one version or the other. And so the unsprung, opposed valve 500 went on sale at the beginning of 1928 with bigger finning around the cylinder block and head, a drum brake on the front wheel, larger and more solid mudguards, a Terry saddle, and an Alfa silencer; it was still painted green and had a 2-spring front fork, along with footrests mounted at cylinder head level. The same year saw the production of a special version with aluminium running-boards, legshields, balloon tyres and a Bosch magneto-dynamo. This model was also painted green and was sold as a *Sport*.

Apart from these variants, the real *Sport 14* had the 3-spring front forks with lateral dampers already mounted on the *G.T.* and the racing bikes. It also had a modified frame with a different steering angle and greater ground clearance: the front hub ran on taper roller bearings and the tyres were 26" × 3.50. The footrests had been shifted aft towards the rocker box cover. Some time afterwards, in 1929, the bike was made available with an electrical system fed by a Miller dynamo which was independent of the magneto and housed in a niche carved out of the crankcase just above the gearbox. It took its power from a pinion which meshed with the clutch ring gear. 1930 witnessed the second series of the *Sport 14*, whose major distinguishing marks included a new drum brake at the front featuring a brake shoe holder with a protective rim to stop mud from gumming up the works, and a toolbox whose lines flowed back towards the saddle.

While the *Sport 14* was in production Guzzi began making more and more use of chrome in place of nickel (chrome brightwork was originally offered as an optional extra and, naturally, it cost a little more). This too is the cause of many doubts and uncertainties on the part of those interested in restoring these bikes. A minor revolution was going on in the motorcycle design

field in those years which was to lead to the introduction of more rounded lines in place of the angular forms popular until then. H.R. Davies and Val Page were the fathers of the new trend: the former was a racing star who had decided to build his own machine after one disappointment too many riding other people's bikes, while the latter was a well known technician who had designed bikes for several leading English marques. These two were responsible for the invention of the so-called saddle tank, that is to say a tank mounted astride the tubes of the frame instead of between them. This idea completely revolutionized the look of motorcycles. It was not long before the designers at Guzzi decided to follow suit and the old fashioned "boxy" look finally disappeared in 1931 when the *Sport 15* took over from the *Sport 14*. This bike was to become the most popular Guzzi of the pre-war era thanks to its outstanding robustness and simplicity. In fact a good number of these are still in circulation and they form the bulk of the bikes on display at every period bike rally. The *Sport 15* remained in production until just before the war and a good 5,979 units were produced.

The principal characteristic which distinguished it from other models was in fact the 11 litre saddle tank with the small tool box recessed into its upper section, access to which was gained by lifting up a cover hinged on one side. The styling of the oil reservoir was also retouched and this container now forsook the old trapezoid shape in favour of a more or less triangular line with two circular protruberances at each side. The classic unsprung Guzzi chassis was kept on, but the front part had to be modified to blend better with the lines of the new tank.

The engine, which invariably had the dynamo separate from the magneto by that time, looked the same as the preceding *14* model but it had undergone a major modification, the adoption of an I-section con-rod with the big-end running on needle bearings instead of the tubular con-rod running on bronze bushings, a feature which had been tried out earlier on the *Quattro valvole*. This led to less friction which in turn made the engine even more resistant to rough treatment inasmuch as the needle bearings required less lubrication than a smooth bearing. This, in combination with a few other touches here and there, produced at least one extra horse if not more and the *Sport* could easily top 100 km/h as a consequence.

THE GOLDEN AGE

The decade preceding the last World War could well be called the "Golden Age" of the combustion engine. It is true that it had not yet reached modern levels of efficiency, but it had never enjoyed so much importance before then, nor had it caught the popular imagination to a similar degree. All the "firsts" of that time were linked to the combustion engine. It seemed to make everything possible: crossing the oceans, connecting distant continents, flying over the poles and breaking all the speed records. The jet engine, the turbine, and the rocket engine had not yet appeared, or were still in the embryonic stage: only the combustion engine seemed able to attain every goal.

The multi-cylinder engines come of age

The same period also saw the birth of some combustion engines which are still admired today, even from an aesthetic point of view. The search for more power led to an increase in the number of cylinders, superchargers were installed, and dual ignition systems were revamped.

This innovational atmosphere also affected the motorcycle. While lots of cheap basic models were created in the aftermath of the world slump of 1929, some very sophisticated models were also built with multi-cylinder engines and all the refinements that the technology of the time was capable of producing. At the same time, the four-cylinder engine began to make itself felt in the world of motorsport. Strange as it may seem, this had not happened before. As a matter of fact, the increase in power which a multi-cylinder unit could provide, with regard to a single of the same capacity, was not enough to compensate for the increase in weight and the handling problems which resulted. For this reason the major manufacturers still preferred to equip their Grand Prix bikes with single-cylinder engines, which were less powerful but lighter and less cumbersome. Things changed

around 1930 when manufacturers began installing superchargers, as the increase in power made it possible to regain in the straights what the awkward handling characteristics had lost in the curves.

So the race began to produce increasingly complex and powerful competition motorcycles. This process actually began in Italy (before spreading all over Europe) with a bike which was well ahead of its time. This was the OPRA, a 500 cc machine with four transverse cylinders, designed by Remor and Gianini.

Guzzi could not remain on the sidelines for long, and by 1931 Carlo Guzzi was busy designing a blown competition bike with four transverse in-line cylinders and a 3-speed gearbox. Even though the cylinders were more or less horizontal, the basic engine design in this case was quite different to what we would now define as a Guzzi-type unit. The aluminium crankcase casting was in the form of a parallelpiped with the gearbox housing, which also supported the blower, bolted on at the back.

The cylinders, in cast iron like the heads, were all separately cast and equipped with straight vertical finning while the three-bearing crankshaft and the con-rods ran on rollers.

The valve gear was a combination of push-rods and rocker arms, with two camshafts (one overhead and the other under the goose neck); the valves had exposed hairpin springs. Carburettor and rotary blower were by Cozette. A tube connected the carburettor to a duct running transversely to the cylinders which was fitted with a safety valve. Four separate 30 mm pipes disposed of the exhaust gases.

Oil circulation was handled by a dual gear-type pump and the lubricant was stored in a special reservoir inside the petrol tank. The circuit was completed by an oil cooler fitted to the front of the frame. A small secondary tank for the supercharger lubrication system was added alongside the rear wheel.

Ignition was by two Bosch magnetos, one for each pair of cylinders. The primary transmission and the supercharger were gear-driven while the clutch was the usual multiplate type. There was also a hand-change gearshift and chain drive. The unsprung frame was still a duplex cradle, but composed of two parts bolted together. The front part was in steel tubing while two large dural plates formed the cradle beneath the engine and the part running down from the saddle. A triangular arrangement of tubes supported the rear wheel.

This design (with its bold use of dural) simplified engine removal and also offered the great advantage of reduced vibration, which was "cut" by the joints of the frame, and was later adopted for production bikes as well. The front forks were the usual parallelogram type with three springs and adjustable dampers; the front wheel carried a 177 mm drum brake and there was a 225 mm stopper at the rear. The bike appeared for the first time at Monza in the September of 1931 and a series of riders carried on testing it for a long time afterwards, but in the end everyone agreed that results had fallen short of expectations and the project was shelved. Effectively speaking one of the major problems lay in the fact that the bike was a mixture of up-to-date features and other items which were obsolete by then, at least as far as Grand Prix bikes were concerned, like the push-rod and rocker arm valve gear and the 3-speed hand-change gearbox. Nonetheless this bike represents an interesting moment in the development of motorcycle technology on the one hand, and of Moto Guzzi on the other. Besides, the experiment had not been entirely fruitless, as was to become clear in the years that followed. More or less at the same time, Carlo Guzzi was also working on a multi-cylinder Grand Tourer, which was introduced in January 1932 at the Milan cycle and motorcycle Show. It had three horizontal cylinders with in-head valves closed by double coil springs and operated by push-rods and rocker arms running on needle bearings. This was also an exceptional motorcycle, because it was the first time this type of four-stroke engine had been fitted to a bike, even though it had been tried out on both planes and motor cars before then. The design makes for balanced running and optimum cyclic regularity, without the bulk and cost of a 4-cylinder engine.

Barrels and heads (with flat combustion chambers and parallel valves) were cast separately in cast iron and had the same finning, and indeed the same bore, as the "Quattro". The engine was still a "long stroker" unlike the usual Guzzi design, but this way it was possible to reuse some of the racing engine components. The crankshafts had the cranks at 120 degrees and ran entirely on needle bearings while the right hand side crank provided power for the dual gear-type oil pump, which was housed in a

A rare shot of Carlo Guzzi and his original 4-cylinder competition bike during a test session at the Monza autodrome. Seated on the bike is Siro Casale, a fine and modest rider of the Twenties who was later to become the head of the repairs department at Mandello. The photo clearly shows the arrangement of the valve springs and the oil radiator, shaped to blend in with the lines of the frame. This was a contradictory and in some ways disappointing bike in which an extremely modern supercharged four-cylinder engine (we are in 1931) was at odds with feeble brakes and a hand-change gearbox with a mere three speeds.

special compartment inside the petrol tank. The right hand side end of the camshaft also drove the ignition distributor. A coil ignition system was chosen in view of the obvious timing difficulties which a magneto would have involved. A sole carburettor fed the three cylinders through a tubular manifold mounted cross-wise above the heads.

The crankcase with the gearbox bolted on at the back was another deviation from the *Quattro cilindri* design. There was nothing new about the geared primary drive and multiplate clutch, but the inborn suppleness of the engine had made it possible to do away with the transmission shock absorber. The slightly smaller flywheel was hidden from view under a metal casting.

The two-part bolted frame was also like that of the *Quattro cilindri*, but in this case it was a sprung, all-steel version. Forks and brakes resembled the standard equipment fitted to the *Sport 15* while the finishing was impeccable, with legshields, crash bars, leather satchels on both sides of the rear mudguard, and so on. The paintwork was a sober but elegant dark brown.

This magnificent bike – which could stand comparison with the most celebrated multi-cylinder bikes of the day, like the English Ariel, Brough Superior, and Matchless; or the American Indian – turned out about 25 hp and could touch 130 km/h. It was put on sale at 9,500 lire but unfortunately it did not meet with public approval. The economy was still in a mess and the price was a high one for the Italian market (for example, the *Sport 15* cost 5,850 lire). Nor can it be forgotten that most motorcycle buyers either wanted a commuter bike or an out and out sports model. For some the *Tre Cilindri* was too luxurious, others had no use for a bike which was the last word in elegance and comfort but not very fast; worse still, the small group of luxury touring enthusiasts remained largely unmoved by its many heterodox features. And so, despite the unconditional praise which the bike had received from technical experts all over the world, people stuck to the familiar single-cylinder thumpers. After a couple of years the *Tre cilindri* was taken off the catalogue.

Some years later however, Guzzi was to return to the 3-cylinder idea for a new Grand Prix bike. At the end of the Thirties the supercharger dominated the international sporting scene and practically every bike was fitted with one. Foremost among these were the Gilera 4-cylinder 500, the BMW twin-cylinder boxer, the NSU 500 twin, the 250 and 350 DKWs, as well as the Guzzi 250 naturally, and there was already talk of a brand new 4-cylinder Benelli 250. After a cautious start, the British were also thinking about changing over to supercharged engines and both Velocette and AJS had blown versions at an advanced stage of development. By that time a half-litre machine with a supercharger running on a petrol-benzole-alcohol mixture was easily capable of developing around 70 hp for top speeds in the region of 230 km/h, which is why Guzzi's competition standby in the 500 class (this was the *Bicilindrica*, which we shall deal with shortly), was liable to lose out in the victory stakes. Guzzi's new creation – without precedent in the history of competition machines – was distinguished by the widespread use of light alloys. Aluminium was chosen for the head and the cylinder barrels (with cast-iron pressed-in liners), which were in-line and tilted at 45 degrees. The two overhead camshafts were driven by a chain which was covered by a triangular electron casting on the right hand side. The valves – two per cylinder - were closed by helical springs while all the timing gear was enclosed and lubricated under pressure.

The 4-bearing crankshaft had the cranks at 120 degrees. The electron crankcase also held the gearbox, which had a good five speeds. The clutch was fitted directly onto the left hand extremity of the crankshaft rather than the gearbox input shaft. Primary drive was still by gears while a chain fed the power to the rear wheel.

There was a Cozette supercharger fitted above the gearbox, and a magneto ignition system which had a distributor splined to the end of the intake camshaft. The dry sump lubrication system was fed by a dual gear-type pump and the oil reservoir was housed in a special compartment in the fuel tank.

The engine was mounted in a composite frame, with a tubular top section and hydronalium pressings at the rear. The rear suspension was the usual Guzzi design while there was a British-built Brampton parallelogram fork at the front, much appreciated for its robust construction and resistance to deformation.

Built in total secrecy, the bike made an unexpected appearance in Genoa at the Circuito di Albaro in the May of 1940, just before war broke out. Although it failed to finish owing to problems with the plugs, the bike showed that it was exceptionally quick, as well as a good sprinter: there were reports – admittedly a little exaggerated – of 80 hp at 8000 rpm.

Guglielmo Sandri was the man riding the *Tre cilindri* that day in Genoa. Born in Bologna in 1906, Sandri had made his competition debut aboard a G.D, before going on to ride for other marques. He joined Guzzi in 1937 and promptly won the Milano-Taranto event and the Italian Championship with the *Bicilindrica*; he also took the 1938 and 1939 editions of the Circuito del Lario and notched up six world records at Brescia. Sandri was also one of the few Italian stars to race outside Italy before the war. In everyday life he was an easygoing chap who loved singing; he even sang on the radio for a while.

The outbreak of war put an instant halt to all forms of motorsport and the *Tre cilindri* had no further opportunities to demonstrate its undoubted potential. When peace returned, superchargers were banned from racing and the fate of this interesting bike was thus sealed definitively. The move to ban the blown engine originated in England. Officially the ban had been imposed for safety reasons (a fair enough point as a matter of fact), but the decision was really a political one. Blown engines were a German and Italian speciality which the English had never completely accepted and, having won the war, they could not miss the chance to remove this ace from their rivals' hand. Woe to the conquered indeed! We might also add that the Germans were banned from international competition until 1950.

In 1933 there was a clear need for a new Grand Prix 500. Practically the leaders in the 250 class (where the agile sohc lightweight built seven years before was harder than ever to beat), in the half-litre category Guzzi had only the *Quattro valvole*, which was getting past it, and the *Quattro cilindri*, which had never really arrived in the first place. It was at this juncture that Carlo Guzzi was struck by one of his periodic brainwaves. Given that the 250 engine went so well, why not find a way to harness a pair of them to the same bike and thus take advantage of its tried and tested abilities?

In order to avoid altering the characteristics of the flat single layout, Guzzi thought a V arrangement would enable him to position the second cylinder as tidily as possible while ensuring optimum cooling at the same time. The result was a very original engine with one cylinder lying flat and the other tilted up towards the saddle so as to form a 120 degree angle between them. The bike was baptized the *Bicilindrica* (twin-cylinder) and went on to become one of the longest-lived racing bikes of all time, since some versions remained in service until 1951. Definitely one of the greatest machines to roll off the lines at Mandello.

Less nimble than the English singles and less powerful than the various supercharged German and Italian "monsters", the *Bicilindrica* nevertheless managed to combine the strong points of these conflicting technical tendencies without falling victim to their weaknesses. Consequently, from 1934 to 1937 it showed that it was more efficient than all of them and that it could adapt splendidly to all kinds of circuits as well as the big road races. It won the Grand Prix of Nations in 1934, '35 and '36; ace rider Omobono Tenni rode it to victory in the Italian Championships

The 1934 version of the sohc *250* with the foot-change 4-speed gearbox and the modern-looking frame and tank. We are at the Italian Grand Prix in Rome, won by Riccardo Brusi (centre). The other members of the team are Biagio Nocchi (right) and Alfredo Panella.

of 1934 and 1935; Guglielmo Sandri won the same title in 1937, followed by Tenni again in 1947, Bruno Bertacchini in 1948 and finally Enrico Lorenzetti in 1949.

It did not do badly in the Milano-Napoli event either, which it won in 1934 (Terzo Bandini), in 1935 and 1936 (Tenni), in 1937 (Sandri in the solo class and Bandini in the sidecar class); but its most epic venture will always be the glorious victory in the 1935 Isle of Man TT, where it broke the British domination of the event which had seemed eternal up that point.

As we have already mentioned, the horizontal cylinder was that of the 250, complete with the sohc valve gear. But the second cylinder had circular finning of a type used by other marques while the finning around the head ran parallel to the axis of the cylinder. Both heads and cylinders were in cast iron and the crankcase, which also housed the gearbox, was made of aluminium. Aluminium was adopted for both heads and cylinders shortly afterwards, while electron was chosen for the crankcase.

The valves, two per cylinder, had a head diameter of 37 mm for the intake and 34 mm for the exhaust, with exposed double hairpin springs. The fuel supply was handled by twin carburettors and the bike was also fitted with magneto ignition. Lubrication was by dry sump with the usual dual gear-type pump.

The first version of the *V*-twin with the rigid frame, prepared for the Milano-Napoli event. It was fully equipped for road use with number plate, silencers, speedometer, horn and toolbox. Standing behind, from the left, Giordano Aldrighetti (who came to Guzzi from the Ferrari motorcycle racing team), "il Moretto" and Pigorini.

The 1934 Italian Grand Prix at Rome's Littorio autodrome witnessed one of the *V*-twin's first great successes; first place went to Omobono Tenni (centre, with the Guzzi sweater) with Amilcare Moretti second. "il Moretto" can also be seen in the group (wearing overalls) as well as the inevitable Fascist bigwig, in this case Generale Teruzzi.

Primary drive was by straight-cut gears and final drive by chain, the clutch was the multiplate type and the foot-change 4-speed gearbox had sliding gears and a pre-selector device. The unsprung tubular chassis had a triangular rear element like that of the 250. The cradle was not a one-piece unit and so the front and rear sections of the frame were bolted to each other and to the engine, which therefore became a stress member within the structure. Brampton forks like those tried out on the *Tre cilindri* were again chosen; weight was around 150 kgs. This first version, which ran on a petrol-benzole mixture, developed 44 hp at 7000 rpm and could touch 190 km/h: in fact at Monza it recorded several laps at an average of almost 178 km/h.

Given the brilliant results obtained almost immediately, Guzzi soon decided to give the new bike a try outside Italy too. Foreign riders were selected for this purpose, as they not only possessed an intimate knowledge of the various European circuits but were also wise to all the tricks of the trade. The choice fell on Stanley Woods, a curly-haired Irishman who was about thirty years old at the time and at the apex of a glorious career which was studded with wins on Nortons and other famous English marques. In particular, Woods was a TT specialist and a six-time winner of that event on Cottons and Nortons. The Irishman had already made the acquaintance of the *Bicilindrica* in 1934, when he had ridden one to victory in the Spanish Grand Prix: the following year he evinced a desire to take on the tough Isle of Man course aboard the new Guzzi.

With this important date in sight the bike was subjected to a thorough overhaul. Tuned to perfection, the engine could pump out roughly 50 hp at 7500 rpm, enough for more than 200 km/h: that Spring Tenni had recorded averages of almost 178 km/h in the famous and very fast Circuito di Tripoli event aboard a machine with no fairing. The most important innovation was the application of rear suspension, which until then had been considered more of a problem than anything else as far as racing bikes were concerned. Bearing in mind the bike's basic structure and the need to reduce its height, a slightly different layout to the one chosen for touring bikes was adopted: the springs (still operating in compression) were housed in two cylindrical downtubes at each side of the wheel, to a point about 15 cms from the ground. The friction dampers were positioned behind the saddle and were connected to the forks by two short struts. These could be regulated with the usual wing-nuts, or alternatively by means of a lever and cable arrangement mounted under the left hand side of the fuel tank, which made it possible for the rider to adjust the suspension while underway without any need to perform acrobatics or, worse still, to stop. The rear mudguard was covered at the sides, so as to form a rudimentary fairing; the wheels had aluminium rims and light alloy hubs.

The race, which had been postponed for one day due to the execrable weather, turned out to be a dramatic affair featuring an epic struggle between Woods and Norton star Jimmy Guthrie, known as the "Flying Scotsman". Guthrie started first and rode like the devil in an attempt to "psych out" his Irish rival. Woods was off a few minutes later (the TT has a staggered start) and it was soon apparent that he was not going to risk a mechanical failure by pushing the bike too hard at the outset.

By the end of the second lap Guthrie had accumulated a 47 second lead over Woods, and it began to look like the British were going to notch up the umpteenth home win. But Woods got his act together in the third lap and the battle was on in earnest. One lap record fell after another, first Guthrie, then Woods, then Guthrie again and finally Woods, and all the while the gap was narrowing between the two. By that point, according to the contemporary press reports, the spectators were going wild, shouting and waving their arms in the air; nobody gave a hoot for what the other competitors were up to because, even though they were good, they were hopelessly behind the two leaders. Guthrie seemed to be hanging on by the skin of his teeth while Woods looked like he still had a little something left in reserve. On the sixth lap the Norton was still 26 seconds ahead and the Guzzi was scheduled to make a refuelling stop. Instead, and to everyone's amazement, Woods flashed past the pits without stopping. Crouched low over his bike, he was about to play his last card.

The seventh and last lap unfolded in an atmosphere of suffering and torment, with all eyes on the stopwatches and all ears alert for the roar of the approaching bikes: at the foot of the mountain Guthrie's lead had slipped to 12 seconds; after the long, mad dash down the hill the word came that Woods, going flat out at a frightening 200 km/h, was a mere six seconds behind. Guthrie arrived at the finish and the silence fell like a tangible thing: everyone had their eyes fixed on the beginning of the final straight. Finally the characteristic roar of the Guzzi was heard and a split second later the red racer came into view with Woods virtually buried in the tank. A thousand stopwatches clicked and feverish calculations were made before the official judgement was handed down: Woods was first by four seconds having lopped one minute and 12 seconds off the lap record and a good seven minutes off the total distance (about 420 kms).

Afterwards, the apotheosis: the English spectators, carried

A very famous photograph taken at the 1935 Tourist Trophy, the race which launched Guzzi to real international fame. Standing around the sohc *250* with the new sprung frame are; first row, from left, Giorgio Parodi, Stanley Woods, Omobono Tenni, Woods's brother-in-law and mechanics "il Moretto" (Carlo Agostini), Bettega and Elsa.

away by enthusiasm, forgot the bitterness of defeat as they thronged around Guzzi, Parodi, Woods, and the mechanics in a display of sporting spirit which those present never forgot.

A few days before, Woods had already won on the Guzzi 250 after another memorable battle, in which he was backed up by Tenni, who was on his TT debut but whose exhilaratingly acrobatic style had immediately made him a favourite with the crowds. After having held second place behind Woods, in the lead virtually from the outset, Tenni was betrayed by the fog and rendered hors de combat as a result of a fall, but the Irishman held on to win three minutes ahead of his closest rival, Tyrell Smith on the Rudge, after a very tough and dramatic race where only 11 out of the 27 starters made it to the finish.

The 1935 TT propelled Guzzi to the heights of international motorsport both from a technical and sporting point of view, a fact which marks a decisive turning point in the history of racing and of motorcycles in general. One result of Guzzi's double triumph was that sprung rear suspension became universal and one short year later there was no Grand Prix bike without it. The unsprung frame was retained for the cheaper models, but by that time even normal motorcyclists, influenced by events on the race track, were turning to "springers" in droves.

In the period leading up to the outbreak of the second World War, the *Bicilindrica* was modified here and there; for example, circular finning was fitted to the rear cylinder head, the frame was lightened with the addition of some parts in hydronalium and the brakes also received some attention. But the predominance of the blown engines was making life very tough for the *Bicilindrica* in those years. After the war was over, this Guzzi twin resurfaced to find its prospects somewhat improved when the supercharger was banned from competition. Riders also had to use ordinary commercial petrol, rated at 72 octane then, which meant that the best output obtainable was reduced to about 42 hp, for a top speed of about 180 km/h.

In 1948 the *Bicilindrica* was radically modified by Antonio Micucci, an engineer who had joined Guzzi during the war years. His new frame was formed by an upper tube with a diameter of 112 mm ending in a cone at the rear, which also served as a reservoir for 5 litres of oil, and was completed by two front downtubes plus the usual light alloy plates at the rear.

The telescopic front forks had built-in hydraulic dampers and an offset axle, an arrangement which is once more all the rage today, while the rear suspension was renewed by fitting a monoarm made of flattened circular section tubing with the "springs in a box" under the engine along with a hydraulic damper; the whole shoot was then covered by a small fairing. Having abandoned the two tier tank, Micucci opted for a model with flowing lines and knee recesses, while the rear mudguard was given a new, arched line.

The V-twin was taller than before, but its more streamlined shape led to a little extra speed even though the power output was more or less unchanged. Manageability and stability were much improved on the other hand, and these were both very important characteristics as far as road circuits were concerned: in fact Tenni held the lead for a good spell in the TT of that year before falling victim to plug problems, but not before he had recorded the fastest lap at almost 142 km/h.

The bike received further attention in 1949, when the engine was slightly improved by the adoption of carburettors with detachable float chambers attached by elastic stays and megaphone exhausts. The front fork was replaced by a *Gambalunga* type fitting, an original model which Guzzi had created in 1946 for competition singles.

The most noticeable modification, which also helped make this the most elegant of the V-twins, concerned the new tank which extended forwards to a point beyond the steering head. Apart from aesthetic considerations, this feature improved the stream-lining in an area which had always been considered "difficult" due to the presence of all the various controls and accessories. The seat and the rear mudguard also received a new look.

Power was now 45 hp at 8000 rpm, still burning commercial grade petrol, while weight had been trimmed to 145 kgs. Thanks to the improved Cd, top speed was now in the region of 200 km/h.

The following year Guzzi decided not to enter an official works team, but it did field some "semi-works" machines which were entrusted to the best riders. A new 350 version of the 1949-type *Bicilindrica* was created; it supplied good if not outstanding results, while its "big brother" was subjected to another round of modifications.

Strictly functional, with its new, more voluminous petrol tank with the recesses scooped out for the arms and knees, this was the most appealing of the V-twins and one of the finest expressions of a basic racing bike constructional concept: i.e. if it makes the bike go faster, it's good. Its strange engine, with one cylinder in the East and the other pointing North-West, the intricate mass of tubes and cables, the tank moulded to the rider's shape (or perhaps it was the other way round?) made this bike a real "ripsnorter" with all the mechanical beauty of an old loco-motive, "...a terribly grotesque machine", as it was described by an English journalist. From another point of view altogether it was functionality on two wheels.

Having returned to the racing fold in 1951, Guzzi managed to squeeze just a bit more from the engine, which could manage 47 hp at 8000 rpm. Top speed was upped to 210 km/h. This was the last version of this bike, which had some slight alterations made to the rear suspension (the friction dampers had been reinstated in place of the hydraulic variant) and the saddle-rear mudguard assembly. Scot Fergus Anderson won the Swiss Grand Prix (a World Championship event) in Berne on this model, while Lo-renzetti took the final event in the Italian Championship at Seni-gallia. At the Monza Grand Prix of Nations, Bruno Ruffo notched up the day's best time with an average of 171.330 km/h. The *Bicilindrica* carried on racing in South Africa, Australia and South America, where it competed in the various meetings held during the European off-season, and where it scored a good number of wins, which were important locally from a publicity point of view. As far as the great Continental Circus was concerned, 1951 was the last season in business, and so a unique chapter in the history of two- wheeled motorsport drew to a close after 18 years.

On the facing page, the start of the 1935 Tourist Trophy. The scene, typical of the world's most famous race, shows Stanley Woods waiting for the off with his Guzzi *250* just before the first of his two fantastic wins. In the background the leader board can be seen; it was operated by a group of boy scouts. Above, Stanley Woods again, at the downhill bend after Governor's Bridge, just before the finish. Here he is riding the *Bicilindrica* (V-twin), with which he won the 500 event after a thrilling and dramatic race.

The legend of Omobono Tenni

Perhaps no other rider could get the crowds on their feet like Omobono Tenni. In an epoch in which the mass media were still in their infancy, with TV virtually unknown and the major news-papers convinced that motorcycling was a sport for a few fanat-ics (and thus not newsworthy), in an age where fame was the re-sult of deeds and not the arbitrary decree of some passing fash-ion, everyone knew Tenni, or had heard of him at least.

His courage on the track, his quasi-foolhardy boldness, the ease with which he defied the laws of physics when cornering, the highly personal riding style which made him seem like a part of the bike, and his crazy acrobatics enthralled the thousands who thronged the edges of the course rightly convinced that they were witnessing a unique spectacle.

A succession of spectacular spills, from which he emerged even more indomitable than ever, had left him with an aura of near immortality which fed his rapidly growing legend. When he wound up in hospital, as he often did, he took the pain stoically with only one thought in his mind; getting back on a racing bike. Many of the anecdotes concerning Tenni have grown somewhat in the telling, but the embroidery with which the truth has been

Omobono Tenni, a "longhair" well before the Beatles, at the time of his early successes with the *G.D.* Idiosyncratic, unorthodox and very brave, Tenni was perhaps the best known and loved rider of his day, a man who could thrill the crowds like no other. He died in Berne in 1948 during practice for the Grand Prix after the driving rain had rendered the cobblestones extremely treacherous.

embellished is often so much in character that it is now difficult to separate fact from fiction. One significant example regards an episode which occurred during practice for the Circuito del Lario. Tenni had made a very early start, around dawn, and was bowling along at a good lick when he had to go off the road into a ditch in order to avoid colliding with a horse and cart. And there he remained until worried stewards mounted a search. He was found half-unconscious with pain groping round in the grass for bits of his finger bones, which he was placing in a handkerchief convinced that the doctors would have been able to put the bits together again.

Tenni enjoyed a 24 year career in motorcycling, and despite this long acquaintance, the start of a race gave him the same thrill it always had. Racing had given him a keen awareness of the risks, but rather than try to avoid danger he welcomed it, flirting with death like a matador in the bullring.

Born in Tirano in Italy's Valtellina region, he moved to Treviso when still very young. He made his racing debut at the age of nineteen, in 1924, aboard a G.D (a popular lightweight at the time) in the Circuito del Piave event. At first he only raced occasionally and so we lose sight of him until 1926, when he popped up at Postumia with his amazing hair barely contained by a crash

helmet worn at a crazy angle. Still on the G.D, Tenni came in ahead of an assortment of 175s and the 250s after a ride which would have made a bald man's hair stand on end.

A series of wins followed and he won at Postumia again, this time in 1928, despite having lost his exhaust pipe. In order to avoid disqualification (the rules demanded that the bike be in a complete state at the finish too) he slung the offending component across his shoulder before taking off like a bat out of hell, stopping only to get a better grip on the refractory pipe which was doing its best to wriggle out of his grasp. That year, G.D gave him a few rides outside Italy and he came third in the Swiss G.P. after a display which had even the stolid locals on their feet. This feat brought Tenni to the attention of people living outside Veneto, his adopted homeland: and at the same time he was given more powerful bikes which improved his chances of success. From 1930 to 1933 he raced for Velocette, Norton and Miller, notching up a total of 15 wins and numerous placings. When he joined Guzzi in 1934 his career was set to take off.

Guzzi had already availed itself of numerous stars of undoubted ability, men like Guido Mentasti, the winner of the first European Championship, Pietro Ghersi, the hero of the ill-fated expedition to the 1926 Isle of Man TT, and Terzo Bandini, who had already won three Italian titles. And if it's true that Tenni found the ideal bike in the Guzzi, then it's equally true that no one else did more than he to promote the fame and popularity of the Mandello product. A man of extremely eclectic tastes, Tenni did not play favourites with either horses or courses: circuits or road races, 250s or 500s, it was all the same to him; the important thing was to race. In 1934 he won the Grand Prix of Nations aboard the wide-angle V-twin to become the Italian Champion while the following year he tested out the sprung version of the same bike, winning the Milan-Naples event at an average of 107 km/h. His first assault on the Isle of Man TT (1935) left the English speechless right from practice. While steaming down Bray hill on the 500 he strayed too far to the left and wound up in a ditch, but he blithely carried on for twenty or thirty yards before he got the bike back on the road under the horrified gaze of the spectators, all of whom were convinced that he was bound to break his neck. "..I could have got her back on the road sooner", he was to say afterwards, "but seeing I was in there I thought I might as well see how well she handled off the road..." Another competitor who stuck to his tail for a long time that day, Rusk, told the pressmen that the "black devil", as Tenni had been nicknamed, had shaved the embankment so close that he had torn out lumps of earth with the handlebars...

More victories followed at home and abroad over the next few years and Tenni also set a series of world records on the blown Guzzi 250. But his most enthralling win of the entire pre-war period was certainly the win in the 1937 junior TT aboard the 250, the first non-British rider to win, and on a non-British bike, the Guzzi, to boot. A fantastic double, which was a bitter pill for the British to swallow, but which was swallowed nonetheless with true sporting spirit.

"...Tenni", the words are those of a radio commentator speaking from a vantage point overlooking one of the most difficult parts of the course, "corners with mad abandon..."

And indeed he must have been a sight to see, crouched over the bike, his head low over the handlebars even in those corners where everybody else had to sit up, with the foot hanging ready to see just how low he could lay her down; both electrifying and chilling at one and the same time. It was a complete triumph, because Tenni also recorded the fastest lap. The same man also became a father in those same days and his cup must have been full to overflowing. The boy was christened Titino after the unforgettable victory in the Isle of Man.

When the war was finally over Tenni was back in action, displaying all the enthusiasm of his younger days. Still a very popular figure, the crowds flocked to watch him just like before. Nor did he let them down, and the string of victories got longer and longer. In 1947 he ended the season as Italian 500 champion; he was back at the TT in 1948 but after scoring the fastest lap with the V-twin he had to slow down due to ignition troubles and was unable to win, despite the fact that "he literally brushed the walls with his shoulder", as an English journalist was to remark.

A few days later he went to Berne for the Grand Prix (scheduled for both cars and motorcycles). Practice was held in the middle of July, under very heavy rain. The bikes went out first and Tenni set off to do a couple of inspection laps. He had to test the new 250 twin, which was still in the experimental phase, and compare it with the *Albatros* single. No one saw him fall, no one witnessed his last accident; perhaps a footrest touched the ground, maybe he was betrayed by the slippy road surface, no one will ever be able to say for sure, not even those who were first on the scene after his absence had been noted.

Shortly afterwards it was the turn of the cars and the best drivers of the day set out to tackle the difficult course. One of these was Achille Varzi, an unflappable veteran of many's the duel (on two and four wheels) with the famous Tazio Nuvolari. Varzi's car went into a slide at a bend, nothing much to worry about it seemed, and Varzi smiled at the other competitors coming up

Some moments from Tenni's career. Above, on the way to victory in the 1937 TT: Tenni was photographed while cornering at Creg-ny-Baa "with mad abandon", as the journalists of the day put it. Below, "wetting his whistle" after this very hard race. Tenni was the first foreigner to win at the Isle of Man, thus breaking the legendary sequence of wins hitherto notched up by British riders.

Overleaf, Omoboni Tenni again. Top, with Guido Corti and Giordano Aldrighetti at the end of the victorious Milano-Napoli race of 1936. Below, with Nello Pagani after the latter's win with the *250* at Monza in 1937. Tenni came second on that occasion. Pagani's wife is standing between the two riders. These two pictures sum up the rough-hewn qualities of the men and their cheerfully unaffected manner.

from behind, but then a wheel went into the ditch causing the car to overturn and the famous racing driver was killed.

And so, in one grey and rainy morning, two of the greatest aces of all time had been killed. Both men had very different styles and neither had ever raced against the other, but a cruel fate was to bring them together for this one final appointment.

Production is renewed

The motorcycle, as we have seen, originated as a motorized bicycle, strengthened and completed bit by bit as motorcyclists got more and more demanding. Immediately after the first World War, a precarious economic climate persuaded manufacturers to go back to square one and sell just the engine, which the public could then fit to common and garden bicycles, the aim being to offer people the cheapest possible transport. Shortly after this, the factories began producing purpose-built moped-type machines as ordinary bicycles cannot stand up to the stresses generated by an engine for very long. Interestingly enough, this progression was to repeat itself after the second World War too. Several factories specialized in producing these motorized bicycles sprang up, like Mignon, Miller, M.M., Piana, Rubinelli, while many other marques were imported, like Evans, DKW, and Alcyon (later built under licence). However sales of these bikes were always fairly limited – in spite of special burocratic concessions made in an attempt to increase their appeal – largely because the contemporary advertising campaign erroneously stressed the sporting aspect at a time when the public was looking for a practical, useful machine. The producers of "real" motorcycles disdained the whole lightweight sector for a long time. It was not until the 1930s, after a steady process of development had begun to transform the motorized bicycle (which could be fitted with an engine of up to 220 cc if a four-stroke, or 132 cc if a two-stroke) into a real lightweight motorcycle, that the big manufacturers began producing their own 125 or 175 cc machines, but these were little different from their "big brothers", even in price. Then, in 1933, the Italian government abolished the tax differences between light motorcycles (*motoleggere*) and motorcycles real and proper (*motociclette*) thus sending the light motorcycle into a rapid decline, as there was no longer any good reason to prefer it to a larger bike.

Guzzi brought out a smart little lightweight in 1932. This was the *P*, a 175 with a 3-speed gearbox which was pretty much a copy of the larger models and to some extent a test bed for some of the stylistic and mechanical features fitted to the *V* series the following year.

The engine had two inclined overhead valves (controlled by pushrods hidden under a tubular cover running alongside the cylinder), and a hemispheric combustion chamber, while the sharply angular lines of the old style crankcase had been smoothed and rounded to satisfy more modern tastes. The shape of things to come, in other words.

The rest of the engine was very much in the Mandello mould: magneto ignition, 18 mm carburettor, separate oil tank with dual pump, straight-cut gears for the primary drive, multiplate clutch, sliding gears operated by means of a stubby hand control and a 30 W dynamo driven by the clutch release bowl. The unsprung frame was a duplex cradle with its three parts (front, rear and lower) bolted together, while the front girder forks had friction dampers mounted at the side. The saddle tank was lower and sleeker than that of the *Sport 15* and was also a forerunner of the model chosen for the *V* series. The following year (1933) Guzzi added a new 250 cc utility version of the *P* to its range. This was a new venture for the Mandello marque, which had only built two other quarter-litre machines before that date: the famous sohc *TT* and *SS* models.

The *P 250* (which really had a 232 cc engine, with bore and stroke of 68 × 64 mm) was obviously a better performer than the 175 (the valves were 33 mm) given that it boasted a couple of horses more, enough to give it 100 km/h-plus performance. The most outstanding exterior difference was the pedal-operated gear change, with the preselector outside the crankcase. Guzzi customers could also buy this engine mounted in a sprung frame, a version known as the *P.E.*

Subsequently, after the war was over, Guzzi added a string of 250s to its catalogue, sometimes with only a few small differences between them, with the result that even experts are occasionally tormented by doubts and confusion. Let us try therefore to re-establish some order in this area in a bid to make life easier for collectors of period bikes.

As well as the machines we have already dealt with, there was the *P.E.S.* (which stands for model P – *Elastico* – Sport) with a 3-speed foot change, tubular frame and girder forks. This was a sporty version capable of more than 115 km/h, only a few of which were built.

In 1937 the swept volume was upped to 246 cc by increasing the bore to 70 mm. Another bike fitted with this same engine was the *P.L.* (*P Leggera*, or "Light") with a 22 mm carburettor, 3-speed foot change and a new rigid frame, whose front-central

Tenni once more, this time at the Milano-Napoli with the *V*- twin. Here he is leaving the Rome checkpoint. Note his anxiety to be off while the mechanic is still trying to finish off. Tenni seems to be receiving some final instructions from the man on the right.

One of the last photographs of Tenni, taken at the famous Ballaugh Bridge during the 1948 Tourist Trophy, a few days before the fatal crash in Berne. The structure of the *V*-twin can clearly be seen; the bike had been retouched by Micucci that year and was nearing its peak.

part was made of rivetted sheet metal pressings while the rear was still tubular. The front girder fork with the fat central spring was made of welded steel pressings. These features were the result of the need to reduce production costs, inasmuch as the motorcycle had to be a cheap means of transport: virtually all chromework disappeared during this period. A sporty version of this bike known as the *P.L.S.* was also planned.

The *P.L.* was renamed the *Egretta* in 1939, when it was put on sale with better finishings and some chromework. At the same time the role of commuter bike was taken over by the *Ardetta*, which had always had the composite frame made up of tubes and pressings, pressed steel forks, the 246 cc engine with coil ignition (the magneto had given way to an integral coil and contact-breaker assembly) and 3-speed hand-change.

The *Ardetta* was intended to be the cheap commuter bike *par excellence*. One curious note worth recording here is that the Italian government was then backing a campaign to produce a "people's bike" which was to be sold through the (Fascist) Party working men's clubs under the terms of a kind of hire purchase agreement.

All the major motorcycle manufacturers conducted research aimed at winning this lucrative contract and the *Ardetta* was the response from Guzzi, who preferred to save as much as possible on the frills (there was no chromework on the *Ardetta*) rather than reduce performance in order to provide the motorcyclist with a cheap machine which was nevertheless reliable and in line with the firm's already established reputation for quality.

The last of the series was a *P.E.* introduced at the end of 1939; this had a 246 cc engine, magneto ignition, 4-speed foot-change gearbox and an all-tubular sprung frame, front fork included. But just as it was about to go on the market the new bike was renamed the *Airone* (Heron), a name we shall come across again in one of the following chapters.

By the beginning of 1934 Guzzi had become the most important Italian motorcycle manufacturer and was also well on its way to becoming the marque with the largest number of units in circulation. The small 300 square metre workshop had become a major factory whose premises continued to expand steadily at the expense of La Grigna, the mountain which towers up sharply behind Mandello. The workforce was around 700, all chosen craftsmen with a grand passion for motorcycles and their work. All the men used to sign their hand-built engines personally while the factory test drivers still consituted the most important source of racing talent for the future.

In this climate of confidence and industriousness, Carlo Guzzi decided to modernize his single-cylinder design in order to bring it into line with the latest technical developments and the exigencies of the market. This decision was to give rise to the *V* series, launched at the end of 1933 and put on general sale by the following Spring.

As far as the engines were concerned, the most important differences between the *V* series and previous models concerned the overhead valves, which were now inclined instead of parallel as they had been on the *2 VT* (thus making it possible to have a hemispheric combustion chamber, which performs better thermodynamically), as well as the four-speed gearbox. Several improvements were made to the tried and tested frame design as well, while the engine and various other components were given a facelift.

Let's take a brief look at these bikes, all of which were to remain in the catalogue in one guise or another right up to the Sixties. The crankcase was still made of two aluminium castings, with a horizontal cylinder in Ni-Cro cast iron with radial fins spaced at 10 degree intervals. The head was also made of cast iron and was fixed to the block by four studs. There was nothing new about the crankshaft (with embodied counterweights) which still ran on rolling bearings with the usual 280 mm external flywheel (weighing 8.2 kilos) and the I-section steel con-rod with the big-end rotating on needle bearings. Ignition was handled by a Bosch magneto with manual advance, while the engine was fed by a 27 mm Amal carburettor. The oil was circulated by a dual pump (vane- and gear-type). There were two exhaust pipes as it was considered very *chic* in those days to have an exhaust running along each side.

Helical gears with transmission shock absorbers were chosen for the primary drive while the multiplate clutch had five steel plates alternating with another five gold bronze friction plates, plus two ferodo plates. The direct-mesh four-speed gearbox had two sliding gears on the mainshaft and ran entirely on ball bearings. For the pedal-operated gearchange there was a drum-type preselector mounted on the right-hand side outer wall of the crankcase connected to a splined shaft which in turn actuated the various shifting forks. The crankcase therefore had an appendage in its upper rear section, which the previous 3-speed models did not possess. All the sharp edges and angles of the crankcase and the various covers were then smoothed and rounded, as had already been done for the *P 175*.

The frame consisted of two parts bolted together, in accordance with the research experience acquired with the racing *Quattro*

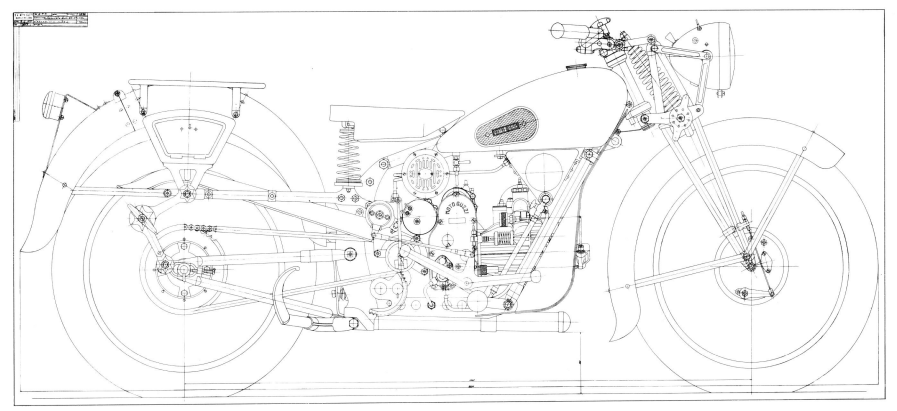

cilindri and the *Tre cilindri*. The front part of the frame was a tubular structure with steel lugs and included the twin ball race steering assembly, and the front downtubes of the cradle. The rear chassis and the cradle beneath the engine were formed by two L-shaped steel plates connected by tubular couplings.

Both a rigid and a sprung frame were available. The rigid version terminated with a triangular arrangement of tubes which supported the wheel and in this case the pressings which ran down from beneath the saddle were arched slightly forwards. The "springer" obviously had the Guzzi swinging arm system. In this case the springs were held in two parallel cylindrical containers which extended almost to cylinder head height. The two horizontal stays which supported the mudguard and the adjustable Hartford-type dampers, with four cork discs, began at the pressings under the saddle. These pressings were not arched (as on the unsprung model), but straight. Trapezoid-shaped metal tool boxes were fixed to both sides of the mudguard; these too had been fitted for the first time to the *P 175* and were to remain a Guzzi trademark for many years.

The parallelogram front fork, with a single spring and friction dampers at each side, was made of decreasing-section telescopic tubing. The petrol tank, still triangular in shape, but lower and less angular than that of the *Sport 15*, was painted red like the rest of the bike, with chrome panels and red shields with the gold decal in the centre bearing the legend Moto Guzzi and the spread eagle. The eagle is always looking forwards, and so the decal on the right hand side is different from the one on the left. The end of the rear mudguard was hinged, to simplify the removal of the rear wheel. Brakes were still 177 mm in front and 200 behind.

At the same time a slightly more powerful version of the engine, known as the *W*, was being prepared.

It had a slightly higher compression ratio (6:1), a different camshaft, a 28.5 mm carburettor and developed 22 hp at 4500 rpm. And that makes four bikes, with various frame and engine combinations: the *V* with the 18.9 hp engine, rigid frame, and 120 km/h performance; the *G.T.V.* with the same engine and performance but a sprung frame; the *W* with the 22 hp engine, unsprung frame and 130 km/h performance; and finally the *G.T.W.* with the 22 hp engine and the sprung frame.

Alongside these machines, which were decidedly sophisticated for that period, Guzzi lined up another opposed valve utility model. More precisely, this was a bike with the *V* model crankcase and 4-speed box, plus the cylinder and head assembly from the *Sport 15*. The cylinder (still made of cast iron, as was the head) was recessed into the crankcase rather more deeply than

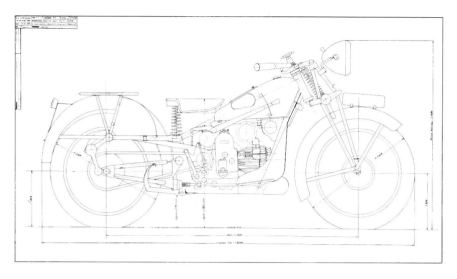

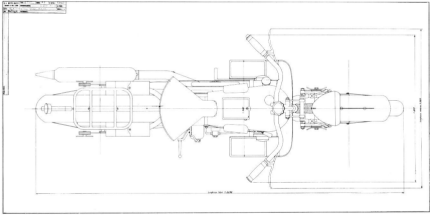

had been the case with the *Sport 15*, and was 4 mm shorter as a consequence, while the three cylindrical elements which served to prevent valves from "dropping in" were kept on.

Here too the bike was offered with a choice of frames, rigid and sprung, from the *V* range, with the result that we have two versions: the rigid *S* and the sprung *G.T.S.* If we include the *Sport 15*, which was still available, this takes the number of 500 cc models in the Guzzi catalogue up to a good seven; these were soon to be joined by a decidedly sporty stablemate.

All these bikes remained in production without any major modifications until war broke out and they made a significant contribution to the growing popularity of the Mandello marque, which had already become the outright Italian market leader by the outset of the Forties, both in terms of production and numbers in circulation.

Production racing

On leafing through newspaper reports of the early competitions from the end of the last century, one is astonished by the number of entrants, sometimes as many as a hundred, so much so that it is tempting to suggest that the owners of cars, motorcycles and motor tricycles were racers to a man. But within a few years things had changed completely, at least as far as motor car racing was concerned. The public thronged to watch the competitors flash past in growing numbers, they camped out all night along the roads and hailed the cars enthusiastically despite the fact they could barely be discerned amid the clouds of dust, but if we peel away the pompous prose beloved of the sporting journalists of the day to get to the bare statistical bones beneath we find that each Grand Prix was contested by a mere dozen competitors or thereabouts at most.

The reason for this rapid change lies in the massive involvement of the manufacturers, who had realized that racing not only "improves the breed" but also represented the perfect advertising vehicle for their products. In order to ensure victory at any cost the producers began entering bigger and ever more powerful cars, with 17 or 18 thousand cc engines and more than 200 hp. As a result private entrants were left with no chance and they very soon decided to stay at home.

Things went differently in the motorcycling field, at least for a while. This was due partly to the fact that different categories for the various engine sizes had been introduced virtually from the outset and partly because the English, who had dominated the international market for years, had a vested interest in production racing. In fact one of the classic competition bikes of the Twenties was still the side-valve Norton 500 single. The wind of change began to blow for the first time around 1925 when all the makers – Guzzi included, as we have already seen – began to adopt overhead valve gear. Things really began to move with the arrival of the blown multi-cylinder bikes which radically changed the face of competition in the space of a few years. Ten years later, in 1935, anyone who was not a works rider had no chance of doing well in the big races and had to be content with the minor meetings, or hang up his helmet. One good solution aimed at raising the level of interest in motorcycle racing seemed to be the introduction of events for "gentlemen racers" riding standard production bikes, that is to say, machines on general sale with a fixed price and complete with registration plates, electrics, stand and kick start. It seemed to the organizers of the day that this would guarantee everyone the same chance of success, given that anyone could buy the same bike as his opponents.

In practice though, things did not go exactly as planned, because instead of promoting the common and garden motorcycle to the rank of racing bike, the manufacturers began producing genuine racing bikes camouflaged with a stand and a headlight at prices which the average amateur could not possibly afford. And this is what has happened every time somebody has tried to revive racing for "sport" or "production-derived" bikes from that day to this. The same phenomenon, on the other hand, has always led to a step forward in motorcycle technology, not only in terms of performance but also lightness, stability and braking.

As soon as word got around about the new competition formula, Guzzi hastened – as did all the others – to bring out a 500 which, while it respected the rules, was a little more powerful than the normal *V* series bikes. Baptized the *G.T.C.* (*Gran Turismo Corsa*) and a "springer" therefore, it was not that different from the type *G.T.W.* bikes: it had a 28.5 mm carburettor like the *W*, a slightly different cam profile, slightly retouched valves and compression ratio, just enough to bring available power up to 26 hp at 5000 rpm. The cycle parts were practically unchanged, apart from the 20" front wheel. In view of the fact that the bike was intended for long distance racing, it was fitted with larger oil (3 litres) and fuel (17 litres) tanks: the petrol tank was identical in shape to the tank on the *G.T.V.* but a little wider. It was easy to spot the difference because it sported a species of chrome sunburst around the hollow of the steering head which the touring version did not have. The legshields were removed, while the tools were kept in leather pouches.

The most obvious difference in terms of styling was constituted by the upswept exhaust pipe, which branched out into two silencers at the height of the rear wheel; the ends of the silencers took the form of a truncated cone. The aim was to simplify the removal of the rear wheel, prevent the silencers from touching the ground when cornering, and to follow the fashion for the upswept double exhaust. However the *G.T.C.* came to have a rather curious look which very soon resulted in the nickname "the wheelbarrow", in a clear reference to the shape of the handlebars.

Thanks to its notable powers of resistance, the *G.T.C.* did rath-

In the pre-war period all the best riders, while they were allowed to carry on their normal activities, were drafted into the Traffic Police, which also organized its own championship (using only Guzzi *Condors* for which the various participants drew lots). Above, the start of an event in Rome, in the April of 1940. On the preceding pages, some drawings of the *G.T.S.* and the *G.T. 17*.

A pre-war production race. Biagio Nocchi, on the *Albatros*, is in the lead ahead of Massimo Masserini. Note the presence of the electrical system, the stand and the other accessories required by the rules.

Two popular figures in the Forties were Ferdinando Balzarotti (left) and Bruno Francisci, shown here with the roadgoing version of the *Condor* at the Circuito del Impero in 1940, a production race. Francisci, a three-time Milano-Napoli winner among other things, raced for fun while Balzarotti went on to become a Guzzi test rider.

An exploded view of the various components of the *Bicilindrica* engine. This is one of the last versions, with the magneto and automatic spark advance. Note the crankshaft and the offset cylinders, each of which had different finning so as to exploit the cooling effect of the airstream to the maximum.

er well in competition, especially in the long road races like the "Raid Nord-Sud" (which was extended as far as Taranto in 1937, the year of the new bike's debut), the Circuito del Lario, etc. But its limitations soon became apparent: it was too heavy, braked poorly and the riding position was still too much like that of a touring machine.

And so the Guzzi engineering team came up with a radical solution to the problem – they simply built a new machine, created with racing bike design criteria in mind. Needless to say, the result closely resembled a contemporary works iron. Known simply as the *Nuova C* at first, the new bike scored a (production class) win on its debut in the 1938 Circuito del Lario event, with rider Ugo Prini also breaking the lap record.

This time many modifications had been made with respect to the basic production model. Externally the engine seemed the same but, apart from the usual contrivances aimed at increasing the power (32 mm carburettor, camshaft, compression), the cast aluminium cylinder barrel and head assembly had much larger finning, there was only one exhaust and the four-speed gearbox was a frontally engaging constant-mesh type, a design which made for easier, safer and quieter gearchanging. As a consequence the rear of the crankcase had to be modified because the new gearbox had the two shafts one behind the other instead of one on top of the other.

The cycle parts were radically different and took their inspiration from the more recent versions of the blown 250. In fact the frame, still a two-piece unit, was a composite structure (tubes and steel pressings) at the front. The two tubes welded to the steering head ran down to straddle the cylinder, but these were bolted directly onto the crankcase rather than the cradle, which was not a one-piece unit therefore. Two superimposed U-section elements were rivetted to the steering head to form the upper part of the frame. The angle plates at the rear were made of hydronalium, a special aluminium alloy. These elements consisted of two plates laid one on top of the other and rivetted together. The rear mudguard and the shock absorbers were supported by light alloy U-section drawn tubes. Steel was chosen for the swinging arm, which had the usual triangular conformation, slightly modified at the ends in this particular case. The front girder fork was made of small diameter tubing while the 21" wheels with light alloy rims had cast electron hubs and drum brake. The fuel tank (with two compartments one on top of the other) was made of sheet steel because it was difficult to weld aluminium in those days. The mudguards were made of aluminium braced by rivetted central ribbing. Complete with its regulation electrical system, the bike weighed 140 kgs and could top 150 km/h.

In the winter of 1938 a small batch of these was put on sale under the name *G.T.C.L.* (*Gran Turismo Corsa Leggera*) but these bikes still had the cast iron cylinder head and barrel. The following Spring, after further major changes (an electron casting for the crankcase, straight-cut gears for the primary drive, special steel forged crankshaft, etc.), the definitive version finally appeared. It was called the *Condor*, the first of the "ornithological" Guzzis, but more importantly the founder of a dynasty of competition motorbikes which was to reign for fifteen years, becoming one of the best known, best loved and most sought-after series in motorcycling history in the process. On sale at 11,000 lire, it became the fastest means of transport on the Italian roads for quite some time to come, and was obviously lusted after by aspiring racers and lovers of speed alike. The *Condor* was to father another two legendary bikes, the *Dondolino* and the *Gambalunga*, of which more anon.

The *Condor* was in the line-up for the "competition" class at the 1939 Circuito del Lario with Nello Pagani – one of the best and most "scientific" riders around at the time – in the saddle. Pagani had entered the racing arena very young, almost certainly after lying about his age, and had become Italian 250 champion (1934) when still only 22 with the Miller. A meticulous rider, it was said that he used to pose in front of a large mirror in an effort to find the most aerodynamically favourable riding position. He was a cool customer who studied every circuit with painstaking care beforehand in order to leave nothing to chance, and in fact he had very few accidents in a long career. World champion with the Mondial in 1949, he also raced for Gilera and MV, for whom he was also racing manager. In 1967, when almost sixty years old, he scored a class win in the Motogiro d'Italia aboard the Norton 750. Once the weight of his years finally obliged him to hang up his helmet, Pagani was one of the few all-time greats who did not disappear from the scene but chose to remain involved in the world of motorsport, thus demonstrating a truly exceptional passion for bikes. He joined Guzzi in 1937 and showed his mettle right from the start by winning the Milan-Taranto race and the Italian 250 championship. In the 1939 Lario, with Tenni *hors de combat* after a ruinous crash during practice, Pagani found himself alone against Serafini on the blown Gilera four and a pair of "Otto bulloni" (Eight bolts) type Gileras ridden by Vailati and Fumagalli. After a clever, tactical race Pagani ran out the winner aboard his agile single – which had less than half the horsepower of the four-cylinder Gilera –

Derived from the *Condor*, the *Dondolino* was one of the most popular racing bikes of the early post-war period and widely used by private entrants. This excellent shot enhances its uncluttered, simple lines. We are at the 1953 Circuito di Faenza: Dante Bianchi is the rider.

Several of the most famous post-war stars began with the *Dondolino*: Bruno Bertacchini (56) and Guido Leoni (26) here shown overtaking Umberto Masetti on the *Gilera Saturno*, another famous bike of the day and one of the *Dondolino's* closest rivals.

while notching up a new best time for the course (84.101 km/h) into the bargain. The record was to remain unbeaten.

Pagani's victory was definitive proof of the *Condor's* role as a genuine racing machine and an official works bike, and this idea was confirmed the following year when Guido Cerato rode a *Condor* to outright victory in the Milano-Taranto at an average of 103 km/h.

After the war, we again find the Guzzi *Condor* in the winner's paddock when Gastone Berardi took the first post-war circuit event (held at Tortoreto degli Abruzzi), and then many other races. In 1946 it was decided to beef up the engine, with a view to using the bike as a works entrant in the minor championships which had taken the place of the defunct production races.

The new version, known jocularly as the *Dondolino* (Rocking chair) because of its less than perfect roadholding, made its debut on the 12th of May at the Circuito del Luino, where Luigi Ruggeri came second behind Bandirolo on the Gilera *Saturno*; but at Reggio Emilia the week after that, the *Dondolino* tasted instant revenge again with Ruggeri (a rider from Bologna who had begun racing when still a child at the insistence of his father Amedeo, the 1925 Circuito del Lario winner). The compression ratio had been uprated to 8.5:1, the valves were 44 mm intake and 40 exhaust, rocker arms and camshafts ran on needle bearings, the carburettor was a 35 mm single barrel Dell'Orto, and the oil feed pump was fitted with an automatic valve. The long pack of springs for the rear suspension, which the *Condor* had inherited from the *G.T.V.*, had been replaced by a single, rather short spring (with counter spring), enclosed by a small fairing which also covered the lower part of the engine. In order to reduce vibration, two small links were added which directly connected the head to the front frame downtubes. The front wheel, still 21", had a new and exceptionally large (260 mm × 35) cast electron lateral drum brake with internal linkages for improved streamlining. The back brake was still the 220 mm × 50 cast electron component from the *Condor*.

The rear mudguard was faired at the sides, while the electrical system was fitted upon request only, for ordinary road use or enduro type races. In this guise the bike weighed in at 128 kgs and could develop 33 hp at 5500 rpm, enough to exceed 170 km/h. Much sought-after by privateers, the *Dondolino* won innumerable races of all types, the second division Italian Championships for the years 1946, 1948, 1950, 1951 and 1954, as well as the third division titles in 1947 and 1948. Then we must add the first division French Championships of 1948, 1949, 1950 and 1951 with Jean Behra and the Swiss titles (1950 and 1951 with Galfetti and Musy). Perfected after a period of long and patient modification which had begun ten years previously with the *G.T.W.*, it was also sold to an élite of customers who, although they took no part in competition, demanded the maximum performance from their motorcycles.

The *Dondolino* was more at home on fast circuits, even though it managed to win in 1949 over the extremely tortuous Sanremo-Ospidaletti course with Geminiani (a win which was later expunged because Geminiani had changed a plug with an undeclared brand in an incident analogous to the Ghersi affair at the Isle of Man TT twenty-three years before). But the bike's speciality was the Milano-Taranto event, the only one of the great long-distance road races to survive the war, in which its robust construction and powers of resistance were to become legendary. Almost always to be found in the middle of the pack up to the halfway stage, the *Dondolino* usually began to climb up the leader board from Rome onwards and then, on the long straights of the Puglia region, it steadily knocked out its rivals one by one. The competing bikes were often faster and more powerful but they were rarely able to take the punishment handed out by 1,400 kilometres of sustained flat out running. This was the way it won the first post-war edition of the race in 1950 with rider Guido Leoni recording an average of 102 km/h. The same event was won in 1951 and 1952 at 112 km/h by Roman star Bruno Francisci; in 1953 by Duilio Agostini, a "home-grown" rider from the Mandello nursery and finally in 1954 (only a class win in the "corsa" group this time) by Sergio Pinza.

Then the years began to take their toll of the *Dondolino* too. Neglected by the powers that be at Mandello, who had turned their backs on private entrants (always pennyless and very demanding), and technically obsolescent, the bike was steadily overtaken by adversaries fitted with more efficient frames and suspension systems until it began to disappear even from the minor events.

A direct descendant of the *Dondolino* was an equally famous bike of the late Forties: the *Gambalunga*, which was reserved for works riders who raced it over road circuits where the less manageable *Bicilindrica* found the going rather tough. The *Gambalunga* made its debut in Genoa in the September of 1946, in the capable hands of Luigi Ruggeri.

The name (which means "Long-leg") derives from the fact that this was a "long stroker" measuring 84 × 90 mm, unlike the classic Guzzi engine dimensions. This feature was adopted in an attempt to diminish the stress on the main bearings during races by reducing the bore and thus closing the angle of the con-rod a little. However the engine was still basically the *Dondolino* unit, changes having been limited to the cylinder casting, the crankshaft and the con-rod assembly, plus some other minor details, like the studs used for the head; even the frame remained the same. The most noticeable novelty was the leading link front fork design, which had tubular fork covers fixed to the base of the steering while the wheel was supported by two lower links. Although the springs and the hydraulic dampers were sealed inside the fork covers, the *Gambalunga* fork, designed by Giulio Cesare Carcano, was clearly a departure from the classic "telescopic" type which had been invented at the beginning of the century, rediscovered by BMW in 1935 after a long period in the wilderness, and then commonly used after the English manufacturers began fitting large numbers of their military models with them.

In this case there were two sheet metal boxes at the base of the fork tubes, which served as a pivot for two forged steel links which passed through the tubes themselves (they were provided with a large slot for this purpose) from which they emerged to support the wheel. The links compressed the springs and the pistons of the hydraulic dampers; the return action was stayed by rubber pads. The geometry of the assembly was such that, when the brakes were applied, the release action of the springs tended to lift the bike, unlike the usual suspension action which caused the forks to "plunge" when the front brake was applied; a characteristic which gave the riders a few headaches at first. Another strange result lay in the fact that the brake had little effect on the fork; the wheel was fixed simply by locking the end of the spindle in the clamp of the links, without any need to use the usual stay to stop the brake shoe holder from rotating. This fork – which spawned various imitations in the years that followed – was later adopted with some variations on all Guzzi's Grand Prix bikes (with the exception of the 1947 and 1948 V-twins) right up to the marque's withdrawal from racing at the end of 1957, and it brought several undoubted advantages in its train. On the debit side travel was inevitably limited and the fork tended to flex due to the smallness of the point of connection with the steering assembly.

The *Gambalunga* also had a large-diameter brake fitted to the rear wheel and a spanking new streamlined petrol tank of a vaguely trapezoid shape; the oil tank was mounted under the saddle between the frame plates, in the place where the battery was mounted in the *Dondolino*. Another revolutionary innovation was the bike's silver coloured metallic finish, a complete break with the shades of "Guzzi red" hitherto used for the racing machines. The nameplate was also new: in blue, it featured a stylized eagle and *Moto Guzzi* in Roman print. The *Gamba-*

Derived from Lorenzetti's conversion of his own *Albatros*, the *Gambalunghino* added new lustre to the aging 250 sohc design, which was nearing the quarter century by that time. The photo shows the new bike at the 1950 Circuito di Sanremo with race winner Lorenzetti on board. Behind him are Grieco on the Parilla and Scopigno with the *Albatros*. Below, a nice shot of Lorenzetti with the 1952 version of the *Gambalunghino*.

lunga weighed 125 kgs, the prescribed limit for a planned *Grand Prix* formula which should have come into being in 1948 in place of the customary subdivision based on engine capacity.

The first *Gambalunga* showed well, but the best results were to come later when Guzzi went back to the "short stroke" engine: effectively speaking this was the *Dondolino* engine with an additional main roller bearing housed in the primary drive cover. The same variation was also adopted for the real *Dondolino* engine, which was known as the "tipo Faenza" from then on. Lorenzetti notched up a string of prestige victories aboard this "hybrid" in 1948, including the Ulster Grand Prix (where he exceeded 180 km/h over a one kilometre stretch), the Swiss and Hungarian Grands Prix etc. Subsequently, the *Gambalunga* had its cycle parts restyled with a view to lowering the line of the bike and thereby improving its streamlining and roadholding. In 1950 the rear pressings were modified, as were the mudguard stays and the rear suspension; the year after that saw the arrival of a Dell'Orto carburettor with a detachable float chamber, while a long saddle with a raked tail was fitted. Naturally the engine was retouched here and there, which brought output up to 37 hp at 6000 rpm.

At the end of 1951 the *Gambalunga* was put out to grass along with the V-twin *Bicilindrica*, when the factory decided on a swingeing renewal programme for the racing division. A few models ended up in the possession of "semi-works" riders who carried on racing them for some while to come. Today they are all highly sought-after collector's items.

We left the 250 racer, complete with a 4-speed box and a rear suspension system, at the Isle of Man TT with victors Woods and Tenni. The competition from the blown German bikes had got steadily stronger until Guzzi too was obliged to fit superchargers to his machines. This was no simple task in that a supercharger – which supplies a constant flow of fuel mixture under high pressure – is not particularly well suited to a single-cylinder engine in which the inlet phases are set well apart from one another, so much so that nobody had so far managed to produce a decent blown single. The Guzzi engineers got round the problem by falling back on a capacious expansion chamber, a species of sac located between the Cozette supercharger and the cylinder, fitted with an automatic safety valve. The blower was mounted above the gearbox and driven by a gear train contained in an extension of the primary drive casing.

Apart from this, the bike also had a new, ultra-light composite frame in steel and light alloy, which was identical to the *Condor*

Top, the Guzzi race shop in 1948. Above, Lorenzetti on the 1952 *Gambalunghino*. Note the central brakes, the anatomical tank and the teledraulic rear dampers.

frame. The only substantial difference lay in the fact that the two front downtubes were bolted rather than welded to the steering head. The wheels had aluminium rims and electron hubs with lateral drum brakes, while the fuel tank (still the type with the two compartments one on top of the other) had been much enlarged to cope with the increased consumption.

In this modified guise, the bike – which was the first supercharged single in the world – weighed in at 132 kgs, but it could call on 38 hp, enough to propel it to over 200 km/h. In fact this bike was also used for several record attempts, which culminated in the simultaneous conquest of the Hour and the flying Kilometre, a feat which entitled the bike to bear that prestigious emblem of international recognition, the "Blue Riband".

The 250 was entered for several international Grands Prix in which it notched up a series of splendid victories, including the German GP, won despite the mighty blown DKW two-stroke which had to be content with third place behind Pagani and Sandri. A series of highly interesting experiments with a fuel injection system then followed, using both electromagnetic injectors developed by Ottavio Fuscaldo as well as a mechanical system, which was taken up again in 1952 (at least the working principle was) and adapted to the 4-in-line engine designed for the 500 events. This research effort came to a halt when war broke out and development of that engine, nicknamed "Gerolamo", was abandoned. Up until 1952 supercharged bikes (with carburettors) were used for various record attempts, and the results were better every time. Blowers, by the way, are still allowed for record attempts. The sidecar version of the bike even managed to beat the record for the 1200 cc class, at a speed of more than 221 km/h.

After the Condor's brilliant debut, Carlo Guzzi thought of carrying out a similar operation for the 250 "sport bike" class, where the Mandello colours were borne by the not exactly unbeatable P.E.S.. Here the solution was even more radical, because in practice they just took the works racing machine – even though it had no supercharger – and added the electrical system and the other equipment required by the rule book. With this move the spirit, if not the letter, of the "formula sport" was virtually knocked on the head, but the result was one of the best machines ever to come out of Mandello, unbeatable just like its three-speed forebear of some years before.

The Albatros (as the bike which "new boy" Carcano had helped bring into the world was called) had an ohc single-cylinder engine, electron crankcase, composite steel and hydronalium frame, four-speed gearbox and aluminium wheels with 200 mm

cast electron lateral brakes both in front and behind. The gear train for the blower was used to drive the dynamo for the lights, while the magneto was retained for the ignition.

A very small number of these was produced before the war (only 25), both because of the imminence of the conflict, and because the rather highly strung sohc engine made its use on the road rather problematic. In other words it was a real racing bike and not a "grand tourer" suitable for a quick "burn-up" of a Sunday morning. The Albatros success story really begins after the war when, following the abolition of the blower in the "racing" class, it also became the Guzzi works mount for all the most important races. The electrical system and the kickstarter having been definitively eliminated, the appendage for the dynamo drive was cut away while the carburettor was uprated from 30 to 32 mm and the inlet valve from 33 to 35 mm. After the various modifications the Albatros weighed 120 kgs and still developed $22 \div 23$ hp, despite the use of normal 72 octane petrol. It was practically the most efficient 250 of its day and it can fairly be said that in those first years it had no serious rivals at all, either in Italy or abroad. On leafing through the contemporary sports reports it is hard to find a race without an Albatros in first place and there were even races with no other marques entered, be-

Several privateers tried to update their own machines using parts taken from works bikes. By way of example, the photo shows Plebani (82) aboard an Albatros fitted with a Gambalunghino tank, alongside Gianni Leoni on a factory racer. The photo is from 1950.

cause all the privateers ran off and bought one just as soon as they could get their hands on the cash.

The list of riders who made their names on board an *Albatros* is pretty impressive and includes all the stars of the day, from Raffaele Alberti to Dario Ambrosini, from Ferdinando Balzarotti to Bruno Francisci, to Gianni Leoni, Lorenzetti, Martelli, Mastellari, Alfredo Milani, Alano Montanari, Bruno Ruffo, Tenni and many, many more. Lorenzetti has the honour of being the first rider to race the *Albatros* in the 1939 Milan-Taranto event, as well as the honour of having renewed it radically in 1948. Still a performer as far as the engine was concerned, the *Albatros* eventually began to look a bit dated in the frame and suspension departments, which were no longer abreast with the times, and when the Benelli team arose from the ashes of the war Guzzi found itself faced with a redoubtable rival.

The Benelli company, stripped to the bone by the retreating Germans, who had taken everything from the machinery to the stores (even the original blown four-cylinder bike had disappeared in the chaos), had been lucky enough to recover some dohc 250 singles, of the type which Ted Mellors had ridden to victory in the 1939 Tourist Trophy ahead of the blown DKW. Smartened up, with modified carburetion, the "new" Benelli was handed to Dario Ambrosini, who had been a faithful Guzzi man until then (and indeed his choice to ride for Benelli was hotly contested by his home fans, who accused him of "treason") but who went on to give the Guzzi singles something to think about in no uncertain fashion.

In the meantime Enrico Lorenzetti had fitted *Gambalunga* forks, brakes and fuel tank to his own personal bike, thus obtaining a modern-looking machine which was far more efficient. The idea, which curiously enough sprang from a road accident (the trailer which Lorenzetti was using to transport the bike broke away from the car sending its burden crashing off the road) and the consequent need to effect repairs, pleased the Mandello engineers who went on to modify the works bikes in exactly the same way.

And so the *Gambalunghino* (Little long-leg) was born. At first the design was a copy of Lorenzetti's original idea, but it soon began to acquire a character all of its own as the modifications began to mount up. In the course of that year (1949) the valve gear was modified, a carburettor with detachable float chamber was fitted and power was increased to 25 hp at 8000 rpm; in 1950 the valves were enlarged to 38.5 mm inlet and 33 mm exhaust while a special horizontal 37 mm (later upped to 40 mm) Dell'Orto with a detachable float chamber was fitted transversely to the frame. A saddle with a raked tail was adopted while the Hartford type rear dampers were mounted backwards in an attempt to improve handling when braking.

In 1951 several experiments were carried out, like the adoption of a five-speed box for some circuits (Anderson at the TT, for example) and the hydraulic rear dampers at the Ulster Grand Prix. Such research blazed the trail for the profound process of renewal which began the following year. In 1952 the engine was patiently retouched as much as possible; for example the offset between the cylinder and the crankshaft (which had existed since the days of the *G.P.*) was eliminated, thus increasing the stroke from 68 to 68.4 mm and gaining a little something in terms of displacement. A new 40 mm carburettor, specially built by Dell'Orto, was fitted; this was a downdraft model with a transverse barrel and incorporated float chamber. A five speed gearbox was mounted and power now stood at 27 hp at 8500 rpm running on a compression ratio of 10:1.

The frame was redesigned, with a tubular upper strut doubling as an oil reservoir, a mono-arm rear suspension system with two elements made up of a hydraulic damper and an external coil spring mounted on either side of the wheel: this was the design first produced by Velocette in 1939 which was then adopted by virtually all of the world's major manufacturers. The diameter of the wheels was reduced to 19" and both wheels received cast electron central drum brakes, the front unit being a twin-cam type. The bike was also fitted with an anatomically shaped fuel tank which extended beyond the steering head, while the shape of the seat and the little tail was slightly altered. The *Gambalunghino* now weighed only 117 kgs and could travel at 180 km/h. This was the last version of the glorious ohc engine which had, among other things, brought Guzzi the World Championship in 1949, 1951 and 1952 with Bruno Ruffo and Lorenzetti, and various world long distance records, still in 1950 and '51. By that time the rise of new adversaries, the German motorcycle industry in particular (finally forgiven by the international Federation), had made radical changes inevitable. Semi-works riders carried on racing the *Gambalunghino* in minor competitions for some time to come, but new machines were being prepared for the world championship races.

The man who was not allowed to win the TT

Born in Verona in December 1920, Bruno Ruffo (whose father was a garage owner) had been messing about with engines since

This page and the preceding pages, some pictures of Bruno Ruffo, the man from Verona who gave Guzzi its first World Championship, in 1949. The photo shows him in victorious action (wearing number 15) at the very tough Ulster event in 1951.

an early age. He had made his competition debut aboard a Miller while still only seventeen and was doing quite well until the war put a halt to his activities. After a spell on the Russian front as an orderly with the transport corps, he returned to racing as a "privateer" with an *Albatros* upon which he notched up a string of victories in the 250 class, which inevitably led to Guzzi inviting him to join the factory team. Second division Italian champion in 1946, he won the Grand Prix of Nations as a member of the works team in 1948. On the 5th of November of the same year a squad comprising Ruffo, Leoni and Alberti broke 19 world records at the Monza autodrome. He won the 1949 and 1951 Italian and World titles with the *Gambalunghino*. In 1951 he also won the French and the Ulster Grands Prix with an instinctive, "hell for leather" riding style which had many comparing him to the great Omobono Tenni. His winning streak would have certainly continued were it not for two serious crashes in 1952 and 1953 which put him out of racing.

Although he was noted for his daredevil style, he is also remembered for an episode in which he demonstrated great self control. Guzzi had shown up "mob handed" for the 1952 Tourist Trophy: Fergus Anderson, Enrico Lorenzetti and Bruno Ruffo. Lorenzetti was the number one rider while Fergus Anderson was on "home turf" before an enthusiastic crowd of his fans. The word was handed down from on high that, if at all possible, Anderson was to win, followed by Lorenzetti and then Ruffo. Ruffo accepted this humble role without a word of complaint but – once he was out on the course – he rode like the devil until he had opened up a lead over the entire field (including his teammates), a position he held until the final lap. Then, having made his point, he slowed down deliberately in order to let his favoured teammates through in accordance with the pre-race plan. But the manoeuvre had escaped neither the experienced Isle of Man spectators nor the sporting press. The following day one paper bore the headline: "Ruffo, the man who was not allowed to win the Tourist Trophy".

Technical contributions: Enrico Lorenzetti.

A very tall man, Lorenzetti was so thin that he was nicknamed *Filaper* (a Milanese dialect word which refers to those long, thin threads you sometimes find clinging to clothes just back from the laundry). He was also one of the most popular and "scientific" Italian riders of his time. A fine rider, he was thorough to the point of fussiness about pre-race preparations. The same person was also a born technician, the best man to tune a new racing bike because he picked up every defect, no matter how insignificant, and reported it with mathematical precision. Lorenzetti also produced several home-brewed specials whose features were later adopted for works machines, in fact he was so talented in this direction that some of Guzzi's most significant victories are inextricably linked to his name. Born in Rome in 1911, but Milanese by adoption, Lorenzetti began his racing career in a 1935 regularity race held in the Bergamo area in which he tied for first place with a Simplex 500. Right after that he bought a biddable Triumph 250 tourer, which was so small that it was a wonder that the lanky Lorenzetti was able to crouch low over the handlebars. Evidently he had a particular physique because he did very well on that bike, winning several fast regularity events straight off the bat. But his most phenomenal exploit of those years, the one which sent his name spinning into the sporting headlines, was his first Milan-Naples race in 1936, which he won after 900 kilometres at an average of 80 km/h – an incredible performance for a touring bike. Lorenzetti used to go racing by road with a rucksack on his back; once he got to the course he would dismantle the headlight, take off the silencer and a section of the mudguard, and then put the parts in his rucksack before taking off in a cloud of dust with the rucksack once more across his shoulders.

The echoes of the Milano-Napoli event had still not died away when Lorenzetti once more had the crowds on their feet: he came first overall at Sondrio, still on the English 250, and then came win after win; in hillclimbs, off-road events, and regularity races, both on the Triumph and other brands like the Sertum, Taurus, and a "special" – the first of several he was to build himself – with a Rudge engine and a frame of his own design which he had built by Miller.

He joined Guzzi in 1939 and rode the *Albatros* on its Milano-Taranto debut. It was a race dogged by a series of valve spring breakages, but Lorenzetti managed to hold the lead almost to the end just the same. A few days later he decided to buy a *Condor* too.

He showed up at Mandello in a van, accompanied by his faithful father-in-law who was his mechanic, manager, trainer and general factotum, and asked for the bike minus its electrical system as he was intending to race it. But Carlo Guzzi was unhappy, he had little faith as yet in the lanky youth and feared that he might make his bikes cut a poor figure. He made it clear that Lorenzetti could have the bike – as long as he had the cash – but he was to do nothing to make it look like a works machine. Loren-

Enrico Lorenzetti in 1940, the year he won his first Italian title with the *Albatros*. Beside him (in the overalls) is his father-in-law, who was also his dedicated mechanic, manager and adviser (as well as unpaid chauffeur).

zetti did not bat an eyelid, but took the bike and drove straight to Lausanne. He entered for the 250 and 500 races (he also had the *Albatros* with him) and promptly came first in both: these were the first wins on foreign soil for the new Guzzis, and demand for them abroad began to grow from then on.

After the war was over, Lorenzetti went back to racing his Guzzis as Italian Champion, having won the title in 1940. He still was not a member of the works team – he was to join a short time after – but he was famous by then and considered highly reliable, and so the factory had begun to take particular care with his bikes: he was, in other words, a "semi-works" rider. He took part in a great number of races in 1946 and 1947, with a considerable number of wins; one famous feat occurred during the dramatic 1947 Grand Prix of Nations event which was held in the streets around the Milan Trade Fair buildings (Monza was still unavailable). Lorenzetti, on the *Condor*, was in the lead in the 500 race but Balzarotti's works *Gambalunga* was still hot on his heels after Tenni and Nello Pagani on the Guzzi V-twin and the Gilera four respectively had both retired with engine trouble. But on the last bend before the finish the two rivals collided and dropped the bikes thus allowing Artesiani on the Gilera *Saturno* to get past. Lorenzetti picked himself up with cat-like speed, grabbed the bike and made it to the line to take second place amid frenetic applause.

In 1948 he "invented" the *Gambalunghino*, as we have already mentioned, when he fitted his *Albatros* with various *Gambalunga* components. The bike handled excellently, so much so that Lorenzetti found himself Italian champion for that class by the end of the season.

And this was the feat which persuaded Guzzi to sign him up as a fully fledged member of the racing team, thus laying the foundation for a long and fruitful working relationship and personal friendship between Lorenzetti and Carcano, who was already in charge of the race shop at Guzzi.

His works career began with a win on the *Gambalunga* over the difficult Ulster GP course in 1948, and he won the Italian Championship again the following year, this time aboard the 500 V-twin. He also took part in his first Tourist Trophy, where he had little luck thanks to engine troubles, although he distinguished himself for scrupulous and methodical preparatory work. He had memorized the course a bit at a time before the race; it took him days and days but he managed to acquire an incredible knowledge of the circuit.

New victories followed as time went by, including the World and Italian Championships of 1952 with the *Gambalunghino*. In this period Lorenzetti was also making a considerable contribution to the tuning of the new competition Guzzis, from the 4-in-line 500, to the various sohc and dohc 250 and 350 singles, the latter being a relatively new class as far as Guzzi was concerned. Indeed, the first wins notched up by the *Quattro cilindri* and the 350 are both connected to his name.

Meanwhile a new danger was arising in the middleweight class in the form of the German marque NSU, which had gone back to racing with a large team (just as Mercedes had done in the motor racing arena) as soon as the Germans were readmitted to motorsport. The Germans had prepared themselves carefully and without fanfare, but they were all ready to explode onto the scene and it looked like trouble was in store for everybody. But despite the awesome power of the German contingent, Lorenzetti managed to do well on several occasions and he wound up the extremely hard-fought 1953 season (during which he took the Italian Championship) with a memorable double at the Monza Grand Prix of Nations, where he won both the 250 and the 350 events.

This was a win with a touch of revenge about it even as far as Guzzi was concerned, because before the race Lorenzetti had asked and received permission to race using the practice bikes, in order to prove that a run of poor results in precedence had been due to the machinery and not the man.

Lorenzetti remained in the works squad for another two years, where he collected a series of wins both in Italy and abroad aboard the 250 and the 350, plus the umpteenth Italian title, in 1955. Then, having reached a certain age, he began to reduce the number of his commitments. He still gave Guzzi the benefit of his experience, but he went back to racing as a privateer. In 1956 he created another splendid motorcycle with the aid of Luigi Lunardon and Eugenio Canova, two gifted and enthusiastic craftsmen.

This machine had a *Gambalunghino* engine with a 5-speed gearbox, a barrel tank, a mechanical petrol pump driven by the oscillations of the rear swinging arm, a full dustbin fairing and a tubular backbone frame. With this bike he took part in various races in 1956 and 1957, winning at Sanremo-Ospedaletti, at Hockenheim, Nuremberg, Salzburg, Sarre and the Saar, as well as taking many top placings in world championship events.

Then, a good 46 years of age, after having established even more records with the works Guzzi 350, he hung up his helmet for good. He worked for a while as a Guzzi dealer before opening a highly specialized cinematographical laboratory, his other passion having always been the cinema. He died in 1982.

On the facing page, two moments from Lorenzetti's career as a test rider; above, riding the *Gambalunghino* with the new frame to victory on its first outing at the 1952 Circuito di Cesena; below, in practice for the Sanremo-Ospedaletti event with one of the first twin-cam 250s, which was fitted with a single carburettor and two valves. Above, Lorenzetti at the 1956 Grand Prix of Nations, riding a "special" derived from the Guzzi 250. After a magnificent race he lost by a whisker to Ubbiali on the works MV, which is still in second place in the photo.

The satisfactions of fame: Lorenzetti interviewed by a RAI sports commentator after the umpteenth win. By this time he was nearing retirement age. After a brief period spent selling motorcycles, Lorenzetti opened a cinematographical laboratory.

THE WAR

The armed forces had become interested in the motorcycle during the first World War, but no one yet had a clear idea of its tactical usefulness. True, some did think of exploiting its agility and manoeuverability for reconnaissance and communications duties, but in general there was a tendency to consider only the economic angle and consequently there were frequent attempts to transform the motorcycle into a species of poor man's tank for armies with liquidity problems.

And so the planners produced a series of assault bikes with machine guns mounted on the handlebars, anti-aircraft bikes with small cannons, and combos for transporting the wounded; in 1930 the French even built a real three-wheeled tank, complete with turret and cannon, whose stability must have been precarious indeed.

That this kind of mentality was deeply rooted among the "experts" in various armies is borne out by the fact that the Germans persisted with their famous (and admittedly well-made) combo units during the last war even though they were shown to be clumsier and less manoeuverable than the Allied forces' jeeps: they probably cost more too.

The situation in Italy was no different and so army bikes had to be big, heavy and if possible, two-seaters, even though off-road riding with a pillion passenger aboard is virtually the equivalent of a circus act.

Bikes for every battlefield

Guzzi's first military order dates from 1928 and it was for a batch of 245 motorcycles with sprung frames; basically, these were slightly modified *G.T.s.* The problem of the specifications was tackled shortly afterwards in a more rational fashion, in a bid to balance the demands of the various Ministries against the need to construct a vehicle which was still light and adaptable to all kinds of terrain.

The result was the *G.T. 17*, which was derived from the civilian *G.T. 16* and made its first appearance in 1932.

This bike had the usual opposed valve engine with magneto ignition, an external flywheel and a 3-speed hand-change gearbox. The combustion chamber was still equipped with the special device which prevented the valves from "dropping in".

The frame was practically identical to that of the *G.T. 16*, with a swinging arm and Hartford-type dampers at the rear; however on the two-seater version (which had a second saddle mounted on the rear mudguard and collapsible handlebars) it was possible to adjust the springs to cope with the extra weight. The system was ingenious: the rear footrest (which could be folded back) was connected by a set of levers to the springs, upon which it acted by means of two racks that varied the degree of preload.

The fuel tank, shorter with more rounded lines, was also different in the two-seater version, because the rider's saddle had been shifted slightly forward.

Compared to the civilian luxury tourer, the army version had a closer set of gear ratios, while other differences included the electrical system (which had no battery), and the exhaust (with the double-barrel silencers).

Wheels, brakes and the footboard-legshield assembly were left unchanged.

Different specifications were prepared depending on the end user's specific requirements: luggage racks or metal panniers of various patterns, attachments for machine guns and their tripods, etc.

In fact light machine guns were very commonly mounted on the handlebars: in this case the seat could be tipped up allowing the gunner to sit on the chassis when shooting; a little less comfort-

Clouds were gathering on the horizon as Europe's armies stepped up their preparations.
Mussolini – we are in 1939 – observes a regiment of Bersaglieri on manoeuvers. The strike force shown in the
photo is equipped with the Guzzi *G.T. 17* which did so well in the Ethiopian war. The *G.T. 17* was the first Guzzi
expressly made for the army.

able perhaps, but far more stable and protected. The *G.T. 17* was delivered to several army groups as well as the *Milizia della Strada*. Adorned with a suitable sand-coloured finish, it had its baptism of fire during Mussolini's African Campaign of 1935-36, where it performed brilliantly on the desert tracks and on the Savannah, filling both natives and Italian soldiery with awe for the way it handled itself over that impossible terrain: "... I left at six for Dembeguinà with a split new bike and brand new boots", wrote E. Novellini in his diary, "after twelve hours I got to my destination. The bike had lost its footboards and I had lost my boots: that ought to give you some idea of what those roads were like..."

At the end of the campaign, several Guzzis were "demobbed" and remained in the Colonies while many of their stablemates went off to the second World War. A case of "out of the frying pan and into the fire" if ever there was one; but some bikes managed to survive both experiences. In 1939 the *G.T.17* was replaced by what was to become the most popular military Guzzi, the *Alce*.

Preceded by a pre-production series denominated the *G.T.20*, the *Alce* – although it had a horizontal cylinder, a two-part frame and a rear swinging arm like all Guzzis – was the result of an entirely unusual design which provided remarkable ground clearance (a good 21 cms) while keeping the wheelbase as short as possible.

This engine was a development of the *S* type unit and had the opposed valves therefore, but the gearbox was a hand-change 4-speed unit with preselector.

The valve stays were retained, largely because military specifications in those days demanded side valves, less of a problem in case of a breakage, and the Guzzi engines were admitted only because they had this safety device. The piston was aluminium, with a good 52/100 of clearance at the crown, which explains the fact that these engines virtually never seized. The crankshaft was still made of steel with embodied counterweights and ran on two roller bearings, while the I-section con-rod rotated with the aid of 33 needle bearings.

The external flywheel was covered by a metal pressing, because the engine was set rather high on the frame and there was a risk of the "bacon slicer" interfering with the rider's leg.

Fuel feed was handled by a 26 mm Dell'Orto with a steel wool air filter, while the spark was provided by a Marelli magneto with manual advance.

The lubrication system was still by dry sump with a twin pressure pump and a vane-type scavenger but, in order to reduce height,

Testing a pre-war experimental tracked vehicle in the outskirts of Mandello. Such vehicles were all powered by 500 cc engines. On the facing page, a division of the Rome city police force equipped with very bellicose-looking armoured bikes fitted with machine guns. The bikes are variants of the *Sport 14* and the year is 1934. The picture after that shows more Bersaglieri in action with the *G.T. 17*, but here we are on the Russian front in 1941. The little Guzzi almost disappears in front of the mighty Mercedes used by Hitler and Mussolini on an inspection of a zone behind the front. Page 61, after the Liberation the Italian Army was equipped with the *Alce* and other vehicles.

the oil tank was housed in the upper part of the frame where it was hidden by the fuel tank.

Primary drive was by helical gears and the multiplate clutch and gearbox were similar to their counterparts in the *V* type drive train. A gear indicator in the form of a slider connected by a flexible cable to the preselector was fitted to the top of the petrol tank. The front end was made up of a forged steel steering head (with two ball races), rivetted metal pressings and a pair of tubular downtubes for the cradle.

This assembly was then bolted to the rear chassis, which was composed of metal pressings. The box for the rear suspension springs formed a stress-member within the lower part of the cradle. The suspension regulation system was done away with although the friction dampers remained.

The tubular girder forks were pretty unusual: in fact the two lateral elements were bolted rather than welded to the central elements so as to simplify repairs. The wheels were interchangeable and both had detachable spindles. The lateral drum brakes were fixed to the hubs by three screws in such a way that the wheels could be removed without disturbing the brakes and the final drive ring gear. In this case too the electrical system was devoid of a battery; a lever was chosen for the throttle as working this type of control was supposed to "come more naturally" to the uninitiated.

Depending on the particular purpose for which the bike was designed, there was the usual assortment of bags, panniers and luggage carriers.

An original device was fitted which made it possible to park the machine on steep slopes: this was formed by a peg which restrained the teeth of the rear wheel sprocket; it was activated by a little lever on the handlebars.

There was also a sidecar version of the *Alce* which was able to transport three soldiers and their equipment. Modifications were few: closer gear ratios plus lugs for the sidecar, which had a four-sided frame made of tubular steel; the wheel was carried on a pressed steel swinging arm with a stubby helical spring working in compression. This swinging arm was then connected to the swinging arm of the bike by means of a torsion bar stabilizer with the dual aim of preventing lateral tipping and skidding when cornering.

Effectively speaking, the peculiar asymmetrical structure of sidecar units always posed knotty problems in terms of road-holding and stability, problems which were exacerbated by the suspension unit (if there was one) fitted to the third wheel. But

designers tended to prefer a rigid frame and even in the Fifties the most famous GP outfits like the Gilera and Norton sidecar units had rigid frames, even for the bike. Therefore it can fairly be said that Guzzi was in the van in this sector too, having been practically the first to show that a completely sprung sidecar combination was both feasible and safe, as well as more comfortable of course.

This vehicle – which had a dry weight of 260 kgs and a good 220 kgs of loading capacity – was constructed in a batch of 669 units which went on to render sterling service, thanks in particular to their lightness and agility (we find that some of today's multicylinder bikes are heavier), but all things considered this should be considered as a transitional motorbike which held the stage while an exceptional new machine was receiving the final touches at Mandello.

This was a combo with a driven third wheel, like the BMW and Zundapp models; but the Guzzi had a completely novel transmission system.

The engine was a *V* derivative: two overhead valves, with a four-speed gearbox and built-in reduction gear; from here the drive was transmitted to the rear wheel by a three-roller chain hidden behind a pressed steel chainguard which doubled as a wheel

support and a suspension swinging arm at the same time. A shaft also emerged from the reduction gear at right angles to the bike; this transferred the power to another three-roller chain (also protected by a chainguard-swinging arm assembly), which drove the third wheel. There was no differential, because the "all-wheel" drive was used for off-road work only, i.e. at moments when the differential would normally be locked to improve traction.

This vehicle, which should have been called the *Trialce* and had three interchangeable wheels, never got beyond the prototype stage as a result of the reverses suffered by the Italian forces; however another *Trialce* was produced. This was an armoured unit obtained by replacing the rearward part of the *Alce* frame with a sheet metal "deck", which could accommodate various kinds of bodies.

In this case the power was fed to the rear axle by a simple chain; the rear axle was also fitted with an aluminium casting which contained the twin triple-chain reduction gear, the recoil stop and the differential, as well as two box-like sheet metal structures for the half-shafts.

The whole thing was connected to the chassis by a swinging arm which acted on a large coil spring.

This *Trialce* was in regular construction from 1940 to 1943 in various guises and there was even a special collapsible version for the parachute regiments which saw action in Corsica, Africa and Greece. It was armed with a light machine gun: as an "assault car" it left something to be desired, but every little bit helped!

After the war was over, research into special vehicles was abandoned and only the solo bike was still produced, in a new version first called the *Alce V* and then rebaptized the *Superalce*. Compared to the wartime version, the most important change consisted of the two overhead valves, which were set at an angle like those of the civilian *V* engines: a definitive goodbye therefore to the glorious opposed valve engine, pensioned off after twenty-five years of honourable service. With its new 27 mm carburettor this engine produced 18.5 hp, while top speed was upped to 110 km/h.

The gears were selected by a pedal: at first they were the frontal engagement type (*Alce V*), which were later replaced by sliding gears (*Superalce*).

The primary drive and clutch were unchanged, proof of the validity of the original design concept.

Likewise, few modifications were made to the frame: the most significant of these concerned the reintroduction of the adjustable rear suspension, which was operated by a control wheel mounted on the lower right hand side of the engine. This bike was in production until 1957, with very few variations: in 1952 a Marelli MCR 4 E automatic advance magneto was fitted in place of the manual advance system; in 1955 a long cylindrical silencer replaced the original double-barrel fitting. Two versions were prepared, one for the Army (dark green) and the other for the *Carabinieri*.

This was a more elegant model with an olive green paint job and chrome brightwork.

The *Superalce* was the last really "military" Guzzi: the machines subsequently supplied to the Italian Army and the various Police authorities were no more than slightly modified civilian bikes, including the *Nuovo Falcone*.

Between 1955 and 1960 research was carried out on various military prototypes, some being *Airone* derivatives fitted with reduction gears and other additions, plus others which were more or less descendants of the *Lodola*, but none reached the production stage.

However they did produce a highly original three-wheeler, the *3 × 3*, which we shall deal with later on.

THE POSTWAR PERIOD

During the dark years of the war the entire Guzzi works was turned over to military production; but people were already thinking of the future and the new motorcycles which would be built when peace returned.

Everybody possesses an innate, atavistic desire for complete freedom of movement and the motorcycle represents a simple form of personal motorized transport which goes some way towards satisfying such a desire. In an Italy whose social structures had been smashed or thrown into confusion by the war, in a country whose roads, railways and transport systems in general were in the grip of virtual paralysis, the motorcycle became an indispensable means of transport as reconstruction got under way. Despite everything however, two-wheeled transport was never really popular in Italy because it had always been seen as a sporting phenomenon, something for athletic and daring young men who were perhaps even a little "tough". This was all very unlike the situation in France or Germany where motorcycle manufacturers had always concentrated largely on producing simple, low-price machines and where the number of bikes in circulation during the pre-war years had already reached notable levels.

By the time the war was over much of the Italian car *parc* had been destroyed and supplies of raw materials like rubber and petrol were drastically limited. Most Italians could do little else but stand helplessly by and watch as their purchasing power was steadily eroded by the raging post-war economic crisis. Within such a scenario the motorcycle represented a potentially ideal means of transport, but it had to be adequately "packaged", and to do that the makers had to divest it of its pre-war image as a dirty, noisy and infernally complex device.

Once again history repeated itself, just like it had done in the aftermath of the Great War: the planners went back to basics and came up with designs for engines which could be fitted to pre-existing pedal bicycles, with the result that most people could afford a personal means of transport. But this time, thanks to technological progress, it was possible to design really small engines, from 30 to 50 cc, that were simple and functional and which gave modest but entirely satisfactory performance.

Sold at prices between 20,000 and 40,000 lire, the "micromotors" were much appreciated by everybody; from cyclists tired of pushing the pedals to motorcyclists who had been "grounded" by the war. Among the many well known Italian marques there were Garelli, who produced the *Mosquito*, a two-stroke 38 cc with roller drive; Siata-Ducati and their *Cucciolo* (Pup), a four-stroke 48 cc moped with a two-speed gearbox and chain drive; the 48 cc *Alpino*, another two-stroke machine with a two-speed box; the *Minimotor*; the *Grim*; the *Aspi*; the *Gazzella*; the *Imex*; the *Leone*; the *Sirio*...

Guzzi gave the matter some thought and produced a very simple little 38 cc two-stroke engine which could be mounted above the rear wheel. It had a horizontal cylinder and rotary inlet valve. The specification also included a two litre fuel tank, a fat exhaust pipe and the frame lugs, with a long lever which made it possible to lift the engine off the wheel in order to disconnect the drive. Built in 1944 and then subjected to prolonged testing, the *Colibrì* (Humming bird) was shelved while still in the prototype stage, in favour of a more ambitious project.

Effectively speaking, a normal bicycle does not really lend itself to being motorized because it is not built to withstand the extra stress involved, nor can it offer a satisfactory level of comfort. As a result the micromotors were soon being fitted to purpose-built frames while vehicles designed and built in one single factory began to make their appearance, like the famous Motom, for example; and probably – since a race to provide improved performance soon got underway – the situation would have led before much longer to a new decline and fall of the moped, if

The photo shows a Customs Police squad mounted on *Falcones* during a riding course held in the Fifties.
The leader is Renzo Alippi, a well known rider in the pre- and post-war periods and subsequently in charge
of testing at Mandello. The *Falcone* represents the maximum expression of Carlo Guzzi's functionalist
constructional philosophy.

suitable legislation had not been passed to make it a special class of vehicle.

At the same time a large number of light and ultralight motorcycles were finding their way onto the market. These had a maximum capacity of 125 cc and, thanks to a wartime regulation, they were not obliged to display registration plates. Obviously these machines were aimed at a class of consumer who could afford something a little more interesting than a moped.

This was the road which Guzzi had decided to take. To some extent perhaps the decision was due to the fact that a micromotor like the one fitted to the *Colibrì* did not seem to offer much in the way of prestige, but in any case it was decided to design something extremely simple and basic but clearly a motorcycle nonetheless, with a 3-speed gearbox, integral suspension, efficient brakes and large wheels.

The 65 cc "Guzzino": a bike for everybody.

Conceived – like the *Colibrì* before it – by Antonio Micucci, the *65* lay outside the Guzzi mainstream in many ways. For a start the swept volume of 65 cc was unusual in itself while the styling was unlike that of its predecessors; not that there was anything whimsical about the design, which was decidedly functional and economical to produce and easy to maintain. Good looking and charming like all truly useful objects, the *65* was an appealing proposition right off the bat. New converts to motorcycling liked its reassuringly clean-cut looks while older hands (who tended to look down their noses at mopeds) were not immune to its appeal either. Undoubtedly the famous Guzzi name was also a major ingredient in its success. The production run extended to tens of thousands of units (it was the first Italian motorcycle to reach such heights) and buyers represented a fair cross-section of society. Sturdy, generous and tireless, it was soon adapted to carry a pillion passenger while sporty variants could "do" the Milan-Taranto event at almost 70 km/h. A sidecar version was also produced. There were some who converted the original 2-stroke engine into a 4-stroke unit while others used it to power three-wheeled minivans.

In 1949, three years after its launch, Guzzi organized an international rally for all "Guzzino" owners. More than 14,000 people showed up from all over Europe bringing 12,660 bikes, a really impressive result and a record for the number of vehicles of the same type which still stands today. It was a memorable occasion resulting in an equally memorable traffic jam which threw the tranquil suburbs of Lecco into confusion for a whole day. That same year witnessed another incredible feat when 25 boy scouts made the 8,000 kilometre trip from Milan to Oslo and back in order to take part in the local owners' rally. The trip went without even the smallest hitch.

Now we come to the construction of the little *65*.

The frame was a single spar type, formed by a fat 50 mm tube which ran down from the steering head at a 45 degree angle; pivoted at its lower end was the pressed steel rear swinging arm, which compressed two biconical springs against two stops welded to the spar itself. The front forks were blade-type units made of pressed steel. The steel wheels were shod with 26" × 1 3/4 × 2 tyres (a size normally reserved for the three-wheeler goods carriers) which had been chosen because they were easier to find than any other type, tyres being still subject to stringent rationing. Brakes were lateral drums.

The extremely simple 2-stroke engine followed the lines of the frame, to which it was attached at three separate points, and had the cylinder inclined at 30 degrees to the horizontal. Made entirely of shell-cast aluminium, it had a two-piece crankcase with the primary drive cover on the right and a plate on the left for the flywheel magneto-alternator. Both cylinder and head had vertical finning, which resembled the pattern chosen some fifteen years before for the racing *Quattro cilindri* and the *Tre cilindri*.

The crankshaft was a three-piece component; in the first models it ran on three anti-friction bearings but later versions used a single roller bearing on the right and a long bronze bearing on the flywheel side. Following the experimental trail blazed by the *Colibrì*, the crankshaft also served as a rotary inlet valve by virtue of a duct carved out of the left hand side port. The one-piece con-rod (made of casehardened steel) ran on 3 mm needle bearings. Two gears in a ratio of 1:3 (fitted on the right) handled the primary drive. These were straight-cut at first but later models had helical gears. The wet clutch had six coil springs arranged in a hexagonal configuration and two friction plates, which later became four. The gearbox was a 3-speeder with sliding gears in direct mesh and was mounted on ball bearings (mainshaft) and bronze bearings (countershaft). Gear selection was effected by means of a lever set on the right hand side of the fuel tank.

Weighing only 45 kilos, the Guzzi *65* could reach 50 km/h, thanks to its 2 hp engine, and could handle gradients of up to 20 %. It consumed a litre of petroil every 40 kilometres and cost 159,000 lire.

The "Guzzino" remained in production until 1954 without any

On the facing page, two shots of the *Colibrì*, the auxiliary bicycle engine designed during the war and then shelved in favour of the *65*. Above, a detail of the Guzzi *65* prototype. It had the carburettor on the right, instead of the left, and a magneto ignition system mounted on the lower part of the crankcase.

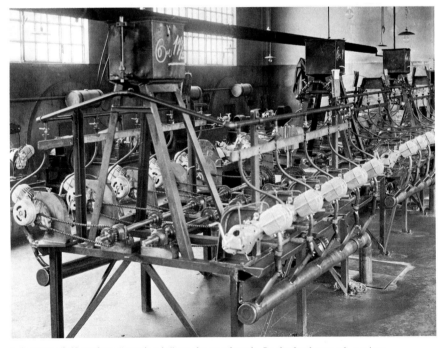

A battery of *65* engines "running in" on the test bench. In the background, engines undergoing power testing. The *65* was the first Italian motorcycle to go into volume production: tens of thousands of units were produced.

great changes being made. The most important modifications regarded the fitting of a stronger swinging arm in 1949 plus a few simplifications, like a cast iron cylinder, blade forks with single rather than double side panels and a simpler type of carburettor, which were aimed at cutting production costs (1953). In a further attempt to curb costs some versions were sold with all-grey paintwork. By way of compensation for all this austerity an elastic pinion (formed by a hub and a crown wheel between which were fitted a series of little cylinders made of special rubber) was fitted to the crankshaft, which functioned as a transmission damper. With these and other minor changes the price fell to a decidedly competitive 107,000 lire.

The following year the price was again reduced, this time to 99,500 lire, and the buyer received an extra in the form of an important modification: the rear mudguard was detached from the swinging arm to become a fixed unit supported by two stays made of box-section sheet metal. A pair of adjustable Hartford-type shock absorbers were mounted between the stays and the swinging arm with the result that the Motoleggera began to look more like its larger stablemates, while the wheel size was reduced to 20" in diameter.

Thus modified, the bike assumed the new name of *Cardellino* (goldfinch - the earlier choice of name *Aquiletta*, or eaglet, having been ruled out) and it remained in production for a considerable number of years to come. During those years it was gradually modified to make it more appealing and to keep costs down in a booming market characterized by some pretty fierce competition. In early 1956 the cycle parts were radically remodelled; the outline of the mudguards and the tank was changed, while the blade forks were substituted by a simple type of undamped telescopic fitment. The original brakes were also replaced by central drums made of cast light alloy.

At the end of that same year the displacement was increased to 73 cc by enlarging the bore to 45 mm, while the hand-operated gearchange (by that time the last of its kind in production anywhere in the world) was replaced by a pedal. Then, the basic *Turismo* model was joined by the new *Lusso* version which had an oval-shaped fuel tank, and a long dualseat. The *Nuovo Cardellino* came out at the end of 1958, with a simplified, lightened swinging fork.

Another major modification consisted of the new light alloy cylinder barrel with chromed liner.

The *Cardellino* was updated for the last time at the end of 1962, when the displacement was once more increased, this time to 83 cc. By that time output was standing at 3.3 hp and top speed at

At the rally organized in Rome by Motociclismo magazine and the F.M.I. for Holy Year (1950) there was no shortage of local colour among the thousands of participants: the photo shows a "chariot" drawn by three *65s* which were controlled by the complex of "reins". The inventor and "charioteer" was Guzzi agent Rino Berton, a good racer in his day. Berton's chariot was a major attraction at many meetings of this type in those years. It had made its debut at the very famous Guzzi-promoted mega-rally held at Mandello in 1949.

about 60 km/h. Other substantial modifications regarded the suspension: the new front forks had springs inside the tubes even though there were no dampers, while telescopic containers had been fitted at the sides of the rear wheels with rubber springing elements which also had a certain shock absorbing effect. The design of the tank had been changed yet again to make it more capacious; the handlebars were also redesigned as were the headlight and the toolbox.

Single and dualseat versions of the 83 cc *Cardellino* remained in the catalogue until 1965, without repeating the success enjoyed by their predecessors. People's tastes and requirements were changing as the industry staggered towards the crisis which followed the rise of the compact car. It was not long before Moto Guzzi also found itself in deep trouble and management hatchet men had to cut out a lot of dead wood on the production side in order to balance the books. And so the *Cardellino* went to the wall after twenty years of honourable service during which it became one of the most popular products ever to roll off the lines at the Mandello works.

The larger capacity classes

As far as the bigger engines were concerned, Guzzi reintroduced the 250 cc *Airone* and the 500 cc *G.T.V.*, after the war, having eliminated all the machines with the rigid frame and the opposed valve engines. Some interesting wartime research, including plans for a 4-stroke 125 cc light motorbike and a 500, both of which would have been fitted with sprung pressed steel frames, remained at the prototype stage and never went into production.

The *G.T.V.* was modified a bit, the most important change being the adoption of a single exhaust, on the right, with the classic fishtail silencer. We have already come across that direct descendant of the *P.E.*, the *Airone*; in this case, the uprated 246 cc engine supplied 9.5 hp at 4800 rpm, ignition was by magneto while the completely redesigned gearbox was a pedal-operated 4-speed constant-mesh unit with an external preselector. The tubular frame was practically the same as the one used by the *P.E.*; additions included the legshields and the rear Hartford-type shock absorbers mounted backwards with the vertex facing forward. Almost immediately however this was replaced by a new, pressed steel frame very like the one used by the *P.E.* and its derivatives. More precisely, the front part was formed by U-shaped elements rivetted to each other and to the steering head,

Top, Enrico Parodi, Giorgio's brother: he joined Guzzi officially in 1942 and managed the firm after the death of the founders. Here he is shown riding a 65 during the 1949 Mandello rally. The photo also shows Umberto Todaro, Carcano's right hand man.

Above, Raffaele Alberti during a successful record attempt with the "Guzzino" on the Saxon-Charrat road (Switzerland) in 1948.
Alberti had already set various records with the blown Guzzi 250 in 1939.

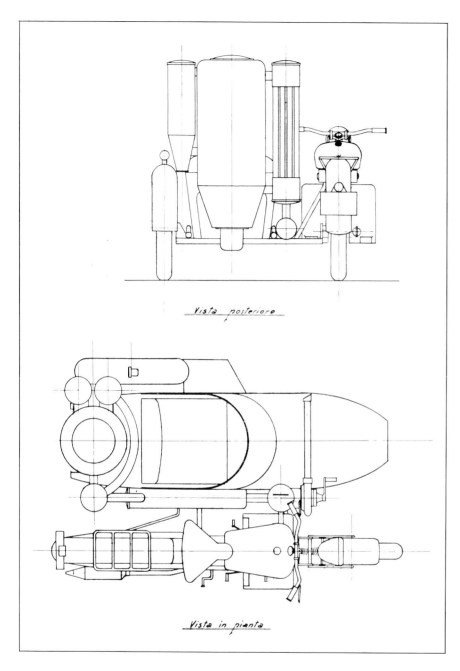

Vista posteriore

Vista in pianta

A wartime plan for a gas-powered sidecar unit. A prototype was also built, using a normal G.T.V. combo. In the period immediately before and after the war, as well as for the duration of the conflict, the petrol shortage stimulated a great deal of research aimed at the creation of vehicles capable of functioning with alternative fuels. Researchers included solo inventors as well as the major manufacturers, like Guzzi and Alfa Romeo. Naturally this kind of equipment proved more suited to motor cars.

while the cradle was completed by the usual L-plates at the back. The parallelogram forks, the swinging arm and the mudguard stays (the one on the right also served as a chainguard) were in box-section pressed steel.

The use of pressed panels, apart from the new design possibilities they offered, helped reduce production costs, which were still high as far as tubular frames were concerned because of the extra manual labour involved. Thanks to the use of deeply valanced mudguards, the *Airone* had an elegant, fashionable look which would not look bad even today, as well as a really competitive price tag. This bike (which weighed in at 135 kgs and could touch 95 km/h) was completed by an 11 litre tank, a 2.5 litre oil tank, a baggage carrier and toolkits at each side of the rear mudguard. This then was the *Airone* which Guzzi began building again in 1945. A very sturdy and tireless bike, it was gifted with a capacity to soak up punishment which was even more impressive than that of the 500 itself. The *Airone* can fairly be considered a smaller copy of the 500, rather than – as is generally the case – a bike obtained by pumping up a smaller model to the bursting point; it was a real utility "workhorse" but it still offered enough genuine motorcycle performance to satisfy a wide range of paying customers. Its limitations, if they may be so described, lay in the use of some components, like the front forks and the exposed valve gear, which were typical of outdated pre-war technology.

The business of updating the bike was not long in getting under way and in fact began in 1947 with the fitting of telescopic front forks and a pair of hydraulic shock absorbers instead of the Hartford-type units. In this case too Guzzi did not stick to the beaten track but blazed new trails. "Classic" telescopic fork designs, still built today, call for the use of weight-bearing internal tubular rods, in a unit with the steering, and sliding external covers, to which the wheel is fixed. Carlo Guzzi's fork turned this design on its head inasmuch as it called for weight-bearing tubes on top, fixed to the steering, with the fork rods inside.

Apart from the difference in terms of styling, this meant greater strength since the part subject to most stress could be made to a considerable diameter (47 mm) and was therefore able to resist flexing far better. Each sliding rod, ground and flash-chromed, was positioned by a bronze bush above while the lower end was positioned by two bronze slides contained in a box welded to the base of the fork tube. One of these two slides was fixed while the other took the form of a roller which rotated on an eccentric spindle so as to recover any play – another exclusive feature of the Guzzi fork. The rod acted upon a long coil spring which had the reloadable dual-action hydraulic shock absorber mounted within it. This design, undoubtedly costly but certainly effective, was also fitted to the *G.T.V. 500* at the end of 1947 and it remained in production until 1967, the year which marked the end of the glorious series of engines spawned by the legendary *Normale* in 1921.

At the rear the suspension was integrated with two hydraulic dampers mounted alongside the wheel in place of the old friction dampers. The springs remained under the engine in the usual cylindrical container and therefore were not linked to the shock absorbers, in accordance with a design which is in common use even today. At the end of 1947 this type of shock absorber was also fitted to the *G.T.V.*, which showed up for the following season sporting a new teledraulic suspension system. Another important update was the adoption of a head with the rocker gear operating in an oil bath and thus protected from damage caused by atmospheric agents. This was introduced at the end of 1948 and put into production the year after that. The aluminium head was accompanied by a new light alloy barrel with larger finning and a cast iron bore. The rocker box was a casting comprising two transverse compartments for the rockers (which pivoted on bronze bearings) and the double hairpin springs. The inlet rocker arm spindle was lubricated via an oilway coming from an oil recovery tube; the oil then ran along a gallery carved out of the casting which led to the exhaust rocker, from where an external line took it back to the bottom of the crankcase.

A sporty version of the *Airone* was then introduced. Guzzi could boast a well deserved reputation in this capacity class and the newcomer soon won enthusiastic acclaim. Manageable, light (140 kgs) and with excellent acceleration for those days, the *Airone Sport* was also very popular abroad, a novelty as far as Italian motorcycles were concerned. In the years leading up to the war the international market was very much dominated by the British industry, which also held a good share of the Italian market. For various reasons – not the least of which was the higher price – Italian products, even though they were appreciated for their technical content, struggled to make themselves known beyond the national frontiers.

After the war the pendulum began to swing in the opposite direction, thanks largely to products like the *Airone*; and if sales were not quite as healthy as they could have been, this was due solely to the rather blinkered mentality then predominant within the Italian motorcycle industry. It is worth observing that such an outlook did not exist in the dynamic new scooter

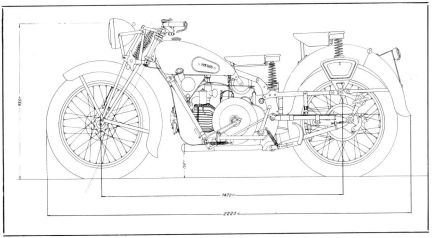

Guzzi has supplied the Traffic Police since that corps was founded. The photo (taken just after the war) shows two policemen on *G.T.V.*s obliging a motorist to pull over. The drawing is of the two-seater version of the same model, built specially for military use. The *Astore* assembly shop is featured in the next photo (1950). In those days the big motorcycles were hand-built one by one without making use of production line systems.

sector, with results that need no further comment here. Compared to the version which from that moment on was known as the *Turismo*, the *Airone Sport* possessed the following variations in the engine room: a different cam profile, a competition-type 25 mm Dell'Orto carburettor and a more compact combustion chamber. Other modifications regarded the stronger clutch spring and the slighly wider gear ratios. The engine developed 13.5 hp at 6000 rpm running on a compression ratio of 7:1, enough to propel the bike to 120 km/h.

The modifications made to the cycle parts were more noticeable because the rear end of the frame (swinging arm and mudguard stays) was a tubular rather than a pressed steel structure; this, along with the two new mudguards, which were sleeker and more compact, conspired to give the bike a far less cumbersome look. The "Guzzi type" telescopic forks were retained, but the old-style friction dampers had reappeared at the rear as, being easily adjustable, they were considered to be better suited to a sporting vehicle in those days. The braking system was improved with the adoption of two lateral light alloy drum brakes (measuring 200 mm in diameter) in preference to the smaller steel units used previously, which were reserved for the *Turismo* from then on. Other variations with respect to the latter bike included wheels with aluminium rims, narrower handlebars and a little pillion pad on the rear mudguard to accommodate the rider's rear when he chose to adopt a sporting riding position.

Sold at 380,000 lire, the *Airone Sport* remained unchanged throughout the 1951 season. A petrol tank with flowing, rounded lines was fitted at the beginning of the following year. This was like the component designed the year before for the *Falcone*; it had a capacity of 13.5 litres and was painted red with two black oval kneegrips. At the same time, the *Turismo* inherited the *Sport* frame, thus sounding the death knell for the all-pressed steel frame, the hydraulic dampers at the rear and the small-diameter brakes. Performance apart, the two versions had different handlebars and wheels (still made of steel for the *Turismo*), while the footpegs had been shifted aft on the *Sport* in the interests of a better riding position. As a consequence, the back brake pedal was operated with the tip of the toe instead of the heel.

In 1952 the manual advance magneto was replaced by the new Marelli MCR 4E instrument with automatic advance and rotary magnet, while in 1954 a new silencer ending in a truncated cone was fitted in place of the noisier fishtail type. This left the easy-going *Turismo* engine unmoved, but it clipped the wings of the *Sport* more than somewhat as output fell to 12 hp and top speed was reduced to a bare 110 km/h. At the same time the *Sport* received chromed tank knee grips in place of the black rubber ovals, while an "army" version was prepared with the *Turismo* engine, legshields, larger tyres and a few other minor differences.

But this period also marks the beginning of the *Airone*'s decline. By that time there were plenty of lightweights on the market offering performance which was just as good if not better than the Mandello single which, as we have seen, had been downgraded rather than improved; even the *Turismo* version no longer had much of a following because few people could see any practical advantage in a big, powerful, but under exploited engine while the majority of riders felt humiliated when overtaken by machines with half the cubic capacity.

At Guzzi the planners were casting around for something new and the *Airone* was allowed to die a lingering death; in 1956 – following the application of a new silencer, which was very effective but even more of a ball and chain in terms of performance – the *Sport* was deleted. The *Turismo* model hung on for another year, thanks to military contracts more than anything else, before it too disappeared, killed off by changing times and demands.

And so we come to the end of an epoch; about fifteen years were to pass before Guzzi once more began producing a machine in this capacity class, even though it was to have characteristics which were in some ways completely different to those of its glorious forebears.

In our section on the *Airone* we also noted that the *G.T.V.* was also equipped with telescopic suspension units at the end of 1947. The aluminium cylinder head with the enclosed valve gear was not fitted to the 500 until the end of 1949, a year after this important innovation had been mounted on the smaller model. In this case, however, it was a pretext for the introduction of a new model, since with this change the Mandello-built "half litre" bike was rebaptized the *Astore* (goshawk), after the powerful bird of prey. Everything else, performance included, remained identical to the *G.T.V.* with the telescopic forks. However it should be said that the *Astore* was the most imposing and perhaps the most refined of the various "old-style" 500s produced by Guzzi: the generously proportioned mudguards, the legshields, the rear shock absorbers and the big engine gave a notable impression of power and strength. The various components, although they were the result of continuous modifications made over the years, nevertheless represented a harmonious

blend which was hard to beat. It was by no means a beautiful bike from a strictly aesthetic point of view, perhaps none of the Guzzis ever were, but it represented the apogee of that essentially functional look which we can trace right back to the very earliest model produced in 1921.

At the end of 1950 Guzzi brought out a new sporty 500 to replace the *G.T.W.* (the production of which had begun again in 1948), based on the *G.T.V.* and in fact resembling it in all but a few details: the light alloy wheels, the more compact handlebars and obviously the more powerful engine. The *Falcone*, as the new bike was called, was very much within the mainstream of the house style, but a few deft touches here and there were enough to give the newcomer the sleek and streamlined look of a greyhound ready to explode into action. The mudguards were slimmer and smaller, the 17-litre tank had a smoothly rounded line, the rear dampers were still the Hartford type, while the narrow handlebars and the footrests set well back made for a typical race-type riding stance. Other differences regarding the cycle parts consisted of the light alloy wheels, the abolition of the legshields and a pillion pad which had appeared on the rear mudguard in place of the baggage carrier.

The engine possessed several innovations in comparison with the preceding production models: the most important of these – which also involved the modification of the crankcase – concerned the adoption of a *Condor* and *Dondolino* type 4-speed constant-mesh gearbox with the shafts on the same level rather than one on top of the other. This was a faster and smoother unit than before which went a good way towards eliminating a typical Guzzi problem, i.e. a certain sluggishness when changing gear. Obviously, other changes had also been made with a view to increasing performance, like a 29 mm carburettor, a domed piston and a different camshaft. The con-rod was made of a lighter special steel, as was the crankshaft. Bikes in the subsequent series were fitted with a one-piece crankshaft without the bolt-up counterweights.

Big-hearted and lively, the *Falcone* engine supplied 23 hp, enough for 135 km/h. It also lent itself well to further development, largely because it was not hard to adapt various *Dondolino* components, like the camshaft, so as to obtain performance levels which would be respectable even by today's standards. Sold at 482,000 lire, it was very much a dream bike at the time, but at least it was a dream which could come true, unlike other much-fancied irons like the *Dondolino*, which at 895,000 lire was a real pipe dream as far as ordinary mortals were concerned; especially

in an age when the moped was a ubiquitous presence and even a light motorcycle turned heads when it went by.

An automatic advance magneto was fitted to the *Falcone* in 1952 while the following year the 500s were standardized in much the same way as the *Airone* had been. This meant curtains for the *Astore* – which had been fitted with a series of different shaped tanks since 1949 – while a *Turismo* version entered the lists alongside the *Falcone*, which was thereafter known as the *Sport*. The new *Falcone Turismo* received Hartford-type shock absorbers at the back and a *Dondolino* gearbox, but it kept the carburettor and rocker gear (and performance therefore) which it had inherited from the *Astore*, as well as the handlebars, wheels, legshields and riding stance.

Around 1955, however, the classic "heavyweights" were in real trouble. The vast majority of utility vehicle buyers, who had made the fortunes of the motorcycle manufacturers in the post-war period by snapping up their scooters and light motorcycles as fast as they came off the lines (Guzzi's arrival in the European big league was largely thanks to the success of the *65*), could now afford a compact car and so many people turned their backs on the big bikes forever. On the other hand motorcycling die-hards could now buy 175 cc (or less) lightweights that could show a clean pair of heels to the lumbering 500s, which had powerful engines but were twenty years out of date in conceptional terms.

And so the big "Cinquecento", which only five years previously had been the queen of the Italian roads, a vehicle which only a few Alfas and the first Cisitalias could overtake, was now being regularly humiliated by pipsqueak 150s and 175s. In the space of a few years the lightweights had made enormous strides, thanks also to a booming market which had encouraged manufacturers to invest in research and development.

In order to make up for lost ground it was necessary to redesign the big bikes. There was no shortage of radically new ideas, since in those days the Italian multi-cylinder bikes were going from strength to strength in the world of motorsport thanks to some very bold technical features which offered amazing performance. What was lacking was the courage or the will to plough back all the enormous quantities of technical know-how which had been acquired through racing into standard production, and so the market continued to splutter along fitfully until it seemed about to give up the ghost altogether. Another ten years were to pass before there was a powerful upsurge of the demand for "maxi-bikes", an urge ably fuelled by the Japanese who were able to carry on – and progress –

Above and on the facing page, two illustrations of the usefulness of motorcycles: a mercy dash for the delivery of a rare medicine and an escort for a wide load. The photographs (from 1954 and 1965) show Transport Policemen aboard the *Astore* and *Falcone* models.

from where the European motorcycle industry had left off. Despite everything, the *Turismo* and *Sport* versions of the *Falcone* remained in production for some years to come, practically until the outset of the Seventies, thanks largely to orders from the Traffic Police and other military corps, which were primarily interested in a bike that was comfortable, robust, and highly resistant to heavy use. The modifications made over the years are not of much importance: a new, quieter silencer was fitted at the end of 1955, but this penalized performance heavily, as had occurred with the *Airone*. Then, in 1958, the headlight on the police bike was set higher in order to accommodate the siren, while a new 60 W dynamo with a separate regulator was mounted in 1964. In 1966 a small series was produced – again for the police – with a stepped saddle, wide, American-style handlebars and a squarish petrol tank with knee recesses.

Some specials are also worth remembering here, like the version with the electric starter supplied to the Presidential Guard for example. For more detailed information, the reader is referred to the catalogue section dealing with military vehicles.

When the last units of the *Falcone* rolled off the lines in 1967 it was the end of the road for Mandello's most classic engine, a direct descendant of the single-cylinder unit conceived and built by Carlo Guzzi all those years before. By now only a few survivors remain from that glorious period during which a handful of enthusiasts threw themselves body and soul into the task of building a new and different motorcycle. But the *Falcone* will always be the symbol of a golden age of romantic motorcycling, one of the highest expressions of one man's brilliance. A symbol which was revived some time later in the form of the *Nuovo Falcone*, built principally to satisfy military orders but aimed also at those who longed nostalgically for the good old days. Although it remained faithful to the flat single layout with the usual over-square (88 × 82 mm) dimensions and the external flywheel, the engine boasted several innovations in comparison with the old *Falcone*, ranging from the wet sump lubrication circuit (with a simple pressure pump), to the coil ignition and the new-concept 4-speed gearbox, the electric starter (optional) with dynamotor, as well as the cleaner, more regular lines which resulted from the fact that all the various accessories, including the flywheel, were hidden under special covers.

The cycle parts were also completely renewed with the employment of a tubular duplex cradle, new telescopic forks, and swinging arm rear suspension with teledraulic units mounted alongside the 18" wheels, which carried centrally-mounted drum brakes. Basically conceived as a military machine, it was the usual mas-

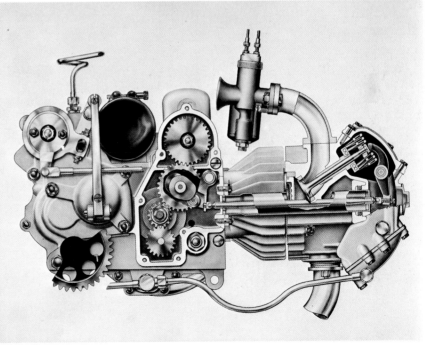

A partial cutaway of the last version (from 1952 onwards) of the *Airone Turismo* engine with the automatic advance magneto.

73

Another shot of the start of the Raid Nord-Sud, from the old customs house in Milan's Rogoredo suburb. We are at the outset of the Thirties and the race has become important enough to attract the attention of the Italian equivalent of a Pathé News film unit.

The finish in Naples. The event was also known as the "Mussolini Cup" in those days. The rather relaxed-looking competitor aboard the *Bicilindrica* is 1934 and 1937 sidecar class winner Terzo Bandini.

sive and excessively heavy bike, so much so that it can more fairly be considered the heir to the Superalce. It had neither the acceleration nor the manageability of the real *Falcone* and it was certainly not bike enough to obscure fond memories of the latter. Its first appearance dates from 1969, while the civilian version with the longer tank and the dualseat made its bow at the end of 1971. The *Sahara* appeared in 1974; this was practically the military bike with a sand-coloured finish and blued (rather than chromed) accessories, intended for heavy duty use in areas where road surfaces were particularly poor. The *Nuovo Falcone* was deleted in 1976.

The great road races

Difficult, dangerous, full of hidden perils but completely fascinating, the great road races have always held a special attraction for spectators and riders alike.

Circuit racing leaves little to chance, the track is studied inch by inch and in the end the race is often no more than a monotonous repetition of identical movements; take the foot off the gas just there, brake just so, sweep through the bend the way you did a hundred times in practice, then open her up and do the same thing all over again. Great for robot-riders, human computers who can do lap after lap without so much as a tenth of a second's variation, this kind of racing certainly did not represent the ideal for idiosyncratic types with a penchant for improvisation like many of the extravagant figures of the past. These were men who competed for the fun of it and because they wanted to measure themselves against their peers and not just to get rich - the money was almost always a pittance in any case. It was no accident therefore that the end of the great road races coincided with a change in the qualities displayed by the riders, who are as cold, detached and even a little unhuman today as they were generous, impulsive and unpredictable before.

Road racing always attracted a large public, precisely for these reasons. In terms of pure spectacle, circuit racing, with its continuous succession of individual duels and dramatic overtaking, represents good value for money whereas a road race offers spectators little more than a fleeting glimpse of their heroes. But in those few brief instants, the spectators could run the gamut of the racer's feelings: his loneliness, his fear of an accident far from any source of aid, as well as the satisfaction which comes at the end of a job well done, when the difficulties have been overcome and the dangers averted. The spectators could see the rider's face as he passed, they could get close (sometimes too close), near enough to tell if he was tired, suffering or elated. Better still, they could cheer him on in the certain knowledge that he could hear every word.

Such events were also run with chronometric precision. For example, the Milano-Taranto event began at the stroke of midnight, from the suburb of Rogoredo before the war and later from the Idroscalo (a large man-made lake on the outskirts of Milan). The competitors waited their turn with their goggles on and their leathers covered by waterproof overalls, which were jettisoned when the sun came up. In order to protect themselves from the nighttime cold, some riders used to cover themselves with anti-rheumatic ointment as such journeys were uncomfortable enough without an attack of rheumatism.

The bikes were padded to an unlikely degree with cushions and foam rubber with a view to mitigating the discomfort of the journey, which could take as much as twenty hours or more for the smaller bikes. Spare parts, wrenches, inner tubes and water bottles were attached in the oddest places with the aid of sticky tape. The spectators began to arrive around eight o'clock in the evening, by bicycle, by car, and naturally by motorcycle, packing the sides of the road in a seemingly endless queue which stretched from the start to the outlying towns of San Donato, Melegnano and Lodi. In the towns and villages on the race route people watched from windows and doorways while rows of seats were lined up in front of the local hostelries, which often stayed open all night for the occasion. It was not unusual for a rider to stop for a quick bite to eat or to make repairs, a fact which attracted swarms of little boys who could not believe their luck at being able to see and touch a real racing bike.

At the stroke of midnight, the tricolour was lowered and the first competitor streaked off down the long straights of the Via Emilia where the most powerful machines regularly set faster and faster times. The great adventure had begun; and it was on to the impossible roads of the Futa and Raticosa passes between Bologna and Florence, the hills and dales of Tuscany, down to Rome and Naples, across the Appenines once more and on to the long straights of Puglia: heat, cold, sometimes rain and fog, bend after bend, up hill and down dale, town after town, roadside crowds and desolate wildernesses, tiredness and hunger, a quick sandwich during refuelling stops, cramps in the hands, arms and back, as the eyesight gets clouded and a little voice inside says what's that noise? Something's getting ready to break, will I be able to repair it? What's that damned dog doing in the middle of the road? I've had enough, I'll have to stop, no, I have

The 1934 Milano-Napoli event: Guglielmo Sandri during a refuelling stop in Rome. The bike is the 4-speed ohc 250.

In an extended version which took it as far as Taranto, the "Raid" began again after the war. Guido Borri (with sideman Lenzi) at the start of the 1953 event with his *Falcone* combo which was to win its class.

to get there... until finally the esplanade at Taranto comes into sight, the white buildings, the palm trees, more people, the chequered flag, I've made it, where am I in the rankings? Who cares, I've made it.

The Raid Nord-Sud, as the race is also known, was first held in 1919 and the route took in Milan - Bologna - Florence - Siena - Rome - Cassino - Naples. Twenty-nine people took part. Miro Maffei was the winner, but he was later disqualified for having strayed off the route and the victory was awarded to Ettore Girardi on the Garelli 350, who took 21 hours and 56 minutes to cover the 865 kilometre course. Maffei got his revenge the following year when he won on an Indian 500 at an average speed of 39.586 km/h.

As we said at the beginning Guzzi made its sporting debut in the 1921 Raid Nord-Sud with riders Mario Cavedini and Aldo Finzi. From then on Guzzis starred regularly in this event, which they won on many occasions. After a lengthy hiatus, the Raid was revived in 1932 and Guzzi immediately scored two victories, one in the 250 class with Riccardo Brusi and the other in the 500 class with Carlo Fumagalli. It was the same story in 1934, 1935 and 1936 with Brusi and Bandini and then with Omobono Tenni and Pigorini.

In 1937 the race was extended to Taranto, thus making the course about 1,300 kilometres long overall. Guzzi continued in its winning ways over this new distance as well, with Guglielmo Sandri and Nello Pagani winning the 500 and 250 classes. Pagani won again in 1938. Then came a straight series of outright wins notched up by the *Condor* and the *Dondolino*, in the years 1949 - 1950 - 1951 - 1952 - 1953, not forgetting a class win in 1954, proof of the fact that the Guzzis were ideally suited to this kind of race, in which robustness and resistance to prolonged stress were decisive factors.

Several other road races deserve a mention here, like the Targa Florio, where Guzzi scored its first win in 1921, and the round Italy race organized by the *Gazzetta dello Sport*; but the most popular event of all, along with the Milan-Taranto event, was the *Circuito del Lario*, which started from Canzo-Asso and ran through Valbrona as far as Onno, before skirting lake Como to Bellagio, from where the route climbed up Mt Ghisallo before running down into Vallassina once more.

The 40 kilometre route had to be covered several times, depending on the capacity class, and so this was not a classic linear road race as such, but its other characteristics made it virtually identical to a normal road event, with all the difficulties which tend to arise from a combination of beaten earth road surfaces, hairpin bends on mountain roads, wooded downhill stretches, and the impossibly narrow and tortuous village streets. The Lario also provided many curious and dramatic episodes which gave rise to some of the most famous anecdotes in motorcycling legendry. Like the stories concerning Tenni's spectacular accidents, for example, or Nuvolari's unorthodox cornering technique (it seems he leaned against the corners of the houses with his elbows). But apart from all this, there remains the reality of a very tough race indeed, which was justly described as the Italian equivalent of the Tourist Trophy, where exceptional riders did not hesitate to pilot even supercharged bikes, despite the dust, discomfort and a host of other hazards, for little else bar the glory. Beset by various difficulties, the *Circuito del Lario* was held fifteen times between 1921 and 1939, with one or two interruptions. The route was home ground as far as the Guzzis were concerned, so to speak, and the race was virtually always monopolized by the Mandello-built machines, which failed to win on only two occasions. The marque also used the race as a species of test bed for its latest creations.

We have already mentioned the victorious debuts of the *2 VT* and the *Quattro valvole*, and so let us turn to the wins notched up by Ghersi (1924) and Ruggeri (1925), both with the 500; and the spectacular straight run of wins in the 250 class, from 1926 to 1939 with only one break, in 1928. This series is largely the work of Ugo Prini, a specialist in the Lario who took part on eleven occasions to rack up an incredible total of eight wins. Born in 1899, Prini had made his debut aboard a Frera in the 1923 Milan-Naples event: he joined the Guzzi team only two years after that (the apprenticeship was not so long then as it was to become). As well as speed races, he also entered and won many regularity events, including the 1932 "Six Days" trophy. Like many other racers of those days he was a member of the *Milizia della Strada* (the present day Traffic Police), a corps in which he remained until he reached retirement age.

The Lario was held for the last time in 1939 and it was to be a triumph for Guzzi who took the 250 Corsa class with Guglielmo Sandri and the 500 Corsa class with Nello Pagani on the *Condor* while the faithful Prini won the 500 Sport class. Pagani's record breaking average of more than 84 km/h, still has a touch of the incredible about it today, despite our completely asphalted roads and modern bikes.

In 1953 the *Motogiro d'Italia* was brought back to life. This was a speed event, divided up into stages, which was limited to 175 cc and under sport bikes for obvious safety reasons. It was a race which generated a lot of enthusiasm among the riders, who en-

Guzzi was always a star of major road races like the *Giro d'Italia*, won by Mentasti in 1923 at more than 40 km/h (the facing page shows him battling his way over an extremely rough stretch), and the Lario, which is portrayed in a romantic shot on the facing page with the church of S. Alessandro in the background. Above, the *Circuito del Lario* again with Ugo Prini on his way to one of his many victories. Top, Aldo Pigorini on his way up Mt Ghisallo in 1935, on his way to victory with the 4-speed ohc 250.

Several prototypes were studied and then abandoned: an honourable mention goes to the 160 cc scooter with electric starter from 1960 (top) and the 49 cc "three-wheeler", also dating from 1960.

tered in droves, and the public, who flocked to watch them race. Unfortunately the Mille Miglia tragedy of some years later was to bring the era of fast road races to an abrupt and final close. Truth to tell, the situation could not have gone on for much longer in any case, as the sport would almost certainly have been killed off by the very progress which it had helped to engender. However we will always remember this period as a fabulous, never-to-be-repeated page in the story of motorcycling, full of a spirit of courage and derring-do, with which the name Moto Guzzi is inextricably linked.

The scooter era: going against the flow?

One of the most noticeable new features on the post-war motoring landscape was the motor scooter.

This strange fully-enclosed vehicle was to attract large numbers of new converts to the idea of two-wheeled transport, that is to say all those people who were looking for a simple and economical means of transport but who did not feel up to the challenge of a traditional motorcycle.

To tell the truth, the motor scooter is not all that recent an invention and examples exist which date from the early years of the century. The scooter even enjoyed a certain vogue in the Twenties, but it failed to catch on in a big way because the majority of people still did not feel the need to procure themselves a private means of transport, while "real" motorcyclists tended to look down their noses at such toys.

By the end of the Forties things had changed and so the scooter – backed up by intelligent advertising and the production "muscle" of the major manufacturers – was ready to begin its triumphal march.

However, apart from the undoubted advantages, like ease of mounting, rider protection and the spare wheel, some disadvantages - or better, some fears - took a long time to die, in particular the idea that the small wheels were neither stable nor safe. On the other hand there had been no shortage of attempts to body ordinary motorcycles with large wheels and there had been a spate of such efforts around the outset of the Thirties, so much so that it is tempting to suggest that, deep down, even diehard motorcycling purists were interested in a little comfort and some protection from the inclemencies of the weather; but all things considered, the results had never really been satisfactory.

In 1950, however, Carlo Guzzi thought that the time was ripe to create a machine representing a compromise between the scooter and the traditional motorcycle which would embody the various advantages of each design while eliminating the respective disadvantages. The result which flowed out from his fertile pencil was the *Galletto* (Cockerel), a bike whose horizontal engine left a certain empty space between the saddle and the handlebars but still left something to grip between the legs, an important factor which conferred a sense of security upon those accustomed to the reassuring presence of the fuel tank between their knees. It also ran on 17" wheels, a "big" size but not so large as to make it impossible to carry a spare wheel for emergencies. The *Galletto* – for which Guzzi had built a life-sized wire mannekin so that he could get an idea of the most rational shape for the bike – had a frame formed by a kind of large upright pressing (incorporating the steering head as well as the fuel tank) at the front, which was rivetted to a horizontal tunnel-shaped engine housing. The rear wheel was supported by a large tubular arm fixed to the tunnel, which made for really simple tyre changes. The rear suspension was handled by a pack of coil springs mounted in a case above the engine, which the fork compressed by means of a sheet metal plate, while the front suspension system had a telescopic leading link fork rather like the one fitted to the *Gambalunga*.

The interchangeable wheels were fixed to the brake drums by four nuts. Dismantling the rear wheel was really very easy, because all that was required was to detach it from the brake drum, which remained attached to the suspension arm by the eccentric spindle used to adjust the tension of the drive chain. Removing the front wheel was a little more complicated, but it was still a relatively easy task all things considered. The engine was enclosed by aluminium pressings at both sides while wide legshields were bolted on to the box-like frontal structure; a valanced rear mudguard formed the rear of the body. Another boxed element supported the saddle, and covered the oil tank and the battery. The space between the front wheel and the front part of the frame was used to house the spare wheel, which did not exceed the transverse dimensions of the legshields and did double duty as a bumper.

The *Galletto* engine which made its world debut at the 1950 Geneva Motor Show had a 150 cc 4-stroke engine with a bore of 60 mm and a stroke of 53 mm. This was a larger capacity engine than that fitted to many similar bikes, which rarely exceeded 125 cc, and it conferred above average performance on the *Galletto*, a fact which made the new Guzzi more than just a two-wheeler suitable for fast hops from one part of town to another, but a genuine roadster in its own right. Various other design features

The engine from the *Zigolo 110* was adapted for various industrial applications, agricultural machinery (cultivators) and for marine use (like the inboard motor shown in this photo). However this did not go into production.

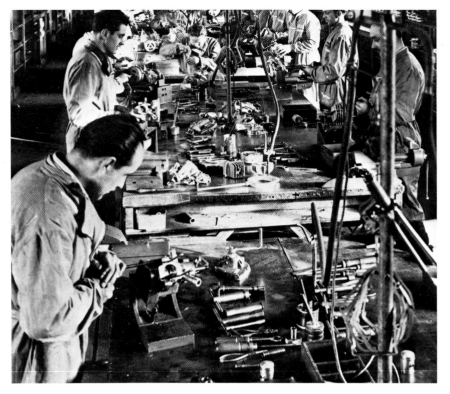

Two views of the Guzzi works in the post-war period: hand-assembling 65 engines in 1949, and the *Galletto*, *Stornello*, and *Zigolo* production lines in 1962. On the facing page, a cross section of the 192 cc *Galletto* engine with 4-speed gearbox and crankshaft running on bronze bushes.

combined to make the *Galletto* engine a little different from the usual Guzzi power unit. The shell-cast light alloy crankcase was a one-piece unit rounded off by a cover on the right hand side and the compartment for the primary drive on the left.

In order to reduce transverse dimensions, the crankshaft was mounted on the left, where it was supported by two roller bearings; the one-piece con-rod ran on needle bearings and was locked onto the crankpin by an endcap and a large screw-in retainer. The aluminium cylinder barrel had a cast iron liner, a good half of which was recessed into the crankcase. Lubrication was by dry sump with a dual feed and return pump. The inclined overhead valves were controlled by push-rods and rocker arms and closed by coil springs. A large flywheel magneto alternator was mounted on the left hand extremity of the crankshaft and this supplied current for the lights and the ignition system. However, the contact breaker with manual spark advance was mounted externally, on the camshaft gear. A pair of spur gears was chosen for the primary drive and the multiplate clutch had six springs. The gearbox was a 3-speeder with sliding gears controlled by a pedal with preselector, although a hand-change unit was also available as an optional. By the time it was put on sale some time later, the *Galletto* had been uprated to 160 cc, a figure obtained by increasing the bore to 62 mm, and this engine remained unchanged throughout 1952. Sales did not reach the levels attained by what we might call the "classic" scooters, the Vespas and Lambrettas, both because of the heftier price tag and the unusual look, but they were still very good and the *Galletto* was a decided success for Guzzi.

After having introduced some design variations to the 160 series at the end of 1951 (arched legshields, smarter, less deeply valanced rear mudguard, a different gear pedal), in the November of 1962 Guzzi presented a new and radically modified version of the *Galletto* at the Milan Show. Just for starters the engine had been uprated to 175 cc (65 × 53 mm), which provided 7 hp and pushed the top speed up to 85 km/h. The crankshaft was now running on a long bronze bush in place of the roller bearings, while the cylinder was made entirely of cast iron. A constant-mesh four-speed gearbox was also fitted. The electrics were still fed by a flywheel magneto, but the ignition system now had an external HT coil mounted under the little instrument panel.

In the first months of 1954 the engine was once more uprated, this time to 192 cc, with bore and stroke of 65 × 58 mm. This meant 7.5 hp at 5000 rpm running on a 6.4:1 compression ratio. The flywheel magneto was replaced by a simple flywheel stabilizer, and electric current was provided by a dynamo mounted

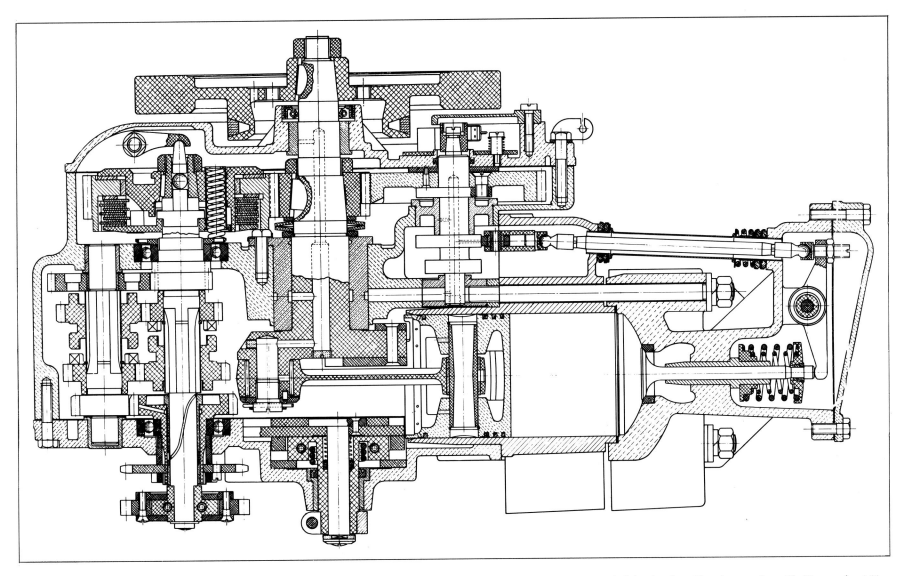

above the engine, which meant that the upper plate of the central tunnel had to be raised as a consequence.

This was probably the best version of the *Galletto*, distinguished by an excellent blend of performance, suppleness, robustness and economical running. The last version dates from 1961 and it sported various modifications to the front chassis, handlebars, rear mudguard, and saddle, as well as new load-adjustable hydraulic shock absorbers at the back in place of the old friction dampers. But the most important change consisted of the electric starter, a 12 V Marelli dynastart unit fitted aft of the engine between the gearbox and the back wheel, and connected to the flywheel by a V belt.

This idea was appreciable in itself, since the *Galletto* (a bike aimed at the utility market) had everything to gain by offering the customer yet another useful feature; but in practice the dynamotor was found to be a delicate and not very efficient instrument which had more than its fair share of problems. Besides, the era of the compact car was dawning and the majority of road users were beginning to turn their backs on two-wheeled transport. The electric-start *Galletto* was therefore unable to repeat the success enjoyed by its forerunners and so, when the great crisis came in 1964 and it was time to cut away the dead wood, the *Galletto*'s name was among the proscribed. It was definitively deleted in 1966.

THE GRAND PRIX ERA

In the immediate post-war period Guzzi could count on the genius of its dynamic founder and on the support of two other talented project engineers: Antonio Micucci, whom we have already mentioned, and Giulio Cesare Carcano. A Milanese with a passion for engines and boats, Carcano also spent his holidays at Mandello, a spot he considered ideal for the pursuit of his various interests. Having thus entered the orbit of the Guzzi clan so naturally, he landed a job in the company in 1936, shortly after taking the equivalent of a first in engineering to become the youngest qualified engineer in Italy. A brilliant and eclectic man with a rather uncompromising character, Carcano's name has become synonymous with some of the most famous models created by Guzzi, especially in the sporting sector. His efforts found their ultimate expression in the creation of the famous 500 cc V8 engine which remains one of the boldest examples of the multi-cylinder motorcycle engine to this day.

Carcano was able to display his considerable talents on the production side too, and his influence would have been greater still had it not been for the thrifty streak in Carlo Guzzi, who ruled out many of the young engineer's ideas saying they were too expensive for the average motorcycle buyer. Carcano's first important job was the creation of the *Albatros*, which was a joint effort with Guzzi himself. The post-war period found him heading the racing division, where he was charged with the specific task of designing the marque's top of the range engines, both the twin-cams and the multi-cylinder units, as well as supervising their development and tuning. Carlo Agostino was in charge of the development of the single overhead camshaft engine. During the decade between 1947 and 1957, the year in which Guzzi retired from the "pure speed" scene, the race shop was a hive of activity which spawned a stream of new or fundamentally renewed bikes and engines with a view to maintaining and consolidating the firm's hard won pre-eminence. It goes without saying that some of the experiments were failures and some of the bikes did not match expectations, yet all contributed to the progress of motorcycling technology and this had a beneficial effect on commercial production as a consequence.

Sophisticated simplicity : the new racers

The first Grand Prix bike we shall deal with is the 1947 250 twin (for the most part designed by Micucci), which can be compared to a certain extent to the 3-cylinder 500 produced in 1940. All things considered, it did not produce the desired results, and so after a couple of years of trials it was discarded in favour of the single-cylinder machine, but it is still an extremely interesting bike with many unusual mechanical and technical features.

The "square" engine, which could be fitted with a blower, had the cylinders in-line and tilted at a sixty degree angle. The cylinders, each one individually cast in electron, had highly unusual finning in order to ensure uniform expansion: the fins at the side and the base ran longitudinally at 90 degrees to each other, whereas the upper fins ran transversely. Special cast iron was used for the cylinder liners and tempered hydronalium for the one-piece head, while the combustion chambers were formed by aluminium bronze castings. The one-piece, three-bearing crankshaft had the cranks at 360 degrees and an external flywheel; the two overhead camshafts were driven by a train of five gears protected by an electron cover. Hairpin springs closed the valves. The electron crankcase casting was in three pieces: a central element which housed the central main bearing, and two lateral compartments. The external walls of the latter housed, on the left, the primary drive gears and the multiplate clutch and, on the right, some parts of the valve gear and the drive for the Bosch magneto, which was mounted below the cylinders. The

The start of the 350 race during the 1956 Grand Prix of Nations event held at the Monza Autodrome. Dustbin fairings, adopted by Guzzi in 1954 and readily imitated by rival manufacturers, radically altered the look of the classic motorcycle, which now looked as though it belonged to a different era. The photo shows Sandford (42) and Hoffman (22) on the 3-cylinder DKWs, Masetti (8) and Roberto Colombo (30) on the 4-cylinder MVs, Lomas (12), Kavanagh (16), Dale (18), Campbell (14), and Duilio Agostini (20) on the single-cylinder Guzzis, Liberati (4), who was to win, and Geoff Duke (2) on the 4-cylinder Gileras. By this time even non-works riders were riding with dustbin fairings.

A rare shot of the 1950 twin-cam 350 single during a race. The rider is Maurice Cann, who is shown leaping the Ballaugh Bridge during the TT.

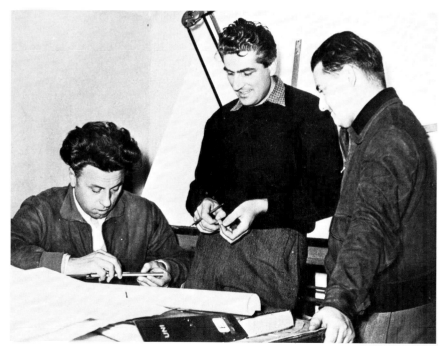

The technical staff responsible for those prestigious creations of the Fifties: from the left, Giulio Cesare Carcano, Enrico Cantoni and Umberto Todaro.

four-speed gearbox could be lifted out of the crankcase without opening up the engine: an advantage when replacing gears. The bike used two Dell'Orto carburettors with a single central float chamber; the lubrication system had its own reservoir and a dual pressure pump with three gears (one pump being for the crankshaft and the other for the valve gear), and a total flow rate of 320 litres/h. Scavenging was handled by a third pump with a flow rate of 400 litres/h.

The engine was supported by a large diameter steel tube strengthened by hydronalium pressings; the tubular swinging arm pivoted on another two double rivetted plates, which formed the rear part of the frame. The suspension consisted of a single cylindrical spring which was housed in a box-like housing mounted under the engine along with the hydraulic shock absorber. The front fork was a classic telescopic design, with an offset axle and electron fork tubes. The lateral drum brakes, also in electron, measured 250 mm in diameter and had shoes mounted on rubber for automatic wheel-alignment when braking.

This motorcycle was tested on several circuits including Sanremo and Treviso, while the following season saw it at Berne and the Isle of Man, with a new look exterior which strongly resembled the 1948 *Bicilindrica* version. Despite its considerable promise, it did not provide satisfactory results, as we have already said, and so it made more sense to back the *Albatros* and the *Gambalunghino* at the time.

A bevel-driven 350 dohc single made a few fleeting appearances at some foreign circuits in 1950 – at Mettet with Lorenzetti and at the T.T. with Maurice Cann. This flat single provided a basis for fruitful experimental work, but its performance on the track was judged unsatisfactory and so at the end of that year it was discarded definitively. These experiments included a cylinder cooling system based on oil circulation as well as a water-cooled exhaust valve no less. The valves were closed by four radially disposed hair springs and controlled by a rocker arm which operated from the middle of the valve clusters. The magneto was fitted both above and below the cylinder. The frame was a *Gambalunghino* component with some slight modifications: for example, the front downtubes straddled the engine from above rather than from below.

At the end of the 1950 season a new twin-cam 250 was introduced. It was, at least initially, a *Gambalunghino* engine with a different head (four valves and coil springs in an oil bath). The fuel supply was handled by two Dell'Orto carburettors with individual float chambers which were tilted backwards at first and then forwards. Ignition was by a single plug, positioned in the middle of the head. This engine – which was also made in an undersquare version, measuring 70 × 64 mm – was first seen at the Locarno Circuit in the autumn, mounted on a *Gambalunghino* frame, where Lorenzetti took third place in a race won by Anderson on his usual sohc mount. It appeared again in 1952 in Berne where, still ridden by Lorenzetti, it recorded the fastest lap and ran out second; the following year the same engine was mounted on a bike with a partial fairing and raced at the TT. A later version was then developed with conventional finning running along the axis of the cylinder (basically this was the rear cylinder from the *Bicilindrica*) but all things considered, the extra performance provided by the four valves did not outweigh the complications and therefore this engine was also abandoned. Quite a different fate was reserved for the two-valve twin-cam engine first built in 1953 and mounted on a bike with a partial fairing. Fairings had been fitted to motorcycles since the Twenties, but their employment had been limited to record attempts, while the fairings themselves were pretty much trial and error affairs. As far as circuit racing was concerned the boldest designers had stuck on a bit of sheet metal here and there and maybe shielded the spokes of the wheels, but this kind of experimentation had soon been abandoned since it compromised stability more than it increased speed. Towards 1950 an embryonic fairing around the steering head could be spotted on some of the Grand Prix motorcycles, but the first truly modern fairings (built in accordance with rigorously scientific principles) were to seen on the 1953 Guzzis.

This was largely due to the experimental possibilities offered by the wind tunnel. Built in 1950, this was the first facility of its kind to be installed by a motorcycle manufacturer and one of the very few that made it possible to test life-size bikes rather than small models.

The installation – naturally still functioning to this day – is an "Eiffel" type open circuit plant, whose total length measures 28.5 metres. It is composed of 3 main sections: the intake shaft (8.20 m in diameter); the test chamber (2.60 m in diameter); where the air reaches its maximum speed and the outlet shaft which houses the fan assembly (a 310 hp electric motor and a 3-bladed variable-pitch airscrew). The vehicle to be tested is placed on a special balance linked up to the instruments in the control cabin, next to the test chamber.

The 1953 Guzzi 250s therefore had a *Gambalunghino* frame from the previous year, with the large tubular upper strut and the teledraulic suspension elements at the sides of the rear wheel. But they also had a large trapezoid-shaped box tank, that

The wind tunnel, a construction of the highest technical importance and to this day one of the few in existence in the world. Among the authorities present at the 1950 opening ceremony were Enrico Parodi (second from the left), Carlo Guzzi (centre) and Giuseppe Guzzi (second from the right). Lorenzetti and managing director Bonelli are standing in the second row. Factory manager Vietone is the first on the left.

Two pictures of the 1953 twin-cam 250 with the first version of the "bird beak" fairing: above, Fergus Anderson streaking towards victory at the Tourist Trophy: below, the bike makes its debut at Siracusa with Enrico Lorenzetti.

ran down nearly as far as the engine, thus obliging the designers to fit a mechanical pump onto the end of the magneto shaft in order to supply the carburettor. The whole thing was then covered by a fairing in electron sheet which began at the steering head and ran back and down along the flanks to the level of the cylinder. The fairing also offered the rider an armrest. At the front it was completed by an appendage rather like a bird's beak, which soon led to the "bird-beak" nickname. This beak cut through the air-stream while the individual streamlines were channelled along the flanks and directed downwards; this gave even better results at the end of that same 1953 season when the side body was lengthened to envelop the rider's legs and feet. The little raked tail on the seat was retained in order to diminish air swirl at the rear.

Fundamentally, the engine was the 5-speed *Gambalunghino* unit, which had been fitted with a special head with two camshafts driven by a gear train enclosed beneath an electron casting fixed to the head by studs. The valves had exposed hairpin springs and the camshafts controlled the valves by means of bucket tappets.

The magneto ignition fed a single spark-plug whilst the carburettor was still the 40 mm Dell'Orto vertical type. The new two-valve 250 twin-cam made its debut at the *Circuito di Siracusa* with Lorenzetti, who came second behind fellow Guzzi rider Ruffo on the sohc *Gambalunghino*. In the course of the season the *250* won several important races, including the TT with Fergus Anderson and the Grand Prix of Nations at Monza, where Lorenzetti managed to snatch victory by the narrowest of margins from Haas on the NSU, who went on to win the world title however.

One direct descendant of the sohc *Gambalunghino* was the 350, also created in 1953. Guzzi had been thinking about this class for some while; it was practically unknown in Italy at the time but enjoyed a considerable following abroad where it was dominated by the English manufacturers: a success would have therefore generated a good deal of interest in Guzzi and would have done the firm's image no harm at all at the same time. The brainwave struck when the team returned from Siracusa, where the "old" sohc had once more defended the colours with honour. By increasing the dimensions as far as the *Gambalunghino's* crankcase would permit, the Guzzi engineers were able to carve out a swept volume of 317 cc (72 × 79 mm) which was enough to guarantee 31 hp at 7700 rpm.

Mounted on the latest frame with a beaked fairing, the new engine found itself in the line-up for the first time at the Hockenheim Grand Prix, where it scored a surprise victory coming in ahead of the large and formidable British contingent led by Norton and AJS. At the next TT it came third, again ridden by Anderson, and the future seemed brighter than ever. At this point therefore the natural thing to do was to carry on and build a new engine with the maximum allowable displacement. The crankcase was enlarged to accommodate the new 75 × 78 mm engine dimensions, which gave a capacity of 345 cc. Subsequently the stroke was further increased to 79 mm, thus uprating the swept volume to 349 cc. The engine was fitted with a 35 mm carburettor fed by a mechanical pump, valves measuring 37 mm at inlet and 32 mm at exhaust, single plug magneto ignition, a built-up crankshaft with con-rods running on needle bearings, and a four or five-speed gearbox depending on the circuits. Running on a compression ratio of 9.5:1 it supplied about 33 hp at 7500 rpm, enough to allow the motorcycle to reach 210 km/h when equipped with the more voluminous version of the bird beak fairing.

In 1953 the "real" 350 therefore had a truly triumphant season: it all started with a win at Assen where the faithful Lorenzetti once more rode a Guzzi to victory on its first outing; then came wins in the Belgian, French and Swiss Grands Prix with Anderson beating the Nortons and the AJS three valvers; then a first place at Monza in a race which saw the Guzzi works team make a clean sweep with Lorenzetti, Anderson and Duilio Agostini in the first three places. The 350 came first again at Barcellona in the 500 race ahead of the larger 4-cylinder Gileras and MVs. Naturally Fergus Anderson and the 350 walked off with the world title.

As far as the 500 class is concerned, we left Guzzi Racing at the end of 1951, when the glorious *Bicilindrica* was pensioned off. This decision probably had more to do with prestige than whether it was possible or not to squeeze a few more horses out of the engine; the fact of the matter is that Giorgio Parodi swore and declared that it would be unspeakable to carry on racing such an antique.

Irritated with his technicians, whom he maintained were irrevocably set in their ways as far as design was concerned, Parodi asked a young engineer from Rome named Gianini – the father of the 4-cylinder OPRA that we mentioned previously – to design him a racing engine which would stand out from the usual Mandello-built models.

Gianini came up with a 4-cylinder unit which was explicitly inspired by the automobile engine. This decidedly undersquare

The first test-runs at Monza on the four-in-line 500 (1952). Lorenzetti, who was involved in the tuning of the new bike, listens to Carcano's and Cantoni's advice. Note the four "pipe organ" exhausts, the oil tank wrapped around the crankcase, the radiator and the water pump, as well as the embryonic fairing. Although Carcano was in charge of tuning, the bike was not designed by him but by a Roman engineer named Gianini, who had already designed another 4-cylinder motorcycle, the OPRA. This was a one-off collaboration whereas Giulio Cesare Carcano's involvement in the engineering of Guzzi's racing models and some touring models was to continue for over two decades.

unit was a water-cooled affair with radiator and pump and had the cranks at 180 degrees.

The electron crankcase casting housed four cylinders with pressed-in liners: the built-up crankshaft with Hearth-type couplings ran completely on caged rollers, both at the mainshaft and at the cranks. The valve gear consisted of two overhead camshafts driven by a gear train set behind the cylinder block; the valves – two per cylinder – were set at right angles to one another and had a diameter of 32 mm at inlet and 30 at exhaust. They were closed by three coil springs.

One interesting feature was the mechanical carburetion system which was roughly analogous to the experiments carried out on the 250 cc *Gerolamo* twelve years before. In practice, the system was made up of a geared pump which took the fuel from the tank and sent it under pressure along an inlet tract running along the front of the intake manifolds. In the tract there were four jets – one per cylinder – whose flow rate was regulated by the throttle control on the handlebars. A small lobe-type pump fitted in the front half of the engine puffed air over the jets, thus creating the fuel mixture which was then introduced into the combustion chambers through the inlet valves. The excess petrol was then sent back to the tank by a scavenging pump.

At first sight many critics maintained that this system was tantamount to a form of supercharging and thus outwith the rules, but that was not the case, inasmuch as one end of the inlet tracts communicated with the open air. Fuel metering was regulated by a butterfly valve while air was admitted at intermittent intervals by a cam-operated valve – driven in its turn by one of the timing shafts – as the throttle was opened or closed. This cam was eliminated at a later stage. Lubrication was by dry sump while the magneto ignition was mounted behind the cylinders just above the four-speed gearbox. The multiplate clutch was splined to an extension of the crankshaft and the cardan shaft for the final drive was housed inside the left hand arm of the rear swinging fork. The frame too was original, formed by a trellis structure made up of small diameter tubing which arched over the engine to link the front to the rear end; the front fork and brakes were those of the *Bicilindrica*. There was a small fairing over the top of the forks which was attached to the petrol tank and the side panels. The bike was seen for the first time at practice for the Grand Prix of Nations at Monza in 1952 and it made its race debut in 1953 sporting a new bird beak fairing. At the end of that year many alterations were made to the frame and a new dustbin fairing was mounted over a trellis-type structure which ran down to cover the front wheel hub. Fuel was stored in the side body of the fairing from where a mechanical pump sent it to a small upper reservoir and from thence to the carburettor by gravity feed.

The 1954 version was fitted with an interesting linked braking system which made it possible to apply both brakes with a single pedal: the pedal in question operated the front brake directly by means of a flexible cable, but the same pedal also worked a linkage and a strong counterspring which in turn activated a brake equalizer with unequal length arms, one of which worked the back brake, while the other was controlled (still by means of a flexible cable) by the handlebar lever. In this way the handlebar lever acted directly on the back brake, and indirectly on the front one because by causing the equalizer to make one more rotation, it released the counterspring with the result that the more pressure was applied to the pedal-operated front brake, the more it was applied to the hand-operated back brake. However, the bike did not give satisfactory results, especially since the longitudinal engine created serious transverse oscillation when accelerating or decelerating (due to the so-called overturning torque), which dramatically reduced manoeuverability and roadholding.

The *Quattro Cilindri* only scored one classic win in 1953, at Hockenheim, a very fast circuit with few bends, at an average speed of over 176 km/h. The rider on that occasion was Lorenzetti, while Anderson broke the lap record at 182.400 km/h. There was another first place in 1954 at the Mettet Circuit in Belgium, this time with Anderson in the saddle. But it was not enough for a machine that sported the prestigious Mandello eagle, and so it was sidelined to make way for a new sensation: the *Otto Cilindri*.

The first foreign racer to join the Guzzi works team was Stanley Woods, who gave the Mandello marque the famous double victory at the TT in 1935. His selection was a good choice, dictated by the necessity to entrust the bikes to someone with a profound knowledge of the difficult Isle of Man circuit in the hope that the name Guzzi would end up inscribed in the honour roll of this prestigious race. In the post-war period, more and more British riders were to be seen on the red Guzzis.

Many were privateers who, attracted by the fame of the motorcycles from Mandello, tried to get their hands on an *Albatros* or a *Dondolino* in order to have a better chance in competition in their countries of origin; others, like the various Fosters, Canns, Barringtons, all old TT hands, were 1directly employed by the firm for specific races; but after

The "bird beak" fairings were used in 1954 too, but in Italy only. This is the start of the 250 race at the Piacenza Circuit. Occupying the front row is the Guzzi team: Adelmo Mandolini (20), Alano Montanari (6), Duilio Agostini, who was to win the race, (2) and Enrico Lorenzetti (4).

Fergus Anderson was one of Guzzi's best foreign riders, and he later became racing manager for the Mandello marque. Here he is at the Governor Bridge Bend (above) during the 1952 Tourist Trophy and (below) being congratulated on his win by Lorenzetti, second place, and by Jimmy Simpson, the famous racer of the Twenties who offered a Trophy for the fastest lap. In the background, Bob Foster, another Guzzi rider.

1950 many riders were also offered a regular seasonal contract. This practice – which was also carried on by the other Italian marques – gave rise to more than one row in those sporting circles which would have preferred to have seen Italian racing riders on Italian bikes. The industry was accused of not taking enough interest in the home-grown product; more or less the same arguments were applied to the engagement of foreign football players in those years.

The fact is that racing is a formidable advertising vehicle, but only for winners, and manufacturers therefore aimed at success first and worried about romantic patriotic notions later. As a result a "circus" of (mostly English speaking) professional riders came into being: men who knew all the tricks of the trade and whose living depended on racing. Such men and their families lived a gypsy existence moving from one event to another in their caravans, and consequently they acquired an expert knowledge of all the courses, which was an additional guarantee of a sound professional performance.

Fergus Anderson, for example, was one of the friendliest and most popular characters in this great international circus. Born in England in 1909, he had begun racing around 1930 and he came to Italy for the first time in 1935 to race at the *Circuito del Lario* with a *350* Velocette. A rider of class and vast technical knowledge, he had a lively, argumentative character which served him well in his other career as a motorcycling journalist. Already quite well known before the war, he reached the apex of his career when peace returned. No longer young by the time he joined Guzzi, he nevertheless enjoyed his greatest career satisfactions with the Italian marque: his victories in Guzzi racing red were legion, ranging from the Swiss G.P. of 1950 and 1951 to TT wins in 1952 and 1953, not forgetting a host of world records. All this culminated in the conquest of two world 350 titles in 1953 and 1954 riding single and twin-cam versions of the single-cylinder model. He also took on the position of race manager at Guzzi and in this role he helped launch Bill Lomas, another worthy English rider. Lomas had been hastily engaged before the start of the 1955 TT, after the works riders – Duilio Agostini, Kavanagh and Dale – had been rendered hors de combat as a result of various accidents during practice. There could not have been a better choice, since Lomas won the 350 race with a record average speed to score the first ever victory in that class for a non-English motorcycle. Lomas went on to enjoy a brilliant career with Guzzi: after the TT he won the 1955 German, Belgian and Ulster Grands Prix against the feared 3-cylinder DKWs and the 4-cylinder MVs, thus becoming a worthy 350 World Champion; he won the title again the following year after wins in Holland, Germany and Ulster, not forgetting Imola and the Floreffe Circuit. He raced the *Otto cilindri* too and with this fabulous motorcycle he set a string of world records, one of which is still unbroken to this day: the standing ten kilometres which he covered at an average of 243.572 km/h on the 26th of February 1957 on the *Fettuccia di Terracina*.

Ken Kavanagh came from Australia to join Guzzi in 1953 bringing with him a good reputation earned in European racing. He was a valued rider, but a highly inconsistent one; when on song he was an exceptionally determined performer, but he was subject to occasional bouts of apathy which left him him indifferent to the outcome of the race. In 1954 however, he won at Hockenheim on a 500 single at an average speed (all the more exceptional given the bike in question) of 182 km/h; he also took the Belgian Grand Prix astride the 350. A series of second places followed behind various Guzzi teammates, until he rediscovered his winning ways in 1954 at Imola, Assen and Hockenheim. In 1956 he won the TT aboard the 350 and he was among the first to race the *Otto cilindri*, with which he achieved the fastest lap at Hockenheim with a spectacular average speed of 199 km/h. The next year saw him riding a Guzzi again, but he had lost form badly and in the end he was substituted by Dickie Dale, with Guzzi since 1955 and winner of the 1957 Imola Gold Cup with the *Otto cilindri*, and Keith Campbell, who became 350 World Champion in 1957.

Italian racing riders were not completely neglected by Guzzi, which took on some young home-grown riders to back up the veteran Lorenzetti and Alano Montanari, an exceptional man from the Romagna region who had done a bit of everything before making rapid progress in motorcycle racing, despite the fact he was no youngster when he first took up the sport. Also worthy of mention are Duilio Agostini, who showed his mettle by winning the 1953 Milano-Taranto before going on to ride the Grand Prix racers; Roberto Colombo, a modest and courageous man from Brianza; and finally Giuseppe Colnago, who switched from Gileras to Guzzis in 1957, just in time to ride the *Otto cilindri* to victory for the first time at Siracusa.

These were really splendid years for Guzzi and, by association, for the racing division which benefitted from lavish financing and the services of the firm's best men, from engineers like Carcano, Todero and Cantoni, to mechanics like Carlo Agostini and his nephew Luigi, Bettega and Pomi; and the results were good. Indeed, it is still hard to understand why all this commitment plus Guzzi's enormous success at home and abroad were never translated into export sales, but the entire Italian motor-

Bill Lomas (top), one of the best and most productive English riders in the Guzzi stable, shown here at Imola in 1957 in front of McIntyre and Liberati, both on Gileras. Above, Alano Montanari, a big-hearted competitor from the Romagna region.

Duilio Agostini aboard the 1953 twin-cam 250 with the oil pump attached to the timing chest, a feature which was discarded after a short time. Below, Ken Kavanagh, an excellent but inconsistent rider, photographed at the 1954 Tourist Trophy astride one of the first 350s to be fitted with a dustbin fairing. Just visible behind him is Todaro, almost hidden by mechanics Fattori and Luigi Agostini, "il Moretto's" nephew.

cycle industry of the day was the victim of a blinkered outlook, from which it was able to break away only many years later, stimulated by the example set by others.

We had left the racing singles at the end of 1953, with the bird beak fairings and engines directly derived from the sohc *Gambalunghino*. At the beginning of 1954 the bikes emerged after a major restyling operation. They were now enveloped by a full dustbin fairing, the prototype of which had first been seen on the *Quattro cilindri* model tested at Monza the previous autumn. This handbeaten sheet electron fairing, originally produced by panelbeaters at the SIAI-Marchetti works in Sesto Calende and then by Guzzi's own staff, was to have a profound impact on the motorcycle racing world.

The increase in the power-speed ratio was remarkable, so much so that the single-cylinder Guzzis found themselves in near parity with multi-cylinder rivals with bigger engines like the Gileras and the MVs. Very light and compact, the Guzzis offered what amounted to minimal fuel consumption for a racing motorcycle (the 350 could do more than 20 km to the litre), which was of the greatest importance in long distance races. In a short space of time, all Grand Prix motorcycles, even those privately owned, sported a dustbin fairing. Not all were scientifically designed like the Guzzi models, which were tested in the wind tunnel, but the advantages were considerable for everybody. The Guzzi fairing also underwent various alterations: the side tanks soon disappeared, to be replaced by a barrel-like tank above the engine, while the outline was made sleeker.

The new Guzzis for the 1954 season had an aircraft type trellis frame (which had also been seen for the first on the *Quattro cilindri*), that extended over the front wheel. The fairing therefore, was no longer an article which you slapped on to a pre-existing bike any old way you fancied; motorcycles and their fairings were now designed and engineered as harmonious wholes.

At the end of 1957, dustbin fairings were abolished by a new regulation, since the steering difficulties at high speeds were really considerable, and Guzzi simultaneously withdrew from competition, therefore the "sharks" from Mandello (which had been painted with a rust-proof green coating since 1955, thus putting an end to the traditional racing red) ended up in a damp attic in Abbadia Lariana.

For the new bikes, Carcano's staff had prepared three new dohc engines: a 250, a 350 and a 500, the latter being intended for use as a back-up for the multi-cylinder machines on the most tortuous circuits. The engines had undergone several alterations with respect to previous models: the valve gear housings had been cast in a unit with the head, thus doing away with the fixed timing chest; the camshafts ran on roller bearings and operated the valves with the aid of bucket tappets. The valves themselves, closed by coil springs, were completely enclosed and worked in an oil bath. The ends of the intake and exhaust cams drove the petrol and oil pumps respectively; the two crankwebs of the built-up crankshaft were joined by a crankpin with a differentiated double screw thread that locked the pieces together automatically. All the con-rods ran on rollers or roller bearings. The ignition system had a coil feeding two 10 mm spark plugs; the gear-box was a 5-speed unit and the primary drive was by straight-cut gears, with a multiplate clutch mounted entirely on rollers.

The 250 model, built with square engine dimensions (68 × 68,4 mm) and in an undersquare variant (70 × 64,8 mm), made a few apppearances in 1954 and 1955, alongside the old version with the bird beak fairing; but by that time this class had fallen more and more under the sway of the rival Mondials and MVs, which had beaten off all competition in short order using racers derived from their twin-cam *175* models.

Guzzi therefore preferred to concentrate on the bigger engines, with an eye also to reducing the expenditure involved in such a massive commitment to racing.

Quite different results were provided by the 350 and the 500. The half-litre machine had a 45 mm carburettor and an engine of classic dimensions (88 × 82 mm) which developed 42 hp at 7000 rpm. This bike won at Hockenheim in 1954 (where it scored the fastest lap at 188.800 km/h) and Ulster, as well as racking up a series of good placings in other Grands Prix; it won the 1956 Imola Gold Cup, coming in ahead of the 4-cylinder Gileras and MVs, as well as a contingent from BMW and Norton; in 1957 it won the Italian Championship with Colnago.

The 350 engine was a "short-stroker" measuring 80 × 69,5 mm with a 37 mm carburettor (subsequently enlarged to 40), a 38.5 mm inlet valve and a 33 mm exhaust. Power output was 35 hp at 7800 rpm, a figure which later became 37 at 8000 rpm. During its brilliant career this bike took three world titles in the years 1954, 1955 and 1956. In 1957 the riders' championship went to Keith Campbell, but the points game stopped Guzzi from taking the constructors' title as well.

Between 1954 and 1957 the bikes underwent a series of modifications. The distributor was shifted from its old place on the top of the magneto to the right hand side of the crankcase; the dual oil pump went back to the right hand side of the engine; the

Lorenzetti at the *Circuito di Faenza* in 1956, with his "special" built in collaboration with Lunardon and Canova. Below, practice at Monza for the 1956 Grand Prix of Nations: Lomas (on the left) looks on while his 350 is tuned; behind, Kavanagh's mount.

valve head diameters of the 350 were enlarged to 41 mm inlet and 36 mm exhaust. In 1957 the magneto and single plug layout was reinstated, but this time it was placed on the right flank where the coil ignition used to be. Whereas in the 1954 versions the petrol had been contained in the barrel tank only, leaving the rider with a box-like structure to lean against instead of the usual tank, the following year's model had a proper tank instead of the "chest rest", which increased the overall capacity up to no less than 30 litres of fuel. In 1956 the frame underwent a major transformation as the part of the trellis below the engine was removed. This meant that the engine now hung from the upper half of the frame and as a result the crankcase connections also had to be moved.

The last year in racing, 1957, witnessed a truly remarkable slimming campaign, given that plastics were not yet in common use. The use of special metals, also employed for the nuts and bolts, brought the 350's weight down to 98 kgs while the 500 weighed in at just over 100 kgs, limits which are difficult to equal even these days.

1958 was to have witnessed the debut of a new single-cylinder 500 designed by Carcano (still with the twin-cam layout but with a longer stroke), but Guzzi's withdrawal from racing brought the project to a halt. It was to resurface "posthumously" a decade or so later, mounted on a 1957-type trellis frame with no fairing, thanks to Giuseppe Mandolini, a rider from Brescia who had been fortunate enough to come into its possession. But engine technology had made giant strides in the interim so there was no chance of obtaining first-rate results with it; however this "special" showed itself to be one of the best privately owned machines around on more than a few occasions, proof of the great qualities of its engine and design.

The fabulous Otto cilindri

At the end of the 1954 racing season the limitations of the in-line *Quattro cilindri*, a rather unstable machine, became obvious to the men running Guzzi racing; the same held good for the 500 single, which was admittedly a marvellous machine but irremediably less powerful than its multi-cylinder rivals, in particular the Gilera and the MV, which were steadily taking over in senior class competition. Even Norton, a strenuous supporter of the single-cylinder motorcycle, was thinking about a multi-cylinder engine (although it got no further than the drawing board) and therefore the feeling at Guzzi was that something new was needed to keep the competition in its place. Carcano thus took to examining all the various possible solutions. A twin-cylinder engine could not do better than a four-cylinder unit and this possibility was therefore discarded straight away. Gilera and MV had been working hard on the transverse four-cylinder layout and they had opened up a considerable lead in this sector by that time. That left the six and eight-cylinder engines: at this point it was clear that the final decision would be based on relative dimensions. Among other things there was also talk of abolishing the dustbin fairing and it was obvious that if that happened then it would have been necessary to design an engine capable of combining the maximum horsepower with the smallest frontal cross section.

The engineers got out their slide rules and discovered that a transverse V engine with two blocks of four cylinders one behind the other need not measure more than 50 cm in width and could be at least 15 cm narrower than a transverse straight six; this layout also offered the same weight distribution as a single-cylinder engine.

Once the decision to use an eight cylinder engine had been made, the choice of a 90 degree V was automatic insofar as this design, in addition to the required narrowness of the engine, also offered the advantage of a robust crankshaft and excellent stability of the moving parts. And so the most sensational motorcycle of all times was born, with a multi-cylinder engine that no one will ever attempt to imitate, not even the Japanese who many today hail as the gurus of modern engineering. Guzzi's withdrawal from racing brought the V8's development to a grinding halt while the bike was still in the delicate tuning phase, but it remains one of the greatest examples of the creative and productive capacities of the Mandello firm's racing division.

Designed and built in record time, the V8 had already made its debut appearance by 1955, during practice for the Belgian Grand Prix, followed by visits to Senegallia and Monza, but another year passed before it was entered as a fully fledged works racer and its main technical characteristics were made known. The crankcase for the engine and the gearbox was a one piece electron casting which incorporated a robust 40 mm rod with a bronze bush to support the swinging arm of the rear suspension system. The two banks of cylinders were tilted at 45 degrees to the vertical and were connected to the crankcase. Screwed into the inside of the cylinder heads were the special cast iron cylinder liners; these were grooved in order to offer a larger surface area to the cooling water and held in place by a special coupling

The two versions of the *Otto cilindri*: above, piloted by Dale at the 1957 Tourist Trophy, with the partial fairing used for certain circuits; below, with Keith Campbell at Francorchamps, again in 1957, with the dustbin fairing. On the facing page, a suburban village on the TT route: heading down towards Quarter Bridge. Dickie Dale (no. 31) on the 500 single.

and synthetic rubber gaskets. The original one-piece forged steel crankshaft was later replaced by a built-up version. The cranks were set at 180 degrees and every crankpin housed two 90 mm Ni-Cro steel con-rods running on needle bearings in dural cages. The crankshaft, which ran on three smooth intermediary bearings and roller bearings at both ends, was made up of 8 disc crankwebs thus making it possible to do away with the external flywheel and the torsional stress it generated; the crank gear was balanced by dovetailing heavy alloy plugs into the crankwebs. The valve gear included four camshafts, driven by a large central gear cluster which took its power from the primary drive gear and transmitted it to the camshaft gears. The whole shooting match was contained in an electron casting mounted on the right hand side of the engine. The central gear cluster also drove the centrifugal pump for the cooling water.

The valves, tilted at a 58 degree angle, had a diameter of 23 mm at inlet and 21 at exhaust, with two-piece guides later substituted by monobloc guides with bucket-type thrust tappets; each valve had two concentric spiral springs. The intake manifolds were inside the V where eight special 20 mm Dell'Orto carburettors had been shoehorned into the space between the two timing cases. Initially there were only two float chambers on one side of the bank of carburettors, then each carburettor was fitted with its own float chamber, so as to obviate certain small fuel feed problems which arose when cornering or accelerating.

The coil ignition system had one contact breaker and one coil for each cylinder; there were two groups of four contact breakers fixed to the left hand extremity of the two intake camshafts and two groups of four coils at the sides of the engine, behind the radiator. The points were made of copper-beryllium and the spark-plugs measured 10 mm.

Lubrication was by dry sump, the oil being contained in the upper strut of the frame; the dual gear pump was on the right. A straight-toothed primary drive gear cluster, with a dry multiplate clutch, was fitted on the outside of the crankcase in order to favour cooling. The gearbox initially had six speeds since it was thought that the engine would have a rather restricted useful range, but it soon became obvious that it was a highly flexible unit, so much so that there was a good amount of power already available at 7000 rpm. A four or five-speed gearbox was therefore chosen (the choice depended on the circuit), in obedience to the principle that, wherever possible, it is best to keep things simple.

The first model developed 68 hp at 12,000 rpm; there were a few problems with overrevs due to considerable vibration caused by the insufficient rigidity of the crankshaft, but these difficulties were later overcome.

The frame was a duplex cradle; the rear swinging arm acted upon two Girling teledraulic suspension units at the side of the wheels. The front fork was the usual leading link type, but in this case the springing was handled by two Girling units identical to those employed at the rear, which were housed in front of the fork tubes. The fork tubes extended up to the steering head and were fixed in two places. This fork was later to be mounted on the single-cylinder models as well, from 1956 onwards. Electron was also used for the brakes, which were concentric drums; the front one had four shoes.

1956 was a year of experimentation aimed at the elimination of some carburetion and ignition problems; but despite the gremlins Kavanagh rode the *8V* round Hockenheim to a new lap record at an average of 199 km/h, a clear demonstration of the bike's undoubted qualities.

The next year began with the conquest of the world record on the *Fettuccia di Terracina*. With a new, more streamlined fairing, the *8V* went on to win the first event on the Italian championship calendar at Siracusa and then the much more important Imola Gold Cup, while the rest of the season was a continuous series of high placings alternating with retirements, inevitable when dealing with a complex vehicle which was obviously hard to keep in a perfect state of tune.

The engine, a 350 cc version of which was also planned at one time, had come to develop around 75 hp, a very considerable figure in those days and much better than any of its rivals could muster, and it seems likely that the following season would have given Carcano and his extraordinary creation a great deal of satisfaction. Unfortunately the ever increasing cost of maintaining a racing department plus a rather jaded market persuaded the major Italian firms to withdraw from competition at the end of 1957 (a common pact was drawn up which bound the signatories not to compete in the speed races).

It has still to be ascertained whether it was a good move to quit motorsport, which had always been a formidable advertising vehicle for the motorcycle, but at the time it appeared a wise decision and so all of the Guzzi racing bikes, including the fabulous *8V*, wound up on the scrap heap until a new understanding of their value as technical-historical artefacts led to their being transferred to a more dignified home in the museum at Mandello. Many models have still not been accounted for however and there are valid grounds for believing that some of them may be secretly preserved in some private collections.

A common scene in the Fifties : the Guzzi victory parade at the finish. This is at Assen, in 1955: Ken Kavanagh crosses the line in the 350 event ahead of Bill Lomas and Dickie Dale.

UTILITY PRODUCTION

In 1953 Guzzi launched a new mass produced light motorcycle, the 98 cc *Zigolo* (Bunting), intended to bridge the gap between the *65* and the *Galletto*. Obviously the newcomer was a utility bike aimed at those customers who wanted something a little more powerful than the miraculous but small "Guzzino" without running into heavy initial expense or increased running costs.

Although it was an essentially simple machine, the *Zigolo* represents an important page in the story of both Guzzi and the evolution of the motorcycle in general. Its most noticeable characteristic was the partially enclosed bodywork which clothed the central part of the bike and the rear mudguard. The body was formed by two metal pressings welded together to form a shell which covered most of the mechanical units without cluttering up the lines of the bike.

As a result the *Zigolo* can fairly be described as one of the most successful examples of a partially enclosed traditional motorcycle produced up to that time.

The Guzzi design team took a lot of trouble to keep costs to a minimum and finishing (at least at first) was decidedly basic. The frame was formed by a wide-section angled tube, like the one fitted to the *65*, which had been bent over backwards in order to cradle the rear end of the engine. In the suspension department the *Zigolo* offered a rear swinging arm which pivoted on the lower extremity of the frame, while rear springing was provided by a large cylindrical rubber element in compression and integrated with twin Hartford-type shock absorbers. The bodyshell supported the baggage carrier-saddle assembly, while a traditional fuel tank represented a rational way of rounding off the lines of this pleasing lightweight.

The 2-stroke horizontal single-cylinder engine was the work of Antonio Micucci and had been derived from the experimental prototype built in 1950 to beat some records for the 75 cc class. The crankcase was a one-piece shell-cast unit, with the primary drive cover on the left and a cast iron cylinder fitted with a light alloy head. The steel crankshaft was supported on the left hand side by one ball bearing and one roller bearing while the con-rod rotated on needle bearings. The free end of the crankpin drove a countersunk cylindrical body which served as a rotary inlet valve.

A flywheel magneto alternator with an external HT coil provided the vital spark, while a pair of helical gears were chosen for the primary drive. Twelve coil springs in an oil bath pressed the 4-plate clutch while the gearbox was a pedal-operated three-speeder. The front fork was an undamped telescopic unit with fixed outer tubes at the top.

New ideas for volume production

In 1954 the original *Zigolo*, with its spartan grey finish, was joined by the *Lusso* version, which had red livery with a chromed tank, a long dualseat and 2.50/2.75-17" tyres. A *Sport* version with a more powerful engine (which provided 6.8 hp at 8400 rpm – enough to propel the bike to 100 km/h) with larger finning around the head, was never put on sale even though it had been displayed at various Shows.

While the *Zigolo* was in production the Italian government passed new road traffic legislation which made it obligatory for motorcycles to be fitted with a luminous stop light. It was not easy to adjust motorcycle electrical systems without incurring excessive costs and the various major manufacturers even began to exchange information in a bid to solve what was only apparently a marginal problem. A certain Vanzetti, then a member of the technical division, came up with a solution which made use of the ignition coil earthing. But a really fundamental innovation was to come along in 1958 with the adoption of a light alloy

A picture which testifies to the importance of goods vehicles in Guzzi production: the final assembly shop with ranks of *Ercole* three wheelers fitted with the 500 cc flat single engine. The photograph was taken at Mandello in 1950.

cylinder barrel lined with a layer of hard chrome plating obtained by a special electrolytic process.

This system led to improved cylinder cooling because chrome does not hinder heat transmission and so expansion is less marked, the result being that piston-to-bore clearances could be made much tighter than before. The chrome layer was made porous in order to make sure that the liner was always coated with a film of lubricant and so less oil was required in the 2-stroke mixture, a fact which led to fuel savings and a net improvement in operating conditions. In fact chrome offers a remarkably smooth finish plus a high degree of surface hardness, and so the coefficient of friction, and therefore wear, is very low.

The undoubted advantages of chromed cylinder bores were the fruit of years of research but considerable production difficulties had always put a brake on their popularity: and so Guzzi is proud of having overcome the problems in this area, and of having made a major contribution to the development of the 2-stroke engine as a direct result.

After the *Zigolo*, chrome bores were fitted to other Guzzi models like the *Cardellino* (goldfinch) as well as various mopeds and 4-stroke engines in the *V7* series.

This innovation soon found its way into bikes manufactured by other marques, in Italy and abroad.

The *Zigolo Series II*, which could call on 4.6 hp, had many features like those used for the preceding *Lusso* model, i.e. 17" wheels, the long dualseat and red paintwork, as well as a set of new light alloy central drum brakes.

The Milan Show of November 1959 witnessed the presentation of the last version of this bike, which remained in production until 1966: the *Zigolo 110*.

The new displacement was obtained with a bore and stroke of 52 × 52 mm, which pushed output up to 4.8 hp at 5200 rpm. The front and rear suspension received hydraulic dampers while tank, engine covers, silencer and mudguards were restyled. The price fell from 169,000 to 135,000 lire despite the various functional and aesthetic improvements, but those were better days for the Italian economy. Around 1953 the old idea of holding competitions for production bikes was taken out and dusted off. Strictly speaking, these new competitions were reserved for "production derived" machines, as the new regulations permitted some small modifications to be made with a view to obtaining a little extra performance.

The event which gave most lustre to this revived category was the *Motogiro d'Italia*, a speed race held in stages over normal roads and the last great event of its type.

First held in 1953, it was abolished for good after the Mille Miglia tregedy of 1957.

Wisely, the *Motogiro* was always reserved for bikes of up to 175 cc in a bid to limit speeds, and hence the element of risk, as much as possible; but, as had happened before, the biddable lightweights which had been built up to then, and which had done so much for private personal transport in Italy, were gradually transformed into costly and complex racing machines.

The event proved to be an excellent advertising vehicle for the factories, which soon found themselves obliged to replace their more economical models with ohc bikes; and double overhead camshafts were never raced simply because the rulebook forbade it.

The first result was an instant increase in performance and in the space of a few seasons the new 175s were going faster than the old-style 500 Sports: Venturi, aboard a Mondial 175, notched up an outright victory in the 1954 Milano-Taranto event coming in ahead of assorted *Dondolinos* and Gilera *Saturnos*, even though it must be said that the latter had had a particularly bad time of it that year as far as mechanical troubles were concerned.

The second result was a certain reduction in the durability and reliability which had hitherto distinguished the best part of Italian production; and it was this fact, which became noticeable just when the motor car was beginning to become more popular, that contributed to the alienation of the utility buyer, who no longer saw the motorcycle as a safe and genuinely economical commuter machine.

Contemporary fashion decreed that the 175 cc lightweight had to have overhead valve gear and commercial reasons obliged Guzzi to enter the lists, even though the factory never participated officially in "production-derived" racing.

The result was the birth of the *Lodola* (skylark), a bike with a whole range of interesting features many of which represented a break with Guzzi tradition: one good example being the engine configuration, which had the engine tilted at 45 degrees instead of lying flat.

The same bike proved to be Carlo Guzzi's swan song as, tired and ill, he relinquished control of "his" factory shortly afterwards.

The decision to produce the *Lodola* had been preceded by some misleading market research. It was the first time Guzzi had made use of such techniques and perhaps the results were overestimated: anyhow the plant tooled up to handle an estimated production run of 30,000 units and the financial commitment involved proved to be a major burden when it became clear that the cost of much of the machinery (which could not be adapted for other models) would have to be amortized by a production total of less than a third of the original estimate.

It was also the first time that Carlo Guzzi had allowed himself to be influenced by "the demands of the market". Although he was only a "technical" partner who had never owned a single share in the firm which bore his name, he had always enjoyed absolute power when it came to deciding which types were to be produced. The *Lodola* was not a failure technically speaking: ten thousand units amount to anything but a failure and the large number still in circulation by the second half of the Seventies is sufficient to forestall any accusations regarding functional shortcomings.

However it was lacking in terms of "image": never completely accepted by the Guzzi faithful, it was only partially successful in attracting new custom.

The chain-driven overhead camshaft fitted to the *Lodola* embodied some really original features. Chains represent a simple and cheap way to drive valve gear and constructors have recourse to them regularly all over the world. But there are several snags due to stretching after prolonged use or the different expansion rates of the various engine parts, which combine to send the timing out of phase. To prevent this, Carlo Guzzi rigged up a kind of tensioner formed by a thin steel strip fixed to a rocker arm which straddled the camshaft. This rocker was supported at the centre by an anchorage fixed to the cylinder head while its other end rested on a steel stud screwed into the base of the aluminium cylinder. The difference in the expansion rate of the stud – which was fixed to a relatively cool part of the engine – and the anchorage fixed to the head (which was hotter) ensured that the rocker lifted itself off the thin steel strip to an extent which was sufficient to keep the chain at a constant tension whatever the temperature of the engine. The camshaft was also fitted with a small flywheel which smoothed out the cyclic irregularities caused by cam throw and load variations, thus ensuring smoother meshing between the teeth of the pinion and the rollers of the chain.

The engine had a three-piece crankshaft, helical primary drive, wet multiplate clutch and a 4-speed gearbox. The primary drive pinion was the same as the one fitted to the *Cardellino* and *Zigolo*, i.e. with a series of small rubber elements serving as transmission dampers. The flywheel was still on the outside, but hidden beneath one of the aluminium covers on the side of the crankcase, which therefore acquired a clean-cut, compact look in the absence of the various accessories normally

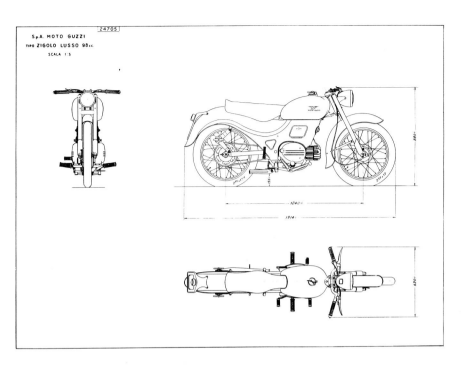

The end of the *Galletto*, *Lodola* and *Zigolo* production lines in 1962. Above, drawings for the 98 cc *Zigolo Lusso*, produced from 1954-1957.

101

exposed to view on the old-fashioned single-cylinder machines. Ignition was by coil and the electrics were fed by a 45 W dynamo; the carburettor was a 22 mm Dell'Orto and lubrication was handled by a dry sump system, with a dual feed and return pump under the saddle.

The full-duplex cradle was made of semicircular section tubing, which offers good resistance despite the modest cross section. The teledraulic front forks had weight-bearing outer covers at the top end while the sprung elements of the rear swinging arm suspension could be set to two positions depending on the load: tilted forward for solo use and upright when carrying a pillion passenger.

The *Lodola* could call on 9 hp, enough for 110 km/h. Some time later, in the April of 1958, a *Sport* version was launched with a more compressed engine (9:1), which could pump out 11 hp and take the bike to over 120 km/h. However, the *Lodola* was basically an honest, unpretentious machine, which followed the fashion of the day but not so far as to risk offending the touring-utility bike buyers who had always formed the bulk of Guzzi's clientele.

In point of fact the bike's performance, although fair, was not good enough to enable the *Lodola* to compete with its rivals on a serious sporting level. And so it seemed worthwhile to forget about sophisticated mechanical features (which had begun to lose favour with the paying customer anyway, due to frequent breakdowns) and concentrate on the essentials.

This was done the following year (1959) when a new version of the *Lodola* was planned. The *Gran Turismo* (which was lined up alongside the two 175s at first, before it replaced them altogether) had a 235 cc push-rod engine (68 × 64 mm) with a cast iron cylinder. Smaller than the *Airone*, of which it was in a certain sense a direct descendant, the *Lodola GT* was light, fast and sprightly and soon became the most popular quarter-litre machine on the market thanks to its equal appetite for touring and sheer hard work.

Later on, the lubrication circuit was improved by the addition of a cartridge-type oil filter – the use of this car-type component being another complete novelty – which improved resistance and kept running costs down.

Some very interesting versions of the *Lodola* were prepared for regularity trials, of which more anon. A *Sport* version was introduced at the 1965 Milan Show with an uprated 247 cc engine (66 × 68 mm), light alloy cylinder with chrome bore, twin exhausts, 2.50-18" tyres in front and 3.00-17" behind. The makers claimed 18 hp and a top speed of 140 km/h. A very handsome machine, it unfortunately remained at the prototype stage and the *Lodola* chapter came to a close shortly afterwards, when the Guzzi works was obliged to rationalize its production.

By the end of the Fifties the world motorcycle industry was in the middle of a full-blown crisis.

A wide stratum of society had "never had it so good" and many people were turning away from the romantic (but often wet and windy) world of two-wheeled transport in favour of the seductive comforts of the motor car.

The newly affluent found that the motor car, once a dream, was suddenly within their grasp and even young people were choosing the open sports car in preference to the big bikes, which were not even up to much in the performance stakes any more because the manufacturers had neither the courage nor the good sense to invest in new models.

In Italy the crisis broke a little later (nothing is ever very punctual in Italy, certainly not even the trains), but even in the stormy economic climate of those years many people had the 400,000 lire which was all you needed to drive off in a spanking new Fiat 500, and so bike sales began to fall off. At the time the best solution seemed to be to cut prices to the bone in a bid to win the lower end of the market and so cost cutting became the order of the day. Guzzi came up with the *Stornello* (starling), a 125 cc 4-stroke lightweight, whose creation had involved the firm's creative personnel to a man. Even Carcano and his specialist racing staff had been drafted into mass production duty when the firm withdrew from motorsport.

The new engine had an almost vertical cylinder (tilted at 25 degrees from the vertical) with parallel overhead valves controlled by push-rods and rocker arms, a configuration which did not make it easy to obtain high performance but which had the virtue of being easy to produce.

The crankcase, the very first of its kind to be fitted to a 4-stroke engine, was die-cast, a method which makes many laborious finishing operations unnecessary. The oil was kept in a sump, another novelty as far as Guzzi was concerned, and this saved the cost of an oil tank, tubing and a scavenge pump. A centrifugal oil filter was fitted coaxial with the crankshaft, which did a lot to improve lubrication conditions and the useful lifetime of the oil. Naturally the factory equipment was also adapted to suit the demands of high volume-low cost production: for example a single machine was used to carry out all the frame welds simultaneously (the frame being an open duplex cradle, consisting of a fat upper tube and downtubes connected to steel lugs). The system

These two pages show some of the trade marks used over the years: they are arranged in chronological order, but their use was not apparently governed by any fixed rule. There were cases in which a preceding mark was revived even when the bulk of production was adorned with a more modern nameplate. The *Alce* and *Trialce* military bikes represent special cases, in which the makers rather coyly omitted the MOTO GUZZI badge, as if it were obvious to all and sundry. Other exceptional cases were the *Gambalunga* and *Gambalunghino* models, which had a very stylized black or dark blue trade mark applied on top of the unusual metallic silver finish chosen for these competition bikes. The trade marks shown here are not actual size.

was so effective that the production cost of the frame was incredibly low, only 5,000 lire per unit.

The bike used teledraulic forks at the front while the swinging arm rear suspension had the usual twin teledraulic units, which were set at a steeply raked angle alongside the wheel. Using a principle borrowed from dirt bike construction, the top end of these units pivoted on the end of the upper frame tube, at a very robust point, while the raked angulation allowed the suspension arm to swing freely even though the units offered only a modest amount of travel.

The tempered steel crankshaft was in threepieces, with a one-piece con-rod running on rollers. The primary drive had three helical gears (and so the engine turned clockwise rather than anticlockwise like all the previous Guzzi models), the second of which also drove the camshaft, mounted transversely behind the crankshaft. The drive train also included a multiplate clutch and a 4-speed constant-mesh gearbox. Ignition was handled by a flywheel magneto alternator, mounted on the right, with an external HT coil. The engine was fed by an 18 mm carburettor and the oil was sent under pressure as far as the rocker gear by a gear-type pump. Seventeen inch wheels went a long way towards diminishing the dimensions of this lightweight, although it had a rather odd look at the front, as if something were missing. A very light bike, the Stornello's seven horses were enough to propel it to around 100 km/h. Various sporty versions were to follow, built around a slightly different engine with a hemispheric combustion chamber and inclined valves.

These were obviously better performers even though more expensive to produce.

In this case the camshaft was still mounted transversely, with the push-rods housed at the rear of the cylinder. As a consequence the valves were inclined on a transverse plane and so the inlet and exhaust manifolds had to follow a dog-leg route on the sides of the head so as to keep the exhaust and the 20 mm carb within the dimensions of the vehicle. This was not the best design from a performance standpoint, but the Stornello Sport – introduced at the end of 1961 – showed itself to be lively and quick just the same, thanks to its 8.5 horses (developed at 7500 rpm running on a compression ratio of 9.8:1). Top speed was around 110 km/h. Three new editions of the Stornello were produced in 1965: the Sport America, a model with a small tank and high, wide, American-style handlebars (originally built for the US market and then sold in Italy too) and a choice of black and silver or black and red finish; the Regolarità, derived from the works machines prepared some time previously for this sporting

speciality; and the Scrambler, whose knobbly tyres also gave it the air of a dirt bike, even though it was less "professional" looking than the Regolarità. Effectively speaking, the Scrambler was a dual-purpose bike which was just as much at home on normal roads as it was in rough country – provided it was not too rough.

At the end of 1967, when major changes were underway at Guzzi, the following versions of the Stornello were in production: the Turismo with the flat head engine, the America version of the Sport and the Scrambler, also built to the America specification. A new 160 version was obtained by increasing the bore and stroke to a uniform 58 mm (which gave a displacement of exactly 153.2 cc), with angled, in-head valves.

The 160, which developed 12.6 hp at 7500 rpm on a 9:1 compression ratio, could reach 118 km/h. Its new look, the fruit of new research into styling, represented an attempt to wed functionality to an attractively modern appearance.

In general, the motorcycles of days gone by were designed by one man, who tended to pay lots of attention to the mechanical side of his creation while neglecting the aesthetic side, and so many bikes wound up with a crudely angular look which appealed to only the most fanatical enthusiasts.

Stylists began working with motorbikes around 1968 in a bid to respond to the rapidly changing market conditions and demands. The Stornello was one of the first bikes to be "facelifted" according to the new design criteria, as can be seen from the last versions which appeared at the end of 1969. The range (which still offered the 125 and 160 cc variants as well as the Scrambler and Normale versions) was fitted with a new 5-speed gearbox which meant redesigning the crankcase; but the design team took the opportunity to "go the whole hog" and the result was a completely new engine block with a heavily finned cylinder barrel and head assembly (the finning was later reduced as it was more abundant than necessary as far as thermic requirements were concerned) and an imposing, quasi-aggressive appearance. The body, mudguards, forks, and the saddle were also modified while the tank acquired a vaguely space-age look. The silencer and the tool box were also remodelled. In all probability this new specification was somewhat lacking in homogeneity while certain elements, like the cylinder head-barrel assembly, owed more to fashion trends than purely functional requirements. However the bike is still an interesting example of what could happen when design principles were finally applied to the motorcycle, and this is another plus point to be added to the many which Guzzi has totted up in the course of its long career. The

Gianfranco Saini negotiates a banking on his *Lodola Regolarità*.

Stornello remained in production until 1975, when it was replaced by the new 2-stroke lightweights which were more in tune with the demands of the younger customer, who is the mainstay of the modern up-to-125 cc market.

The regularity races

Perhaps there is no word quite so inappropriate as "regularity" in the motorcycling field, nor one which does less to express the particular nature and difficulties of this sporting speciality. Regularity racing began a long time ago as an alternative to pure speed events in an attempt to show that even a normal touring bike could cover long distances at a good speed, and above all to prove that motorcycles could cover these distances without too many mechanical problems, barring those occasional little troubles which every good motorcyclist ought to be able to handle without any assistance.

These races obliged riders to travel for some hundreds of kilometres on normal roads (which were often pretty awful in those days) at an average of around 40-50 km/h. In the event of mechanical problems competitors had to make their own repairs (or face disqualification) while they also had to show up at the various checkpoints along the route at the exact time (to the minute) shown in the timetable.

Everything worked very well as long as the roads were not asphalted; afterwards it became child's play to maintain an average of 50 km/h, a figure which could hardly be changed on the other hand, otherwise the race would have become a speed event.

It was then decided to make use of unmetalled tracks, muletracks and the like until competitors finally found themselves in an authentic off-road landscape complete with mountainsides, riverbeds and marshland.

At this point regularity racing had become a species of motocross competition, made even more arduous and demanding by the far longer courses and the requirement to make repairs without assistance and without using practically any spares, because virtually all the major components were marked before the off. This is now known as "enduro" racing, an exotic and presumably more gratifying title.

Regularity racing has therefore developed into one of the most complete sporting disciplines, because participants must possess excellent riding skills, first class reflexes and eyesight, physical fitness, a profound mechanical knowledge and the intelligence to follow a race strategy with split-second precision, especially in team events. It is no accident that the "Six Days", the world's major event in this speciality where an international field of entrants competes over a 2,000 km long course, is known as the motorcycling Olympics. This soubriquet is fully merited because the event arouses worldwide interest and is extremely hard on the entrants, who compete for a few, largely symbolic prizes in the form of cups or at most gold medals. Logically, the bikes had to be adapted to the ever more difficult courses and it was not long before they were being provided with entirely specialized features like purpose-built frames, and the cunningly tuned special engines you need for such long and tough competitions. Since Guzzi was no longer involved in speed events, it was decided to take an interest in regularity racing – something the other Italian manufacturers had already done. The famous agreement to abstain from Grand Prix racing did not apply to *Regolarità* events, which did not require the construction of extremely expensive, highly strung racers, and so the necessary financial commitment could be made without too much soul-searching. In 1958 Mandello already had a bike which, suitably modified, filled the bill very well: the *Lodola 175*. This was a light, sturdy machine with only a reasonably powerful engine, which was

nevertheless a supple performer able to supply a deep-chested shove at low speeds. All the members of the golden-age race shop (Carcano, Todaro, Cantoni and the various mechanics) got down to business and the first race of the season – Bergamo's Reda Trophy, one of Italy's senior regularity races – witnessed a victorious debut for the Guzzi squad, which was equipped with *Lodolas* ridden by Gianfranco Saini, Sergio Cremaschini and Brunone Villa – three of the best specialists around at the time. The bikes differed but little from the standard production versions: stronger forks, vertical rear shock absorbers with exposed springs, high handlebars, raised mudguards and silencer, studded tyres, a different saddle plus a few other minor particulars. However that season was dedicated to experimentation and preparation on an organizational level too, since entry into such a different sector presented new problems even for competition veterans; but results were not long in coming.

The bikes were modified on the basis of the experience acquired and in 1959 they reappeared with two engines, an ohc 175 and a push-rod 235 cc unit with a light alloy cylinder barrel and chromed bore.

The frame was then strengthened in the steering area with the application of special stays and sheet metal gussets and the rear fork was shortened for improved manageability. Then larger brakes were fitted and finally the 175 received 2.75-19" and 3.25-18" tyres at front and back respectively, while the larger bike was fitted with 3.00-19" and 3.50-18" tyres.

Other useful features included: a carburettor air intake shielded against mudsplash, a quick-change tank, a retractable kickstarter and carefully scaled gear ratios. The 175 weighed 107 kilos and developed 12 hp at 7500 rpm, while the 235 weighed one kilo more and could count on 12.5 hp at 6000 rpm. After a few races however, the 235 was also fitted with an overhead camshaft, with the result that output was upped to 14 hp at 7500 rpm on a 9:1 compression ratio. A 24 mm carburettor was also fitted. Results were satisfactory, a fact amply borne out by the four gold medals won at the "Six Days" event held that year in Gottwaldov, Czechoslovakia.

In 1960 the 235 cc ohc version of the *Lodola Regolarità* was placed on general sale thus providing amateurs with a bike which could help them put up a good show in a sport which was becoming more and more sophisticated and exclusive. This was another extremely good year for the Mandello-built single, which won the "Valli Bergamasche" Italian team Championship, six gold medals at the Bad Ausse "Six Days" and many other less important competitions.

One of the works *Stornellos*, which won the Silver Vase at the 1963 "Six Days". The Guzzi works team was Carlo Moscheni, Giuseppe Panarari and Luigi Gorini.

The works *Lodolas* were further improved for the following seasons. First of all the engine capacity was uprated to 247 cc (68 × 68), then a 5-speed gearbox was added which was better able to exploit the power of the engine, now able to produce about 16 hp at 7500 rpm running on a 11:1 compression ratio. A few adjustments were also made to the frame and the suspension. This version of the *Lodola* also racked up a string of successes together with its 175 cc stablemate, which was reserved for the Guzzi works team: gold medals at the 1961 and 1962 "Six Days", individual and team wins in the 1962 and '63 "Valli Bergamasche", as well as the usual hatful of minor wins. But the most important success of all was to come in the 1963 "Six Days", again hosted by Czechoslovakia, where an Italian team mounted on Guzzi *Lodolas* and *Stornellos* walked off with the "Silver Vase". In 1962 Guzzi decided to turn its 125 cc lightweight into a regularity bike, so as to extend the firm's involvement to the smaller capacity classes which offered the advantage of lower average speed requirements among other things.

The *Stornello Regolarità* was fitted with a tweaked version of the Sport type engine with inclined valves and a 24 mm carb. The compression ratio was 11.3:1 while output stood at 12 hp at 8000 rpm.

The right hand side engine cover was divided into two pieces in order to afford faster access to the sprocket, the oil filler cap was shifted to a more accessible position on the left and the exhaust pipe was steeply upswept. The sump was protected by a tubular structure which also helped to strengthen the frame; the brakes and front forks were taken from the *Lodola*.

The bike was fitted with a complete enduro-style specification, including a sheltered air intake, quick-change tank, dual ignition circuit with two coils which could be swiftly integrated in the event of a breakdown, quick-change wheel spindles and so on. The wheels were shod with 2.75-19" and 3.00-18" tyres at front and rear respectively. Weight was around 95 kilos.

The *Stornello* made an important contribution to the Guzzi success story from 1962, when Gianfranco Saini scored a win straight off the bat at Varese in the first event on the Italian Championship calendar, right through to 1964, when Guzzi decided to withdraw even from regularity racing. A special 98 cc works version was also prepared for some events. Guzzi's withdrawal from the field corresponded to the launch of the *Stornello 125*, in a version which was rather different to the works machine in that it was powered by the less powerful *Sport* version with the 22 mm carburettor. The rear wheel was 19 inches in diameter. The *Stornello Regolarità* remained in the catalogue until 1967, when it was replaced by the *America* version of the Scrambler, which looked similar but was inferior from a sporting point of view.

From the three-wheeler to the heavy-duty motocarro

Attempts to employ motorcycle-based vehicles for carrying goods date from the earliest days of motor transport, but results were poor at first and the paying customer remained unconvinced for a long time.

This was due partly to the long standing prejudice which decreed that motorcycles were fundamentally sporting vehicles and therefore unsuitable for working purposes and partly to the empirical nature of the early efforts, which were based on asymmetrical affairs like sidecar combinations or other imaginative but inherently unstable designs.

Even the machines based on the classic pedal tricycle design (i.e. with the body in front and a single rear wheel) were not very practical, because the load was limited by the need to ensure forward visibility. Another disadvantage lay in the fact that the steering tended to get heavy when the vehicle was fully loaded, while braking could easily result in the tricycle tipping over onto its nose.

On the other hand the goods motortricycle, or "motocarro" as the Italians subsequently baptized it, clearly possessed considerable potential in practical terms – what was needed was a truly rational design. The said advantages can be summed up in terms of low construction costs, a favourable useful load-to-tare relationship combined with the excellent manoeuverability typical of three-wheeled vehicles, which are also ideal for crowded city conditions.

Guzzi first tackled the problem in 1928 and came up with a simple but brilliant solution based on the normal *Sport* model. The front end (forks, cradle, tank and engine) was left unchanged while the rear triangulation was removed and replaced with a framework of pressed panels and tubular stays which were attached to two long leaf springs that in turn supported either a deck with wooden sides or a closed metal body. The whole assembly was completed by a car-type rear axle equipped with a differential and spoked wheels.

Power was transmitted to the wheels by a long heavy-duty chain supported in the middle by a sprocket which doubled as a tensioner, while a strap-type brake controlled by the usual pedal on the left hand side acted on the differential ring gear. The Guzzi motocarro had a precise steering system similar to that of a normal motorcycle, while the load bearing down on the drive wheels ensured excellent grip, which made it possible to exploit the available power to the full. The weight was rationally distributed and so abnormal braking and cornering behaviour were not very likely.

The dimensions of the loading platform (1.25 × 0.75 m) were not exceptional, but they were sufficient to carry more than six hundredweight of goods, enough for the needs of many small firms, tradesmen and shopkeepers.

The very first models were built over the *Sport*, which was soon abandoned in favour of the *Sport 14*. Since the frame for the loading platform was simply bolted on to what was otherwise a normal motorcycle, Guzzi would supply a normal motorcycle rear wheel on request, complete with the necessary triangulated elements, which enabled the owner to convert his motocarro into "a powerful touring motorcycle" as the contemporary advertising puff had it, and all in the space of a few minutes!

The motocarros remained in production ever since, and their evolution naturally followed that of normal motorcycle production. An improvement on the original *14*-type model came along in 1936. This machine, powered by the *S*-type engine, was then replaced by the *E.R.* (1938), which had an engine derived from the ohv V series power unit. The *E.R.* represented a quantum leap forward in comparison with its predecessors. By then the motocarro had overcome all the doubts and mistrust which it had previously aroused, while certain specific requirements of the national economy, following the world slump and the economic sanctions which had followed Italy's African war, had set the seal on its success. Such was the demand that all the motorcycle manufacturers began producing three-wheeled goods vehicles and firms were established which catered wholly for this specialist market.

The *E.R.* retained the design with the single wheel at the front and the two driven wheels at the rear, but the all-new pressed steel chassis was much stronger. Pressed steel was also used for the parallelogram front forks and lateral friction dampers, the engine cradle and the loading platform. The front wheel was a motorcycle-type fitment but the rear wheels were pressed steel discs supported by swinging arms, also made of pressed steel. Semi-elliptic leaf springs were used for the suspension system. The gearbox, in a unit with the engine, had three speeds plus reverse, an indispensable feature given the motocarro's considerable overall weight.

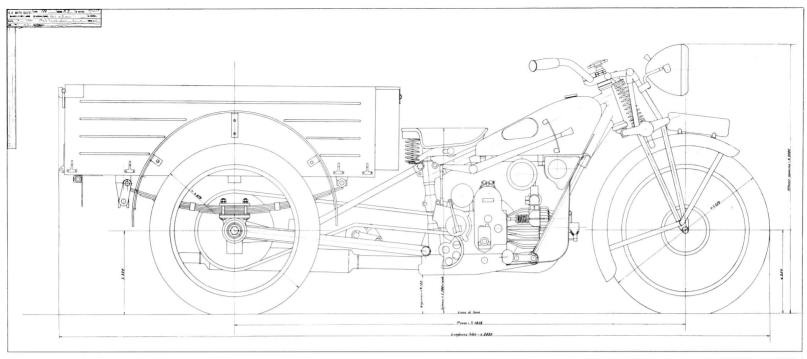

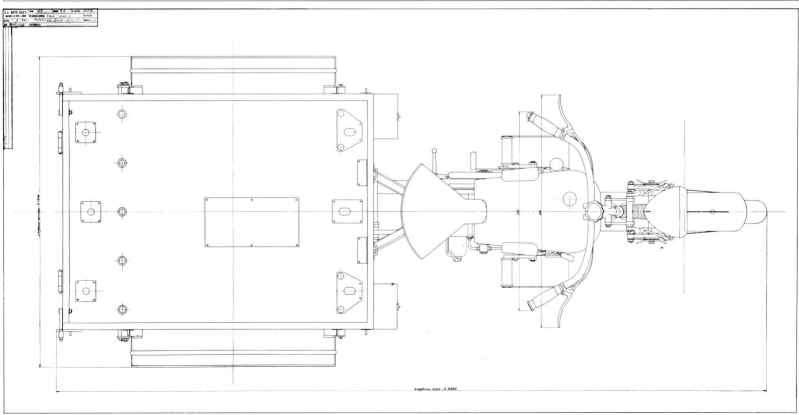

109

Carrying capacity was uprated to a thousand kilos. The power was still fed to the wheels by a chain drive with a pressed steel rear axle and differential but the strap-type brake had been replaced by two mechanically controlled drums.

The driving seat was still uncovered as the various types of cabins were made by independent coachbuilders and were purchased separately.

In 1942 the *E.R.* was replaced by the *U* model (the *U* stood for "Unified"). Shortly before war broke out the Italian government had passed a series of rigid laws governing the construction of motor vehicles which obliged all manufacturers to eliminate variety as much as possible, both in terms of the finished product and individual spare parts.

The advantage of this was that if the factory had to be requisitioned the number of necessary spares and other supplies would have been correspondingly reduced.

The *U* motocarro was built in accordance with these legal restrictions, which did nothing to impair the classic Guzzi design in any case. On the contrary the new model was considerably improved both mechanically and in terms of performance. Cold air was conveyed to the hottest part of the cylinder (the area around the exhaust valve, in the lower part of the cylinder head) by a

Above, the civilian version of the *109-32* motocarro. The drawings on the previous page refer to the military version. Practically speaking, the only difference was in the size of the body. This vehicle was the link between the original 1928 model and the later *S* type. 1,068 units were produced between 1933 and 1936.

centrifugal fan mounted on the flywheel, while a reduction gear was fitted to the differential housing (the *U* still had a chain drive), which made it possible to have six forward and two reverse gears in all. The front forks were strengthened and the front wheel was bolted to the brake drum. Wider section tyres were fitted to the back wheels. Large numbers of the *U* were ordered by the Army, which found many uses for the versatile three-wheeler.

The immediate post-war years were more or less the golden age of the motocarro because the demands of a rapid reconstruction programme made beasts of burden seem even more anachronistic than they already were, while lorries were extremely costly and virtually unobtainable. At a time when everything was in short supply and spare parts lists regularly offered inner tubes with "up to or more than three patches", saving a tyre or a few litres of petrol became a major consideration. This situation lent considerable impetus to the production of three-wheeled vehicles, which ranged from pedal tricycles fitted with micromotors to "mototreni" complete with trailers.

Guzzi decided to concentrate on medium-large capacity vehicles, given the firm's long experience in this sector and the proven versatility of the half-litre engine.

Two new vehicles were introduced in 1946, the *Ercole* and the *Edile*. The *Ercole* (Hercules) was a shaft-driven development of the *U* type, fitted with five forward gears plus reverse, which could carry 1,500 kilos.

The gearbox, a beautiful piece of engineering, was a car-type unit (controlled by a gated gear selector on the right hand side of the tank) mounted in a separate housing at 90 degrees to the crankshaft, so as to be in line with the drive shaft. Power was transmitted to the gearbox by a bevel gear pair with the drive pinion mounted on the shaft of the wet multiplate clutch.

The *Ercole* motocarro, which remained in production until 1980, was gradually modified in the course of its long career; in 1950 it was fitted with a light alloy cylinder barrel-head assembly and enclosed rocker gear; in 1953 it received the automatic advance magneto, while hydraulic rear brakes were fitted in 1955. The electric starter with the motor which meshed with the flywheel ring gear, and the coil ignition came along in 1957. A version adapted to run on methane gas was also produced.

The *Edile* was designed as a direct substitute for the horse-drawn carts used in the building trade. As with the carthorses it was built to replace, speed was never a major factor and in fact Guzzi put its money on carrying capacity. The result was a vehicle (with a pressed steel frame) capable of carrying a good 3,600 kilos despite a tare of only 1,350 kilos, an unheard of weight-to-carrying capacity ratio for a motor vehicle. An *Ercole*-type drive train with a 5-speed box plus reverse and shaft drive was fitted. Gear ratios were extremely close of course, so much so that the *Edile* could manage a top speed of no more than 25 km/h. There was a worm and roller type steering system which was connected to a steering wheel inside a species of cabin formed by a roof and a big sheet metal panel at the front, with neither windscreen nor doors at the side. Given the low speeds in play it was not considered necessary to fit suspension, the fat tyres being considered springy enough. The *Edile* was not much of a success however, because of the low speed and the difficulties involved in driving a vehicle with no suspension. Men who had finally got rid of the horse and cart wanted to savour the convenience of the horseless carriage to the full, with no half measures, and so the *Edile* was soon struggling to find a market and was deleted definitively after only a few years.

In 1956 Guzzi brought out something new in the goods vehicle field in the form of the *Ercolino*. This was a motocarro with a small carrying capacity (350 kilos) built over a modified version of the 192 cc *Galletto*, which had received a 4-speed gearbox with a reverse gear and shaft drive. The frame was made up of a large tubular stress-member to which the brackets for the bodywork were welded. At first the newcomer was built with medium diameter disc wheels (3.25-14" in front and 4.25-15" behind) but from 1959 onwards it was fitted with fat 5.00-10" tyres. A version able to carry 590 kilos was also on sale with a reduction gear and 5.00-10" tyres. The *Ercolino* was also available with an electric starter.

Other models came along some years later, with engines derived from the *Zigolo 110* (the *Aiace*, which carried 250 kilos) and with 50 cc engines (the *Dingotre* and later the *Furghino*), the last two being in the moped class, which meant they could circulate without number plates – nor did the driver have to have a licence. The *Furghino* had an interesting glassfibre cabin. But these little goods vehicles were not very successful and they were soon deleted from the catalogue. The situation today is unlike the immediate post-war period and the many advantages possessed by the conventional van have led to its being preferred over the motorcycle truck despite the latter's undeniable cheapness. This is particularly true in the case of the heavy-duty three-wheelers where the handlebar steering gets very heavy beyond a certain weight limit and where driver comfort has traditionally been sacrificed in the interests of obtaining additional useful space. Furthermore, a 500 cc engine cannot guarantee the

kind of speeds which are expected of today's commercial vehicles, especially when fully loaded. This does not mean that the motocarro has reached the end of the road, because it still offers some interesting advantages: all that is required is a thorough-going face-lift and a more modern range of applications than those currently envisaged.

SEIMM: from the agreement to the relaunch

Forty years after it was established in 1921 with a staff of twelve working in a 300 square metre shed, Guzzi had become a vast, flourishing concern which employed over 1,500 people in a 24,000 square metre factory. Subsidiary companies were operating in Spain and Turkey.

Perhaps more importantly, the same company was also a leader in terms of both technology and organization.

The work was carried on with the most modern and accurate machinery available; every product was subjected to rigorous checks throughout the manufacturing process. The research centre and the race shop, which was practically a offshoot of the former, tested and experimented with techniques and new mate-

An aerial shot of the Guzzi plant in 1970. The Milan-Sondrio railway line and Mandello station can be seen in the foreground. The test track is in the background.

rials aimed at improving the product, which was manufactured virtually entirely at Mandello, in the sense that very few components were ordered from external suppliers. Two hydroelectric power stations satisfied the factory's energy requirements while exclusive facilities like the wind tunnel allowed the firm to carry out research which was unique in the motorcycling field.

A network of carefully selected dealerships and sales points guaranteed customers quality after-sales service even in the most isolated areas.

At the same time the company took care to develop all those social services which, even in the era of assembly line production, combined to generate a family spirit and a particularly strong sense of company loyalty.

Apart from all the normal factory facilities like the medical centre, shops, canteens, libraries and so on, the firm also provided workers with housing close to the works at rents which amounted to only 6.5% of wages. Seaside resorts were created for the children and the works was involved in a number of sporting activities; the Mandello "nursery" did not just produce star riders, it also produced athletes of some note in several other sporting disciplines.

Worthy of particular mention is the factory canoing team whose

A partial view of the shop floor in 1970. The installation of the first numerically controlled machine tools has already begun.

haul includes a number of national and international titles as well as Olympic gold medals. But around 1964 a series of circumstances began to make this rosy picture look rather faded. A serious internal crisis, concerning both personalities and methods, plus the changing conditions within the motorcycle market conspired to unleash a combination of body blows which soon had Guzzi reeling on the ropes.

The founders, the old warriors whose blend of brilliance and parsimony had steered the firm through many's the storm had all disappeared from the scene by that time: Emanuele Vittorio Parodi had died during the war at almost the same time as his nephew Angelo; his son Giorgio died suddenly in 1955; Carlo Guzzi, old and unwell, went into retirement after having lost a bitter boardroom battle with the new men to maintain control of his own factory.

He was to die aged 75 in the November of 1964.

That left Enrico Parodi, Giorgio's brother, who had joined the company as recently as 1942, but who had already held a series of managerial positions. He was a brilliant man but not as careful as his brother. Some cases of poor judgement, a few unlucky foreign contracts plus a series of mistaken investments outwith the motorcycle industry combined to shake the Parodi empire (shipping companies, real estate and utilities) which staggered under the crisis just when Guzzi found itself faced by the bitter realities of a shrinking market. In order to save the sinking ship, Guzzi management decided to put their money on the moped, in the belief that it was still possible to tap the vast lower end of the market. In a bid to enter this segment immediately the Mandello concern bought up a batch of mopeds from a small Milanese company which was in financial difficulties and sold them under the Guzzi trademark; then came the *Dingo*, a genuine Guzzi product introduced in 1963. Based on a pressed steel single-spar frame with a 2-stroke engine and 3-speed gearbox, the original *Dingo* can fairly be described as an honest get-to-work machine which was not much different from the average product on the market at that time. Two versions were built: the *Turismo* was fitted with pedals, cycle-type saddle and a small ovoid tank which left an open space in front of the saddle; while the *Sport* had no pedals and a tank which had been extended to link up with the dualseat, a design which gave this little bike the look of a light motorcycle.

But the *Dingo* alone was not enough to solve a problem which was getting more and more complex as time went by.

The Parodi family had to sink their entire family fortune into the business in order to stave off bankruptcy, but even more money was urgently required in order to keep the flag flying. The old family firm was in very poor shape to meet the industry-wide crisis of the Sixties: even though it could still count on the services of first class engineers it lacked a modern-minded sales management team capable of understanding the new levels of production which were required if Guzzi was to become a contender on a world level. Plant and machinery were obsolete and too many workers were producing too little. On the 25th of February 1966 the firm was put into the hands of a receiver, a situation which lasted for roughly one year during which the firm was run by a provisional board chaired by Arnaldo Marcantonio, a fiduciary for the group of creditor banks and a large building society known as IMI (*Istituto Mobiliare Italiano*) in particular. One of Marcantonio's first moves was to make staff cuts at all levels. Inevitably these drastic cuts involved sacrificing some men of the highest calibre who could still have done a good job for the firm, like Carcano and Cantoni. A man of great discretion, Carcano has never disclosed the reasons for the termination of his contract, limiting himself to an appreciation of the gifted Carlo Guzzi, who he described as "a self-taught man and an acute observer".

When asked to give a summarized account of his long career at Mandello, he would only say that it had been a "unique and marvellous experience".

The significant fact remains that since then, even though he was still in his creative prime, he never worked again in the mechanical engineering field, preferring to dedicate himself to designing revolutionary sailing boats.

On the 1st of February 1967 the holding company known as SEIMM (*Società Esercizio Industrie Moto Meccaniche*) was founded. This new company rented the plant and other assets formerly owned by Guzzi for a three year period with an option to buy, which it exercised within two years. SEIMM was still owned by IMI, which possessed virtually all of its shares. In the March of 1967 Luciano Francolini and Romolo De Stefani were nominated chairman and managing director of the new company. Francolini resigned after the first year and was replaced by Donato Cattaneo, who occupied the chairman's seat until the beginning of the De Tomaso takeover. De Stefani had a solid background in the motorcycle industry with Edoardo Bianchi and Ducati, which had been followed by a brief spell in the motor car industry as head of ASA. He was responsible for bringing former Bianchi design supremo Lino Tonti to Guzzi. In 1970 Guzzi also brought in Giorgio Araldi, a scooter engineer from Innocenti, who ran the technical division for three years: in

The record-breaking *Cobra* vetturette built by Gino Cavanna (at the wheel), Carcano, Cantoni and ing. Bazzocchi of Aeronautica Macchi, and powered by the pre-war blown 250 Guzzi engine. In May 1959 it set various records on a stretch of the *Autostrada del Sole*, reaching 232 km/h. The driver lay prone; the rear wheels (with no differential) were very close together, but sufficient to class the vehicle as a four-wheeler.

113

practice his job was to liaise between the design team and the sales management.

The SEIMM board operated on the basis of emergency criteria, if we can put it like that, but those same citeria were based on sound management concepts. All the models which the public had clearly forsaken (the *Cardellino*, the *Zigolo*, the *Galletto*, and the *Lodola*) went to the wall while production was concentrated on the mopeds and the *Stornello*. Furthermore the development of a new heavyweight, the *V7*, was stepped up. Guzzi management realized that the *V7* , first planned as a police bike, had a good chance of success on the civilian market abroad, especially in the USA, now that that market was finally moving under the impact of the Japanese "invasion". For the first time, in other words, Guzzi was attempting to play the export card, a move which had brought success to many other Italian industries at the time.

Results were not long in coming, thanks also to a gradual change in market conditions. Young people, particularly young men, enjoyed greater freedom and independence than ever before and the desire to own a bike, or at least a moped, was gaining ground rapidly. At the same time a goodly number of people in higher socio-economic brackets were beginning to "discover"

The *Nibbio II* set motoring records in 1956 and 1957 and, on the facing page, a view of the Guzzi 350 twin-cam engine with the pipe for the cooling system.

the motorcycle – partly in imitation of the American biking vogue and partly because the motor car was now seen as a badge of conformity which lay within the financial grasp of the masses. Such people wanted big, heavy, expensive bikes. Exclusivity, in a word.

This led to a demand, in Italy too, for powerful prestige machines, the so-called "maxi-bikes".

Guzzi's new management found itself with the right product at the right time, and the results of this were a real breath of badly needed oxygen for the firm's flagging finances. The *V7* was a big success on the international market, not only in the States but also in Germany, where the passion for *kolossal* bikes had never really died out. And so the old works at Mandello calmly began to recover its former position of pre-eminence.

In an attempt to underline the efficiency of the new SEIMM management Guzzi introduced various new products between the end of 1965 and the beginning of the following year. The Milan Show of November 1965 was the stage chosen for the prototypes of the civilian *V7* and the *Lodola 250 Sport* (which never got off the ground however), as well as two new mopeds in the *Dingo* series, the *Super* and the *Cross*, which had an interesting raised tubular duplex cradle frame resembling the unit designed for the last Grand Prix singles.

Despite the legal limitations regarding moped performance, the youngsters loved the new lightweights, which not only looked like their higher-capacity stablemates but were also particularly well finished, with chromed mudguards, dualseat, knee recesses on the tank, and efficient suspension systems. The *Dingo Cross* received a publicity boost in 1967 when Roberto Patrignani (a singular figure – half racer, half journalist – and an old hand at such exploits) rode one across Africa from South to North.

Shortly afterwards, the *Dingo* was further perfected with the adoption of a 4-speed, pedal-operated gearbox, which was undoubtedly sportier and easier to use on an off-road bike, while a *Gran Turismo* variant was also launched with raised handlebars, baggage carrier and 2.50-17" tyres, a genuine light motorcycle perfect for work and short-distance touring. The *Dingo* was restyled in 1970, along lines introduced at the same time for the *Stornello*. These last *Dingos* were the single-speed model, with the automatic clutch and pressed steel frame, and the 3-speed version.

The *Trotter* came along in the Spring of 1966. This was a very cheap moped (it cost only 54,000 lire) which enjoyed instant success and did much to keep the Mandello concern afloat during the difficult transitional phase. Effectively speaking this really was an invitingly low price, one of the lowest on the market, and with it Guzzi won a considerable number of customers who had never ridden a motorcycle before: cheap or not it was still a Guzzi, and what else could you buy with a few thousand lire after all? The launch of the *Trotter* marked the renaissance of the moped, a means of transport which continues to enjoy considerable popularity in virtually all consumer categories. Apart from its simplicity (it resembled a woman's bicycle with a frame made of welded steel pressings and no suspension), the *Trotter* was fitted with an automatic centrifugal clutch, a device calculated to please the mechanically inexpert because it reduced riding to a matter of controlling the throttle and the brakes. It did have a 2-speed option however, which was very useful in mountainous areas: in normal conditions the bike moved off directly in the longer gear and so it was unnecessary to change gear. The chain drive was mounted on the left while the cycle-type pedals (necessary for starting) were equipped with their own chain on the right.

There was another element worthy of note, in that it was rarely used in motorcycle construction: the engine was fixed to the frame by two rubber silentblocs which neutralized the vibration. More versions were to follow in the next few years as the original model was steadily improved upon: the *Super* was fitted with telescopic front forks (1968); the *Special M* sported leading link forks and an automatic clutch; the *Special V* had the automatic stepless transmission (i.e. an automatic transmission with an expanding belt and pulley) while the *Mark M* and *Mark V* used swinging arm rear suspension.

These last four models were powered by a new belt-driven engine with a horizontal cylinder. By the beginning of 1977 Guzzi moped production also included the *Chiù*, a direct descendant of the *Trotter Mark*, the 3-speed *Dingo 3V* and the automatic *Dingo MM*, both of which had a new tubular frame and telescopic forks; the *Nibbio* and the *Cross 50* with the Benelli-derived 5-speed power units, and finally the *Magnum* with the fat single-spar frame, 4.00-10" tyres and 5-speed gearbox.

With the end of Guzzi's Grand Prix racing involvement, Carcano and his technical staff dedicated themselves to commercial production, beginning with the *Stornello* project. But the business of turning out simple, cheap machinery was certainly not enough to satisfy the man who had produced the *Otto cilindri*, the most fantastic motorcycle ever built. And so the idea of a big V-twin began to form in his mind, firstly as a means of escaping the daily routine and then more seriously. He wanted a powerful 4-stroke machine which could be built without incurring exces-

sive costs; a push-rod engine therefore, with crankshaft and con-rods running on smooth ball bearings. For normal use two cylinders were more than sufficient, while a 90 degree configuration would ensure good balance by reducing vibration to more than acceptable levels.

At that particular time it seemed too risky to commit the firm to a heavyweight motorcycle project and this application of the V engine was shelved. Instead, Guzzi management thought to adapt it to the new Fiat 500 with a view to turning the little compact into a real sportster. The engine, built at first in a 500 cc and later in a 650 cc version, fitted perfectly inside the bodyshell of the little Fiat, whose gearbox and other drive train components were also compatible.

The more powerful version (fitted with a twin carburettor) developed about 34 hp, enough to boost the little car to 140 km/h with ease. Testing continued for a long time, but just when everything seemed to be going well Fiat backed out and the whole project had to be abandoned.

3 × 3: the "mechanical mule"

More or less at the same time the Italian Ministry of Defence encharged Guzzi with a project to build a special vehicle for the country's alpine troops. Based on an idea of General Garbari's, the *3 × 3* was a completely new conveyance with some exceptional features : three drive wheels, of which the rear pair were fitted with variable track in order to cope with the narrowest bridle paths. A species of "mechanical mule" in other words, capable of carrying a 500 kilo load over any kind of terrain, no matter how rough.

This vehicle, baptized the *3 × 3* in accordance with the typical military formula (three wheels, all driven), was powered by a biddable version of the V engine. The 754 cc power unit developed a mere 20 hp at 4000 rpm (at the crankshaft), but max torque was a good 4.7 kg at only 2400 rpm. The engine was fed by a single 26 mm Weber carburettor and had forced air cooling (fan), shielded coil ignition, dry sump lubrication with dual feed and return pumps driven by the two camshafts, a dry clutch on the flywheel and electric starter, plus the possibility of adding an emergency battery in case of need.

The frame resembled the type used for the motorcycle trucks with large-section tubes and pressed panels; the two rear wheels were supported by box-type arms hinged on the tubular structure. The engine was housed in the central part, behind the driv-

The first V-twin, designed by Carcano and intended for the Fiat 500 compact, whose transmission it used. A forced air system was used to cool the engine.

er, who sat on a motorcycle-type saddle but drove with the aid of a wheel and car-type pedals.

The drive train was made up of the following elements in order: the 6-speed and reverse gearbox (handchange), the epicyclic central differential (with a pawl to prevent the machine from slipping backwards), which assigned the torque in a proportion of 1/5 to the front wheel and 4/5 to the back wheels, the rear wheel differential and finally the two halfshafts with universal couplings for the drive, and gear pairs with Gleason teeth for the final reduction drive.

A cardan shaft also branched out from the central differential; this shaft passed between the V of the cylinders to join the steering box.

Here, with the aid of a Gleason gear pair and a train of three spur gears, it drove another shaft (running in the weight-bearing telescopic tube alongside the front wheel) which terminated in another Gleason pair.

Gearbox, differential and the device for varying the track were all contained in a single aluminium box. The device for varying the track (the limits ran from 1.30 m to 85 cm) included a drive for the rear wheels which came from the differential and which was formed by a pair of spur gears, a constant-mesh type bevel-driven reverse gear controlled by a sliding coupling and frontally meshing gears with neutral in a central position, a safety coupling calibrated to prevent overloading the drive train when adjusting the track, a jointed telescopic connecting shaft, a worm screw type reduction gear pair and finally a coupling with a double spiral thread – right and left – which controlled, by means of linkages, the arms supporting the wheels. Track adjustment was carried out with the vehicle in motion and could be accomplished after travelling a maximum of 25 metres; in emergencies this manoeuver could be carried out manually with the aid of a special lever.

The steering was by spur gears and the turning radius was barely 2.20 metres. The drum brakes were hydraulically controlled at the rear while the front brake was operated by a manual lever and cable system.

It was possible to fit the back wheels with tank-type tracks, which were tensioned by rollers fixed by an arm and a coil spring mounted directly around the hubs. The front suspension had a spiral spring inside the telescopic wheel arm; rear springing was provided by elastic rubber elements.

The *3 × 3* could reach a top speed of 50 km/h. In first gear (it normally moved off in third on the flat) it could handle very steep slopes until it reached the critical overturning angle. It of-

A photo which clearly demonstrates the practical possibilities of a fully loaded *3 × 3*. Note the remarkable "angle of approach" to a vertical obstacle! The system for mounting the rear tracks is also clearly visible; the tensioning roller pivots on a mobile arm (preloaded by a coil spring) which is free to rotate through a wide sector. The system ensured that the tracks were always in contact with the ground, no matter how steep the slope. Mechanically over complex, the vehicle – which was intended for Italy's Alpine regiments – never really found any practical application.

fered a particularly good "angle of approach", i.e. the ability to clamber over steep obstacles from a standing start.

However, on various mountain tracks even the *3 × 3* showed it possessed all the limitations of three-wheeled vehicles: very powerful as long as it was free to move straight ahead and tackle slopes and alpine meadows head on, it was always in danger of tipping over sideways as soon as it had to traverse steep slopes, while on the bridle paths all it took to stop it in its tracks was a particularly tight hairpin or a boulder of modest dimensions, which a more orthodox mule simply stepped over.

On a practical level then, the *3 × 3* simply did not measure up to expectations, as was predictable, but it is still a bravura piece of engineering.

Some time later another government tender announcement finally provided Guzzi with the chance to design a real motorcycle powered by Carcano's V engine. The *Polizia Stradale* – although still fairly content with the good old *Falcone* – needed a new, more modern machine which could keep pace with the majority of cars which were in production by that time. The new police mount had to be a very robust machine, capable or running for at least 100,000 kilometres without any major repairs, easy to maintain and simple in structure, so as to keep dead time in the

repair shop down to a minimum. While the 90 degree V with the unit construction light alloy crankcase were left unchanged, the engine was a completely different unit in comparison with the versions fitted to the vetturette and the *3 × 3*. A single camshaft was fitted in the centre of the V, which had a wet sump lubrication system. The one-piece steel crankshaft still ran on smooth ball bearings, lubricated in parallel, so as to avoid the pressure drops which occur when the oil is fed to the bearings one after another. For the first time in such a large engine, the cylinders were fitted with chrome bores. The overhead valves were at an angle of 70 degrees with the valve diameters set at 38.6 mm inlet and 34.6 exhaust.

Two 29 mm Dell'Ortos were fitted while the coil ignition system with the rotor arm distributor was retained.

Another completely new element was the drive train.

The car- type dry clutch on the flywheel had twin discs; the gearbox, contained in a separate aluminium housing, had a cluster of four speed gears in constant mesh engaged by sliding sleeves. Between the clutch shaft and the gearbox there was a helical gear pair with a flexible coupling which helped to supply a modest reduction in engine revolutions. The final drive was provided by a shaft with a constant velocity joint at the gearbox output, a coulisse and a bevel gear pair.

This came naturally given the longitudinal configuration of the engine and resulted in reduced maintenance at the same time because the chain, which had to be coddled in continuation, was eliminated.

The engine was fitted with a 12 volt, 300 W dynamo, the biggest ever to be mounted on a motorcycle, which – along with the 32 Ah battery – made for a really efficient electrical system. Thus it was possible to solve the age-old problem of motorcycle electric starting systems by fitting an automobile-type starter motor, which was far more reliable than the dynamotors and other systems experimented upon so far, while there was plenty of juice left over for all those onboard services required on police bikes (siren, radio, etc.).

The tubular full-duplex cradle, reinforced with sheet metal in the upper part, had swinging fork rear suspension with the drive shaft running in the right hand side arm, and adjustable (three-way) teledraulic suspension units on either side of the rear wheel. The front forks were also the teledraulic type. In this version, the engine capacity was 703.3 cc. Output was around 35 hp, which was good for 150 km/h despite the respectable weight of 250 kilos.

The traditional links with the Polizia Stradale carried on: after the *V7* the police took delivery of the *850 T3* and the *850 T5*, which obviously had to be built to particular specifications. This bike has the light blue and white finish used by the Italian state police since 1976.

CHANGED DAYS AND NEW FACES

The first research on the *V7* (as the first version of this bike was called) began in 1964 and Guzzi and Police test riders began the long, tough testing process the following year. In the meantime the new bike was publicized abroad where both private individuals and various police authorities, like the Californian state police, expressed considerable interest.

It was decided therefore to produce a slightly more powerful civilian version which could be sold on the Italian market too, in the event of a favourable response.

International class: the V7

The civilian *V7* made its debut at the Milan Show of November 1965. The engine had been uprated to produce 40 hp at 5800 rpm and the top speed had risen to about 164 km/h. Stripped of its various military accoutrements, the weight had dropped to 230 kgs. The *V7* went into production the following year, at first for the Police and the export market; it was put on sale in Italy in 1967 at 725,000 lire.

The *V7*, whose gestation period corresponded with Guzzi's "rough patch", was also the last bike designed by Giulio Cesare Carcano, who left the industry altogether after the bitterness and disappointment of those dark days.

The job of developing and perfecting the *V7* was given to Lino Tonti, a gifted engineer from the Romagna who had taken a radio engineering diploma before the war and had joined Benelli almost by chance to become one of the country's most prolific motorcycle designers, working for a succession of firms including Aermacchi, Bianchi and Gilera, for whom he also produced various racing and record machines like the Patons and the Lintos. He joined Guzzi in 1967 and it was not long before he made his mark. In 1969 a *Special* version of the *V7* came along, with

an uprated 757 cc, 45 hp engine, improved gearing, black and white paintwork and a new, more complete instrument pack. A lightened version of this bike, fitted with a partial fairing and a tweaked 68 hp engine, was used to beat various records for the 750 and 1000 cc classes in the course of two sessions held at the Monza autodrome in June and October of that same year.

The *California* and *Ambassador* versions followed, with trim and accessories specially designed for the American market (big saddle, apehanger handlebars, lateral panniers and so on) plus the variants with the bigger 850 cc engine, 5-speed gearbox and twin-leading shoe front brake: the *V 850 GT* and the *California V7 850*. But it was with the arrival of the *V7 Sport* that Lino Tonti's genius was fully revealed. Up to then the *V7* had been a fine grand touring machine, sturdy and comfortable, but the general structure (i.e. the weight and the dimensions) made for limited manageability and therefore limited effective performance. It was not at all easy to get the best out of such a "buffalo", as German motorcyclists described it. At the same time long distance road races for heavyweight production bikes were beginning to become fashionable and more than a few Guzzi enthusiasts wanted to take part astride a machine bearing the Mandello eagle, providing it could be made competitive. For some time Guzzi even toyed with the possibility of forming a works team for these events, which looked promising from a publicity point of view, and therefore a project for a high performance bike in the *Dondolino* or *Albatros* mould was promoted with considerable determination.

The *V7 Sport*, which was seen for the first time at the Monza "500 km" of June 1971 (where it came third), was completely different from its older stablemates. The engine (whose displacement had been reduced to 748 cc to keep within the limits for the capacity class) had a new crankcase with ample external ribbing for extra strength, twin contact breakers and twin coils, plus two 30 mm Dell'Orto carburettors. Modifications had also been made to the valve gear and the con-rod assembly with a view to reducing the weight of the various organs and improving performance. Power went up to 52 hp at 6300 rpm. Other novelties included the alternator fitted to the front extension of the crankshaft and the 5-speed gearbox.

But the most interesting part was the beautiful and rationally constructed frame: Lino Tonti has always been rightly famed for his frames. The compact tubular duplex cradle fitted the engine like a glove, so to speak, leaving no gaps anywhere. In fact the fit was so close that the lower left hand rail of the frame had to be detached before the engine could be removed. The look was low, sleek and racy, a result which hardly seemed possible for a transverse V engine of those dimensions, with lines which gave an immediate impression of power and speed. Above all it proved to be an exceptionally stable mount, the best on the market in its class and the best thing to roll off the Mandello production lines up to then. The bike – rounded off by a new telescopic front fork and adjustable rear suspension units, plus twin-leading shoe front brakes – was also finished with great attention to detail: it should suffice to mention the adjustable hydraulic steering damper, the clip-on handlebars with both fore and aft and up and down adjustment and the wealth of well laid out instrumentation. Kerb weight was 206 kgs and top speed was in excess of 200 km/h.

The *Sport*-type frame and engine were fitted to all the subsequent versions of the *V7*, even the less sporty variants, all of which used the disc braking system in one form or another. The list includes the *750 S*, launched in November 1973, which differed from the previous *Sport* because it had two front discs and a drum at the back, as well as some variations in the colour scheme, saddle and trimming in general; the *850 T*, more of a touring bike, had an 844.05 cc engine, 5-speed gearbox, single-disc front brake with a drum at the rear, and also came out in November 1973; the *850 T3*, the improved version of the *850 T* (1975) had the triple-disc integral braking system, of which more later; the *750 T3* and the latest sporting version of the V-twin, the *850 Le Mans*, introduced at the Milan Motorcycle Show of November 1975; the *850 T3 California* and finally the *1000 I Convert*, with the automatic torque converter, another 1975 debut. All of the last four models were fitted with the linked braking system.

Up to then, motorcycle braking systems had been composed of one disc or drum brake per wheel, independently controlled by a lever on the handlebars (front wheel) and a pedal (back wheel). This was a very simple system to construct and it also allowed a good rider to gauge and assign the required degree of braking force to the two wheels (based on his assessment of factors like load, grip and speed) with more accuracy and sensitivity than any automatic device, no matter how well designed. Unfortunately however, good riders are thin on the ground and the braking system was often used "unscientifically", without exploiting its potential to the full. Many people were afraid to use the front brake because they felt the wheel might lock thus causing a skid, despite the fact that this is certainly not the result under normal road conditions, even though it can happen in certain specific circumstances (on unmetalled roads, for example). A single control, as in car braking systems, seemed one way of solving the problem, because it obliged the rider to use both brakes whether he liked it or not. Various attempts in this direction had already been made, even in the pioneering days, but all had been systems based on mechanical linkages and their failure was due to the difficulty of constructing a really synchronized control able to assign the braking force conveniently between the front and back wheels. Even the system used by Guzzi for the racing *Quattro cilindri* of the Fifties had failed to produce satisfactory results.

Tonti decided to tackle the problem in 1972, partly because the modern heavyweights had reached limits of weight and performance which put existing braking systems under the maximum stress thus obliging designers to pursue any path which might result in improved efficiency. Disc brakes require a hydraulic control circuit, given the considerable pressure which has to be applied to the pads, which are not self braking like the shoes in a drum brake system: besides, a hydraulic system made it easier to solve the age-old problem of splitting the braking load between the two wheels.

The new system, which was improperly but effectively described as "integrated" (improperly, because any vehicle equipped with brakes on all wheels may be braked integrally, whatever the nature of the control system), was introduced with little fanfare during the 1971 "Premio Varrone" fitted to a *V 850* competition prototype.

The system had a pedal with a hydraulic pump which operated both the rear disc brake and one of the two front discs at the same time. The other front disc brake was controlled by a lever on the handlebar, which actuated a second hydraulic pump. Thus the system offered normal, workaday braking, with two discs (one per wheel) plus an extra brake on the front wheel only – which takes most of the load when braking – to be used at high

With the *V7*, Guzzi made a brief return to production bike racing, more out of a desire to test the bike to the full than anything else. Above, a shot of the *Special* in 1969 and, below, the debut of the *Sport* at the Monza autodrome in 1971. Raimondo Riva is the rider in both cases.

speed or as an emergency brake. This linked braking system was fitted to all the Guzzi heavyweights from 1975, including the *850 Le Mans* and the *1000 I Convert*. This latter pair deserve a more detailed description.

The *850 Le Mans* was directly derived from the prototype which had appeared at the "Premio Varrone". During the three years following its debut the bike was modified and improved to ensure that it would be very quick and sporty, but also able to double as a touring bike. With this requirement in mind it was fitted with 36 mm carburettors and cast iron cylinder liners (easier to overhaul) in preference to the light alloy unit with chromed bores and a five-speed gearbox with helical-cut teeth. This version developed 71 hp, which enabled the bike to touch 210 km/h. Some special components were available for competition purposes, like 40 mm carbs, capable of boosting top speed to 240 km/h, as well as straight-cut gearing with closer ratios, a different number of teeth on the final drive gear pair and so on. As far as looks were concerned, the *Le Mans* was a beautiful piece of work in line with the latest styling criteria: cast light alloy spoked wheels, streamlined bikini fairing and black-painted exhausts slightly upswept at the end. The tank, saddle and side panels were all characterized by sharply angular contours.

The *1000 I Convert* was born to satisfy the requirements of several American police authorities, which had already taken delivery of various *V7* series. They wanted a vehicle which could crawl along at walking pace for parade and escort duties without the need to use the clutch continuously and risk overheating the engine. Many attempts had been made in the past to build bikes with stepless gearboxes, even torque converters, but no one had produced a successful result, largely because of the modest power outputs of the engines used. A hydraulic torque converter has a rather low degree of mechanical efficiency and requires very powerful engines if adequate performance is to be obtained.

First of all, the generous and extremely robust V engine was uprated to 948.8 cc, obtained with a bore and stroke of 88 × 78 mm. This not very compressed engine (9.2:1) developed 61 hp at 6500 rpm (measured at the shaft), enough to guarantee good performance without losing too much flexibility and pulling power at low speeds.

The cylinders were fitted with cast iron liners.

The engine was linked up to a torque converter produced in cooperation with Sachs, which had been specializing in clutches of all types for years. It is a classic layout, in which a centrifugal pump driven by the crankshaft impels the hydraulic fluid into a coaxial turbine fixed to the transmission input shaft. When the fluid leaves the turbine it passes into the stator vanes which redirect it back to the impeller so that the whole cycle can be repeated. The hydraulic fluid is kept under pressure by a special trochoidal pump mounted above the alternator and driven by the engine. Mounted behind the torque converter was a dry multiplate clutch controlled by the usual handlebar lever and a pedal-operated gearbox with two-speeds, one for town use (for faster acceleration) and uphill work and the other for normal fast running. Final drive was by shaft.

This bike also sported a wealth of accessories which, in a certain sense, made it Guzzi's most prestigious product: an adjustable steering damper; a parking brake connected to the side stand; a system which prevented the engine from starting in gear; a comprehensive battery of warning lights for the lubrication system, brakes, fuel reserve, neutral etc; two lateral hazard flashers; streamlined windscreen and front spoiler plus crash bars and capacious panniers on both sides. All this brought the weight up to over 260 kgs, but the bike was tailor made for the American market for which it was intended. It was a decidedly high-tech product with many exclusive features which enhanced the fame of the Mandello marque.

Ernesto Brambilla astride the *V7 Sport* in 1972, during a brief return to racing. His brother Vittorio had also raced for the Guzzi works team in the days of the *V7*, before dedicating himself to motor car racing. Below, Riva again – this time in tandem with Carena – at the 1972 Liège "24 Hours", where he was assisted by Luigi Agostini. Note the twin discs at the front, later adopted for series production.

The De Tomaso management

The "De Tomaso era" began for Guzzi in 1973. Rumours had been circulating for some time to the effect that SEIMM considered the salvage operation to be successfully completed and its job over. There was even talk of shipping the entire plant and equipment to a foreign buyer who had made an interesting offer. Alejandro De Tomaso had been operating in Italy for some time by then: an Argentinian of Italian descent, he had been a brilliant racing driver in the not so distant past. A born businessman, he also raised bulls on the pampas and collected antiques. His Italian career had begun some years before with a factory producing sports and luxury cars. Subsequently he bought up 85% of the shares in the Benelli company of Pesaro, which was in financial trouble and badly in need of new blood. De Tomaso had understood the enormous potential of the international motorcycle market and he saw no reason why this should become an exclusively Japanese fief. The strength of the Japanese industry lay in excellent organization and massive production capacity, as well as in their excellent creative and technological gifts. Technology and imagination were abundantly available in Italy too, what was lacking were the first two fac-

tors. A merger between Guzzi and Benelli looked like a good place to begin: De Tomaso's expert management would do the rest.

At first, De Tomaso's offer to acquire Guzzi aroused a good deal of perplexity and did not meet with approval at Mandello, where people feared a leap in the dark and a possible reshuffle. In point of fact early relations between the workforce and the new owner were by no means idyllic. But all the wrinkles were eventually ironed out, largely because the initial results achieved by the new management were promising.

De Tomaso's first move was to harmonize the production of the two factories, which together amounted to western Europe's largest motorcycle manufacturing concern. The basic processing and the assembly of the various models were rationally subdivided between the two plants, and it was immaterial under which name the bikes were eventually sold. Although this decision displeased older fans, mindful of the many hard-fought battles between the two marques in the sporting arena, it was nevertheless in line with modern concepts of industrial management.

Then, De Tomaso went on to widen the range of products on offer. At that time the public were very keen on four-cylinder engines, which the Japanese were selling in greater and greater quantities, and so it was decided to give the paying customer what he wanted – but made in Italy.

Time was at a premium and it was necessary to beat the Japanese rival to the punch: and so two bikes (a 350 and a 500) were prepared in the space of a few months. Ironically enough, these finished up by resembling the competition they were supposed to be beating off, but for the time being there was little to be done about that.

The two bikes, powered by transversely mounted 4-cylinder overhead camshaft engines, both had practically the same structure: the bigger model was sold under the Benelli name, while the Guzzi badge was reserved for the smaller 350.

The technical features were decidedly up to date, even though they obviously resembled the Japanese product: a die-cast light alloy gearbox-crankshaft assembly split horizontally (rather than vertically), primary drive by Morse chain in the middle of the crankshaft and cylinders cast in a single block with pressed-in liners.

The crankshaft was also a one-piece component with the con-rods running on smooth ball bearings; the overhead camshaft was driven by a chain mounted in the middle of the cylinders. Other details included four 20 mm Dell'Orto carburettors, coil ignition with twin contact breakers, wet sump lubrication, mul-

tiplate clutch, 5-speed gearbox and electric starter. The engine, undersquare in accordance with modern orthodoxy and the good old Guzzi tradition, supplied 31 hp for a top speed of around 150 km/h. Introduced in the course of 1973, the *GTS 350* was joined in 1975 by a version with a larger 400 cc engine (50 × 50.6 mm × 4), which offered superior performance, at low speeds in particular. Power output was uprated to 40 hp at 9500 rpm and top speed was 170 km/h. The *400 GTS/FD* was fitted with a 260 mm front disc brake in place of the twin leading shoe drum brake carried by the 350.

Along with the 4-cylinder 350, another sprightly and youthful motorcycle made its appearance. This was a 2-stroke 250 twin derived from a similar model previously sold under the Benelli trade mark. A 2-stroke engine, especially if it has more than one cylinder, offers bags of acceleration and power, so much so that this is currently the most popular configuration for competition bikes: it was only logical therefore that it be adopted for a sporty machine. Yet again a very up-to-date design was produced, with light alloy chosen for the horizontally split die-cast crankcase, the cylinders with chrome bores (separated from each other in order to accommodate the play caused by thermic expansion), and the heads. The built-up crankshaft had one-piece con-rods and ran on roller bearings and needles. Fuel was fed to the engine by two 25 mm Dell'Ortos, while the ignition system was a sensible electronic set-up with a pick-up and no moving breaker points. The gearbox offered five speeds while there was a multiplate clutch and geared primary drive. Given the modest weight in play, the bike was fitted with a simple kickstarter, which was also more in character with its sporting temperament. The frame was a traditional duplex cradle with telescopic forks. In 1975 the front drum brake was replaced by a disc brake. Output stood at 30 hp, enough for a good 140 km/h.

Another product of the Guzzi-Benelli merger was a 125 cc lightweight with a 2-stroke single-cylinder engine. This was built in two versions, the *Turismo* and *Tuttoterreno*, the latter being intended for undemanding off-road use. Although these were cheap bikes aimed at people interested in a reasonably priced product this did not prevent Guzzi from offering a good level of finishing, a fact which is borne out by the front disc brake, the 5-speed gearbox and the chromed cylinder liners. Otherwise the bike was a traditional affair: vertically split crankcase, flywheel magneto ignition with external coil, helical-cut gears for the primary drive, wet multiplate clutch, tubular duplex cradle and telescopic suspension. The engine developed 15.4 hp; the *Turismo* version could do 118 km/h while the *Tuttoterreno* with the closer gear ratios had a top speed of 110 km/h. But the De Tomaso management showed itself to be most innovational in the field of styling. In the old days motorcycles used to be designed by one man, whose principal concern was the mechanical efficiency of his creation. Generally speaking the same man's understanding of styling was heavily influenced by a strictly engineering tradition dominated by exclusively "utilitarian" concepts. When, despite everything, a "good looking" product emerged, this was due to an unconscious creative capacity which accompanied the purely mechanical talents of the best designers: as was the case with Carlo Guzzi. In particular, no one dreamed of involving suppliers of electrical accessories, mechanics, coachbuilders or anybody else in schemes aimed at producing vehicles which were harmonious wholes. Besides, even the public was unaccustomed to the idea of being able to insist on specific requirements: it was already hard enough to find a bike which worked well... never mind worrying about the looks of the thing. And so the motorcycle had remained a tool which stubbornly resisted all attempts to beautify it.

In recent years, however, it has been a different story. The motorcycle no longer represents the lowest rung on the motoring ladder, but has become a means of escaping into the great outdoors whenever we have a moment's free time. Undoubted technological progress has ensured that problems related to merely mechanical aspects are now of secondary importance: today we all take it for granted that a motorcycle will start at the first kick and come to a smooth stop when the brakes are applied. Furthermore, the public has become far less traditionally minded and exterior appearances now count for far more than they did in the past. Thus, as people's aesthetic sensitivity continues to develop, stimulated to a large degree by the aggressive competition which characterizes the international market, motorcycle engineers have had to take more and more account of those factors once considered to be of secondary importance at best and vaguely sinful at worst. Lines, "look" and colour schemes now form a species of visual code aimed at nourishing that impression of youthfulness, the good life and often of prestige which the modern buyer wishes to acquire along with his chosen motorcycle.

At first the stylist's job was limited to the treatment of certain secondary details (largely because of the need not to "rock the boat" as far as production was concerned): the form and finish for tanks and mudguards, the shapes of saddles and accessories. Styling acquired more importance later on with the advent of fairings and "bodywork".

Born in Buenos Aires in the July of 1928, Alejandro De Tomaso moved to Italy in 1955, where he began a career as a racing driver before going on to build sports cars. In precedence he had worked for the family farming concern and with a specialist newspaper dealing with financial and economic matters. Blessed with a considerable personal fortune and undoubted entrepreneurial gifts, he erupted onto the motoring scene at Turin and Modena with all the shattering force of a meteor, revitalizing placid little businesses which, had they been left to themselves, would have never got beyond the cottage industry phase and then boosting them into the orbit of the great American financial and commercial corporations. And so, surprisingly, it was the little De Tomaso car company, in its role as advanced sports car design centre, which became the Ford company's European bridgehead. After having produced a large number of competition models, the De Tomaso company found its vocation constructing GTs built over redesigned Ford engines. As soon as success began to take concrete form, De Tomaso bought the Ghia and Vignale coachworks, transforming the former into an advanced design centre for Ford and the latter into a factory for the production of the *Pantera*, a car which Ford was to make its own in 1972, when the US colossus acquired a majority shareholding in De Tomaso Inc., a firm in which it had held a minority interest since the very beginning (1970). It was at this point that Alejandro De Tomaso realized the enormous potential of the Italian motorcycle industry.

Two perspectives, from front and rear, of the *V 50* and *V 35* drive train. The partially cut away specimen units are complete with cardan shaft drive and the rear braking system.

On the facing page an unusual view of the same assembly from above, which clearly shows the innovational features possessed by this design: the quadrangular section light alloy swinging arm (which pivots directly on the gearbox housing thus guaranteeing considerable rigidity and resistance to torsional stress) and the disc brake, perfectly integrated with the rear bevel pair assembly.

126

The "clothed" bike, able to protect the rider from atmospheric and mechanical agents, and which also represented a breath of fresh air in design terms, was an old dream at Guzzi, as we have already seen in the case of the *Zigolo* and the *Galletto*; but it is only very recently, with the arrival of the ultra-sporty bikes, replicas of the grand prix racers and the great GTs, that bodywork has become an essential component actively required and appreciated by the majority of motorcycle buyers.

Nevertheless it must be pointed out that from a construction point of view there is nothing really new around at the moment, inasmuch as the market is merely offering basically traditional designs which have been faired with varying degrees of skill: research into bikes with bearing bodies or other unorthodox structures has recently entered a period of stagnation.

But let's get back to Guzzi. The De Tomaso administration underlined the importance of design considerations right from the outset, thus running the risk of a conflict with those who upheld the conservative streak which had traditionally characterized the firm's production in the past.

And so early initiatives were limited to a few changes in trim and specifications. One result of this first phase was the *254*, a refined bike with an exceptional engine seen for the first time at the Milan Show of November 1975.

This bike represented another production first for Moto Guzzi: no other marque has yet produced a standard production quarter-litre machine with four cylinders.

In the case of the 254, the integral design of the tank-saddle-rear mudguard assembly managed to avoid giving that impression of having been thrown together almost at random conveyed by certain other quality makes. The sleek and sporty look was enhanced by the cast light alloy wheels with six twin spokes, a feature which was just beginning to appear on roadsters after an outstanding success in the world of competition. For some mysterious reason, which continues to elude even the best technicians and market analysts, the public did not greet the *254* with particular enthusiasm, but it still represents an important motorcycle from both a technical and a design point of view.

Another example of the inherent potential of the collaboration between engineers and stylists can be seen in the major restyling operation which was to lead to the *V7 Sport*. In this case, some design suggestions from Lello Gandini (a member of the Bertone school of design) were assimilated into the structural engineering real and proper. The result was a vehicle with powerfully expressive lines, a little hard-edged perhaps, but consistent with the required image.

A further goal was the creation of that group of motorcycles equipped with the "small" version of the by now traditional transversely mounted 90 degree V engine, which represents the marque's most recent engineering effort.

This engine, the result of modifications (aimed at reducing costs and dimensions) made to the original *V7* design by Lino Tonti and his team, was introduced for the first time in 1977 in 350 and 500 cc versions, which were later uprated to 650 and 750 cc in order to keep pace with changing trends within the market. You can get a rough idea of the extent of this transformation by considering the total weight of the first *V 50*, a mere 150 kgs: an incredibly low figure for a twin complete with lights, electric starter, silencers and so on.

Various expedients were tried in order to reduce production costs, like the use of flat heads with parallel valves controlled by push-rods and rockers. The precision design of the combustion chambers nevertheless made it possible to obtain very respectable performance: for example, the original 500 cc version supplied 45 hp at 7500 rpm, i.e. an output comparable with the Grand Prix twin-cam singles of the Fifties.

This series had wet sump lubrication and a horizontally split crankcase, cylinders with quadrilateral finning and chrome bores, a one-piece steel crankshaft running completely on smooth bearings, and one crankpin. The power was fed through the dry single-plate clutch to the gearbox by a helical gear pair: the gearbox was a 5-speeder and the shaft for the final drive ran inside the right hand fork of the cast light alloy swinging arm. The latter pivoted on the gearbox housing, a design solution resembling the one used years before on the *Otto cilindri*. The power unit thus formed a stress member within the rather original tubular duplex frame, of which the upper part (running from the steering head to the rear mudguard) was equipped with two elements extended downwards to support the gearbox, plus two front downtubes (again starting from the steering head) which cradled the engine from beneath to terminate at the level of the rear footrests without rejoining the upper frame elements at the back. The lower part of the cradle had detachable rails, to simplify the removal of the engine. The teledraulic front forks were a Guzzi design, while the rear suspension comprised the usual adjustable telescopic units on both sides of the wheel, supplied by various specialist manufacturers.

Spoked light alloy wheels were fitted to all bar the off-road versions. Naturally the bikes also used the linked braking system, like their bigger stablemates, again with the exception of the dirt bikes, where specific circumstances made it more practical to fit normal brakes with independent controls.

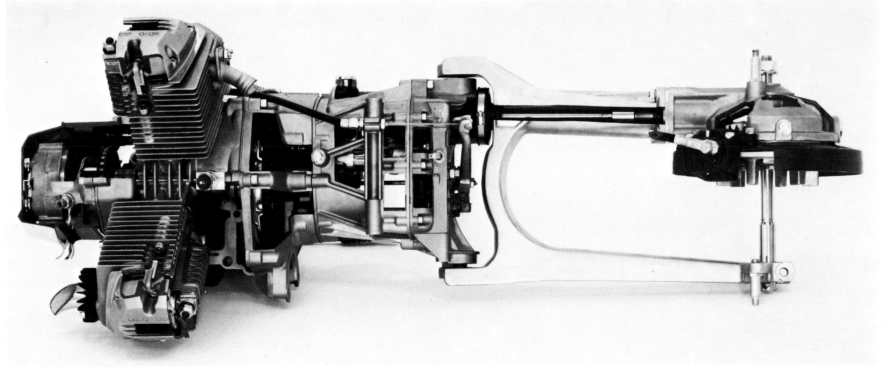

Born with more or less orthodox looks, the *V 35* and *V 50* have spawned a notable range of models, that differ in terms of performance and specific applications (like the dirt bikes we have already mentioned), but above all in terms of styling. This new family of bikes is the result of the fact that stylists have now been given a free hand to create bikes which are very unlike one another, even though the difference is often merely skin deep.

The same process has been going on for some time in the motor car industry, where at the end of the day a new model almost always boils down to a case of old wine in new bottles, the "old wine" here being mechanical units which have already been tried and tested and whose cheapness and reliability have already been amply proven. It is no exaggeration therefore if we maintain that, for the time being at least, the importance of styling at Guzzi has acquired – or at least equalled – the importance of mechanical engineering.

Apart from anything else, the motorcycle market, afflicted by recurring crises for the most disparate reasons – competition from the compact car industry, the speed with which young people's tastes change, the obligation to wear crash helmets, and so on – does not invite repeated doses of major investment. Today therefore the Guzzi catalogue includes – leaving aside the little Benelli-derived 125 stroker – the models in the 350 to 750 cc range fitted with the "small" V engine designed by Lino Tonti, and the bigger models, from 850 to 1000 cc, fitted with the older "big" V engine derived from Carcano's original design. Obviously these models have been improved and updated with the passage of time, thanks to technical contrivances like electronic ignition and four-valve heads right up to the indirect injection systems supplied – upon request – for the *California*. Until a short time ago production was divided up between Mandello (the bigger engines), Milano (the engines in the "Tonti" series, at the Innocenti works in Lambrate) and Pesaro (assembly, in the Benelli works), but now that the Milan and Pesaro plants have been sold off the bikes are once more being manufactured in Mandello, to the satisfaction of all old Guzzi fans, who never appreciated the previous division of labour much in any case.

Times are harder today: many glorious names have gone to the wall, both in Italy and even more so abroad (the great English marques for example), because they were unable to adapt to changing tastes and market conditions. Guzzi has managed to survive and fight off the new overlords of the motorcycle market, the Japanese, thanks to the quality of its products which, although they have a strongly traditional content, nonetheless represent something different and original on the international production landscape. And in a world where uniformity often tends to get the upper hand, this can be a winning card. The Mandello marque has made this generous yet difficult choice: let us hope that it will be able to continue travelling down its chosen road, remembering that it is still the same road which was chosen all those years ago by a handful of bold, farsighted men led by Carlo Guzzi and Giorgio Parodi.

Normale 500 cc

esemplare del 1922 / a model from 1922

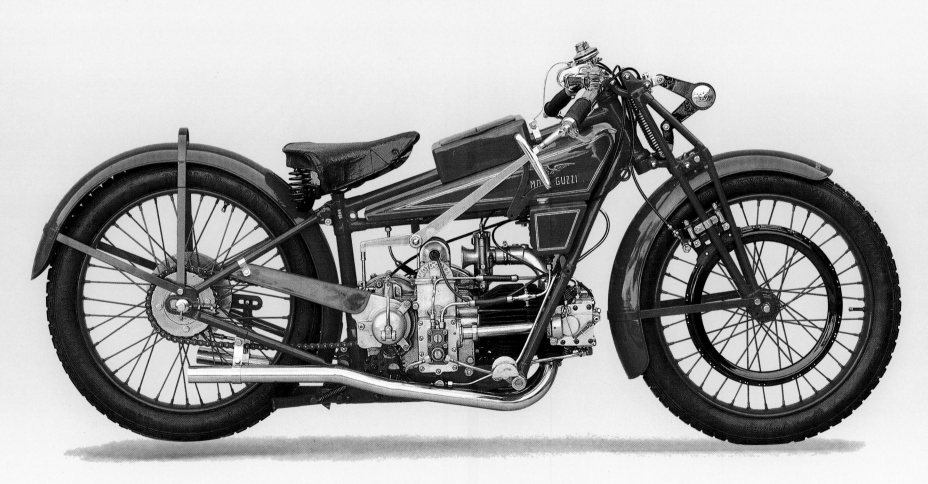

esemplare del 1926 / a model from 1926

1928 - 1929
G.T. "Norge" 500 cc

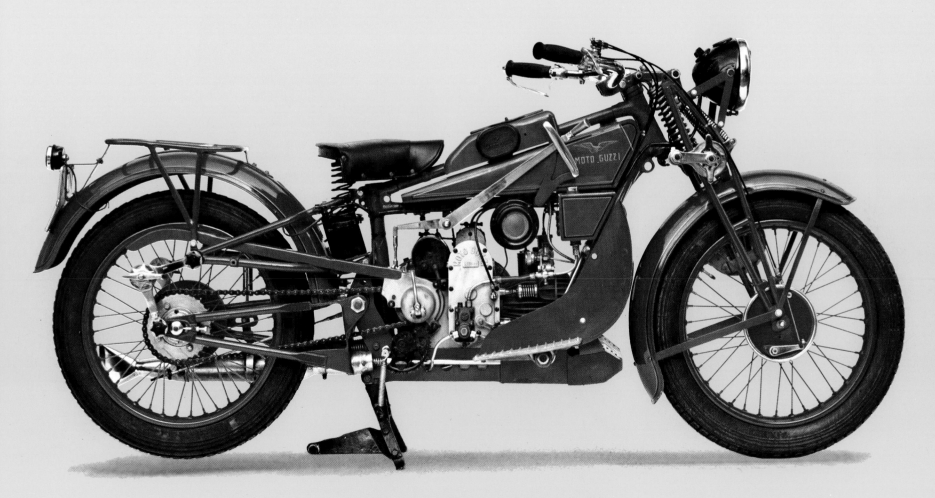

esemplare del 1928 / a model from 1928

1929 - 1930
Sport 14 500 cc

esemplare del 1929 / a model from 1929

250 cc S S

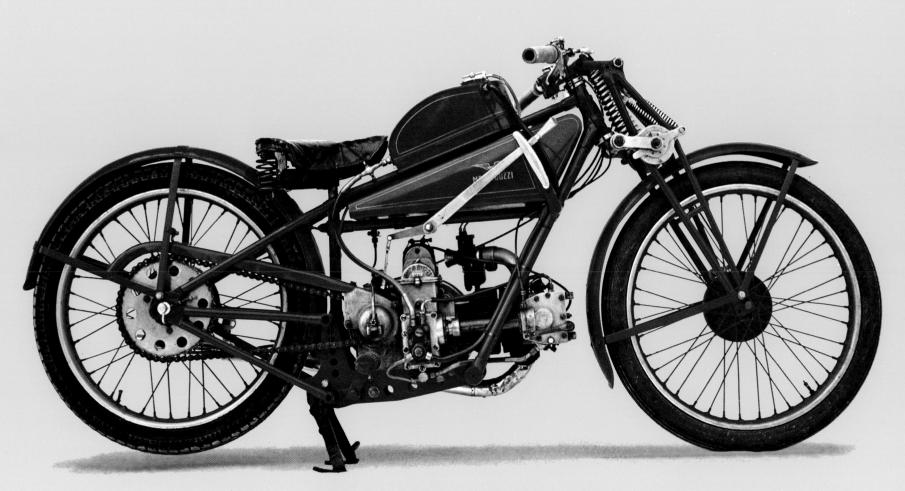

esemplare del 1930 / a model from 1930

1931-1934
G.T. 16 500 cc

esemplare del 1931 / a model from 1931

esemplare del 1932 / a model from 1932

1932 - 1939
G.T. 17 500 cc

esemplare del 1933 / a model from 1933

Sport 15 500 cc

esemplare del 1935 / a model from 1935

1938
250 cc "Compressore"

esemplare del 1938 / a model from 1938

1939 - 1948
Albatros 250 cc

esemplare del 1945 / a model from 1945

1933 - 1951
Bicilindrica 500 cc

esemplare del 1947 / a model from 1947

Motoleggera 65 cc

esemplare del 1947 / a model from 1947

1949 - 1953
Astore 500 cc

esemplare del 1949 / a model from 1949

1946 - 1951
Dondolino 500 cc

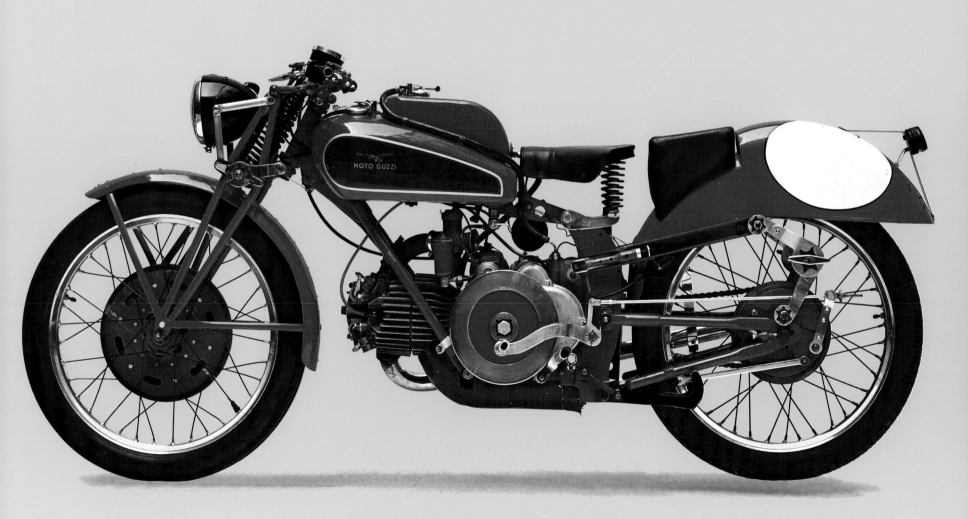

esemplare del 1948 / a model from 1948

Gambalunga 500 cc

esemplare del 1951 / a model from 1951

1949 - 1952
Gambalunghino 250 cc

esemplare del 1951 / a model from 1951

1946 - 1957
Superalce 500 cc

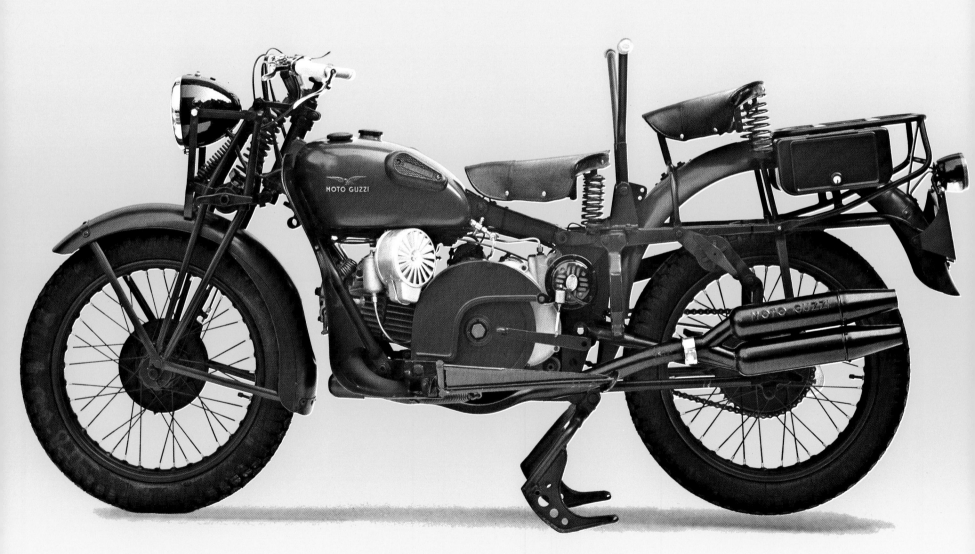

esemplare del 1951 / a model from 1951

1950 - 1967
Falcone 500 cc

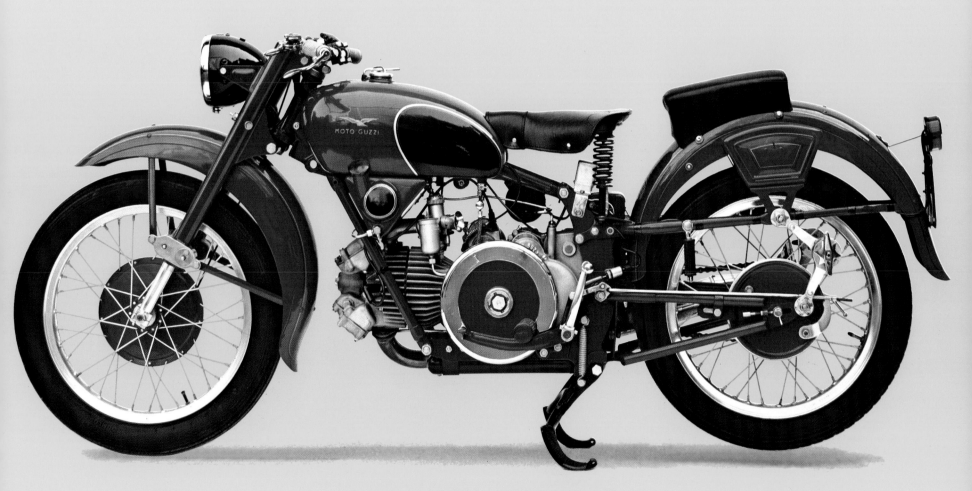

esemplare del 1952 / a model from 1952

1939 - 1957
Airone 250 cc

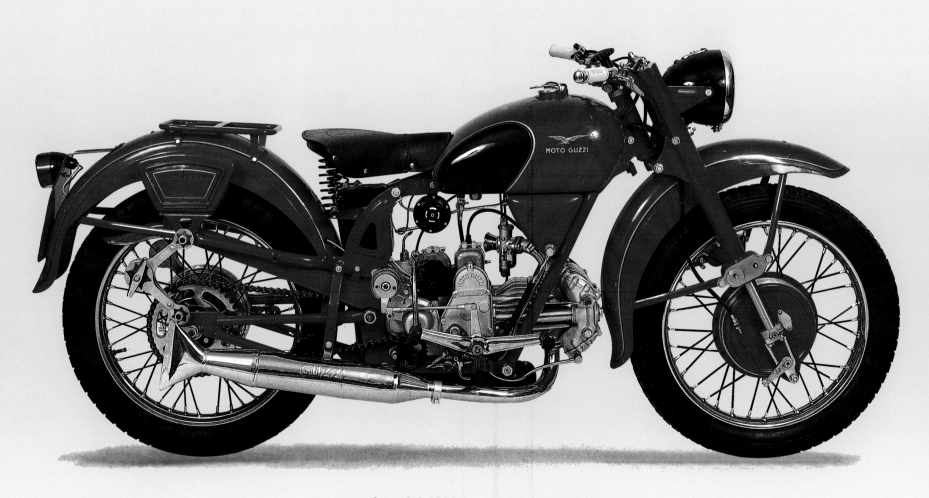

esemplare del 1953 / a model from 1953

250 cc Bialbero

esemplare del 1954 / a model from 1954

1954 - 1957
350 cc Bialbero

esemplare del 1956 / a model from 1956

Otto Cilindri 500 cc

esemplare del 1957 / a model from 1957

1950 - 1966
Galletto 160 - 192 cc

esemplare del 1958 (192 cc) / a model from 1960 (192 cc)

1959 - 1965
Lodola Regolarità 235 cc

esemplare del 1960 / a model from 1960

1969 - 1971
V7 Special 757 cc

esemplare del 1970 / a model from 1970

1971-1974
V7 Sport 750 cc

esemplare del 1972 / a model from 1972

1977 - 1986
V 50 500 cc

esemplare del 1977 / a model from 1977

1988 - ...
750 NTX 750 cc

esemplare del 1988 / a model from 1988

1000 California III 950 cc

esemplare del 1990 / a model from 1990

1988 - ...
1000 SP III 950 cc

esemplare del 1990 / a model from 1990

Daytona 1000 cc

esemplare del 1990 / a model from 1990

SERIES PRODUCTION

N.B.: In the "catalogue" part of this book, the length of time during which a motorcycle was in production is indicated by a pair of dates in the title of each section (when the second date is missing, it should be understood that the bike was still in production at the time of printing). Vice-versa, the period of production shown in the technical specifications refers to the more limited period of validity of the date contained in the table. Given the frequency with which variations appeared when series were changed, we decided to supply the dates of the first or the most important versions of each machine in the technical tables, and to refer the reader to the text or the captions for the data regarding the different series or any special versions.
Some of the titles in the catalogue section contain an arbitrary summary of several models when these share a basic design and components.

G.P. and Normale

Carlo Guzzi first began thinking of building a motorcycle during the first World War. Thanks to the financial support provided by Giorgio Parodi, one of his comrades in arms, the first Guzzi began to take shape in 1920. Its creator intended it to be a safe, practical means of transport, inexpensive to produce but strong, and free of the defects which dogged the motorcycles of the day. Some of its features directly influenced Guzzi production for over fifty years; some indeed were so well designed that they can arguably be described as modern to this day. Features like the horizontal cylinder, the external flywheel, the geared primary drive, and the unit construction gearbox can still be seen in recent machines. The original prototype had an engine with four valves actuated by an overhead camshaft and dual ignition. The first mass-produced model dates from 1921. It was known as the *Normale* (standard), and had therefore an opposed valve engine with a 3-speed gearbox; a layout which, with only a few minor modifications, was to remain in production for a long time and to make a considerable contribution to the reputation for sound engineering and commercial honesty which Moto Guzzi products enjoyed right from the outset.

Model / year	Normale / 1921-1924
Engine	four-stroke flat single 88 × 82 mm / 498.4 cc
Compression ratio	4:1
Output	from 8 hp at 3200 rpm to 8.5 hp at 3400 rpm
Cylinder head	cast iron
Cylinder	cast iron
Valve arrangement	opposed; inlet at side; exhaust overhead
Valve gear	inlet, tappet; exhaust, push rod — rocker arm
Ignition	Bosch ZE 1 shielded magneto
Carburettor	Amac 15 PSY 1 in.
Lubrication	geared pressure pump; vane type scavenge pump
Clutch	wet multiplate type
Gearbox	hand-change 3-speed sliding gears
Transmission	primary, gear driven; final drive, chain
Frame	tubular duplex cradle
Wheelbase	1380 mm
Front suspension	girder fork
Rear suspension	rigid
Wheels	spoked with 26 × 2 1/4 rims
Tyres	26" × 3.00
Brakes	single rear wheel expansion brake with pedal and manual control
Weight	130 kgs
Max speed	85 km/h
Normal consumption	3.5 litres per 100 kms
Fuel tank capacity	10 litres
Lubricant capacity	2.5 litres

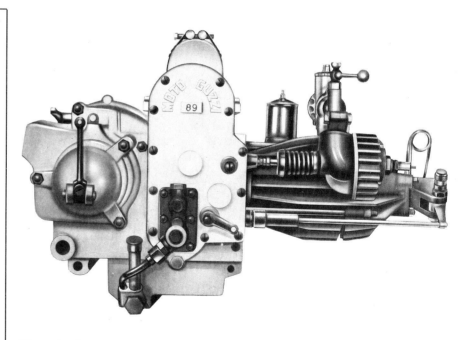

The engine from the *Normale*, which went into production in 1921. The unit shown was one of the first to be built, it is still without the oil scavenge pump, which was fitted the following year. This model had dual ignition, a feature which remained an optional extra until the end of 1925.

The prototype built by Carlo Guzzi in 1920, still on show in the Guzzi Museum, with the 4-valve engine. The triangulated rear section of the frame was bolted together — a feature which was to be taken up again a decade later — while the section of mudguard immediately behind the engine was part of the weight-bearing structure. There was only one brake, a band-type unit on the rear wheel. One interesting feature was the double drive (sprocket and pulley) for the speedometer on the front wheel. The paintwork was a very dark grey-green and the bike bore the initials G.P. (Guzzi and Parodi) instead of the later MOTO GUZZI logo.

The *Normale* model which went into mass production in 1921 differed from the prototype in several ways: apart from the engine, the all-welded frame had a robust box-type element which took the weight previously borne by the section of mudguard. Sheet steel was used for the horizontal arm of the triangle and the rear brake was a dual-control drum. An olive green paint job was highlighted by gold pin-striping and nickel plated controls. The cooling fins welded to the exhaust pipe were another original feature (protected by patent number 495-197).

This longitudinal section along the centre line of the cylinder highlights the simplicity of the Guzzi engine and its principal features, like the shape of the combustion chambers, the exhaust valve hairpin springs, the tubular con-rod running on bronze bushings and the gearbox wheelwork with the selector fork for the sliding gears. Although the crankcase was a one-piece unit, it had two sections for the crankshaft and the gears, separated by a bulkhead which was later eliminated. Note the cylinder, which was offset in a bid to reduce the lateral thrust of the con-rod during the expansion stroke.

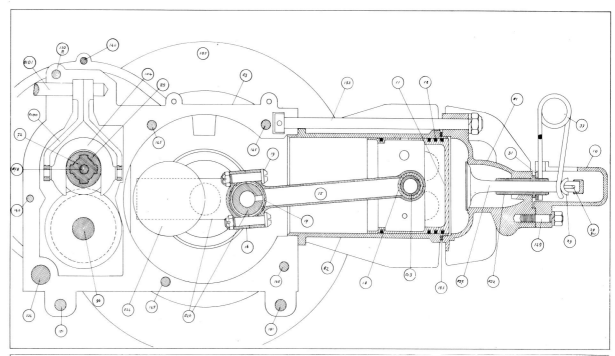

The second diagram, a cross section along the axis of the side inlet valve, shows the tappet-operated overhead exhaust valve and the push rod for the inlet valve. Both ran on rollers which were in direct contact with the camshafts. The primary drive pinion (with the hexagonal nut) drove the oil pump, fitted below, and the camshaft mounted above it, which in its turn drove the magneto. Note the cam used to work the valve lifter. The kickstart quadrant can just be seen beneath the clutch lever.

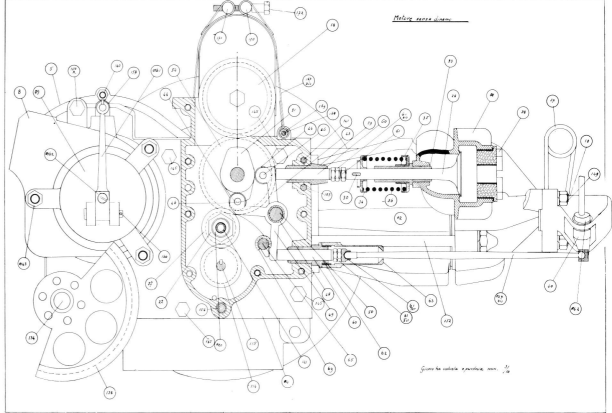

164

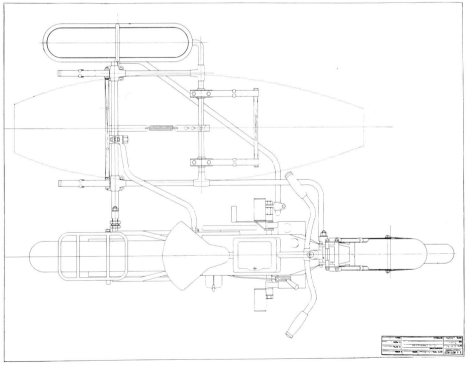

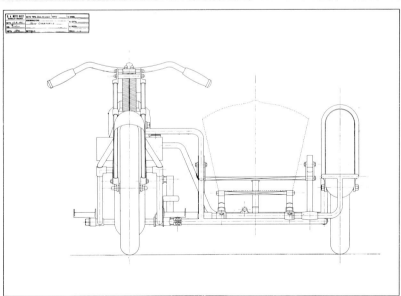

The 1923 *Normale* (top). Some details had been changed compared to previous versions, the toolbox for example. Above and left, diagrams of the sidecar chassis planned by Guzzi around 1925. Sidecars were a very fashionable accessory in those days and the sturdy Guzzis were well suited to the task of pulling them.

Sport

The new longer, lighter frame introduced for the *C 2V* was chosen — still in 1923 — to house the biddable opposed valve engine, thus giving rise to a new *Sport* model which took over from the earlier *Normale*.

It had only taken a few years for Guzzi to convince people of the worth of his own design ideas and the marque was earning itself a solid reputation for excellent, robust construction, so much so that Guzzis began to be used to pull sidecars, a task which had been reserved for bikes with at least a litre of displacement until then. The *Sport* — which cost 8,750 lire — could be fitted with a Bosch lighting system, including a 30 Watt dynamo and battery, in exchange for an extra 1,000 lire. This machine was to be followed by the so-called *Sport 14* which was later baptized the *Sport 13* by motorcyclists and period bike collectors; but this designation was never official and cannot be found in any House publication.

As far as Guzzi is concerned the opposed valve model built between 1923 and 1928 is invariably referred to as the *Sport* and nothing else. All in all 4,107 of these were made, some with a front brake.

Model / year	Sport / 1923-1928
Engine	four-stroke flat single 88 × 82 mm / 498.4 cc
Compression ratio	4.5:1
Output	13 hp at 3800 rpm
Cylinder head	cast iron
Cylinder	cast iron
Valve arrangement	opposed; inlet at side; exhaust overhead
Valve gear	inlet, tappet; exhaust, push rod — rocker arm
Ignition	Bosch ZE 1 shielded magneto
Carburettor	Amac 15 PSY 1 in.
Lubrication	geared pressure pump; vane type scavenge pump
Clutch	wet multiplate type
Gearbox	hand-change 3-speed sliding gears
Transmission	primary, gear driven; final drive, chain
Frame	tubular duplex cradle
Wheelbase	1430 mm
Front suspension	girder fork
Rear suspension	rigid
Wheels	spoked with 26 × 2 1/4 rims
Tyres	26" × 3.00
Brakes	single rear wheel expansion brake with pedal and manual control
Weight	130 kgs
Max speed	100 km/h
Normal consumption	3.5 litres per 100 kms
Fuel tank capacity	10 litres
Lubricant capacity	2.5 litres

The *Sport* sprang from a combination of the *Normale* engine and the *C 2V* frame. It was painted green with gold pinstriping and had nickel plated controls. The characteristic rubber knee grips, which appeared for the first time on the *C 2V*, were attached to the sides of the tool box. In order to reassure those worried about possible breakdowns, the second spark plug (by that time supplied on request only) had been replaced by a retaining fork fitted to the combustion chamber which made it impossible for the exhaust valve to drop into the engine, a feature which was retained until the last war.

A version of the *Sport* fitted with optional electrics. The eye for the attachment of the Guzzi-built sidecar can be seen under the steering head. The sidecar version was equipped with a front brake operated by a lever mounted on the right handlebar. The two-spring forks, without damper, were practically identical to those of the *Normale* of previous years.

G.T. and G.T. 16

The biggest shortcoming which afflicted motorcycles in those years was the lack of rear wheel suspension, insofar as no manufacturer had yet solved the problem of making a sprung chassis with the required torsional rigidity.

The design created by brothers Carlo and Giuseppe Guzzi however was a brilliant success and in 1928 they managed to build the first real Grand Tourer in motorcycling history without any significant increase in weight. The new bike was very stable and far more comfortable than any other.

Constructed with painstaking care, its sales price was decidedly modest at 8,650 lire. Despite this it struggled a little to get established, because the sprung chassis was popularly believed to jeopardize the bike's stability and it took a memorable demonstration in competition a few years later to convince a rather sceptical public of the convenience and absolute safety of this desirable new feature.

The original *G.T.*, 78 of which were sold between 1928 and 1930, was then replaced by the *G.T. 16* version with engine and frame derived from the *Sport 15*. This variant was produced until 1934 for a grand total of 754 bikes.

Model / year	G.T. 16 / 1931-1934
Engine	4-stroke flat single 88 × 82 mm / 498.4 cc
Compression ratio	4.5:1
Output	13.2 hp at 3800 rpm
Cylinder head	cast iron
Cylinder	cast iron
Valve arrangement	opposed; inlet at side; exhaust overhead
Valve gear	inlet tappet ; exhaust, push rod — rocker arm
Ignition	Bosch type shielded magneto
Carburettor	Amal
Lubrication	geared pressure pump; vane type scavenge pump
Clutch	wet multiplate type
Gearbox	hand-change 3-speed sliding gears
Transmission	primary, gear driven; final drive, chain
Frame	duplex cradle in tubes and sheet metal
Wheelbase	1430 mm
Front suspension	girder fork with friction dampers
Rear suspension	swinging arm with friction dampers
Wheels	spoked with 19 × 2 rims
Tyres	3.50 - 19"
Brakes	expansion type; front manual, rear pedal
Weight	150 kgs
Max speed	100 km/h
Normal consumption	3.4 litres per 100 kms
Fuel tank capacity	11 litres
Lubricant capacity	3 litres

The original sprung frame perfected in 1928 by Carlo and Giuseppe Guzzi. The pressed steel box containing the four springs in compression was an integral part of the structure.
The swinging arm made of rods and steel plate was very rigid and resistant to deformation.

The *G.T.*, nicknamed the "Norge" after Giuseppe Guzzi's epic trip to the Arctic circle on a bike of this type, was finished with painstaking care. It had the three-spring fork which had been designed for the racing department the previous year, footrests with wide legshields, an Alfa silencer, a Brooks or Terry saddle and 26" × 3.50 tyres. The rear dampers were the "B & D" type and rear suspension travel was 11 cm. Painted red, it could be supplied with an optional electric starter. At first it was powered by the *Sport* engine and then by the *Sport 14* unit: in this latter case the tool box was tapered towards the saddle.

In 1931 the *G.T.* was replaced by the *GT 16*, which used an engine and frame derived from the *Sport 15*. It was fitted with a saddle tank therefore, while the footrest-legshield assembly and the oil tank were also different. The rear part of the frame also differed from the *G.T.* design: there was only one fork to support the mudguard and dampers instead of the previous double triangle arrangement. Note the kickstart which has been moved to the right. The colour scheme included two shades of amaranth red with black, red and gold pinstriping, like the *Sport 15*.

Sport 14

The *Sport 14* represents the natural evolution of the *Sport* and it embodied all the modifications which over five years in the business had suggested. The growing tendency to use motorcycles for heavier work resulted in a larger cylinder barrel-head assembly while competition experience suggested the adoption of new forks and steering geometries. The brakes and the electrical system were also improved, the latter being fitted with a dynamo separate from the magneto.

In 1929 Guzzi was on its way to becoming Italy's best selling marque because it had shown that its products were really ideal for all uses. Production of the *Sport 14* thus reached very high levels for those days: 4,285 bikes in just over two years (it should be remembered that in 1921 Guzzi made only 17 machines in all!). The assembly line was organized to produce about 50 bikes a week. This allowed the factory — which employed more than 500 people — to keep cutting prices as production gradually increased.

The 1928 price tag of 6,900 lire for the *Sport* became 6,250 lire for the *Sport 14* of the early Thirties: a very competitive price even in comparison with inferior products.

Model / year	Sport 14 / 1929-1930
Engine	4-stroke flat single 88 × 82 mm / 498.4 cc
Compression ratio	4.5:1
Output	13.2 hp at 3800 rpm
Cylinder head	cast iron
Cylinder	cast iron
Valve arrangement	opposed; inlet at side; exhaust overhead
Valve gear	inlet tappet ; exhaust, push rod — rocker arm
Ignition	Bosch type magneto
Carburettor	Amac
Lubrication	geared pressure pump; vane type scavenge pump
Clutch	wet multiplate type
Gearbox	hand-change 3-speed sliding gears
Transmission	primary, gear driven; final drive, chain
Frame	tubular duplex cradle
Wheelbase	1430 mm
Front suspension	girder fork with friction dampers
Rear suspension	rigid
Wheels	spoked with 26 × 2 1/2 rims
Tyres	26" × 3.50
Brakes	expansion type; front manual, rear pedal
Weight	130 kgs
Max speed	100 km/h
Normal consumption	3.4 litres per 100 kms
Fuel tank capacity	11 litres
Lubricant capacity	3 litres

According to a contemporary advertisement the *Sport 14* boasted a good thirty improvements over the *Sport*, almost all of which concerned the engine. The most noticeable of these changes regarded the larger finning and the rocker gear lubrication system plus a special housing which could accommodate a dynamo separate from the magneto.

A 1930 version of the *Sport 14*, also known as the "new series". Unlike the previous series it had a little protective rim surrounding the front brake while the toolbox was tapered instead of angular. The most noticeable modifications with respect to the *Sport* regard the three-spring forks and the position of the footrest, which had been shifted aft. This model does not have the special housing for the dynamo and therefore could only be fitted with the old Bosch magneto-dynamo.

A *Sport 14* from 1930, with an electrical system fed by a Miller dynamo, driven by a pinion which meshed with the clutch ring gear (the appendage can be seen on the primary drive cover). In this case the engine number was preceded by the letter L, for "light". The 1930 *Sport 14* was painted red with gold stripes on the tanks only: some models belonging to the previous series were occasionally painted green.

171

Sport 15

The *Sport 15* was an important turning point in the history of Moto Guzzi design thanks to the introduction of the saddle tank mounted astride the tubular elements of the frame. This innovation, which originated in England, can be seen as the definitive line of demarcation dividing the products of the pioneering days from those of the early modern age, in the sense that it radically changed the look of the vehicle. The other major innovation introduced with the *Sport 15*, the substitution of the tubular conrod with an I-section component with the big-end running on needle bearings, was a feature which had been adopted some time before on the *Quattro valvole*. Simple and robust, the *Sport 15* was a real favourite with many motorcyclists, to the extent that this Guzzi became the best selling bike of the pre-war era: 5,979 of them were made. It came in two shades of amaranth with red, black or gold stripes and (after 1933) a "de-luxe" version was launched with tank, wheel rims and other details in chrome. A few rare red-painted versions were also produced. Until 1937 the typical — and awkward — Bowden levers for the clutch and brake were mounted on the handlebars. These were replaced with controls of a more ergonomic design at a later date.

Model / year	Sport 15 / 1931-1939
Engine	4-stroke flat single 88 × 82 mm / 498.4 cc
Compression ratio	4.5:1
Output	13.2 hp at 3800 rpm
Cylinder head	cast iron
Cylinder	cast iron
Valve arrangement	opposed; inlet at side; exhaust overhead
Valve gear	inlet tappet ; exhaust, push rod — rocker arm
Ignition	Bosch type shielded magneto
Carburettor	Amal type 6/142
Lubrication	geared pressure pump; vane type scavenge pump
Clutch	wet multiplate type
Gearbox	hand-change 3-speed sliding gears
Transmission	primary, helical gear; final drive, chain
Frame	tubular duplex cradle
Wheelbase	1430 mm
Front suspension	girder fork with friction dampers
Rear suspension	rigid
Wheels	spoked with 19 × 2 1/2 rims
Tyres	3.50 - 19"
Brakes	expansion type; front manual, rear pedal
Weight	150 kgs
Max speed	100 km/h
Normal consumption	3.4 litres per 100 kms
Fuel tank capacity	11 litres
Lubricant capacity	3 litres

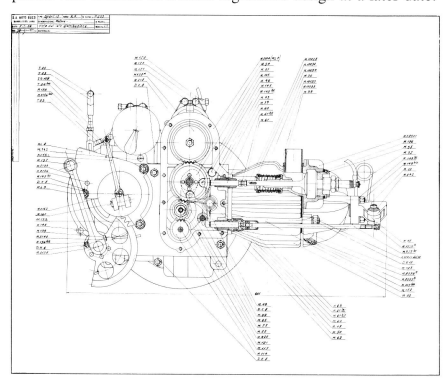

The "assembly drawing" of the military version of the *Sport 15*.

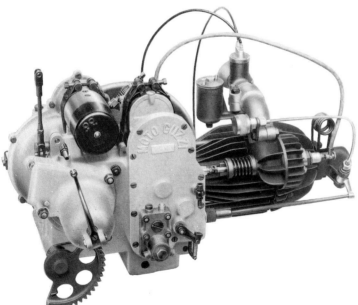

Above, the all-painted version of the *Sport 15*; the version shown below has chrome plated sections on the tank. The engines shown in these photographs are fitted with Dell'Orto carburettors, which replaced the Amal instruments used until 1935. The drum brakes had a diameter of 177 mm (front) and 200 mm (rear) respectively.

173

Tre Cilindri

After a four-cylinder racing model which never got beyond the prototype stage, in 1932 Carlo Guzzi designed this magnificent Grand Touring machine whose engine (three horizontal cylinders) could be said to be a fairly direct descendant of the earlier prototype. The frame, made of two parts bolted together, was also inspired by the four-cylinder model, with the addition of a Guzzi-type rear suspension layout which had been redesigned with sleeker, more elegant components. It was fitted with coil ignition, considered more suitable for a multi-cylinder touring bike, and a single carburettor, which was mounted on the right at first and then on the left. The gearbox had three speeds, more than enough, given the flexibility of the engine. This elegant, beautifully finished bike was probably a bit too far ahead of its time and it never enjoyed the success it undoubtedly deserved. Only a few preproduction units were built, which all differed from one another in minor details, like the position of the carburettor and the gear lever whose control rod ran inside the petrol tank in the last version.

Only one of these bikes has survived and it is presently on show in the Guzzi Museum at Mandello.

Model / year	Tre Cilindri / 1932-1933
Engine	4-stroke transverse three-in-line 56 × 67 mm / 494.8 cc
Compression ratio	4.9:1
Output	25 hp at 5500 rpm
Cylinder head	cast iron
Cylinder	cast iron
Valve arrangement	parallel overhead
Valve gear	push-rod and rocker arms
Ignition	coil
Carburettor	Amal
Clutch	wet multiplate type
Lubrication	geared pressure and scavenge pumps
Gearbox	hand-change 3-speed sliding gears
Transmission	primary, gear driven; final drive, chain
Frame	duplex cradle in tubes and sheet metal
Wheelbase	1440 mm
Front suspension	girder fork with friction dampers
Rear suspension	swinging arm with friction dampers
Wheels	spoked with 19 × 2 1/2 rims
Tyres	3.25 - 19"
Brakes	expansion type; front manual, rear pedal
Weight	160 kg
Max speed	130 km/h
Normal consumption	–
Fuel tank capacity	11.5 litres
Lubricant capacity	3 litres

The frame used for the *Tre Cilindri* heralded the lines of the *V* series and its derivatives, which were to follow soon after. Note the more compact arrangement of the rocker arms and the valves with the coil springs; the enclosed flywheel; the location of the oil pump and the distributor as well as the single silencer on the right hand side. This bike was the first to be fitted with the Guzzi rear friction dampers (held by wing nuts), instead of the "B & D"s with the control wheel.

P 175, P 250 and their descendants

In 1932 Moto Guzzi decided to move into the lightweight market. This size of engine had been virtually snubbed by the major manufacturers, even though its production was accompanied by several advantages, not least of which was a favourable taxation class. Guzzi came up with the *P 175*, a lively little bike with plenty of new technical and design features which were adopted by the larger production machines shortly afterwards. When the burocratic advantages hitherto enjoyed by owners of smaller bikes were abolished the public began to lose interest in the 175 cc class, and so Guzzi decided to increase the displacement of its little *P 175*. The new *P 250* (which was really a 232, to be exact) was instantly joined by a stablemate with a sprung chassis, the *P.E.*, and a later by a sporty model, called the *P.E.S.* In 1937, when economic self sufficiency was rigidly enforced by government sanctions, Guzzi introduced the *P.L.* This had a 246 cc engine, but was equipped with a cheaper tubular and pressed steel frame. In its turn, the *P.L.* fathered the *P.L.S.*, the *Egretta*, and the *Ardetta*. Finally, in 1939, we come to the birth of a new *P.E.* with four gears, which was sold under the name *Airone* (Heron).

Model / year	P 175 (P 250) / 1932-1937
Engine	4-stroke single 59 × 63.7 mm / 174 cc (68 × 64 mm / 232.3 cc)
Compression ratio	6:1
Output	7 hp at 5000 rpm (9hp at 5500 rpm)
Cylinder head	cast iron
Cylinder	cast iron
Valve arrangement	overhead inclined
Valve gear	push rod and rocker arm
Ignition	Bosch type magneto
Carburettor	Amal or Dell'Orto SB 20 mm (22 mm)
Lubrication	geared pressure pump; vane type scavenge pump
Clutch	wet multiplate type
Gearbox	hand-change 3-speed sliding gears
Transmission	primary, helical gear; final drive, chain
Frame	tubular duplex cradle
Wheelbase	1320 mm
Front suspension	girder fork with friction dampers
Rear suspension	rigid
Wheels	spoked with 19 × 2 1/4 rims
Tyres	3.00 - 19"
Brakes	expansion type; front manual, rear pedal
Weight	115 kgs
Max speed	90 (100)km/h
Normal consumption	2.9 litres per 100 kms
Fuel tank capacity	10 litres
Lubricant capacity	2 litres

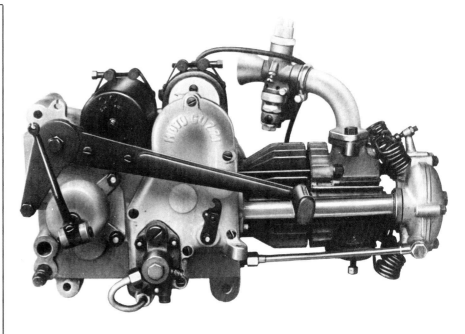

The arrival of the *P* series with the two inclined overhead valves rounded off and modernized the lines of Guzzi engines. This is the 238 cc version with the pedal-operated 3-speed gearbox.

The *P* was a lively 175 cc light motorcycle built between 1932 and 1937. It boasted several mechanical innovations (the valve gear in particular) while the restyling of the frame, tank, and headlamp was later extended to the entire Guzzi range. It had an amaranth finish and 1,503 units were built. The price was 4,250 lire.

In 1934 the *P* was joined by a 250 stablemate (whose effective displacement was only 238 cc however) of which various versions were produced. This was the sprung *250 P.E.*, 1,568 units of which were built up to 1939. It weighed 135 kgs, had 3.00-19" tyres and could touch 100 km/h. A new version was launched at the end of 1939 with a 247 cc engine (70 × 64 mm instead of 68 × 64) and a 4-speed gearbox. This newcomer was baptized the *Airone* just before its introduction. There was also an unsprung variant known as the *P 250*, 1,886 units of which were made until it was deleted in 1937.

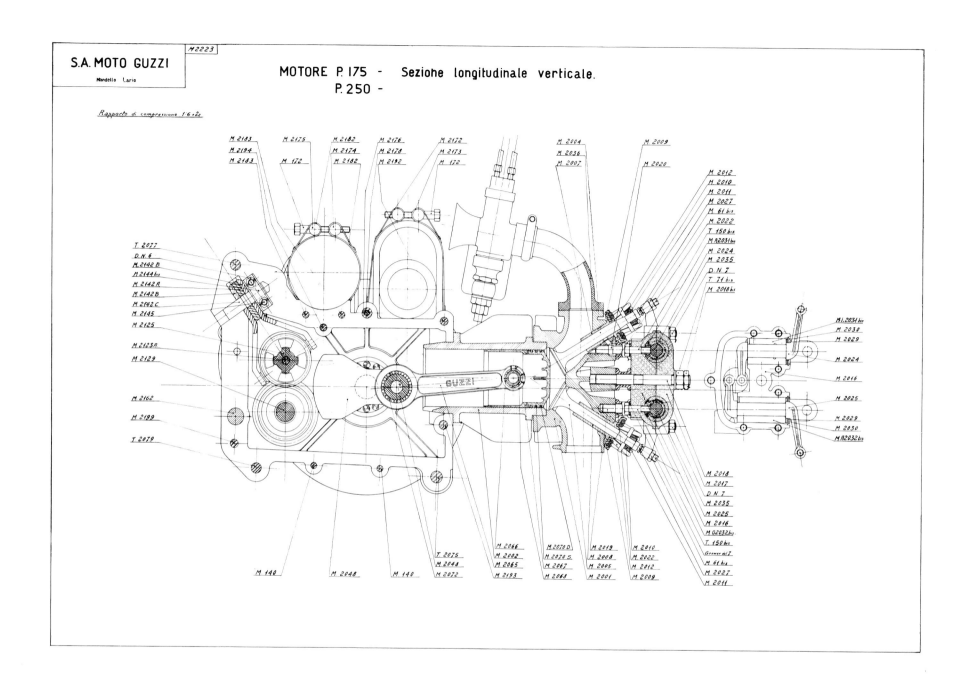

MOTORE P. 175 - Sezione longitudinale verticale.
P. 250 -

S.A. MOTO GUZZI
Mandello Lario

M2223

Rapporto di compressione 1·6·óc

The cross section of the *P* engine displays the layout of the various organs and the route taken by the gas tracts in the hemispheric head. The steel crankshaft, with a diameter of 27 mm, was a built-up two-piece assembly running on two bearings (a ball bearing on the right and a roller on the left). The one-piece con-rod ran on 3 × 16 mm needle bearings, the tappets were the finger-follower type with roller bearings, while the rocker arms ran on bronze bushings. The valves (angled at 31 degrees) were 32 mm in diameter and were closed by exposed double hairpin springs. The clutch had four steel plates alternating with four friction plates, while the 3-speed sliding gears were hand-operated in the 175 cc version and pedal-operated in the 232 cc version, with external preselector. Note the simple, essential lines of the crankcase with the ribbing for extra strength, as well as the cylinder barrel which is recessed into the block.

The *P.E.S.* with the 238 cc engine and the 3-speed foot-change gearbox was the sporty version of the Guzzi 250. Weighing in at 135 kg, it had 3.00-19" tyres and could touch 115 km/h. Only 75 units were built between 1938 and '39 but some were raced in minor events, after suitable modifications had been made.

A rare photograph of a *P.E.S.* specially prepared by Guzzi for the Milan-Taranto event. The engine was slightly modified while the frame and accessories had been lightened. This version could exceed 125 km/h.

This *P.L.* is from 1937, with the 246 cc engine and the 3-speed gearbox. In the interests of economy the chromework was eliminated and pressed steel was chosen for the frame. Production continued until 1939 and 1,474 units were built, as well as 744 units of the sporty *P.L.S.* version. It was fitted with 3.00-19" tyres, weighed 105 kgs and had red paintwork with mudguards and part of the tank in black. In 1939-40 it was replaced by the *Egretta* (in the photo) which had better finishing and some chrome work.
It cost 4,300 lire and 784 units were built.

In 1939-40, the *Ardetta* was the cheapest model in the Guzzi range. This "people's bike" cost 3,950 lire cash down or 170 lire a month on hire purchase. It had a 246 cc engine with coil ignition and a 3-speed hand-change gearbox (foot-change available on request) mounted on an unsprung frame made of tubular and pressed steel elements. This motorcycle, 599 units of which were built, had grey paintwork with white pin-striping.

179

V, G.T.V., G.T.W. and G.T.C.

The *V*-type ohv engines with the 4-speed gearbox, introduced at the end of 1933, marked another milestone for Moto Guzzi, both in terms of performance and design, after the Italian marque had definitively turned its back on the angular design which had distinguished its earlier models. Mounted at first on two different types of frame, sprung and rigid, both of which had also been modernized, the *V*-type engine was produced over a thirty year period, during which time it was repeatedly renewed and perfected. Its numerous descendants range from the robust *G.T.V.* and the *Astore* to the sporty *G.T.W.*, *G.T.C.* and *Falcone*, and from the

army bikes and delivery tricars down to the *Condor*, *Dondolino* and *Gambalunga*, genuine competition machines which were not really intended for sale. After the war, as far as solo bikes were concerned, only the sprung *G.T.V.* (and briefly the *G.T.W.*) which had been improved in the winter of 1947 with the adoption of teledraulic suspension was still in production. The choice of an aluminium cylinder barrel-head assembly, with enclosed valve gear, resulted in the birth of the new *Astore* and *Falcone* series, which are dealt with in another section of this book along with their racing derivatives.

Model / year	V / 1934-1940
Engine	4-stroke flat single 88 × 82 mm / 498.4 cc
Compression ratio	5.5:1
Output	18 hp at 4300 rpm
Cylinder head	cast iron
Cylinder	cast iron
Valve arrangement	overhead inclined
Valve gear	push rod and rocker arm
Ignition	Bosch type magneto
Carburettor	Amal or Dell'Orto MD 27 27 mm
Lubrication	geared pressure pump; vane type scavenge pump
Clutch	wet multiplate type
Gearbox	pedal operated 3-speed sliding gears
Transmission	primary, helical gear; final drive, chain
Frame	duplex cradle in tubes and sheet metal
Wheelbase	1400 mm
Front suspension	girder fork and friction dampers
Rear suspension	rigid
Wheels	spoked with 19 × 2 1/2 rims
Tyres	front 3.25 - 19", rear 3.50 - 19"
Brakes	expansion type; front manual, rear pedal
Weight	160 kgs
Max speed	approx. 120 km/h
Normal consumption	4.5 litres per 100 kms
Fuel tank capacity	12 litres
Lubricant capacity	2.5 litres

The 500 cc single-cylinder V type engine with the two inclined overhead valves, hemispheric combustion chamber and 4-speed gearbox. This is a post-war version with a single exhaust pipe and a few modified components.

The new engine with the two inclined overhead valves gave rise to a new series of motorcycles which remained in production with various modifications until the outset of the Seventies. This is the *V* with the rigid tubular and sheet metal frame and twin exhausts, 2,119 of which were built between 1934 and 1940. It came with a red finish and cost 6,950 lire. The *W* type with the 22 hp, 130 km/h engine looked identical. 159 of these were sold before the outbreak of the war.

The *G.T.C.* was a *V* series derivative first produced in 1937 for racing in the recently established Sport category. It had a beefed-up engine which produced 26 hp at 5000 rpm, a 28.5 mm carburettor, sprung frame, larger 17 litre fuel tank, 3.00-20" tyres in front and 3.50-19" behind, and weighed in at 160 kgs. The paintwork was red and the engine number was preceded by the letter C. It could hit 150 km/h but braking and roadholding were on a par with the standard models. Guzzi built 161 of these, and production ceased in 1939.

The version with the sprung frame bore the initials *G.T.V.* (*G.T.W.* for the version with the 22 hp engine). Performance, apart from comfort, was practically identical to that of the unsprung models. Above, the pre-war edition with twin exhaust pipes; on the right, a version with a single pipe which appeared after the war and was produced until 1947. It had red paintwork with black and gold pinstriping. The legshields were standard equipment.

182

At the end of 1947 the *G.T.V.* was updated with the addition of the telescopic forks and the hydraulic rear dampers, which had been fitted to the *Airone* some months before. The front mudguard was also modified. Performance remained the same but weight went up to 180 kgs. The red paintwork was retained. The photographs on this page are from 1948 and show the new 200 mm front brake while the first models to be fitted with the telescopic forks still had the small 170 mm pre-war brakes. The *G.T.V.* was produced until 1949, when it was replaced by the *Astore*.

In 1948 and 1949 production of the *G.T.W.* was restarted and this bike was also updated with the brakes and suspension from the renewed *G.T.V.* It had light alloy wheels and the narrower sportier handlebars were different too. The engine, fed by a 28.5 mm carburettor, supplied 22 hp at 4500 rpm, enough to power the machine to 130 km/h. The bike was painted red. The tyres were 3.25-19" in front and 3.50-19" behind.
On the facing page: the "motocarrozzetta", very popular before the war, virtually disappeared after the end of hostilities when it was replaced by smaller utility vehicles. The version shown is a "hybrid" from 1948: a *G.T.V.* linked to a sidecar with a sprung wheel but whose body dates from the Thirties.

184

S and G.T.S.

The needs of the sporting clientele having been catered for with the new *Vs* and *Ws* and their derivatives, all very quick, snappy performers, Guzzi turned its attention to those more peaceful souls who needed a bike to get to work — people concerned with practical matters like fuel economy and robust construction. And so the company prepared two new bikes, basically *V*-type variants with the option of rigid or sprung frames, which had modern four-speed gearboxes together with the classic opposed valve layout: a marriage between the advantages of progress and the proven reliability of the firm's tradition. What's more these bikes sold pretty well, a sure sign that the formula was the right one. The first units of the *Milizia della Strada*, as the Italian traffic police were then called, were given these Guzzis to patrol the country's major arterial routes. The *Alce*, the legendary army bike, could also be said to be derived from the *G.T.S.*, as we shall see later.

Production of opposed valve engines was discontinued after the war, even for heavy duty machines: technological progress and the demands of the new market had definitively buried this last relic of the marque's prehistory.

Model / year	S / 1934-1940
Engine	4-stroke flat single 88 × 82 mm / 498.4 cc
Compression ratio	4.6:1
Output	13.2 hp at 4000 rpm
Cylinder head	cast iron
Cylinder	cast iron
Valve arrangement	opposed; inlet at side; exhaust overhead
Valve gear	inlet tappet ; exhaust, push rod - rocker arm
Ignition	Bosch type magneto
Carburettor	Amal 6/142 type or Dell'Orto MCS 25
Lubrication	geared pressure pump; vane type scavenge pump
Clutch	wet multiplate type
Gearbox	manual or pedal operated 4-speed sliding gears
Transmission	primary, helical gear, final drive, chain
Frame	tubes and sheet metal
Wheelbase	1400 mm
Front suspension	girder fork and friction dampers
Rear suspension	rigid
Wheels	spoked with 19 × 2 1/2 rims
Tyres	front 3.25-19"; rear 3.50-19"
Brakes	expansion type: front manual, rear pedal
Weight	147 kgs
Max speed	approx. 105 km/h
Normal consumption	3.4 litres per 100 kms
Fuel tank capacity	12 litres
Lubricant capacity	2.5 litres

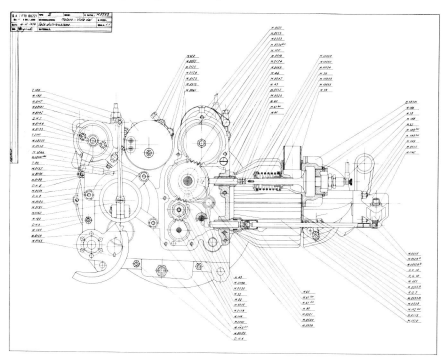

A partial cross section of the *S* type engine, with the opposed valves.

The *S*, built from 1934 to '40 for the most conservative clients and lovers of the traditional opposed valve engine. Intended as a "get to work" machine, it could be supplied with the hand-change gear lever, assisted by a preselector: as a result there was no need for the usual gated gear beside the tank because the lever, recalled by the spring, always returned to its original position, as happens with a pedal control.

The *G.T.S.* had the opposed valve engine linked to the four-speed gearbox and the sprung frame from the *G.T.V.* Both the models in the *S* series were painted in a dark shade of amaranth and there was no difference in performance. Production amounted to a total of 4,004 and 2,652 units respectively and ceased on the outbreak of the war. Prices, again respectively, were 6,700 and 7,700 lire.

Airone

First built in 1939 as a development of the *P.E.*, and then updated with the 246 cc engine and four-speed gearbox (in fact when it was first launched it still bore the *P.E.* nameplate), the *Airone* was soon given a new sprung chassis in pressed steel (1940), directly derived from the *P.L.* frame. The result was to become the most popular Italian middleweight for the following fifteen years, a successful blend of practicality and high performance. Guzzi spent a lot of time and effort making sure that this bike remained abreast of the times: it received teledraulic forks in 1947. In 1948 it was fitted with new aluminium head and cylinder barrel castings and enclosed rocker gear. A peppy sporting version was produced in 1949. This was distinguished by a new combination, frame partly made up of pressings, which was adopted for the touring version in 1952. However the *Airone* was gradually overtaken by more modern lightweights with smaller engines until, no longer competitive, it was pensioned off in 1957. The *Airone* sported a red paint job with black and gold stripes. In 1939 it cost 6,200 lire, a price which had become 370,000 by 1949. In 1956 prices were 349,000 lire for the *Turismo* version and 364,000 for the *Sport*.

Model / year	Airone / 1939-1946
Engine	4-stroke flat single 70 × 64 mm / 246 cc
Compression ratio	6:1
Output	9.5 hp at 4800 rpm
Cylinder head	cast iron
Cylinder	cast iron
Valve arrangement	overhead inclined
Valve gear	push rod and rocker arm
Ignition	Marelli BL1 type magneto
Carburettor	Dell'Orto SBF 22
Lubrication	geared pressure pump; vane type scavenge pump
Clutch	wet multiplate type
Gearbox	foot-change 4-speed constant mesh
Transmission	primary, helical gear, final drive, chain
Frame	tubular duplex cradle
Wheelbase	1370 mm
Front suspension	girder fork with friction dampers
Rear suspension	swinging arm with friction dampers
Wheels	spoked with 19 × 2 1/4 rims
Tyres	3.00-19"
Brakes	expansion type; front manual, rear pedal
Weight	dry weight 135 kgs
Max speed	approx. 95 km/h
Normal consumption	3.3 litres per 100 kms
Fuel tank capacity	10.5 litres
Lubricant capacity	2.5 litres

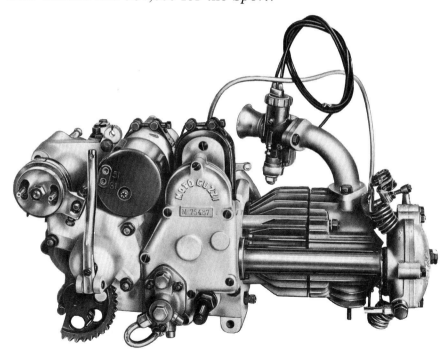

The first version of the *Airone* with cast iron cylinder and head. The one-piece crankshaft measured 26 mm at the crankpin and 25 mm at the mainshaft and ran on two rolling bearings. The bolt-up con-rod ran on 30 roller bearings.

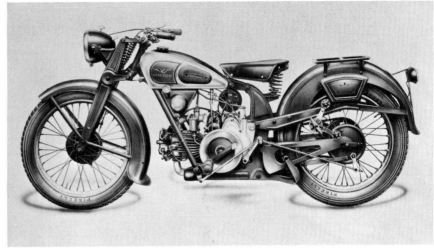

Above, the first *Airone* type with the tubular frame from the *P.E.* Between 1939-40 997 of these were built. The gearbox was a four-speed constant-mesh unit. A new sprung frame made entirely of pressed steel (top, right) was adopted in 1940. By the time this version reappeared after the war it was the only Guzzi middleweight in production.

The factory drawing shown here highlights the construction characteristics of the *Airone*'s pressed steel frame. As can be seen, the front part is composed of elements which were first bolted together and then fixed to the forged steel steering post. The rear pressings and the arms supporting the mudguard and the dampers were then bolted to the front part of the frame. The rear suspension arm was also in pressed steel.

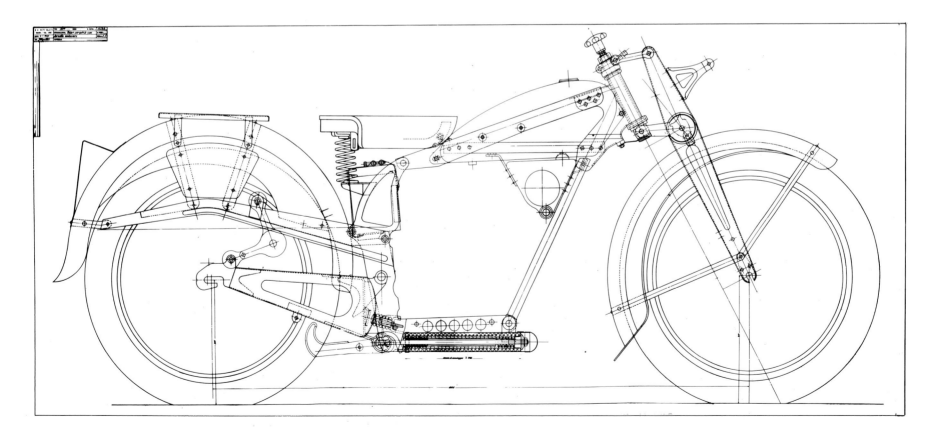

189

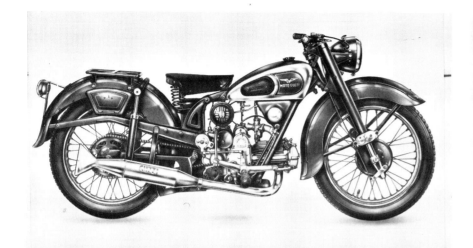

190

On the facing page: in 1947 the *Airone* was fitted with original hydraulic forks designed by Carlo Guzzi, and with hydraulic rear dampers (top, left). At the end of 1948 the bike was equipped with a new aluminium cylinder-head assembly with enclosed valve gear (top right). The *Sport* version (below) was introduced at the same time with a pressed steel and tubular frame, and aluminium wheel rims. The engine, fed by a 25 mm Dell'Orto SS carburettor, had a compression ration of 7:1 and developed 13.5 hp at 6000 rpm.
Top speed was 120 km/h.

On this page, successive versions of the *Airone*: top left the 1952 *Sport* with the new (painted) tank and magneto with manual advance control; top right the *Turismo* (1952). Above, the 1954 *Sport* which developed 12 hp at 5200 rpm; it had a magneto with automatic advance and a chromed tank. Right, the Turismo from 1956-57 with the cigar-shaped B.G.M. silencer; this side, the last *Sport* (1956), again with a B.G.M. silencer.

191

Motoleggera 65

Italy's rebirth from the ashes of the war was assisted by two-wheeled vehicles like mopeds, scooters and lightweight motor cycles.

Such conveyances supplied the mobility necessary for reconstruction which the bigger vehicles used by the public transport systems were unable to guarantee: this is a fact which many people refuse to recognize but it is true nonetheless.

Guzzi made its own particular, and essential, contribution to all this in the form of a very light motorcycle which, thanks to its uncomplicated aspect plus the undoubted quality guaranteed by the Guzzi name, soon earned itself a vast clientele ranging from workmen to doctors. First launched in the spring of 1946, 50,000 units of the 65 had already been built by 1949, an all-time high for the Italian motorcycle industry. Shrewd construction policy allied to soaring sales resulted in the price coming down from 159,000 to 107,000 lire over the years. In 1954, following some modifications made to the frame, it was rebaptized the *Cardellino*, which we will deal with later. The 65 was normally painted red with black and gold pinstriping; some models from 1953 were ash-grey with no pinstripes.

Model / year	Motoleggera 65 /1946-1954
Engine	2-stroke inclined single 42 × 46 mm/ 64 cc
Compression ratio	5.5:1
Output	2 hp at 5000 rpm
Cylinder head	light alloy
Cylinder	light alloy with pressed-in liner
Valve arrangement	—
Valve gear	—
Ignition	Marelli or Filso type flywheel magneto
Carburettor	Dell'Orto MA 13
Lubrication	20:1 mixture
Clutch	wet multiplate type
Gearbox	hand-change 3-speed constant mesh
Transmission	primary, helical gear; final drive, chain
Frame	single tube
Wheelbase	1200 mm
Front suspension	blade forks
Rear suspension	swinging arm
Wheels	spoked with 26 × 2 3/4 rims
Tyres	moped type 26 × 1 3/4 × 2
Brakes	expansion type; front manual, rear pedal
Weight	45 kgs
Max speed	approx. 50 km/h
Normal consumption	2 litres per 100 kms
Fuel tank capacity	6.5 litres
Lubricant capacity	—

The 1953 version of the 65 engine with the cast iron cylinder. On the facing page the 1948 model with horn, new chain guard and new silencer; right, the 1949 model with the reinforced forks.

Guzzi set several world records on several occasions with bikes derived from the *65 motoleggera*. Left, the speedster used in 1948, at Saxson and at the Monza Autodrome. All in all 27 records were set, from the flying kilometre at 96.051 km/h, to the 1,000 kilometres at 75.571 km/h with riders Alberti, Gianni Leoni and Ruffo. The engine had been uprated to 73 cc (46 × 46 mm) and ran on a 7:1 compression ratio for a power output of 3.6 hp at 6300 rpm. The standard tank was fitted only for the long distance runs. The photos above show the bike used for the Montlhéry record attempts (1950) both "undressed" and clothed in its special shell. The ultra-sleek shell hid a special 75 cc engine which was the forerunner of the *Zigolo*. At Montlhéry the Guzzi team set more records, in some cases bettering the existing 100 cc class records. The average speed recorded over the 1,000 kilometres was 105.3 km/h.

Cardellino

The *Cardellino* was a *65* derivative, produced to keep pace with a changing market. By the time the law exempting lightweights from the need to display registration plates was abolished in 1951, motorcycle buyers were already turning to bigger machines and so attempts were made to stimulate demand for the "Guzzino" by lowering the price and thus increasing its appeal as a utility bike. The *Cardellino* was launched in 1954 and, thanks to the changes made at the rear, it also looked more like a "complete" motorcycle. On a more practical level, it was also easier to carry a pillion passenger. The new bike — sold at 99,000 lire — was updated and modified as time went by. In 1956 the bodywork and front forks were changed, while at the end of the same year the displacement was increased to 73 cc and two versions were made available, the *Turismo* and the *Lusso*. At the end of 1958 it was equipped with a new aluminium cylinder with a chromed liner while the rear part of the frame was simplified. Finally, in the November of 1962, the displacement was again upped (this time to 83 cc), and new suspension was added. When Guzzi was reorganized in 1965 the *Cardellino* was put out to grass due to falling demand.

Model / year	Cardellino / 1954-1956
Engine	two stroke flat single 42 × 46 mm / 64 cc
Compression ratio	5.5:1
Output	2 hp at 5000 rpm
Cylinder head	light alloy
Cylinder	cast iron
Valve arrangement	—
Valve gear	—
Ignition	flywheel magneto
Carburettor	Dell'Orto MU 14B2
Lubrication	20:1 mixture
Clutch	wet multiplate type
Gearbox	constant mesh 3-speed hand-change
Transmission	primary, helical gear; final drive, chain
Frame	central tube and two rear arms
Wheelbase	1200 mm
Front suspension	blade forks
Rear suspension	swinging arm with friction dampers
Wheels	spoked with 20 × 2 rims
Tyres	2.25-20"
Brakes	expansion type; front manual, rear pedal
Weight	55 kgs
Max speed	approx. 55 km/h
Normal consumption	2 litres per 100 kms
Fuel tank capacity	6.5 litres
Lubricant capacity	—

The *Cardellino* represents the evolution of the *65*. The photo shows the engine with the aluminium cylinder and chromed barrel, built in 73 and 83 cc versions.

Top left, the first version of the *Cardellino* (1954) with a cast iron 65 cc engine and blade forks: top right, the 1956 edition, still 65 cc but with the new mechanical telescopic forks, a different shape for the mudguards and tank, and light alloy central drum brake. At side, an early *Cardellino* conversion for the Italian postal service.

On the facing page, top left, the *Lusso* version of the 1958 *Cardellino 73*. The cylinder is still in cast iron with bore and stroke of 45 × 46 mm. The carburettor measured 14 mm, output was 2.6 hp at 5200 rpm, top speed was 60 km/h. There was a foot-change gearbox. Top right, the *Nuovo Cardellino* from November 1958. The 73 cc engine had an aluminium cylinder with a hard-chromed barrel. This is the *Turismo* version. Finally, at the foot of the page, the last version of the *Cardellino*, with the 83 cc engine, built between November 1962 and 1965. The cylinder still has the chromed liner and bore and stroke of 48 × 46 mm. Other vital statistics: carburettor 14 mm, compression 7:1, 2.9 hp at 5200 rpm, 65 km/h. The suspension was a new design.

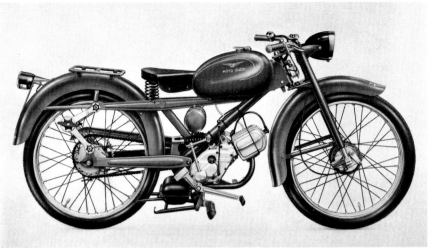

197

Astore

With the adoption of the light alloy cylinder head and barrel at the end of 1949, the *G.T.V.* bike — which had received its telescopic forks a couple of years previously — was renamed the *Astore*.

Made rather massive looking by the new front mudguard (like the one fitted to the smaller *Airone Turismo*, where it looked really incongruous), the *Astore* (Goshawk) was without a doubt the most important of the 500 cc machines directly descended from Carlo Guzzi's original design, and in a certain sense it also represented the maximum expression of his idea. Launched at a time when the small bike market was booming, the robust, powerful and very springy *Astore*, with its incredibly supple and deep chested engine, was in a class of its own as far as contemporary production was concerned. It was appreciated by a chosen few, all fans of "real" grand touring machines capable of tackling the higher Alpine passes. The *Astore* remained in production until 1953, when it was replaced by the touring version of the *Falcone*.

The *Astore* was painted red with black and gold pinstriping; it cost 462,000 lire.

Model / year	Astore / 1949-1953
Engine	4-stroke flat single 88 × 82 mm / 498.4 cc
Compression ratio	5.5:1
Output	18.9 hp at 4300 rpm
Cylinder head	light alloy with valves in oil bath
Cylinder	light alloy with pressed-in liner
Valve arrangement	inclined overhead
Valve gear	push rod and rocker arm
Ignition	Marelli type magneto
Carburettor	Dell'Orto MD 27F
Lubrication	geared pressure pump; vane type scavenge pump
Clutch	wet multiplate type
Gearbox	foot-change 4-speed sliding gears
Transmission	primary, helical gear; final drive, chain
Frame	duplex cradle in tubes and sheet metal
Wheelbase	1475 mm
Front suspension	teledraulic fork
Rear suspension	swinging arm with hydraulic dampers
Wheels	spoked with 19 × 2 1/2 rims
Tyres	studded 3.50-19"
Brakes	expansion type: front manual, rear pedal
Weight	180 kgs
Max speed	approx.120 km/h
Normal consumption	4.5 litres per 100 kms
Fuel tank capacity	13.5 litres
Lubricant capacity	3 litres

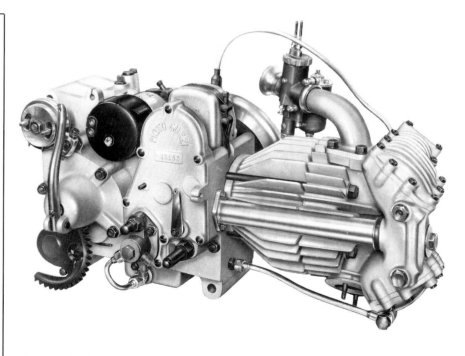

The powerful *Astore* engine with aluminium cylinder barrel-head assembly and enclosed valve gear. This is the last version, dated 1953, with the new Marelli MCR 4 E magneto with automatic advance and rotary magnet.

The original version of the *Astore* first presented at the end of 1949. The hydraulic dampers at the rear were fixed to the fork and to a tubular element which formed an arch across the mudguard to connect the two fixed arms (as in the *Airone Turismo*).
The "springs in a box" under the engine still followed the *G.T.V.* layout.

The *Astore* was a particularly comfortable bike to ride. As well as the very soft suspension and the relaxed riding stance, there were some other ingenious touches like the handlebars with the height adjustable levers. The legshields were standard. Another well designed component was an extremely light and user-friendly stand.

This side, an *Astore* plus an elegant "gran turismo" sidecar with sprung wheel. Below, the 1952 *Astore*, with the tank painted red and black. Chrome was in short supply on the international market in those years and therefore many components had to be painted, blued or cadmium plated rather than chrome plated in order to keep costs at a reasonable level.

On the facing page, the last version of the *Astore* (1953), with a tank rather like the one on the *Falcone* and a magneto with an automatic advance/retard device. This is a fairly rare machine, because it was replaced almost immediately by the *Falcone Turismo*. Some models were given an amaranth finish.

Falcone

In the early Fifties the *Falcone* was the most sought-after of the big Guzzis. Powerful and not all that simple to ride, it was the sportster parexcellence, more at home — like most Guzzis — on a fast straight rather than a mixed stretch. When the *Astore* was deleted in 1953, the *Falcone* was produced in a *Sport* and *Turismo* version to remain the only half-litre machine in Guzzi's civilian catalogue.

Somewhat dated by this time, the *Falcone* slowly lost favour with the public, who preferred lighter, faster bikes.

However it remained in production until 1967, for the benefit of the few who still loved the unmistakable thump of the half-litre engine and of course the military, especially the Traffic Police, who still thought the *Falcone* provided unbeatable value in many respects. Special versions were produced for the *Guardia di Finanza* (Customs and Excise Police) and another army regiment, the *Corazzieri*. Sold at 482,000 lire in 1951, the price later fell to 419,000 for the *Sport* and 399,000 for the *Turismo*. The *Falcone* had red paintwork with black and gold pinstriping; models from 1952-53 had the panels of the two tanks painted black in order to save on the expense of chrome.

Model / year	Falcone Sport / 1950-1967
Engine	4-stroke flat single 88 × 82 mm / 498.4 cc
Compression ratio	6.5:1
Output	23 hp at 4500 rpm
Cylinder head	light alloy with valves in oil-bath
Cylinder	light alloy with pressed-in liner
Valve arrangement	inclined overhead
Valve gear	push rod and rocker arm
Ignition	Marelli type magneto
Carburettor	Dell'Orto SS 29A
Lubrication	geared pressure pump; vane type scavenge pump
Clutch	wet multiplate type
Gearbox	foot-change 4-speed constant-mesh sliding gears
Transmission	primary, helical gear, final drive, chain
Frame	duplex cradle in tubes and sheet metal
Wheelbase	1500 mm
Front suspension	teledraulic fork
Rear suspension	swinging arm with friction dampers
Wheels	spoked with 19 × 2 1/2 rims
Tyres	front, ribbed 3.25 -19"; rear, studded 3.50-19"
Brakes	expansion type: front manual, rear pedal
Weight	167 kgs
Max speed	approx.135 km/h
Normal consumption	4.5 litres per 100 kms
Fuel tank capacity	17.5 litres
Lubricant capacity	3 litres

The *Falcone* engine. It was equipped with the *Dondolino* constant-mesh gearbox and it also used the latter's crankcase therefore, although this was in cast aluminium instead of electron. The engine shown is the post-1952 *Sport* version with the automatic advance/retard mechanism.

The original *Falcone* as it appeared at the end of 1950, with manual advance/retard control and chromed tank with painted stripe. The brakes measured 200 mm, like those of the *Astore*; the springs of the rear suspension, under the engine, were shorter and stiffer, better suited to the higher speeds which the *Falcone* could attain.

All it took to give the *Falcone* an extraordinarily pantherish and streamlined look was a a minimal degree of restyling: the size of the mudguards was reduced, the legshields abolished and the footrest shifted aft. As in the *Airone Sport*, the designers went back to the adjustable Hartford-type dampers.

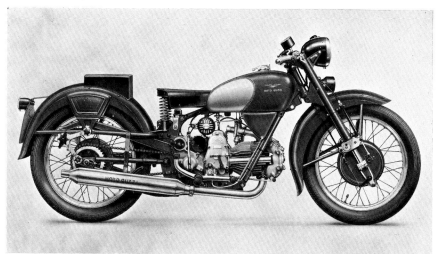

Left, the last version of the *Falcone,* known as the *Sport* after the creation of the *Turismo* variant, in production between 1964 and 1967. Characteristic features include the raised headlamp, the tank with the chromed panels, the cylindrical silencer and the voltage regulator straddling the battery. The photo shows a model destined for the Traffic Police, which was therefore fitted with a siren.

Below, the last *Turismo* version of the *Falcone* engine. The crank shaft was a one-piece component (with embodied counterweights), with a 29 mm crankpin and a 35 mm mainshaft. The big-end ran on thirty-three 3 mm roller bearings. The valve diameters were 43 mm inlet and 42 mm exhaust. The carburettor was a Dell'Orto MD 27 F and power output stood at 18.9 hp at 4300 rpm. Compression was 5.5:1. The *Sport* version differed in that it had a lighter con-rod, a different cam profile, a Dell'Orto SS 29 A type carburettor, and a 40 mm exhaust valve. Compression was (6.5:1) and output 23 hp at 4500 rpm.

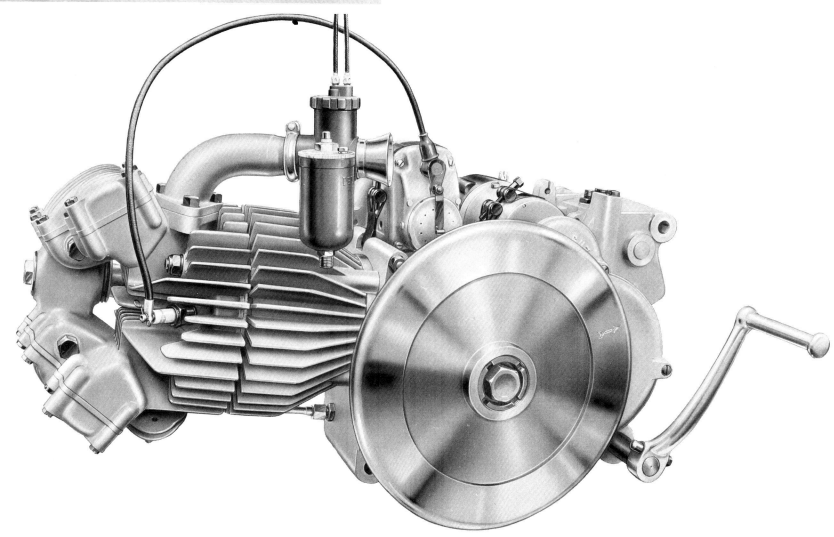

The first version of the *Falcone Turismo* which replaced the *Astore* in 1953. The frame came from the *Falcone* and so did the engine with the *Dondolino* type gearbox. This bike inherited carburettor, compression ratio, camshaft, timing gear, and hence performance, from the *Astore*. The 3.50-19" tyres were another bequest from the same source.

The handlebars, footrest and legshields on the *Falcone Turismo* came from the *Astore*, and so the riding position was the same in both cases. Note the different route (as compared to the *Astore*) taken by the rod linking the gear pedal and the preselector. This was due to the need to keep the order of the pedal movements unchanged even with the new gearbox.

Galletto

The *Galletto*, devised and built by Carlo Guzzi in 1950, represents probably the most successful attempt to combine the strengths of the scooter with those of the classic motorcycle while eliminating their respective weaknesses at the same time. The rider was offered a good degree of protection, a user-friendly machine and a spare wheel along with the kind of performance, comfort and roadholding normally associated with a conventional motorcycle. It was planned to fit the Galletto with a 150 cc 4-stroke engine and a 3-speed gearbox, but it went on sale with a 160 cc engine, uprated to 175 cc and linked to a new 4-speed gearbox at the end of 1952. In 1954, the engine was again uprated, this time to 192 cc, while the electric starter with dynamotor was added in 1961, together with some modifications to the bodywork. The *Galletto* was painted in ivory and could be bought with the spare wheel mounted cross-wise behind the front wheel so as to form an efficient bumper, or protected by a specially shaped cover: the price difference was 4,000 lire. The last version, with electric starter, was painted grey or, upon request, in Guzzi red. The price remained steady at around 265,000 lire until 1966.

Model / year	Galletto / 1950-1952
Engine	4-stroke flat single 62 × 53 mm / 159.5 cc
Compression ratio	5.6:1
Output	6 hp at 5200 rpm
Cylinder head	light alloy with valves in oil-bath
Cylinder	light alloy with pressed-in liner
Valve arrangement	inclined overhead
Valve gear	push rod and rocker arm
Ignition	Marelli or Filso type flywheel magneto
Carburettor	Dell'Orto MA 18 BS 1
Lubrication	geared pressure and scavenge pumps
Clutch	wet multiplate type
Gearbox	foot-change 3-speed constant-mesh sliding gears
Transmission	primary, helical gear; final drive, chain
Frame	tubular main spar, pressings
Wheelbase	1310 mm
Front suspension	telescopic leading link forks
Rear suspension	swinging arm with friction dampers
Wheels	spoked with 17 × 2 1/4 rims
Tyres	studded: front 2.75-17"; rear 3.00-17"
Brakes	expansion type: front manual, rear pedal
Weight	107 kgs
Max speed	approx. 80 km/h
Normal consumption	2.6 litres per 100 kms
Fuel tank capacity	7 litres
Lubricant capacity	3 litres

The *Galletto* engine (first series), with swept volume of 160 cc and 3-speed gearbox, was fitted with flywheel magneto ignition which had a separate contact breaker and manual advance/retard. The Dell'Orto carburettor was a new type, with an extra jet for the choke instead of the usual shutter which blocked off the airflow when cold starting.

The 1951 version of the *Galletto 160*, with the optional spare wheel. Unlike the first models sold in 1950 this had a heel and toe rocking gear change pedal. At the end of 1951 the *Galletto 160* gained the new look rear mudguard and legshields as shown in the photo below. Light alloys were widely used for the body.

The *Galletto 192* built in early 1954, with 4-speed gearbox. November 1952 saw the *Galletto 175* make its debut, also with a 4-speed box. Externally, the *192* model differed from its *175* predecessor in that the plate covering the engine was set higher due to the need to accommodate the dynamo. The diameter of the headlamp was increased by 20 mm to 150 mm.

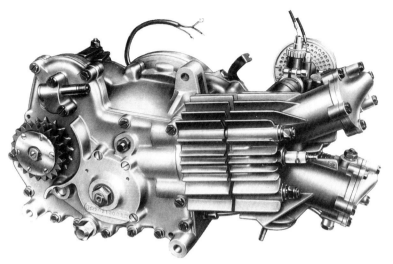

The *Galletto 175* propulsion unit with 4-speed gears

The *Galletto 192* propulsion unit with dynamo.

A version of the *Galletto 192* made for the Italian post office with large panniers astride the rear wheel.

Cutaway of the *Galletto 192* showing the principal mechanical members.

The last version of the *Galletto 192* with dynamotor ignition.

The same version viewed from the left: the dynamotor can just be seen

Zigolo

Intended to fill the gap between the *65* and the *Galletto*, the *Zigolo 98* was also the first enclosed bike to find favour with the public, that had been somewhat unwilling to accept the advantages of enclosure until then, largely on aesthetic grounds. First introduced in 1953 as a low-priced popular conveyance (the first version was practically devoid of chromework and bore drab grey livery, handlebars included), the *Zigolo* was later to come to the attention of engineers all over the world when, in 1958, it was fitted with a light alloy cylinder and chromed liner, a very advantageous feature from a functional standpoint, but which had been applied only rarely until then due to practical difficulties regarding its production on an industrial scale.

The basic *Zigolo* (later named the *Turismo*) was joined by an upmarket version in 1954. The *Lusso* had a red finish with chromed panels on the tank and 17" wheels, and by 1956 it was the only *Zigolo* still in production. At the end of 1959 the displacement was upped to 110 cc and stayed at that level until 1966, when the *Zigolo* was deleted. Over the years its price had fallen from 169,000 to 135,000 lire, despite the numerous important improvements which had been made to it.

Model / year	Zigolo Turismo / 1953-1956
Engine	two stroke flat single 50 × 50mm / 98 cc
Compression ratio	6:1
Output	4 hp at 5200 rpm
Cylinder head	light alloy
Cylinder	cast iron
Valve arrangement	—
Valve gear	—
Ignition	flywheel magneto
Carburettor	Dell'Orto MAF 15 B 1
Clutch	wet multiplate type
Lubrication	20:1 mixture
Gearbox	foot-change 3-speed constant-mesh
Transmission	primary, helical gear; final drive, chain
Frame	single spar with enclosed partially unitized body
Wheelbase	1240 mm
Front suspension	telescopic forks
Rear suspension	swinging arm with friction dampers
Wheels	spoked with 19 × 2 rims
Tyres	2.50-19"
Brakes	expansion type; front manual, rear pedal
Weight	78 kgs
Max speed	approx. 76 km/h
Normal consumption	2.2 litres per 100 kms
Fuel tank capacity	13.5 litres
Lubricant capacity	—

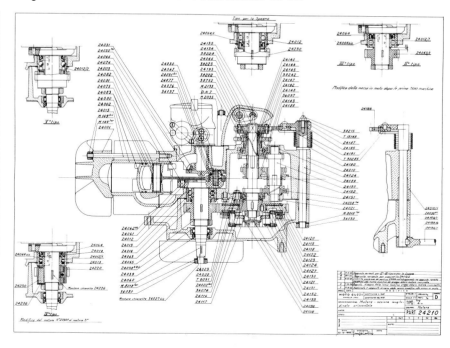

Assembly diagram of the *Zigolo 98* with the cast iron cylinder. The details added to the drawing show the successive modifications made to the main bearing and the starter assembly.

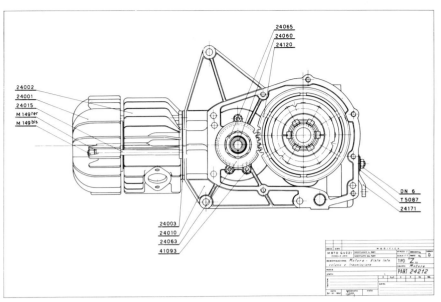

Another assembly diagram showing the flywheel side of the first *Zigolo*-type engine with the cast iron cylinder. Below, the original *Zigolo* from 1953 was painted grey, with blued exhaust and rear dampers.

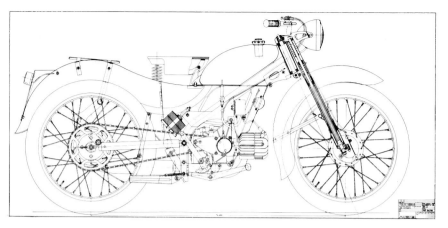

A diagram of the *Zigolo* frame showing the layout of the various mechanical units. The body was partially unitized. The interesting rear suspension design had a large rubber pad working in compression.

The last *Zigolo* engine had a light alloy cylinder with chromed liner and a displacement of 110 cc. In 1954 the *Zigolo 98* with the 19" wheels was baptized the *Turismo*. It had a black and grey tank with chrome-plated handlebars, exhaust and dampers. It was deleted in 1956 (photo below).

The *Zigolo Sport* was introduced in 1954 with a larger head and red paintwork. It developed 6.8 hp and could reach 100 km/h but it never went into production. The *Zigolo Lusso*, with the same body but the standard engine, was chosen instead. It ran on 17" wheels and was produced until 1957.

The *Mk II Zigolo* of 1958-59 (above), with chromed cylinder liner and central drum brakes. The tank was red and white. Below, the *Zigolo 110* of 1960-66. Apart from the engine, still with the chromed liner, there were telescopic forks plus several other new details (exhaust, headlamp, tank, front hub etc.).

Lodola

The *Lodola* was the first 4-stroke motorcycle to break decisively with the traditional Guzzi flat single design. Introduced when sporty *175*s were in fashion, it was launched in 1956 complete with all the features which the public of the day demanded (like the single overhead camshaft valve gear), without any sacrifice in terms of the robustness and good value for money for which Guzzi was famous.

It embodied several interesting technical features, like a timing chain fitted with a small damping stabilizer which was kept at the correct tautness by a self-adjusting tensioner. In 1959, the original 175 cc models, the *Normale* and *Sport*, were followed by the *Gran Turismo* with the 235 cc push-rod engine.

The *Lodola* also gave rise to some very important Regularity racers, with 175, 235 and then 247 cc engines, still with the sohc timing gear (apart from the first works 235s).

The 235 cc sohc version of the *Lodola Regolarità* was also sold to the public. In the catalogue until 1966, the *Lodola* was the last bike designed entirely by Carlo Guzzi, who was to hand over the reins of the firm's technical management a short time afterwards.

Model / year	Lodola / 1956-1958
Engine	4-stroke flat single 62 × 57.8 mm / 174 cc
Compression ratio	7.5:1
Output	9 hp at 6000 rpm
Cylinder head	light alloy with valves in oil-bath
Cylinder	light alloy with pressed-in liner
Valve arrangement	inclined overhead
Valve gear	overhead camshaft
Ignition	Marelli-type coil
Carburettor	Dell'Orto UB 22 BS 2A
Lubrication	geared pressure and scavenge pumps
Clutch	wet multiplate type
Gearbox	foot-change 4-speed constant mesh sliding gears
Transmission	primary, helical gear, final drive, chain
Frame	duplex cradle in tubes and sheet metal
Wheelbase	1314 mm
Front suspension	teledraulic fork
Rear suspension	swinging arm with teledraulic dampers
Wheels	front: spoked with 18 x 2 1/4 rim; rear, 17 x 2 1/4
Tyres	front: ribbed 2.50-18"; rear, studded 3.00-17" R
Brakes	expansion type: front manual, rear pedal
Weight	109 kgs
Max speed	approx. 110 km/h
Normal consumption	(Cuna stds.) 2.7 litres per 100 kms
Fuel tank capacity	12 litres
Lubricant capacity	2.5 litres

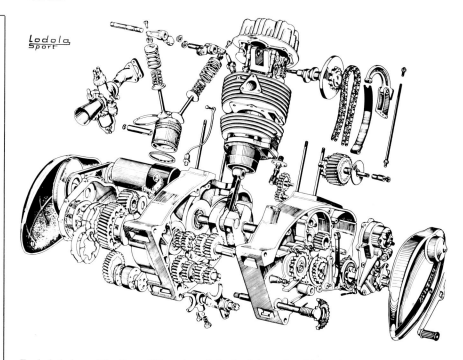

Exploded view of the *Sport 175* version of the *Lodola* engine (1958-59). The characteristics of the various mechanical units are clearly visible. The 175 cc *Normale* and *Regolarità* engines were virtually identical.

Above, the original *Lodola 175* appeared in the Spring of 1956 and was known as the *Sport* at first. It had chain driven sohc valve gear, a 4-speed gearbox, 18" wheels in front and 17" behind, and lateral drum brakes. It was painted red with black panels, cost 249,000 lire and was in production until 1958.

The last models had ivory white panels and a different tank. Below, the *Lodola Sport 175* of 1958-59, the "bike designed by the wind", as the advertising puff of the day had it. Output was 11 hp and top speed 120 km/h. The front brake and the tank were new. Below, the 1959 *Lodola Gran Turismo*, with the push-rod engine. It developed 11 hp at 6500 rpm, and ran on a compression ratio of 7.5:1. Top speed was 115 km/h. The model shown was fitted with a cartridge-type oil filter, which was a later addition.

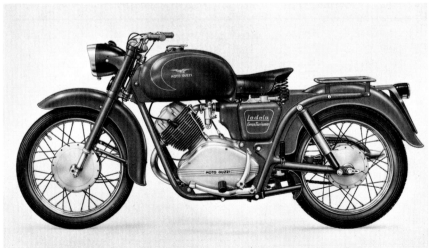

215

Right, one of the first versions of the *Lodola*, prepared in 1958 for regularity racing. It had a sohc 175 cc engine with a 4-speed gearbox and was reserved for the Guzzi works riders. Below, the 1959 factory *Lodola Regolarità*. As can be seen, several rational modifications had been made. The bike was available in 175 and 235 cc versions, both with single overhead camshaft and 4-speed gearbox. The first 235s were built with the push-rod engine intended for the *Gran Turismo* model.

On the facing page, the 1960 *Lodola Regolarità* with the 235 cc sohc engine: it developed 14 hp at 7500 rpm, had the 4-speed box, could hit 130 km/h, weighed 110 kgs and rode on 2.75-19" tyres at the front with 3.50-18" behind.
Far right, the 1961 works machine, with the 247 cc sohc engine and 5-speed gearbox. Still on the facing page, two beautifully clear cross sections of the sohc *Lodola* engine.

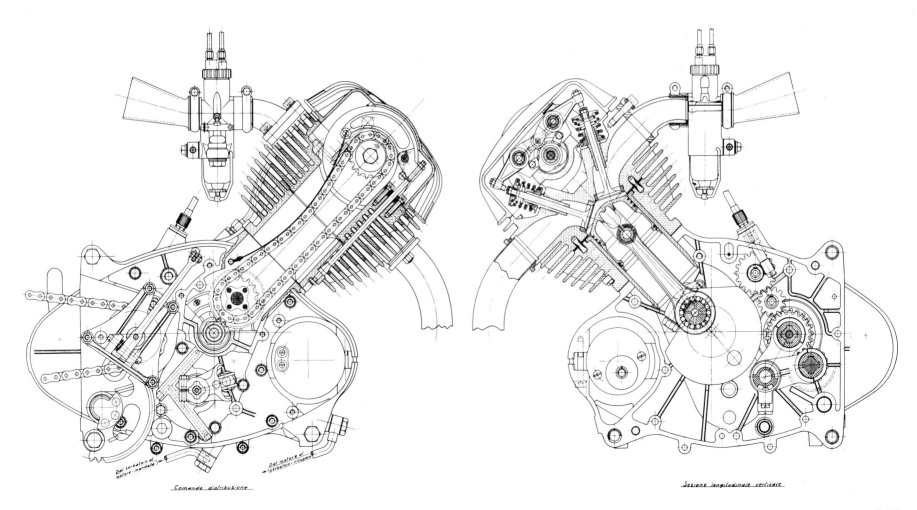

Comando distribuzione

Dal serbatoio al
motore-mandata

Dal motore al
serbatoio-ricupero

Sezione longitudinale verticale

Stornello

Introduced at a time when the motorcycle industry found itself in the grip of a minor crisis, the *Stornello 125* was designed with maximum cheapness of construction in mind: parallel overhead valves, wet sump, pressure die-cast crankcase, etc. Given the healthy sales, a new and more powerful engine with inclined valves was built and fitted to various racers: the *Sport*, the *Scrambler*, and the *Regolarità*.

At the end of 1967 the *160* version was introduced; in early 1970 the *Stornello* was given a 5-speed gearbox and new styling. It was produced from 1960 to 1975.

Model / year	Stornello Turismo / 1960-1968
Engine	4-stroke inclined single 52 × 58 mm / 123.1 cc
Compression ratio	8:1
Output	7 hp at 7200 rpm
Cylinder head	light alloy with valves in oil-bath
Cylinder	light alloy with pressed-in liner
Valve arrangement	parallel overhead
Valve gear	push rod and rocker arm
Ignition	flywheel magneto
Carburettor	Dell'Orto ME 18 BS
Lubrication	wet sump and gear driven pressure pump
Clutch	wet multiplate type
Gearbox	foot-change 4-speed constant-mesh
Transmission	primary, gear driven; final drive, chain
Frame	tubular duplex cradle
Wheelbase	1250 mm
Front suspension	teledraulic fork
Rear suspension	swinging arm with teledraulic dampers
Wheels	spoked with 17 × 2 1/4 rims
Tyres	front: ribbed 2.50-17"; rear, studded 2.75-17" R
Brakes	expansion type: front manual, rear pedal
Weight	85 kgs
Max speed	approx. 100 km/h
Normal consumption	(Cuna stds.) 2.3 litres per 100 kms
Fuel tank capacity	12.5 litres
Lubricant capacity	1.9 litres

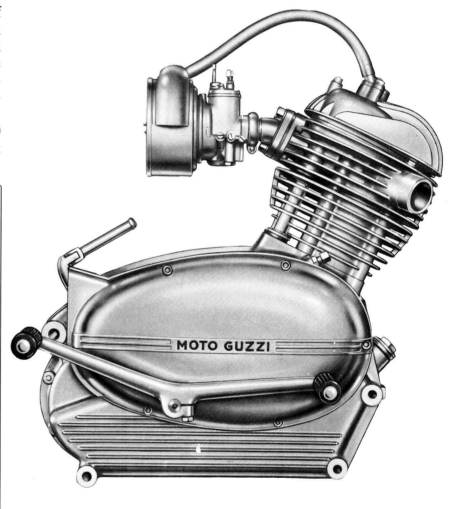

The original (1960) version of the *Stornello* engine (later known as the *Turismo*), with parallel overhead valves, flywheel magneto ignition and foot-change 4-speed gearbox.

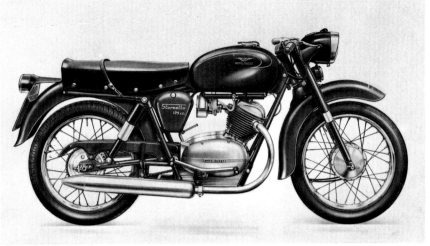

Above, the 1960 *Stornello 125*. It was styled the *Turismo* when the *Sport* model was introduced and stayed in production until 1967. It was painted red and cost 179,000 lire. The very first models had the horn mounted on the toolbox. At side, an exploded drawing of the engine handed out by the makers at the press conference held for the launch of the new lightweight. Top left, the 125 cc *Stornello Sport* with the inclined valve engine, introduced at the end of 1961. This was the version built until 1967. It cost 195,000 lire.

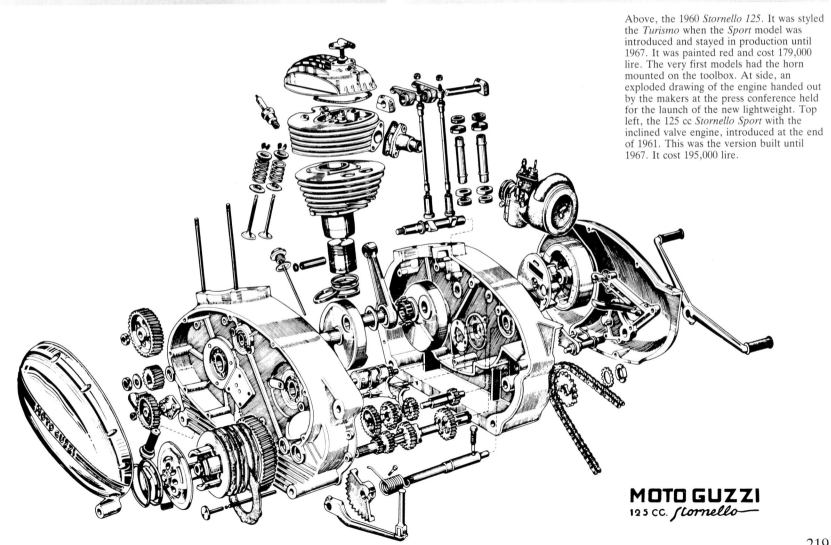

MOTO GUZZI
125 CC. *Stornello*

From top left: the 1967-69 *Scrambler America 125*; the *Sport America* from the same period; the *160* from 1968-69. Above, the *Stornello 125* from 1970-75. Below, a cross-section of the new engine with the 5-speed gears.

On the facing page, top right, the *Stornello Regolarità 125* in the version which was sold to the general public; left, the prototype from 1965. Below, the 5-speed *Stornello 160* from 1970-75.

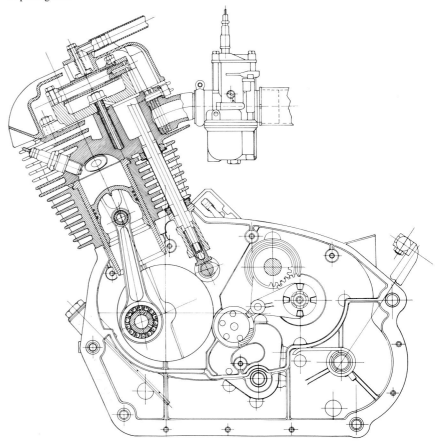

Dingo

In a bid to overcome the crisis of the Sixties, Guzzi decided it was worth producing a moped in the hope of attracting more customers. This was done with the launch of the *Dingo* at the 1963 Milan Trade Fair. First produced with a 3-speed gearbox, the *Dingo* was further developed over the years as Guzzi turned out a series of sporty little bikes aimed at the youth market; these were fitted with a new engine and a 4-speed box. Towards the end of its development the *Dingo's* designers again went for more economic versions, both with and without the 3-speed gears, but with automatic transmission. In 1963, the basic version cost 80,000 lire.

Model / year	Dingo Sport / 1964-1965
Engine	two stroke flat single 38.5 × 42 mm / 48.9 cc
Compression ratio	7.5:1
Output	1.4 hp at 4800 rpm
Cylinder head	light alloy
Cylinder	chrome plated light alloy
Valve arrangement	—
Valve gear	—
Ignition	flywheel magneto
Carburettor	Dell'Orto SHA 14.9
Clutch	wet multiplate type
Lubrication	50:1 mixture
Gearbox	hand-change 3-speed constant-mesh
Transmission	primary, helical gear, final drive, chain
Frame	pressed steel single spar chassis
Wheelbase	1130 mm
Front suspension	telescopic forks
Rear suspension	swinging arm with friction dampers
Wheels	spoked with 18 × 1.20 rims
Tyres	2.00-18"
Brakes	expansion type; front manual, rear pedal
Weight	48 kgs
Max speed	approx. 40 km/h
Normal consumption	(Cuna stds.) 1.3 litres per 100 kms
Fuel tank capacity	6.5 litres
Lubricant capacity	—

The 4-speed version of the 49 cc *Dingo* engine (1967-70). It had no pedals.

Above, the *Dingo Turismo* with 3-speed hand gearchange, from 1963-66.

Above, the *Dingo Sport* with 3-speed hand gearchange and no pedals, from 1963-67.
Below, the *Dingo G.T.* with 4-speed pedal-operated gearchange, from 1967-69.

The *Dingo* "pack" is composed of a large number of models all with the same engine. Top: the *Dingo Super* with the 4-speed foot-change from 1967-69.
It ran on 2.00-18" tyres at the front and 2.25-18s at the back.
Above, the *Dingo Cross* with 4-speed pedal-operated gearchange from 1967-69. It had 2.50-17" studded tyres. On the right, from top to bottom; the 1966 *Dingo Super*, with 3-speed hand gearchange; the 1968-75 *Dingo Turismo* (called the *50-3 Marce* in 1971 and *50-3V* in 1973); the 1970-75 *Dingo 50 MM* (or *50 Monomarcia*), had no gearchange, but an automatic centrifugal clutch and pedals. Tyres were 2.25-16".

Above, the 1970-73 *Dingo Super Sport*, with 4-speed pedal-operated gearchange. Right, the *Dingo Cross* from 1970-73, with 4-speed pedal-operated gearchange. This side, an exploded view of the 1970-73 version of the 4-speed *Dingo 49* engine. Compared to the previous 4-speed model, there were differences in the finning, crankcase and gearbox. This engine was fitted to the *Super Sport, Granturismo* and *Cross*.

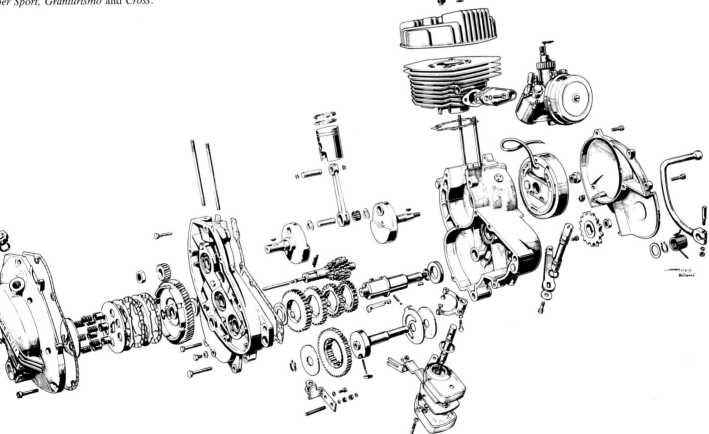

Trotter

The *Trotter* first entered the world in 1966, during the delicate transitional phase between Parodi and SEIMM ownership. Very simple and very cheap (54,000 lire) the *Trotter* was an instant success, so much so that it made an important contribution to the company's succesful bid to restore its flagging fortunes. At the end of 1967, the original model with the completely unsprung frame and automatic friction clutch, plus a special ratio for gradients, was joined by the *Trotter VIP* (painted in livelier colours) and the *Super*, which had telescopic front forks. The *Trotter* was subjected to major modifications at the end of 1969, when the 49 cc cylinder barrel was laid on its side and linked to a V belt primary drive. Changes were also made to the frame. This resulted in four new versions of the moped: the *Special 1* (later known as the *Special M*) a single-speed automatic with leading link front forks; the *Special 2* (later baptized the *Special V*) which had the stepless transmission powered by a V-belt drive; the *Mark 1* (later the *Mark M*) single- speed, with girder forks at the front and swinging arm rear suspension; finally there was the *Mark 2* (later the *Mark V*) with the *Mark 1* frame and the stepless transmission. The four versions remained in production until 1973.

Model / year	Trotter / 1966-1969
Engine	two stroke single 37 × 38 mm / 40.8 cc
Compression ratio	7.5:1
Output	1.2 hp at 5000 rpm
Cylinder head	light alloy
Cylinder	chrome plated light alloy
Valve arrangement	—
Valve gear	—
Ignition	flywheel magneto
Carburettor	Dell'Orto SHA 14.9
Lubrication	50:1 mixture
Clutch	wet automatic centrifugal single plate type
Gearbox	hand-change 2-speed constant-mesh
Transmission	primary, gear driven; final drive, chain
Frame	pressed steel single spar chassis
Wheelbase	1035 mm
Front suspension	rigid
Rear suspension	rigid
Wheels	spoked with 16 × 1.20 rims
Tyres	2.00-16"
Brakes	expansion type; front manual, rear pedal
Weight	35 kgs
Max speed	approx. 36 km/h
Normal consumption	(Cuna stds.) 1.5 litres per 100 kms
Fuel tank capacity	2.5 litres
Lubricant capacity	—

The first *Trotter* engine with the inclined cylinder (40.8 cc), automatic centrifugal clutch and selectable low gear option for steep gradients. It was fixed to the frame with a silentbloc mounting.

The original *Trotter* from 1966 had sober black livery which was a perfect match for the spartan lines of the pressed steel frame. Nevertheless this was the first production Guzzi available in different colours. At the end of 1969 the *Trotters* painted in brilliant colours were known as *VIP*s: they cost 1,800 lire more than the basic model.

The 1970-73 *Trotter Special*, with the leading link suspension. It also came with the single-speed transmission or an automatic converter. This was the last version: the engine fairing on the first model was slightly different.

The 1970-73 *Trotter Mark*, with integral sprung frame. This bike too was available with or without automatic transmission. The model shown is the last version: the first had a slightly different frame and engine fairing.

Above, the 1970-73 *Trotter* engine, with the 48.8 cc horizontal cylinder (bore and stroke 38.5 × 42 mm). It was available with or without the stepless transmission linked to the automatic centrifugal clutch.

227

V7 and derivatives

The idea of producing a large V-twin engine arose at the end of the Fifties, but at first it was reserved for the automobile and military markets as the public seemed to have lost interest temporarily in high performance bikes. It was only after an order from the Italian police that a bike was finally fitted with this engine, which Guzzi then thought it would sell in the normal way given the interest the machine had aroused abroad. The civilian V7, introduced at the end of 1965, went on sale in Italy two years later and did much for the rebirth of interest in big bikes. Sold at first with the 703 cc engine at 725,000 lire, it had red and silver finish, chromed panels on the tank and a black frame. The V7 was replaced in 1969 by the V7 Special which had an uprated 757 cc engine and various other mechanical (gearbox) and design improvements (wider tank, complete instrument pack, white paintwork with red stripes). Special models were prepared for the American market with names like Ambassador, Eldorado, and California.

The evolution of the V series is still in progress and has resulted in the creation of numerous other models, with different frames and various sizes of engine.

Model / year	V7 / 1967-1969
Engine	4-stroke 90 degree V-twin 80 × 70 mm / 703.3 cc
Compression ratio	9:1
Output	40 hp at 5000 rpm
Cylinder head	light alloy with valve seat inserts
Cylinder	light alloy with chromed liner
Valve arrangement	inclined overhead
Valve gear	push rod and rocker arm
Ignition	coil
Carburettor	Dell'Orto SS I 29 DS, SS I 29 D
Lubrication	wet sump and gear driven pressure pump
Clutch	dry dual plate type
Gearbox	foot-change 4-speed constant-mesh
Transmission	primary, gear driven; final drive, shaft
Frame	tubular duplex cradle
Wheelbase	1445 mm
Front suspension	teledraulic fork
Rear suspension	swinging arm with teledraulic dampers
Wheels	spoked with 18 × 3.00 rims
Tyres	4.00-18"
Brakes	expansion type: front, manual (twin-cam); rear, pedal
Weight	230 kgs
Max speed	approx. 164 km/h
Normal consumption	(Cuna stds.) 7.3 litres per 100 kms
Fuel tank capacity	20 litres
Lubricant capacity	3 litres

The first version of the V7 engine (703 cc) seen from the flywheel side.

The prototype of the *V7*, introduced with a silver-grey finish in 1965.

The 703 cc *V7*, which went on sale in 1967.

The version produced at the end of 1968, before the arrival of the *V7 Special*.

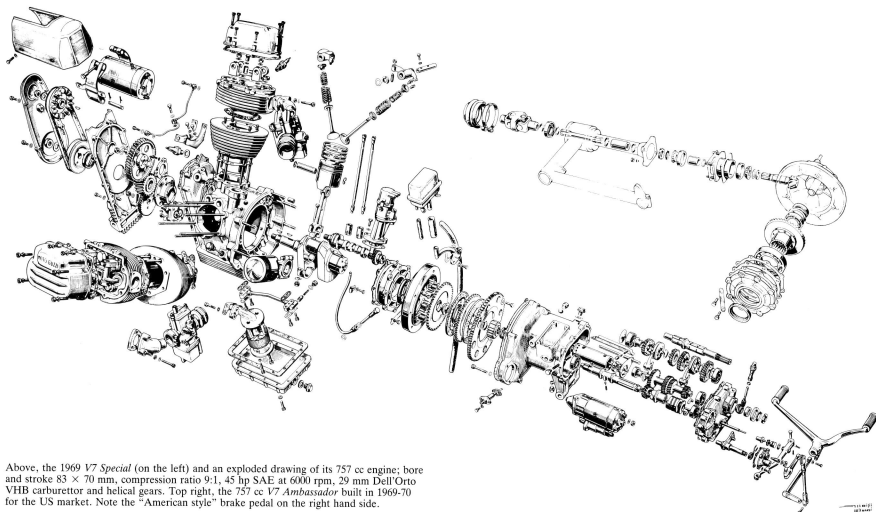

Above, the 1969 *V7 Special* (on the left) and an exploded drawing of its 757 cc engine; bore and stroke 83 × 70 mm, compression ratio 9:1, 45 hp SAE at 6000 rpm, 29 mm Dell'Orto VHB carburettor and helical gears. Top right, the 757 cc *V7 Ambassador* built in 1969-70 for the US market. Note the "American style" brake pedal on the right hand side.

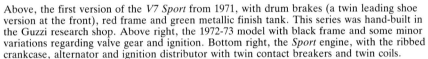

Above, the first version of the *V7 Sport* from 1971, with drum brakes (a twin leading shoe version at the front), red frame and green metallic finish tank. This series was hand-built in the Guzzi research shop. Above right, the 1972-73 model with black frame and some minor variations regarding valve gear and ignition. Bottom right, the *Sport* engine, with the ribbed crankcase, alternator and ignition distributor with twin contact breakers and twin coils.

Model / year	V7 Sport / 1972-1974
Engine	4-stroke 90 degree V-twin 82.5 × 70 mm / 748 cc
Compression ratio	9.8:1
Output	52 hp at 6300 rpm
Cylinder head	light alloy with valve seat inserts
Cylinder	light alloy with chromed liner
Valve arrangement	inclined overhead
Valve gear	push rod and rocker arm
Ignition	coil
Carburettor	Dell'Orto VHB 30 CD, VHB 30 CS
Lubrication	wet-sump and gear driven pressure pump
Clutch	dry dual plate type
Gearbox	foot-change 5-speed constant-mesh
Transmission	primary, helical gear; final drive, shaft
Frame	tubular duplex cradle
Wheelbase	1470 mm
Front suspension	teledraulic fork
Rear suspension	swinging arm with teledraulic dampers
Wheels	spoked: front, WM 2/1.85 × 18; rear, WM 3/ 2.15 × 18
Tyres	front 3.25-18", rear 3.50-18"
Brakes	expansion type: front manual (four shoes); rear pedal
Weight	206 kgs
Max speed	approx. 200 km/h
Normal consumption	(Cuna stds.) 8.5 litres per 100 kms
Fuel tank capacity	22.5 litres
Lubricant capacity	3.5 litres

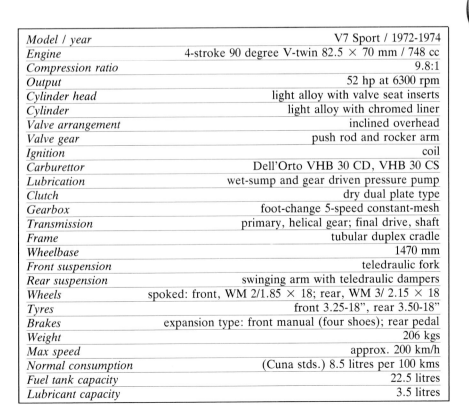

The 1974-75 *750 S*. This model had the twin-disc front brake, operated simultaneously by the hydraulic handlebar control.
Some design details differed from the *V7 Sport* (big single/dual seat, silencers, finish), while the gearbox and the state of tune were also slightly different.

The *750 S3* introduced at the November 1975 Milan Motor Show. It was equipped with the three disc "integral" braking system: one of the front units and the rear brake were actuated simultaneously by the pedal, the other front disc was hand-controlled. The flashing indicators and the left hand side gear pedal were standard equipment.

In the June and October of 1969 Guzzi set various world records in the 750 and 1000 cc classes with this *V7*-derived machine which was ridden by Bertarelli, Vittorio Brambilla, Mandracci, Alberto Pagani (Nello's son), Patrignani, Tenconi, Trabalzini and Venturi. Two engines had been prepared: one was a 739.3 cc unit (82 × 70 mm × 2) and the other 757.5 cc (83 × 70 mm × 2), in order to stay within the limits set for the two classes.
Power output was practically the same, 68 hp at 6500 rpm on a compression ratio of 9.6:1.

Dell'Orto SSI carburettors were fitted. The 4-speed gearbox was stock with a modified final drive ratio.
After several accessories were removed, the weight fell to 158 kgs, including the glassfibre fairing and the 29 litre light alloy tank. The most significant results obtained on the Monza speedbowl were 100 kms at an average of 218.426 km/h, the Hour at 217.040 km/h and the 1,000 kms at 205.932 km/h.

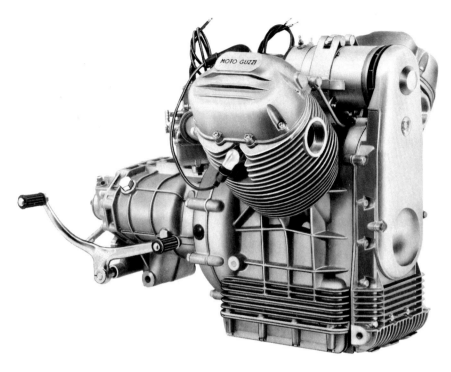

The 1971-1974 *V7 California 850*, specially prepared for the American market with a wealth of accessories. A number of these were also sold in Italy and in Europe. The first units (1971) had the 757 cc engine from the *V7 Special* with a 4-speed gearbox.

Model / year	V 850 GT / 1972-1974
Engine	4-stroke 90 degree V-twin 83 × 78 mm / 844 cc
Compression ratio	9.2:1
Output	51 hp at 6000 rpm
Cylinder head	light alloy with valve seat inserts
Cylinder	light alloy with chrome bores
Valve arrangement	inclined overhead
Valve gear	push rod and rocker arm
Ignition	coil
Carburettor	Dell'Orto VHB 29 CD, VHB 29 CS
Lubrication	geared pressure pump
Clutch	dry dual plate type
Gearbox	foot-change 5-speed constant-mesh
Transmission	primary, gears; final drive, shaft
Frame	tubular duplex cradle
Wheelbase	1470 mm
Front suspension	teledraulic fork
Rear suspension	swinging arm with teledraulic dampers
Wheels	cast light alloy with WM 3/2.15 × 18 rims
Tyres	4.00 - 18"
Brakes	expansion type:front, manual with 4 shoes; rear, pedal
Weight	253 kgs
Max speed	approx. 180 km/h
Normal consumption	(Cuna stds.) 6.5 litres per 100 kms
Fuel tank capacity	22.5 litres
Lubricant capacity	3 litres

The 1972-1974 *V 850 GT* with the *Special* frame, 844.05 cc engine and 5-speed gearbox. The gearbox had external ribbing like that of the *Sport*, but the bike still had a dynamo instead of an alternator. The model shown carries a *Sport*-type twin leading shoe front brake; the earliest models used the leading shoe unit from the *Special*.

On this page, top left, the *Eldorado* version, with front disc brake and, right, the *California* version, with single-dual seat of the type popularized by the great Harleys. Both these versions were intended principally for the US market. Below, the exploded drawing of the 844.05 cc engine with 5-speed gearbox and dual contact breakers, subsequently fitted to the *850 T* and the *850 T3*.

On the facing page, top left, the 1974 *850 T* with single disc front brake and rear drum brake. Right, the *850 T3* with the triple disc system. Both bikes had the 844.05 cc engine mounted on the *Sport*-type frame. The engine developed 59 hp at 6800 rpm and gave a top speed of 182 km/h. Below, the *California* version of the *850 T3* model, which differed from the basic model only as far as some trim details were concerned.

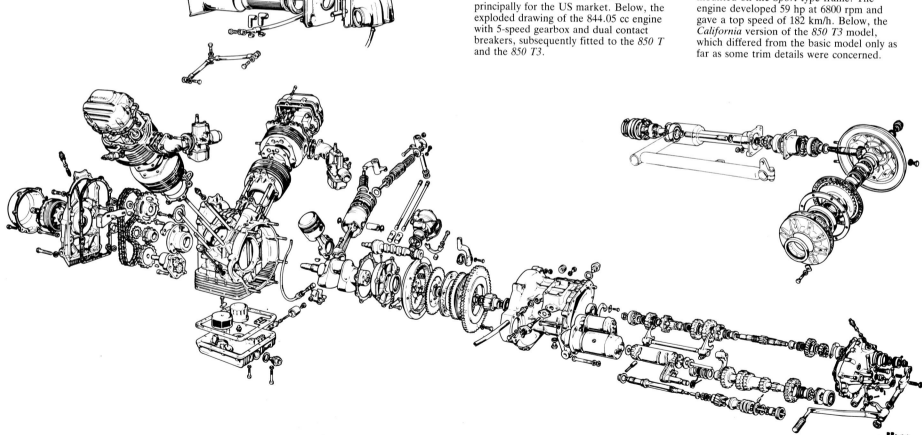

In 1975 the *850 T* spawned the *T3*, so called because of the Guzzi three-disc integral braking system; the following version, which appeared in 1980, had to be called the *T4*, even though there were still only three discs obviously. Number two is missing from this numerical series. Unlike its predecessor, the *T4* was fitted with a bikini fairing with a wide windscreen (previously mounted on the *1000 SP*), and cast light alloy wheels, which had in reality already been fitted to the last few units of the *T3*. The silencers were also slightly upswept. As far as the technical side is concerned, the *T4* had light alloy cylinder barrels with Nigusil coated bores (a Guzzi patented electrolytic process using nickel and silicon), 41 mm intake and 36 mm exhaust valves angled at 70 degrees to each other, Dell'Orto VHB 30 CD (and CS) carbs, coil ignition with two pairs of points, a five speed gearbox, and a 100/90H -18" tyre at the front with a 110/90H-18" tyre at the rear. The front brake calipers were shifted to a position behind the fork stanchions and a pressure equalizer was added. The factory claimed 68.5 hp at 7000 rpm; compression was 9.5:1 and speed approx. 190 km/h; weight was 215 kgs. The *T4* was supplied to various military clients and police authorities, as the previous *T* and *T3* had been, with some variants in the specification which depended on the end user's specific requirements (saddle, panniers, fairings, etc.).

In 1983 the *850 T4* was followed by the *850 T5*, which had been radically reviewed both mechanically and stylistically. There was a new mini fairing plus a new tank and saddle; the mudguards, side panels and grab rail were also modified. Other changes concerned the cylinder block and head finning, which was no longer rounded but angular like the units fitted to the smaller *V 35* and *V 50* models. The diameter of the wheels (now with five spokes) having been reduced, the tyres obviously needed to be changed: 110/90 H-16" at the front and 130/90 H-16" behind. The Guzzi air-assisted front fork was fitted with a pressure equalizer, while "compensated" air-assisted shocks were chosen for the rear. The retouched engine now ran more sweetly: output was claimed to be 67 hp at 7000 rpm, with 7.5 kgm of torque at 5800 rpm; weight was 220 kgs. Some minor details were again altered in early 1984, as can be seen from the photo below.

Still in the course of 1984, the *850 T5* underwent further development, aimed principally at improving stability and handling. The *Nuova 850 T5* had different fork measurements, while the designers went back to the 18" format for the back wheel. Tyres were therefore 110/90 H-16" (or V-16") in front and 120/90 H-18" (or V-18") at the back. The fairing was also new, still in a unit with the fork but with a taller windscreen. Performance and weight were unchanged: the tank held 26 litres and claimed consumption was 5.4 litres per 100 km (Cuna Regs). The *Nuova 850 T5* was produced until the first months of 1989 when it was replaced by a model with a bigger engine.

Technologically speaking, the 1975 *V 1000 I Convert* is considered by many to be the most prestigious Guzzi of all. The 948.8 cc (88 × 78 mm) engine was linked to a hydraulic torque converter (made by the German firm of Sachs), as well as a dry clutch and a two-speed semi-automatic gearbox. The cylinders had cast iron liners. This bike was intended especially for police patrol duties, but was also on general sale. It was discontinued in early 1985.

Model / year	V 1000 I Convert / 1975-1984
Engine	4-stroke 90 degree V-twin 88 × 78 mm / 948.8 cc
Compression ratio	9.2:1
Output	61 hp at 6500 rpm
Cylinder head	light alloy with valve seat inserts
Cylinder	light alloy with pressed-in liner
Valve arrangement	inclined overhead
Valve gear	push rod and rocker arm
Ignition	coil
Carburettor	Dell'Orto VHB 30 CD, VHB 30 CS
Lubrication	geared pressure pump
Clutch	dry multi-plate type
Gearbox	2-speed automatic hydraulic converter
Transmission	primary, helical gears; final drive, shaft
Frame	tubular duplex cradle
Wheelbase	1470 mm
Front suspension	teledraulic fork
Rear suspension	swinging arm with teledraulic dampers
Wheels	spoked with WM 3/2.15 × 18 rims
Tyres	4.10-18"
Brakes	discs: front, d/disc manual-pedal; rear pedal
Weight	261 kgs
Max speed	175.6 km/h
Normal consumption	(Cuna stds.) 6.3 litres per 100 kms
Fuel tank capacity	24 litres
Lubricant capacity	3.5 litres

The drive train of the *I Convert* model was fitted with a Sachs hydraulic torque converter. This device was an established regular in motor car drive trains, but virtually unknown in the motorcycle sector. The illustration shows an assembly which has been partially cut away for teaching purposes. All that can be seen in this bird's eye view of the engine is the block minus the cylinders.

239

"American style" trim is now a regular feature in the Guzzi catalogue which lists the *California* heavyweight as well as the *Florida* and *Custom* models. This is the 1982 *California* II, with a 950 cc engine and 5-speed manual gearbox. The engine had square finning, a larger sump and a more sophisticated system for the recirculation of the oil vapour, necessary in order to stay in line with US emission regulations. Standard trim included a windscreen, side panniers, buddy seat, chromed mudguards with a painted central strip, footboards and various other accessories. Colour schemes included white, black or Madera red. The engine ran on a 9.2:1 compression ratio and developed 65 hp at 6750 rpm; the valves, angled at 70 degrees to each other, were 41 mm intake and 36 exhaust. The engine was fed by two 30 mm Dell'Orto VHB carbs; the tank held 25 litres and ignition was by coil with a double set of points. The cast light alloy wheels were shod with 120/90 H-18" tyres at front and rear while weight was 250 kgs. Top speed was 180 km/h. Obviously it was on sale both on the home and the export markets.

The *California III* appeared in July 1987 fitted with a power unit which was more or less identical to that of the *California II* (850 cc and 65 hp at 6700 rpm). However the bodywork had been subjected to a major restyling operation with some parts (tank, saddle) looking very much like "chopper" components. Apart from the abovementioned details, which conspired to give the bike an even more "laid-back" riding position, the side panels were also altered while the drive train received a coat of black paint. The bike was available with spoked alloy wheels or the classic spoked wheels, which were better suited to this kind of machine. Tyres were still 100/90 V-18" in front and 120/90 V-18" behind. Naturally the 3-disc linked braking system was also fitted (300 mm discs in front with 270 mm at the rear) to the models with spoked wheels too. The *California III* weighed in at 250 kgs and top speed was about 190 km/h.

The *California III* was first introduced in the November of 1987 at the Milan Show. This version represented an ulterior development of the luxury touring style of this series, which was on a par with the best Japanese and German marques. The new specification featured a larger one-piece front fairing fixed to the frame (i.e. goodbye bikini fairing and windscreen which turned along with the handlebars) and a matching set of three rear-mounted panniers (photo above). But, and this was far more important, a version was also presented in which the traditional 30 mm carbs had been replaced by a Weber-Marelli indirect electronic ignition system managed by a computerized control module which decided the correct ignition timing on the basis of throttle status, revs, engine temperature and atmospheric temperature and pressure (photo below). The engine developed 67 hp, still at 6700 rpm. Top speed was about 175 km/h and the bike weighed 270 kgs. In 1989 available versions of the *California III* included: the *RL*, with light alloy wheels and no fairing; the *CIRR*, with spoked wheels and integral fairing; the *Iniezione*, with integral fairing and a choice of wheels.

242

For more traditionally-minded motorcyclists, Guzzi produced the *V 1000 G5* (at side) and the *1000 SP* (below); both were derived from the *V 1000 I Convert* and equipped with a traditional 5-speed manual gearbox. The power unit was identical to that of the *Convert*, and so were performance and other characteristics: bore and stroke were 88 × 78 × 2 mm, displacement 948.8 cc, compression 9.2:1, and the engine produced 64 hp at 6200 rpm. The carburettors were 30 mm Dell'Orto VHB 30 CD (CS) instruments, and the coil ignition system used two sets of points. The wheels were shod with 100/90 H-18" tyres in front and 110/90 H-18" behind; weight was 220 kgs and top speed 180 km/h. The integral braking system was made up of two 300 mm front discs with dual action Brembo calipers and a 242 mm rear disc, which was also fitted with a braking-force limiter so as to prevent the rear wheel from locking up.

In comparison with the *V 1000 G5*, the *1000 SP* had different trim and a different three-piece fairing which was the result of experimentation in the Mandello wind tunnel.

The mini fairing turned along with the steering. Other variations regarded the footrests (further aft on the *SP*), the panniers and the mudguards.

Until May 1983 there were two versions of the *1000 SP*: the first series (shown in the photo) and the second (the *NT 80*), which can be recognized by the gloss finish used for the frame and by the straight pipe instead of the previous slightly upswept version. The *V 1000 G5* and the *1000 SP* were presented at the Milan Show in the November of 1977 and went on sale the following year.

243

At the end of 1984 Guzzi brought out the *1000 SP II*, with a slightly modified engine which produced 67 hp at 6700 rpm, with max torque of 7.7 kgm coming in at 5200 rpm on a compression ratio of 9.2:1. The bodywork had also been modified, the bikini fairing (still connected to the handlebars) and the saddle in particular. However the most eyecatching alteration was the 16" front wheel; the tyre measurements were therefore 110/90 H-16" (or V-16") in front and 120/90 H-18" (or V-18") at the rear. Weight was 220 kgs, top speed approx. 200 km/h and consumption was 5.8 litres per 100 kms. The price was 12,559,400 lire.

The *1000 SP III* was presented in 1988 with a new look featuring a wide one-piece fairing fixed to the frame, and therefore without the mini fairing attached to the handlebars. The rear end had also been clad in new panelling; this model comes with side panniers as standard fitments. The saddle has also been restyled and its shape now emphasizes the vertical elevation of the rear chassis. Both wheels are once more 18 inchers, shod with 110/90 V-18" tyres in front and 120/90 V-18"s behind.
The bike weighs in at 230 kgs, and top speed is 195 km/h.

The *Mille GT*, which could be described as a more spartan version of the *1000 SP*, appeared in 1987: this is an essential, no-frills machine created for people who do not want to be coddled overmuch and who prefer the exhilaration of the wind in their hair. No fairing therefore and no windscreen, but by way of a reward there is plenty of lovely engineering on view to delight the eye. *RR*-type spoked wheels round off this "old-fashioned" look even though it is still possible to have light alloy *RL*-type wheels fitted as an optional extra. The engine is a 948.8 cc unit with two 30 mm Dell'Orto PHF carbs, coil ignition, Guzzi air-assisted forks with pressure equalizer, Koni rear dampers, and 100/90 H-18" and 120/90 H-18" tyres at front and rear respectively. Weight is 215 kgs and top speed about 200 km/h. Various colour schemes are available.

The *1000 S*, presented at the Milan Show in November 1989, is a faithful expression of Guzzi's current construction philosophy, which can be summed up in the expression "evolution within the tradition". The new bike is in fact the *730 S3* revisited. It has been fitted with a modern 948.8 cc engine and Sixties style tank and side panels; the paintwork is black and red and there is an abundance of chrome. Output is 82 hp at 6250 rpm and there are two 40 mm Dell'Ortos, coil ignition and a 5-speed gearbox. The spoked wheels are shod with 100/90 V-18" tyres at the front and 120/90 V-18s at the rear. Weight is 215 kgs and top speed is around 230 km/h.

Although it had the traditional two-valve V engine, the *Quota 1000*, an off-road bike also introduced at the 1989 Milan Show, is well outside the Guzzi design mainstream as far as the cycle parts are concerned: the frame is a duplex cradle (made of rectangular section steel spars with detachable bottom rails), which rides on Marzocchi teledraulic offset axle forks, and a variable section swinging arm with Marzocchi monoshocks. The 948.8 engine is fed by a 36 mm Weber twin carburettor and supplies 72 hp at 5200 rpm. There is also a Motoplat electronic ignition system and max torque is 7.9 kgm at 5200. Wheels are spoked with 90/90 - 21" tyres in front and 130/80 - 17" behind; there is a 300 mm floating disc brake at the front, and a 22 litre tank. Weight is 210 kgs and top speed about 200 km/h.

The *V 850 Le Mans* introduced in the November of 1975 at the Milan Motor Show was derived from the prototype which had appeared at the end of 1971. Robust and very fast, its performance could be improved even more with the aid of a competition kit supplied by the makers. The engine, a descendant of the previous *Sport* models, had cast iron cylinder liners and Dell'Orto carbs with an accelerator pump; the lubrication system included a cartridge filter previously used on the *850 T3*. Naturally the *Le Mans* was also fitted with the three-disc linked braking system.

Model / year	V 850 Le Mans / 1976-1978
Engine	4-stroke 90 degree V-twin 83 × 78 mm / 844 cc
Compression ratio	10.2:1
Output	71 hp at 7300 rpm
Cylinder head	light alloy with valve seat inserts
Cylinder	light alloy with pressed-in liner
Valve arrangement	inclined overhead
Valve gear	push rod and rocker arm
Ignition	coil
Carburettor	Dell'Orto PHF 36 BD, PHF 36 BS
Lubrication	geared pressure pump
Clutch	dry dual plate type
Gearbox	foot-change 5-speed constant-mesh
Transmission	primary, straight-cut gears; final drive, shaft
Frame	tubular duplex cradle
Wheelbase	1470 mm
Front suspension	teledraulic fork
Rear suspension	swinging arm with teledraulic dampers
Wheels	cast light alloy with WM 3/2.15 × 18 rims
Tyres	front, 3.50 - 18"; rear 4.00 - 18"
Brakes	discs: front, d/disc manual-pedal; rear pedal
Weight	215 kgs
Max speed	205 km/h
Normal consumption	(Cuna stds.) 9.7 litres per 100 kms
Fuel tank capacity	22.5 litres
Lubricant capacity	3.5 litres

Towards the end of 1978 Guzzi brought out the *Le Mans II*, which had an original fairing with a built-in spoiler at the front (see photo at top right). The braking system had been modified: a species of load divider was added while the front brake calipers had been shifted aft of the fork stanchions. Optionals included a gearbox with closer ratios and straight-cut gears. Tyres were 100/90 H-18" at the front and 110/90 H-18" at the back.

The Le *Mans III* appeared in 1981 with a much smaller fairing. The design of the cylinders — with Nigusil liners — and the heads resembled that of the *V 50* and *V 35* engines. It was the first Italian engine to be built according to American anti-emission regulations, which meant a slight drop in performance. It was still possible to have the straight-cut gears and there was also a choice of various bevel pairs for different ratios. Available colours: red-black, white-black, metallic grey-black.

A thoroughly renewed *Le Mans 1000* was introduced at the Cologne Show in the September of 1984 (photo above): the engine had been uprated to 948.8 cc (88 × 78 mm × 2), and output was 81 hp (at the crank) at 7000 rpm running on a 10:1 compression ratio. It also had two 40 mm Dell'Orto PHM carbs, a 16" front wheel and a slightly different front chassis therefore. This bike sported a new mini fairing and new side panels incorporating the rear mudguard while the sump was fitted with a bellypan. Other features included the Guzzi air-assisted forks with equalizer, Koni dampers at the rear, tubeless 120/80 V-16" tyres in front and 130/80 V-18s behind. The entire drive train was painted black (and not just the exhausts) while a two-tone white and red colour scheme was available for the body (photo below). January 1985 price: 8,280,000 lire.

In 1987 a new version of the *Le Mans 1000* was fitted out which differed from its predecessors in a few details: the front wheel was once more an 18 incher (and so the suspension had to be slightly revised) while a new front end had been fitted with a built-in fairing which meant the latter no longer moved along with the steering. The drive train was once more aluminium coloured (photo above). Performance and other characteristics were unchanged: 100/90 V-18" tubeless tyres in front and 120/90 V-18s behind. The bike received new red and black livery (which enhanced its extremely sporty looks) in time for the Milan Show in the November of 1987.

1000 Daytona

The *1000 Daytona* is a bike which has come a long way: it is derived from the specials which John Wittner, an American ex-dentist who has dedicated himself body and soul to motorbike racing, has been building for some years with brilliant results — read first place in the 1987 Ama Pro-Twin championship with rider Doug Brauneck. Convinced of its fine qualities, Guzzi management decided to produce a limited series of this bike which, from a technical and performance standpoint, represents the top of the current Mandello range.

The classic V-twin engine has been uprated to 992 cc and topped off with a 4-valve head and a single overhead camshaft driven by toothed belts. Fuel is metered by either a carburettor or a digital electronic injection system; there is an electronic ignition system and a 5-speed gearbox.

Other very interesting features include the ultra-light rectangular-section single spar frame (weight, 8.5 kgs) of which the engine forms a stress-member, and the rear suspension. An exceptional bike, it is intended for a restricted circle of enthusiasts, both for technical and financial reasons (understandably it is rather expensive).

Model / year	1000 Daytona/1990-...
Engine	4-stroke 90 degree V-twin 90 × 78 mm / 992 cc
Compression ratio	10:1
Output	92 hp at 7400 rpm (94 hp at 7500)
Cylinder head	light alloy with valve seat inserts
Cylinder	light alloy
Valve arrangement	inclined overhead, four per cylinder
Valve gear	raised camshafts
Ignition	double Motoplat system (Weber-Marelli digital)
Carburettor	twin Dell'Orto PHB 40 (Weber-Marelli digitial electronic injection)
Lubrication	geared pressure pump
Clutch	dry dual-plate type
Gearbox	foot-change 5-speed constant-mesh
Transmission	primary, gears; final drive, shaft
Frame	rectangular-section spar with engine semi-load bearing
Wheelbase	1440 mm
Front suspension	adjustable teledraulic Marzocchi fork
Rear suspension	rectangular s/arm with Marzocchi monoshocks
Wheels	cast light alloy
Tyres	front 120/70 ZR 17"; rear 160/60 ZR 18"
Brakes	discs: front, floating d/disc; rear, normal fixed unit
Weight	205 kgs
Max speed	245 km/h (250 km/h)
Normal consumption	(Cuna stds.) 5.6 litres/100 kms (5 litri/100 km)
Fuel tank capacity	22.5 litres
Lubricant capacity	4 litres

The *1000 Daytona* engine with belt-driven sohc timing gear; the four valves are actuated by rocker arms and ultra-short push rods.

The *1000 Daytona*, the fastest bike in the Guzzi catalogue. It looks like a typical racer: the fairing, the fruit of painstaking wind tunnel research, favours high speed performance without making the bike unsuitable for ordinary road use. The entire body, tank included, may be rapidly dismantled for easy access to the mechanical members. Note the handsome light alloy wheels, the powerful disc brake assembly with the Brembo calipers, and the upswept exhausts. Given the particular use for which this bike is intended it was not thought necessary to fit the linked braking system. The filler cap is the rapid-action type, for high pressure refuelling. Light alloy was used for the pedal controls.

Stripped of its fairing, the *1000 Daytona* shows off its its powerfully compact muscles. The tubular frame is rounded off by big cast light alloy plates which support the rectangular section swinging arm. The latter acts (through a triangulated tubular structure) on the Marzocchi mono-arm shock absorber mounted under the saddle. The drive shaft rotates in full view. The engine forms a stress-member within the lower part of the structure. This is the version with indirect injection. As well as the inlet tubes and the complex of air filters, the camshaft housing on the cylinder head can also be seen. In effect, the valve gear is not exactly a sohc layout, in that the valves are controlled by rockers and very short push-rods: a better definition would therefore be "raised cam valve gear".

Nuovo Falcone

The *Nuovo Falcone*, initially designed for the Army and the Police, was later sold to the general public as soon it was realized that lots of people were still interested in big singles along the lines of the classic Guzzi design. Seen for the first time at the end of 1969, the civilian version real and proper went on sale in 1971 priced at 612,000 lire, characterized by sleeker lines and dynamotor electric starter.

Compared to the old *Falcone* (1950-1967), it boasted several innovations both as far as the engine room (the wet sump for example), and the cycle parts were concerned. But its military ori-

gins were still evident, in terms of weight and performance. Despite its many modern features the *Nuovo Falcone* was unable to do better than its predecessors in either manoeuverability or acceleration.

A new version, known as the *Sahara*, first saw the light in 1974. Its designers saw it as a touring bike suitable for particularly difficult routes. In practice it was no more than the military version with side panniers, a blued exhaust and sand-coloured finish. Production, which never reached satisfactory volumes, ceased in 1976.

Model / year	Nuovo Falcone / 1971-76
Engine	4-stroke flat single 88 × 82 mm / 498.4 cc
Compression ratio	6.8:1
Output	26.2 hp at 4800 rpm
Cylinder head	light alloy with valve seat inserts
Cylinder	light alloy with pressed-in liners
Valve arrangement	inclined overhead
Valve gear	push rod and rocker arm
Ignition	coil
Carburettor	Dell'Orto VHB 29 A
Lubrication	wet sump and gear-type pressure pump
Clutch	wet multiplate type
Gearbox	foot-change 4-speed constant mesh
Transmission	primary, helical gear; final drive, chain
Frame	tubular duplex cradle
Wheelbase	1450 mm
Front suspension	teledraulic forks
Rear suspension	swinging arm with teledraulic dampers
Wheels	spoked with 18 x 3.50 rims
Tyres	3.50-18"R
Brakes	expansion type: front manual (twin cams), rear pedal
Weight	214 kgs
Max speed	127 km/h
Normal consumption	(Cuna stds.) 4.1 litres per 100 kms
Fuel tank capacity	18 litres
Lubricant capacity	3 litres

The civilian *Nuovo Falcone*, painted red with white tank and side panels.

The *Sahara* model, on sale from 1974 onwards, with a sandy beige finish.

As from 1974 the *Nuovo Falcone* was sold with chromed mudguards and various colour schemes.

250 TS

One of the first bikes produced during the "De Tomaso era" was the *250 TS*. This was a 2-stroke twin with a 5-speed gearbox directly derived from a similar Benelli model and produced in order to give Guzzi an immediate foothold in the middleweight segment. The most important difference with regard to the Benelli version lay in the light alloy barrel castings with the bores in chrome rather than cast iron, which made for a considerable increase in output in exchange for a handy weight loss. The *250 TS* — which represented a major turning point in Guzzi styling and technology — was launched in the Spring of 1973 and put on sale the following year, enriched by a new electronic capacitor-discharge ignition system with the generator mounted on the left of the drive shaft.

In 1975, the twin leading shoe front drum brake was replaced by a hydraulic disc brake, which was more in line with recent technological developments. Given the bike's decidedly sporting characteristics and in an attempt to avoid excess weight and complexity, it was decided not to fit an electric starter. The *TS* was sold with a black frame, chromed mudguards and metallic finish tank in various colours.

Model / year	250 TS / 1974-1975
Engine	2-stroke twin 56 × 47 mm / 231.4 cc
Compression ratio	9.7:1
Output	24.5 hp at 7570 rpm
Cylinder head	light alloy
Cylinder	light alloy with chrome bore
Valve arrangement	—
Valve gear	—
Ignition	electronic with flywheel magneto
Carburettor	Dell'Orto VHB 25 BD, VHB 25 BS
Lubrication	25:1 mixture
Clutch	wet multiplate type
Gearbox	foot-change 5-speed constant-mesh
Transmission	geared primary; final drive, chain
Frame	tubular duplex cradle
Wheelbase	1330 mm
Front suspension	teledraulic forks
Rear suspension	swinging arm with teledraulic dampers
Wheels	spoked: front, WM 2/1.85 × 18; rear, 3/2.15 × 18
Tyres	front 3.00-18"; rear 3.25-18"
Brakes	expansion type; front manual (4 shoes); rear, pedal
Weight	137 kg
Max speed	131 km/h
Normal consumption	(Cuna stds.) 7 litres per 100 km
Fuel tank capacity	17 litres 2-stroke mix
Lubricant capacity	—

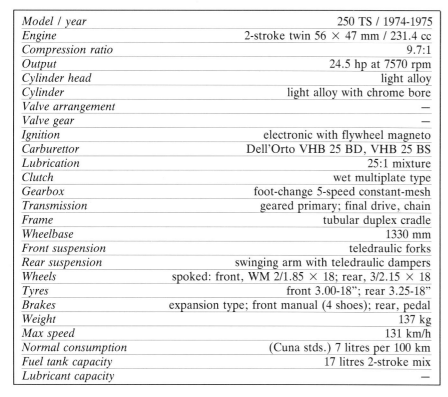

At side, the original *250 TS* twin with twin leading shoe front drum brake. Below, the 1975 model, with a disc brake at the front and the drum at the back. Among other innovations brought in with the new series, there was also electronic ignition. The previous page shows the engine (note the separate cylinder heads), in light alloy with chrome-plated bores. Unlike the Benelli fitted with the same engine, the Guzzi twin had a bigger 25 mm carburettor.

125 Tuttoterreno and 125 Turismo

The *125* lightweight with the 2-stroke engine and 5-speed gear-box first sold in 1975 is another product of the Benelli-Guzzi association, which began when the two firms were incorporated under the leadership of Alessandro De Tomaso. In this case too the power unit was of Benelli origin and derived from earlier small-engined models, while the styling looks like a product of what might be described as the Nippo-Italian design school. At first, the *Tuttoterreno* (All-terrain) version, basically built for off-road touring rather then competition moto-cross, but still useful enough to give learners a taste of the real thing, was for export only; then the *Turismo* version was brought out in 1975. This was intended for normal road use and had slightly different styling from the *Tuttoterreno* (saddle and tank, for example), as well as different transmission ratios and a hydraulic disc brake at the front.

It was a bike aimed at the utility clientele as well as at youngsters impatient for promotion from the moped class who wanted a quick sprinter without having to break the bank: all characteristics which had been rendered obligatory by the fierce competition in Italy and the Common Market countries.

Model / year	Tuttoterreno / 1974-1981
Engine	2-stroke single 56 × 49 mm / 120.6 cc
Compression ratio	9.9:1
Output	11.5 hp at 6700 rpm
Cylinder head	light alloy
Cylinder	light alloy with pressed-in liner
Valve arrangement	—
Valve gear	—
Ignition	flywheel magneto alternator
Carburettor	Dell'Orto VHB 22 BS
Lubrication	20:1 mixture
Clutch	wet multiplate type
Gearbox	foot-change 5-speed constant-mesh
Transmission	geared primary; final drive, chain
Frame	tubular duplex cradle
Wheelbase	1300 mm
Front suspension	teledraulic forks
Rear suspension	swinging arm with teledraulic dampers
Wheels	spoked: front, 21 × 2; rear, 18 × 2 1/2
Tyres	front 2.50- 21"; rear 3.50 -18"
Brakes	expansion type; front manual; rear, pedal
Weight	105 kg
Max speed	83.7 km/h
Normal consumption	(Cuna stds.) 7.4 litres per 100 km
Fuel tank capacity	8.5 litres
Lubricant capacity	—

A profile shot of the *Tuttoterreno* lightweight with the Benelli-derived engine. Although the bike was not intended to be a competition iron, it was still well equipped: hydraulic steering damper, adjustable rear suspension, plastic mudguards etc.
The brakes were drums.

The *Turismo 125* lightweight. Frame and engine were identical to those of the *Tuttoterreno*; but differences included the gear ratios, bodywork, the non-knobbly 2.50 - 18" tyre at the front and the 2.75-18" incher at the rear, the exhaust pipe, the front disc brake and some other details.

350 GTS and 400 GTS

The series of 4-cylinder engines dates from 1973 and originally included a 350 model sold under the Guzzi name plus a 500 sold as a Benelli. Later, the Guzzi range was enlarged with the addition of a slightly faster 400 version. Conceived and created in a very short time, these engines ended up by resembling the Japanese machinery they had set out to challenge, even though there were a goodly number of differences — especially as far as the Guzzis were concerned. The *400 GTS* (1975) came with an (optional) front disc brake, which was also offered as an optional for the *350*.

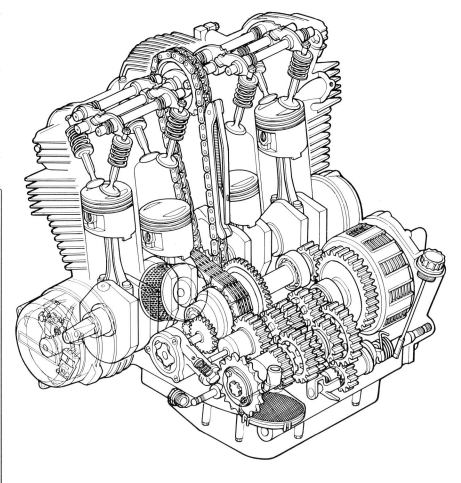

Model / year	350 GTS / 1974-1975
Engine	4-stroke 4-cylinder 50 × 44 mm / 345.5 cc
Compression ratio	10.2:1
Output	31 hp at 9200 rpm
Cylinder head	light alloy with valve seat inserts
Cylinder	light alloy with pressed-in liners
Valve arrangement	inclined overhead
Valve gear	overhead camshaft
Ignition	coil
Carburettor	Dell'Orto VHB 20 D
Lubrication	trochoid gear pump
Clutch	wet multiplate type
Gearbox	foot-change 5-speed constant-mesh
Transmission	primary, chain and gear ; final drive, chain
Frame	tubular duplex cradle
Wheelbase	1370 mm
Front suspension	teledraulic forks
Rear suspension	swinging arm with teledraulic dampers
Wheels	spoked: front WM 2/1.85 × 18; rear WM 3/2.15 × 18
Tyres	front 3.00-18"; rear 3.50-18"
Brakes	expansion type: front, manual (4 shoes); rear, pedal
Weight	198 kg
Max speed	150 km/h
Normal consumption	(Cuna stds.) 7.4 litres per 100 kms
Fuel tank capacity	17 litres
Lubricant capacity	3 litres

A very clear explanatory drawing of the engine architecture of the *350-400 GTS* series sohc 4-cylinder engine. Despite the fact that it was inspired by Japanese technology, especially in the transmission department, this engine possesses some unusual characteristics, like the undersquare bore and stroke measurements. The coil ignition system had two sets of points and an electric starter.

The 1975 version of the *350 GTS* had a 300 mm front disc with a dual action hydraulic caliper. The original fitting was a drum brake with twin leading shoes and two 180 mm cams.

The *400 GTS*, presented in 1975 with a front disc brake, was effectively identical to the *350 GTS*; of which it was a more powerful version. Its characteristics were: bore and stroke 50 × 50.6 mm (397.2 cc), compression ratio 10.2:1, max power 40 hp at 9000 rpm, torque 3.7 kgm at 8000 rpm, weight 175 kgs and top speed 170 km/h.

Cross 50 and Nibbio

At the 1973 Milan Motorcycle Show, Guzzi introduced two new lightweights whose capacity and performance made them mopeds in a technical sense, but which were light motorcycles in all other respects.

These were the *Cross 50* and the *Nibbio*, both equipped with the 2-stroke engine / 5-speed gearbox drive train which Benelli had been building for some time by then.

As the name suggests, the *Cross 50* was an off-road bike with goodish performance despite the laws governing mopeds in those days, while the *Nibbio* was designed for normal street use. The styling of various details was distinctive; for example the *Cross* exhaust and the tank on the *Nibbio* both resembled the designs used for the *Tuttoterreno* and *Turismo* lightweights. Levels of finish were very high given the size of the engines. Like all Guzzi production bikes the frame was painted black while various colour schemes were available: the days of "any colour will do as long as it's Guzzi racing red" were long gone by that time! The *Cross* received a facelift in 1976 which included an upswept exhaust, new air filter, mudguards, tank, as well as different side panels, etc.

Model / year	50 Cross / 1974-1982
Engine	2-stroke single 40 × 39 mm / 49 cc
Compression ratio	8:1
Output	1.1 hp at 3750 rpm
Cylinder head	light alloy
Cylinder	light alloy with chrome bore
Valve arrangement	—
Valve gear	—
Ignition	flywheel magneto alternator
Carburettor	Dell'Orto SHA 14.12
Lubrication	20:1 mixture
Clutch	wet multiplate type
Gearbox	foot-change 5-speed constant-mesh
Transmission	geared primary; final drive, chain
Frame	tubular duplex cradle
Wheelbase	1210 mm
Front suspension	teledraulic forks
Rear suspension	swinging arm with teledraulic dampers
Wheels	spoked: front, WH 1/1.6 × 19; rear WH 1/1.6 × 17
Tyres	front 2.50-19"; rear 3.00-17"
Brakes	expansion type; front manual; rear, pedal
Weight	81 kg
Max speed	34.5 km/h
Normal consumption	(Cuna stds.) 2.9 litres per 100 km
Fuel tank capacity	9.5 litres
Lubricant capacity	—

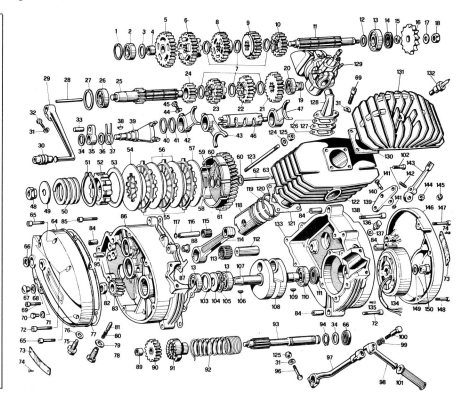

The *Cross 50* was introduced at the end of 1973. Note the characteristic double rear wheel sprocket which made it possible to select one ratio for the road and a closer ratio for off-road work. In 1976 the body, the exhaust (now bent up over the cylinder head), the frame, etc., were all altered. The wheels fitted to the last series were 2.50 × 21" (front) and 3.00 × 18" (rear).

Apart from some trim details like the tank, saddle and side panels, the *Nibbio* differed from the *Cross 50* for its chromed mudguards, the exhaust, the (non-knobbly) 2.50 - 18" tyres and the larger diameter front brake. The double rear wheel sprocket had also disappeared. Weight was 77 kgs and performance was identical, given the legal restrictions which forbade vehicles without registration plates to exceed 40 km/h.

Chiù

The *Chiù* also made its first appearance at the Milan Motorcycle Show in November 1973, and it may be considered the direct heir to the last versions of the *Trotter*, with which it had features in common, especially the pressed steel frame with the built-in fuel tank.

The rear end was virtually unchanged while the front had mechanical telescopic forks (without the hydraulic dampers) instead of the pressed steel leading link forks used for the *Trotter*: this made little difference to comfort, but was more modern as far as styling went.

The engine had been fairly thoroughly redesigned on the other hand, even though the cylinder remained horizontal. The transmission was a single-speed box with an automatic centrifugal friction clutch, which made this bike very easy to drive.

There were two chains, both on the left, for the engine and for the pedals.

The front "grocery basket", so useful for carrying lightweight articles around town, was a stock fitting. Various colour schemes were on offer. The bike originally cost 120,000 lire but this price had risen to 245,000 lire by early 1976.

Model / year	50 Chiù / 1974-1976
Engine	2-stroke flat single 40 × 39 mm / 49 cc
Compression ratio	8.5:1
Output	1.5 hp at 4400 rpm
Cylinder head	light alloy
Cylinder	cast iron
Valve arrangement	—
Valve gear	—
Ignition	flywheel magneto alternator
Carburettor	Dell'Orto SHA 14.9
Lubrication	20:1 mixture
Clutch	wet automatic type
Gearbox	single-speed
Transmission	geared primary; final drive, chain
Frame	sheet metal single spar
Wheelbase	1130 mm
Front suspension	telescopic forks
Rear suspension	swinging arm
Wheels	spoked with WM 0/1.5 × 16 rims
Tyres	2.25-16"
Brakes	expansion type; front and rear manual
Weight	48 kg
Max speed	38.4 km/h
Normal consumption	(Cuna stds.) 1.5 litres per 100 km
Fuel tank capacity	3.3 litres
Lubricant capacity	—

The *Chiù*, an automatic single-speed moped built from 1974 to 1976, had a pressed steel frame which was very like the last version of the *Trotter*.

Magnum

A recurring vogue in the motorcycle industry, following the precedent created by the scooters used by the allied forces paratroops, is the fashion for small vehicles which can be folded up and stowed away in any small space; a car boot, for example. This is a trend which has never quite taken off however, because the practical difficulties have always outweighed the advantages. By way of compensation, the idea of the mini-bike itself has enjoyed a certain success.

Today's mini is no longer collapsible, but is tiny instead, with small wheels and generally rather idiosyncratic lines; an unor-

thodox fun bike rather than a utility machine. Guzzi's offering in this sector was the *Magnum*, also constructed in association with Benelli. It was characterized by a fat banana-shaped tubular frame which doubled as a fuel tank and a two-stroke engine linked to a good five gears. Also typical were the spoked cast light alloy wheels shod with balloon tyres. The *Magnum* was supplied in various shades of metallic finish while the drive train was painted black; a fact which, apart from improving cooling, gave the bike the look of a pro sport iron, according to the colour codes then in fashion.

Model / year	Magnum / 1976-1979
Engine	2-stroke inclined single 40 × 39 mm / 49 cc
Compression ratio	8.2:1
Output	1.2 hp at 5400 rpm
Cylinder head	light alloy
Cylinder	light alloy with chrome bore
Valve arrangement	—
Valve gear	—
Ignition	flywheel magneto alternator
Carburettor	Dell'Orto SHA 14.9
Lubrication	20:1 mixture
Clutch	wet multiplate type
Gearbox	foot-change 5-speed constant mesh
Transmission	geared primary; final drive, chain
Frame	tubular single spar
Wheelbase	1040 mm
Front suspension	telescopic forks
Rear suspension	swinging arm with teledraulic dampers
Wheels	spoked with 10 × 2.10 rims
Tyres	4.00-10"
Brakes	expansion type; front and rear manual
Weight	58 kg
Max speed	39.6 km/h
Normal consumption	(Cuna stds.) 2.2 litres per 100 km
Fuel tank capacity	3 litres 2-stroke
Lubricant capacity	—

The *Magnum* was a typical minibike which enjoyed a certain popularity with the young and fancy free.

254

Along with its badge-engineered Benelli "stablemate", the *254* was a surprise exhibit at the Milan Motorcycle Show of November 1975, where it aroused a good degree of excitement not only for its bold mechanics but also for its well assembled and stylish fitments.

In point of fact this was the first time a 4-cylinder layout had been proposed for commercial production of an engine of less than 250 cc (it was 231 cc to be exact), even though there had been plenty of 125 twins.

The state of the art sohc engine with four carbs, electric starter and 5-speed gearbox was clad in a decidedly modern "body". One noteworthy feature was the instrument console set above the petrol tank; the location was sheltered from the elements but not ideal as far as instrument visibility was concerned.

The simple tubular cradle frame had been designed for lightness and resistance to flexing and torsional stress. The cast alloy wheels had six double spokes.

After a long proving period, the bike was launched in the Spring of 1977. The frame was painted black and the bodywork bright red.

Model / year	254 / 1977-1981
Engine	4-stroke 4-in-line 44 × 38 mm / 231.1 cc
Compression ratio	11.5:1
Output	27.8 hp at 10,500 rpm
Cylinder head	light alloy with valve seat inserts
Cylinder	light alloy
Valve arrangement	overhead inclined
Valve gear	ohc
Ignition	coil-battery
Carburettor	four Dell'Orto PHBG 18 B
Lubrication	lobe pump
Clutch	wet multiplate type
Gearbox	foot-change 5-speed constant-mesh
Transmission	primary, gears and chain; final drive, chain
Frame	open tubular cradle
Wheelbase	1270 mm
Front suspension	teledraulic forks
Rear suspension	swinging arm with teledraulic dampers
Wheels	cast light alloy: front, WM 1/1.6-18 R; rear, WM 2/1.85-18
Tyres	front 2.75-18" R; rear 3.00-18" R
Brakes	front disc (manual); expansion type at rear (pedal)
Weight	126 kg
Max speed	138 km/h
Normal consumption	(Cuna stds.) 7 litres per 100 km
Fuel tank capacity	10 litres
Lubricant capacity	2.2 litres

The *254* was unusual, both in terms of trim and construction techniques: the bike was clad with a normal frame and tank, before being fitted with a body made of a thermoplastic material whose component parts snap-locked together and unsnapped just as easily thus permitting easy access to the "guts" of the machine. The capacity of the fuel tank, which had never been great, was further reduced by the instrument panel. The location of the latter had caused some problems as it was impossible to read the instruments and keep one's eyes on the road at the same time. A badge-engineered version of the same bike was marketed as the Benelli *Quattro* when the two marques were merged.

125 2C 4T

After having introduced the *254*, a unique, avant-garde machine with a single overhead camshaft 4-cylinder engine of a mere 231 cc and highly original lines, Guzzi thought that "halving" the engine would enable them to produce a 125 twin able to fill a gap existing at that time (in the Italian market anyway) at the top end of the 1/8 litre market.

All the cycle parts — frame, wheels and suspension — and the bodywork were taken from the *254*, as were most of the mechanical members.

The result was an unusual lightweight, with an electric starter and a very high-revving engine (which could be pushed up to 11,000 rpm with impunity) and a rather sharp power curve, all of which demanded a decidedly sporty riding style accompanied by heavy use of the 5-speed gearbox. The bike was sitted with an electric starter.

Like the *254*, the tank itself (in plastic) was hidden by the bodywork, but the instrument console was mounted in the traditional place above the steering head.

The *125 2C 4T*, introduced at the 1979 Milan Show, was painted in metallic silver with dark and light blue flashes.

Model / year	125 2C 4T / 1979-1981
Engine	4-stroke twin 45.5 × 38 mm / 123.57 cc
Compression ratio	10.65:1
Output	16 hp at 10,600 rpm
Cylinder head	light alloy with valve seat inserts
Cylinder	light alloy monobloc with pressed-in cast iron liners
Valve arrangement	inclined overhead
Valve gear	overhead camshaft
Ignition	coil
Carburettor	two Dell'Orto PHBG 20 B
Lubrication	lobe pump
Clutch	wet multiplate type
Gearbox	foot-change 5-speed
Transmission	primary, mixed ; final drive, chain
Frame	open tubular cradle
Wheelbase	1290 mm
Front suspension	teledraulic forks
Rear suspension	swinging arm with teledraulic dampers
Wheels	cast light alloy: front WM 1/1.60 × 18; rear WM 2/1.85 × 18
2/1.85 x 18 Tyres	front 2.75 × 18" R; rear 3.00 × 18" R
Brakes	front, disc; rear, expansion
Weight	110 kg
Max speed	130 km/h
Normal consumption	(Cuna stds.) 3.3 litres per 100 kms
Fuel tank capacity	8.5 litres
Lubricant capacity	2.2 litres

The *125 2C 4T* had an open cradle frame; the fork was a Guzzi unit with 125 mm of travel while the Sebac rear dampers had a total travel of 70 mm and three-way adjustment.
The front disc brake was a 260 mm fitting with Brembo calipers.
The photo of the engine, on the preceding page, highlights the clean, compact lines of the power unit; note the location of the cartridge-type oil filter, the filler cap and the sump.
Valves were 22.5 mm inlet and 18 mm exhaust. By way of comparison, we should point out that the famous *Otto cilindri*, with the same bore, had 23 and 21 mm valves respectively, as well as 20 mm carburettors.

V 50

The "small" V engines designed by Lino Tonti, the 350 and 500 versions of which were presented for the first time in the Autumn of 1976, represent the fruits of Guzzi's more recent creative efforts. Although they were inspired by Carcano's V engines, they had been completely redesigned with a view to reducing dimensions and costs alike, so that they could be produced on a large scale in fully automated plants. The engines were then mounted in duplex cradles of which they formed an integral (and therefore partially load bearing) part: for example, the rear fork, one of whose arms was used to house the drive shaft, pivoted directly on the gearbox casing. The first bikes in this series were the 500 cc *V 50* and the 350 cc *V 35*; both were well finished machines with compact lines and both had the three-disc linked braking system. The frame was black while various bright colour schemes were available. In the first series the hydraulic pump for the front brake was housed in a very sheltered position under the tank.

Subsequently the engine was uprated to 650 and then to 750 cc, thus resulting in lighter, more compact bikes which easily outperformed the primitive *V7*.

Model / year	V 50 / 1977-1980
Engine	4-stroke 90 degree V-twin 74 × 57 mm / 490 cc
Compression ratio	10.8:1
Output	45 hp at 7500 rpm
Cylinder head	light alloy with valve seat inserts
Cylinder	light alloy with chrome bore
Valve arrangement	parallel overhead
Valve gear	push rod and rocker arm
Ignition	electronic coil
Carburettor	Dell'Orto VHB 24 FD, VHB 24 FS
Lubrication	lobe pump
Clutch	dry single plate
Gearbox	foot-change 5-speed constant-mesh
Transmission	primary, helical gears; final drive, shaft
Frame	tubular duplex cradle
Wheelbase	1410 mm
Front suspension	teledraulic fork
Rear suspension	swinging arm with teledraulic dampers
Wheels cast light alloy: front WM 3/1.85 × 18 CP2; rear WM 3/2.15 × 18 CP2	
Tyres	front, 3.00 S-18"; rear 3.50 S-18"
Brakes	discs: front, d/disc manual-pedal; rear pedal
Weight	152 kgs
Max speed	165 km/h
Normal consumption	(Cuna stds.) 4 litres per 100 kms
Fuel tank capacity	16.5 litres
Lubricant capacity	2.2 litres

The drive train of the *V 50*, with the 2-cylinder push-rod engine and Heron heads, dry single-plate clutch, 5-speed gearbox, electronic coil ignition and electric starter. Note the large intake filter and the rear swinging arm which pivoted on the gearbox casing. The *V 50* was a highly individual, modern bike with detachable lower frame tubes for easy engine removal. The rear swinging fork, whose right arm housed the cardan shaft, was in cast light alloy, as were the spoked wheels. The brakes were controlled by the Guzzi linked braking system.

The *V 50*, introduced in 1977, was followed by two successive versions, both updated and improved obviously: the *V 50 II* (1979), and the *V 50 III* (1981), which is shown above. The *V 50 II* was fitted with innovational cylinder liners in Nikasil (a nickel-silicon coating patented by Mahle); and in the course of production the electronic ignition was abandoned in favour of a traditional points system. The sump was also enlarged. On the *V 50 III* the cylinder liners were coated with Nigusil (a Guzzi-patented nickel-silicon treatment): the valves were 34 mm inlet and 30 exhaust; the valve-gear was driven by a double chain. Air-assisted hydropneumatic dampers were added to the suspension system. Tyres were 3.00-S-18" in front and 100/90 S-18" behind.

At the end of 1981 the *V 50* — along with the *V 35* — was restyled to look like the American-style "choppers" which had been made famous by the film *Easy Rider*: eyecatching and provocative, these bikes were decidedly anti-conformist even as far as the extremely heterodox riding position was concerned. In a few words, the styling was calculated to appeal to all those unconventional souls who were rich enough to parade their "rejection of contemporary social values". Naturally the various Custom models on offer — not only the Italian models — avoided the excesses frequently produced by American home-brew enthusiasts while the riding position was much more relaxed than usual and therefore suitable for long distance cruising. The major manufacturers limited themselves to adopting just a few ingredients of the recipe, like the ape hanger handlebars, the stepped saddle and the fat rear wheel. And so, with no changes having been made to either frame or engine, the Guzzi *Custom* models received 100/90 H-18" tyres in front and 130/90 H-16" tyres behind, a large 15 litre petrol tank, upswept pipes and other modifications which can easily be seen in the photos. The front end is the same as that of the *V 65* — which we shall be looking at on the following pages — while the rear swinging arm was lengthened by 40 mm. The wheelbase was increased to 1,460 m as a result. Speed was slightly less than the standard model: about 155 km/h.

The improvements made to the *V 50 III* were then transferred to the *Custom* version (1984), which enjoyed slightly uprated performance as a result: 47 hp at 7500 rpm and 165 km/h. The carbs were 28 mm PHBH-type Dell'Ortos. There were few styling changes on the other hand, the most notable of these being the two-tier saddle with the passenger backrest — all very American. This version also had a small rear luggage carrier.

In the November of 1981 Guzzi presented this *V 50 TS* or *Tuttostrada* at the Milan Show; this was a machine aimed at the new dirt bike market which was emerging at the time. This market segment was occupied by bikes which were just as much at home on the street or the dirt track, even though they were obviously not intended to be competition machines. The engine was taken from the *V 50 III*, while modifications were made to both frame and suspension with this new role in mind: note for example the offset axle front fork. But this bike never got beyond the prototype stage, Guzzi having opted to develop other capacity classes, as we shall see, for this kind of machine.

V 50 Monza

As was the case with many other models, even the "small" V-engined bikes were to spawn sporty variants, all aimed at that section of the clientele which was particularly interested in performance. Introduced at the 1980 Monza Motor Show and named *Monza* after the famous autodrome, the sporty *V 50* had a distinctive bikini fairing with built-in rectangular headlight and indicators. Another typical feature was the saddle with its streamlined tail.

The improvement in performance was obtained by modifying the pistons, the valves and the size of the carburettors; the timing chain was reinforced and nigusil-lined cylinder barrels were fitted. The front forks were hydropneumatic: the action of the metal springs was air-assisted, while the damping effect was provided by the usual hydraulic system.

When this spanking new sportster was introduced, production of the *V 35* and *V 50* engines began at the Innocenti works in Milan — which has been a part of the De Tomaso group for some time now — with notable advantages accruing in terms of production volumes and cost effectiveness, thanks to the highly automated Innocenti production lines.

Model / year	V 50 Monza / 1980-1984
Engine	4-stroke 90 degree V-twin 74 × 57 mm / 490 cc
Compression ratio	10.43:1
Output	45 hp at 7600 rpm
Cylinder head	light alloy with valve seat inserts
Cylinder	2 light alloy barrels with chromed liners
Valve arrangement	parallel overhead
Valve gear	push rod and rocker arm
Ignition	coil
Carburettor	Dell'Orto PHBH 28 DB, PHBH 28 BS
Lubrication	lobe pump
Clutch	dry single plate
Gearbox	foot-change 5-speed
Transmission	primary, helical gears; final drive, shaft
Frame	removable tubular cradle
Wheelbase	1420 mm
Front suspension	hydropneumatic fork
Rear suspension	swinging arm with hydropneumatic dampers
Wheels	cast light alloy: front WM 2/1.85 × 18; rear WM 3/2.15 × 18
Tyres	front, 3.25-S 18" or 90/90 S-18"; rear 3.50 S-18" or 100/90 S-18"
Brakes	discs: front, d/disc manual-pedal; rear pedal
Weight	60 kgs
Max speed	175 km/h
Normal consumption	5.06 litres per 100 kms
Fuel tank capacity	16 litres
Lubricant capacity	2.5 litres

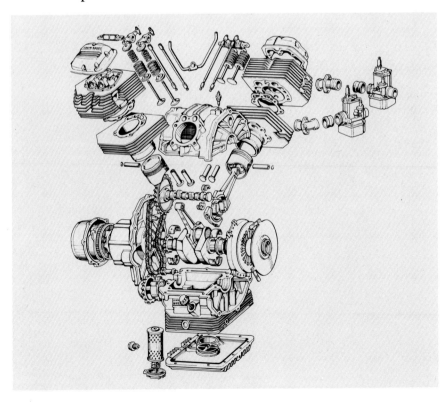

The engine of the *V 50 III* was modified along the lines suggested by the changes made to the *V 50 Monza* beforehand: valves were 34 mm inlet and 30 mm exhaust and the compression ratio was 10.4:1. The more streamlined shape of the bike and the bikini fairing made it possible to lengthen the gear ratios a little, by working on both the primary drive and the secondary bevel pair. The result was a touch more speed. The linked braking system used 260 mm discs in front and a 235 mm fitting at the rear. The more markedly oblique upward slant of the silencers made it possible to lay the bike farther over when cornering. As well as a classic Guzzi red colour scheme, the bike also came in metallic grey and blue finish.

V 35

Right from the outset the new *V* series had been based on the 350 and 500 cc format but at first all the attention was drawn to the bigger version.

But then changes in Italian tax legislation made the 350 version a much more interesting proposition as far as the home market was concerned and the development of the *V 35* was speeded up as a direct consequence.

Structurally it was very like the *V 50* both in the drive train (cylinders in a transverse V with push rods and rocker arms, five-speed box, drive shaft running inside the light alloy rear swinging arm) and the chassis (cradle and crankcase in an integral unit). The differences lay in the bodywork and the finishing, as well as the lesser performance of course. The *V 35* was fitted with the three-disc linked braking system, which was carried on spoked light alloy wheels.

Production of the *350* began in 1977, after the indispensable preparatory work on the test-bench. The frame was painted black, with various colour options. The *V 35* marks the return to grand touring standards for an capacity class which had been neglected in Italy for a long time.

Model / year	V 35 / 1977-1979
Engine	4-stroke 90 degree V-twin 66 × 50.6 mm / 346.2 cc
Compression ratio	10.8:1
Output	33.6 hp at 8100 rpm
Cylinder head	light alloy with valve seat inserts
Cylinder	light alloy with chrome bore
Valve arrangement	parallel overhead
Valve gear	push rod and rocker arm
Ignition	electronic
Carburettor	Dell'Orto VHB 24 FD, VHB 24 FS
Lubrication	lobe pump
Clutch	dry single plate
Gearbox	foot-change 5-speed constant-mesh
Transmission	primary, gears; final drive, shaft
Frame	detachable tubular duplex cradle
Wheelbase	1410 mm
Front suspension	teledraulic fork
Rear suspension	swinging arm with teledraulic dampers
Wheels	cast light alloy: front WM 3/1.85 × 18 CP2; rear WM 3/2.15 × 18 CP2
Tyres	front, 3.00 -18" R; rear 3.25 -18" R
Brakes	discs: front, d/disc manual-pedal; rear pedal
Weight	152 kgs
Max speed	150 km/h
Normal consumption	(Cuna stds.) 3.5 litres per 100 kms
Fuel tank capacity	16.5 litres
Lubricant capacity	2.2 litres

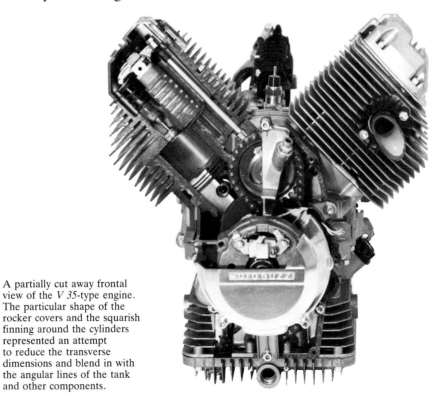

A partially cut away frontal view of the *V 35*-type engine. The particular shape of the rocker covers and the squarish finning around the cylinders represented an attempt to reduce the transverse dimensions and blend in with the angular lines of the tank and other components.

The V 35 arrived in the showrooms a few weeks before the 1977 Motorcycle Show along with the V 50, which had been penalized by a very high purchase tax rating and the (then) age restriction which meant that under-21 year-olds could stand and drool over it, but not ride it. This left the smaller model with more room for manoeuvre on the other hand, as its price was very competitive even in comparison with the Japanese bikes. The V 35 and its larger stablemate were virtually identical, in accordance with the dictates of a sensible production policy, and differences were restricted to a few minor details.

The *V 35*, designed after the *V 50* — even though a series of commercial considerations eventually combined to make it a more interesting proposition than the latter — also benefitted from a longer testing period, one reason for the fact that only two series were necessary to catch up with the *V 50*. And so the corresponding model to the *V 50 III* is the *V 35 II*, which was presented at the Milan Show in November 1979 and put on sale a few months later. Running on a 10.1:1 compression ratio, the *V 35 II* developed 35 hp at 8100 rpm; it was fitted with Dell'Orto VHB 26 FD (FS) carbs with a 26 mm choke tube and a classic coil ignition system with two pairs of points. The gear ratios were slightly shortened with a view to obtaining better pick-up and more flexible responses. The front forks had 125 mm of travel and the preloaded three-way rear suspension units had from 67 to 69 mm of travel. The tyres were 3.25-18" in front and 3.50-18" behind. The bike weighed 155 kgs and top speed was 145 km/h. Slight styling differences included the front mudguard, the silencers (at a sharper angle) and the rear swinging arm paintwork.

The November 1985 Milan Show witnessed the baptism of the next version of the *V 35*, the *III*, which had a radically different appearance thanks to the mini fairing attached to the steering head, the new tank and a new side panel-saddle assembly linked with the rear mudguard. The front mudguard was also modified, as were the wheels (with a 16", five-spoke version at the front). Other data: 10.5:1 compression ratio, two 26 mm VHBZ Dell'Orto carbs, electronic ignition with magnetic pick-up, Guzzi air-assisted forks with pressure equalizer, hydraulic rear dampers, integral braking system with two drilled 260 mm discs in front and a 235 mm disc at the rear, 100/90 H-16" tyres in front and 110/80 H-18" tyres behind, 17 litre tank, weight 160 kgs, 35 hp at 8100 rpm, 150 km/h and 4 litres per 100 kms consumption. The showroom price was 4,838,000 lire.

The *Trentacinque GT* made its first appearance at the same time as the *Mille GT* (see previous pages) in the Autumn of 1987. This bike was built in accordance with a similar, no-frills philosophy and aimed, why not?, at those who prefer their bikes without too many concessions to the latest trends. Differences with regard to the *V 35 III* concerned the bodywork only: the bikini fairing was no more. But there was new instrumentation and a new tank plus a grab rail at the rear. Performance, suspension, wheels and the braking system were unchanged.

The *V 35* was also given the *Custom* treatment, as we mentioned before, using the same components as were fitted to the *V 50*, i.e. forks, front wheel, headlight and instrumentation from the *V 65*, handlebars from the *California II*, etc. In this case too the rear fork was lengthened by 40 mm in order to accommodate the fat rear tyre. The rear wheel rim is offset with respect to the hub and the spokes are slightly angled to the right as a result. The mudguards are chrome plated while the rear dampers are hydropneumatic units with 5-way regulation exactly like the ones fitted to the *V 65*. Length is 2200 mm; width 960 mm and weight 165 kgs. Top speed is around 145 km/h.

In 1984 the *V 35 Custom* was restyled along the same lines as the *V 50*; i.e. a stepped saddle with backrest and rear grab rail plus baggage carrier, as well as other minor details.

In 1986 the *Custom* was joined by the *V 35 Florida*. At first sight this bike looked like just another chopper variant, but it possessed some radical differences. First of all the engine had been redesigned and was now markedly undersquare: where the other *V 35* engines had a bore and stroke of 66 × 50.6 mm, this model had measurements of 74 × 40.6, and an overall displacement of 349.2 cc. Compression was 10.3:1. Ignition was electronic with magnetic pick-up, and the engine was fed by two 28 mm Dell'Orto PHBH carbs. The drive train was painted black and the bike stands tall at the front because of the longer forks. Other details include the peanut tank and 90/90 - 18" tyres in front and 120/90 - 16" behind. Weight was 170 kgs and top speed 150 km/h.

The *500 Tutta Strada* having been sidelined, as we mentioned earlier, Guzzi returned to the enduro theme in 1984 with the *V 35 TT* and the *V 65 TT*, which stood out for their highly individual styling, aided and abetted by the V-twin engine, and the presence of certain accessories like the electric starter (which was by no means a standard fitment on this kind of bike in those days). Other important changes included the closer gear ratios, obtained by modifying the final drive bevel pair, a stronger weld between frame and steering, the long Marzocchi forks (as previously fitted to the *Tutta Strada*), the hydraulic rear dampers with external reservoir and an independent disc braking system, more suited to off-road duty. The 346.2 cc engine (66 × 50.6 mm) developed 33 hp at 8300 rpm running on a 10.5:1 compression ratio. There were also two 26 mm Dell'Orto VHB carbs, spoked wheels with aluminium rims (3.00-21" tyres in front and and 4.00-18" behind), 260 mm drilled discs (the earliest models had a 180 × 30 mm drum brake at the rear), and a 16 litre tank: Weight was 160 kgs, speed 140 km/h and paintwork was white and red.
The 1984 price was 4,307,000 lire.

In 1987 the *V 35 TT* was replaced by the *V 35 NTX*, which had a more "professional" look, thanks to the generously proportioned fuel tank which blended in with the lines of the fixed fairing and the new-style saddle. This new bike also had the undersquare 349.2 cc (74 × 40.6 mm × 2) engine previously fitted to the *Florida*. Compression was 10.3:1, giving an output of 35 hp at 8400 rpm, and the engine was fed by two 28 mm Dell'Orto PHBH carbs. Other features included electronic ignition, spoked wheels with 3.00 S - 21" tyres in front and 4.00 S - 18" fittings bringing up the rear, two 260 mm drilled disc brakes (the rear disc was on the left), "upside down" rear dampers with upper reservoir, a 32 litre fuel tank, wheelbase 1480 mm, minimum ground clearance 230 mm, weight 170 kgs and top speed 140 km/h. The colour scheme was white-yellow-black, with the drive train painted black. The 1987 price was 5,947,000 lire.

V 35 Imola

Naturally there was also a sporting version of the *V 35*: as a matter of fact it came into the world before the *V 50 Monza*, as it was introduced at the 1979 Milan Motorcycle Show. In this case too the name had been chosen in honour of an arena which had witnessed many of the Mandello marque's glorious sporting triumphs: Imola.

It is also worth drawing attention to the return of the famous spread eagle badge to its place on the sides of the fuel tank, almost as if to underline the sporting vocation of this bike.

Engine modifications (pistons, valves, carbs) were the main source of the improved performance here; other differences included the fatter front tyre, as well as the race-style riding position.

Bodywork components (bikini fairing, tank, saddle, mudguards) were lifted wholesale from the *V 50 Monza*.

The first Imola models had electronic ignition, but a more traditional coil system was adopted later.

Another important innovation was the adoption of Nicasil-coated bores for the (light alloy) cylinders. The 1979 price was 2,565,000 lire.

Model / year	V 35 Imola / 1979-1984
Engine	4-stroke 90 degree V-twin 66 × 50.6 mm / 346.22 cc
Compression ratio	10.5:1
Output	36 hp at 8200 rpm
Cylinder head	light alloy with valve seat inserts
Cylinder	2 light alloy barrels with hard chrome bore
Valve arrangement	parallel overhead
Valve gear	push rod and rocker arm
Ignition	coil
Carburettor	Dell'Orto VHB 26 FD, VHB 26 FS
Lubrication	lobe pump
Clutch	dry single plate
Gearbox	foot-change 5-speed
Transmission	primary, gears; final drive, shaft
Frame	detachable tubular duplex cradle
Wheelbase	1420 mm
Front suspension	teledraulic fork
Rear suspension	swinging arm with teledraulic dampers
Wheels	cast light alloy: front WM 2/1.85 × 18; rear WM 3/2.15 × 18
Tyres	front, 3.25 S-18"; rear 3.50 S-18"
Brakes	discs: front, d/disc manual-pedal; rear pedal
Weight	158 kgs
Max speed	160 km/h
Normal consumption	5.22 litres per 100 kms
Fuel tank capacity	16 litres
Lubricant capacity	2.5 litres

The piston crowns of the *V 35 Imola* were scooped out more to encourage the flow of fresh gas and increase turbulence; the valve diameters were 30.5 intake and 27.5 exhaust. The silencers were far more upswept than those of the touring version. The frame, which still had the detachable lower tubes for easy engine removal, had the steering tube inclined at 28 degrees. The discs were made by Innocenti and measured 260 mm (front) and 235 mm (rear); both were drilled for better cooling, a feature later adopted for all *V 35* and *V 50* models; the calipers were by Brembo. The forks were Guzzi units (as were the wheels), and the 32 mm diameter stanchions had 125 mm of travel; the Sebac three-way adjustable rear dampers had an average travel of 69 mm.

Four years after its introduction, the *V 35 Imola* was replaced by the *V 35 Imola II*, presented in November 1983 at the Milan Show and put on sale the following Spring. The big novelty in this case was the 4-valve per cylinder layout with a pent roof head and the spark plug in the middle. A double push-rod and rocker arm assembly did the donkey work. This innovation did more than merely raise output (up to 40 hp at 8800 rpm), it also increased the torque and made for smoother and more regular delivery of power to the wheels. The bike also looked radically different, with its new bikini fairing, tank, side panels and saddle plus a bellypan and a species of mini spoiler below the tank like the one fitted previously to the *Le Mans II* and *III*. Compression was 10.5:1 and there were two 28 mm Dell'Orto PHBH carbs, coil ignition with a double set of points, spoked wheels shod with 100/90 V-16" and 120/90 V-16" tyres at front and rear respectively, hydropneumatic suspension, and 18 litre tank. Weight was 168 kgs and top speed 170 km/h. Colours: red, white and metallic grey.

The Milan Show of November 1987 witnessed the appearance of a very interesting motorcycle, the *V 35 Falco*, in which traditional Guzzi twin engineering had been enriched by the addition of double overhead camshafts and integral plastic bodywork. The frame had been redesigned with square section tubing. The four valves per cylinder obviously remained while the double overhead camshafts were driven by toothed belts. Compression was 10.5:1 and there were two 30 mm Dell'Orto PHBH carbs. A variable advance electronic ignition system was also fitted. The suspension comprised Guzzi air-assisted forks in front and hydropneumatic dampers at the rear. The spoked wheels ran on 100/90 V-16" and 120/90 V-16" tyres at front and rear respectively, and the wheels carried the usual integrated braking system with 270 mm drilled discs at the front and a 235 mm disc at the rear. The bike weighed in at 179 kgs and top speed was 175 km/h.
Changing market conditions, which had seen a fall-off in 350 sales following the abrogation of the age limit (21), persuaded Guzzi management not to develop this really modern bike any further and it remained at the prototype stage.

V 65

With the progressive increase in the capacity of the major models, a certain gap began to emerge between these and the smaller bikes.

The gap was bridged with the *V 65*, three versions of which were prepared: *Normale, Speciale (SP)* and *Custom*.

The *V 65s* — seen for the first time at the 1981 Milan Show — were derived from the *V 50*, whose frame they inherited. The drive train had been modified somewhat: increases were decreed for bore and stroke, carburettor and valve diameters, crankshaft and con-rod dimensions; the rear swinging arm was lengthened. Gear ratios were also altered. The front fork was strengthened using stanchions from the *Le Mans*, while the rear suspension sported 5-way adjustable dampers.

Other modifications regarded steering geometry and some bodywork details. Available colours were Guzzi red, or green and silver metallic finishes.

At first the *V 65* was constructed jointly by the entire De Tomaso group: the engines were built by Innocenti and the frames by Maserati of Modena while assembly was handled by the Benelli works in Pesaro.

Model / year	V 65 / 1981-1987
Engine	4-stroke 90 degree V-twin 80 × 64 mm / 643.4 cc
Compression ratio	10:1
Output	52 hp at 7050 rpm
Cylinder head	light alloy with valve seat inserts
Cylinder	light alloy
Valve arrangement	overhead
Valve gear	push rod and rocker arm
Ignition	coil
Carburettor	Dell'Orto PHBH 30 BD, PHBH 30BS
Lubrication	lobe pump
Clutch	dry single plate
Gearbox	foot-change 5-speed
Transmission	primary, helical gears; final drive, shaft
Frame	removable tubular duplex cradle
Wheelbase	1440 mm
Front suspension	hydropneumatic fork with pressure equalizer
Rear suspension	swinging arm with hydropneumatic dampers
Wheels	cast light alloy: front WM 2/1.85 × 18; rear WM 3/2.15 × 18
Tyres	front, 100/90 H-18"; rear 110/90 H-18"
Brakes	discs: front, d/disc manual-pedal; rear pedal
Weight	165 kgs
Max speed	175 km/h
Normal consumption	5.5 litres per 100 kms
Fuel tank capacity	16 litres
Lubricant capacity	2.5 litres

At side, the *V 65*, and, (below) the faired version of the *SP*. The frames of these bikes had remained substantially identical to the frames used for the smaller models, but the rear swinging arm had been lengthened by 25.5 mm and trail was increased to 99 mm (it was 86.5 mm on the V 50). The Guzzi-built fork (with stanchion diameter of 34.77 mm) had 140 mm of travel, while the Paioli rear suspension units were fitted upside down in order to enable their connection to a pressure compensation tube (they were hydropneumatic units, like the front forks), the total travel in this case being 75 mm.

Here too the braking system was fitted with Brembo calipers and Innocenti discs of 260 mm diameter (front) and 235 mm (rear); thickness was 6 mm. The silencers were derived from those of the *Le Mans III*. Naturally the *V 65 SP* offered a slightly different riding position compared to the *V 65* (footrest position, etc.) as we have already seen with the *1000 SP*. The *V 65* and the *V 65 SP* were deleted in 1987.

As well as the *Mille GT* and the *Trentacinque GT*, there was also the *Sessantacinque GT*, which had the same simple, essential styling as its two stablemates. As far as general characteristics and performance are concerned there was little difference between this and the previous model with the 650 engine; but the different riding position and the bike's greater overall height (the forks had longer stanchions) had shaved a little something off the top speed, claimed to be around 170 km/h. Components included two 30 mm Dell'Orto PHBH carbs, an electronic ignition system, spoked wheels with 100/90 H-18" and 110/90 H-18" tyres at front and rear respectively, Guzzi air-assisted forks, hydropneumatic rear dampers, and a 17 litre tank. Weight was 165 kgs.

The *V 65 Florida* (1986) was built along the same lines as the *V 35 Florida*. Here the standard specification included a traditional windscreen fixed to the handlebars, and two capacious rear panniers. The dualseat had a hint of a backrest for both rider and passenger. The drive train was painted black. Mechanical characteristics were the same as those of the *Sessantacinque GT*, including the tyres. Weight was 170 kgs. Top speed was around 170 km/h, without windscreen and panniers; the said accessories slowed the bike down by about 20 km/h. Price at time of launch was 6,941,000 lire.

As we have already mentioned, the *V 65 TT* was fitted out at the same time as the *V 35 TT*, presented in Milan in November 1983 and put on sale the following year. The same considerations therefore hold good for this bike, especially as far as the styling (practically identical) is concerned. In this case too gear ratios had been reduced by modifying the final drive bevel pair. Compression was 10.1, power was 48 hp at 7400 rpm and there were two 30 mm Dell'Orto PHBH carbs, offset axle Marzocchi forks, Marzocchi hydropneumatic rear suspension units with external fluid reservoir, spoked wheels with 3.00-21" and 4.00-18" tyres at front and back respectively, and an independent braking system comprising two drilled 260 mm discs. The weight was 165 kgs and top speed 165 km/h.

In 1985 it looked like Guzzi was beginning to take a greater interest in enduro racing, given the good results which their French importer had achieved using some specially prepared machines. In the November of that year the Milan Show was the stage for the introduction of the *V 65 Baia*, built over *TT* mechanics but with a strengthened frame, 42 mm Marzocchi forks, Marzocchi race-type rear dampers, a special steel swinging arm, Akront rims and a 50 litre aluminium tank. The engine had also been modified with a view to obtaining more torque and power, which had been uprated to 45 hp at 7000 rpm. Tyres were 90/90-21" and 140/90-17" at front and rear respectively. This bike was very promising, at least on paper, but it never went into production and Guzzi subsequently abandoned the idea of taking part in competition enduro events.

The *650 NTX* replaced the *V 65 TT* in 1986, and received the same bodywork as its contemporary the *V 35 NTX*, whose large petrol tank followed the vogue for "African" styling which had been popularized by the big desert races like the Paris-Dakar. In this case too the componentry was identical to that fitted to the smaller bike; the black-painted drive train sported a lower bash plate. Colours were white and blue with red flashes; the spoked wheels had gold-coloured anodized aluminium rims. Weight was 170 kgs and speed 170 km/h.

V 65 Lario

The *V 65 Lario* was first shown at the 1983 Milan Show (held in November), along with the *Imola III*, and like the latter bike it sported a major innovation in the form of 4-valve heads, even though the push rods and rocker arms remained. The body was practically identical to that of its predecessor. The *Lario* is a very vivacious performer which has often been called the "little *Le Mans*", a really accurate comparison not only as far as regards looks, but also performance. Obviously the *Lario* is not as quick as the *Le Mans* but it is just as agile and very surefooted. The frame was restyled to accommodate the 16" wheels and to improve roadholding, but the traditional look was preserved more or less intact.

As we mentioned before, the body is very like that of the contemporary *Le Mans*, including the spoiler and the aerofoils under the fuel tank which wind tunnel testing had revealed to be conducive to improved driveability.

The suspension is a hydropneumatic system with pressure equalizers. The comprehensive instrument pack includes a speedometer, rev counter and voltmeter plus a battery of warning lights. In 1984 the *V 65 Lario* cost 5,747,700 lire.

Model / year	V 65 Lario / 1983-1989
Engine	4-stroke 90 degree V-twin 80 × 64 mm / 643.4 cc
Compression ratio	10.3:1
Output	60 hp at 7800 rpm
Cylinder head	light alloy with valve seat inserts
Cylinder	two light alloy barrels with Nigusil liners
Valve arrangement	inclined overhead, 4 per cylinder
Valve gear	push rod and rocker arm
Ignition	Bosch distributor with double contact breaker
Carburettor	Dell'Orto PHBH 30 D, PHBH 30 S
Lubrication	force-fed by lobe pump
Clutch	dry single plate
Gearbox	foot-change 5-speed
Transmission	primary, helical gears; final drive, shaft
Frame	removable tubular duplex cradle
Wheelbase	1455 mm
Front suspension	hydropneumatic fork with pressure equalizer
Rear suspension	swinging arm with air-assisted hydropneumatic dampers
Wheels	cast light alloy: front MT H2-2/1.15 × 16"; rear MT H2-2.50 × 16"
Tyres	front, 100/90 V-16"; rear 120/90 V-16"
Brakes	discs: front, d/disc manual-pedal; rear pedal
Weight	184 kgs
Max speed	190 km/h
Normal consumption	(Cuna stds.) 5.6 litres per 100 kms
Fuel tank capacity	18 litres
Lubricant capacity	2.5 litres

The engine from the *V 65 Lario*. The presence of the four valves is revealed — as it was on similar models — by the "slab" type, squarish heads.

The 1983-84 version of the *V 65 Lario*. The four valves, controlled by a double push-rod and rocker arm arrangement, were angled at 48 degrees to each other and therefore a pent roof head had to be fitted. The diameter of the inlet valves was 34 mm while the exhaust valves measured 23.5 mm. Pistons and cylinders were slightly different with the barrels less deeply recessed into the cylinder block. The steering head had been raised by 55 mm and pivoted on tapered roller bearings; the Guzzi forks had 38 mm stanchions instead of the 35 mm version; the rear suspension units offered a five-way adjustment feature and 75 mm of travel. The wheelbase was lengthened. The instrument pack included a racing-type rev counter, speedo, voltmeter and warning lights for headlamps, oil, fuel, neutral, brakes and battery. Cost at time of launch was 5,747,700 lire.

V 75

First seen at a sneak preview at the 1984 Bologna Motor Show and put on sale the following year, the *V 75* represents — for the time being at least — the maximum expression of the "small" V engine designed by Lino Tonti, who had thus equalled the cylinder capacity of Carcano's original V design. Naturally this displacement was not arrived at merely by changing the bore and stroke, but by a thorough modification of the engine dimensions in order to keep them in proportion with the notable increase in output. Despite the touring style riding position, the *V 75* was fitted with a sporty engine, a fact borne out by the choice of the 4-valves, still controlled by the faithful push-rod and rocker arm layout. The electronic ignition system was new, with a Bosch pick-up unit and Motoplat control module. The front wheel, with five twin spokes, was a 16 incher, while the designer went back to the 18" size for the rear wheel. The wheelbase had been increased again in comparison with the *Lario*. Bodywork was crisply essential, a bikini fairing over the steering head being the only concession to aerodynamics. The *V 75* was the product of a protracted gestation period and was not included in the catalogue until 1986, priced at 6,762,000 lire.

Model / year	V 75 / 1985-1986
Engine	4-stroke 90 degree V-twin 80 × 74 mm / 743.9 cc
Compression ratio	10:1
Output	65 hp at 7200 rpm
Cylinder head	light alloy with valve seat inserts
Cylinder	two light alloy barrels with Nigusil liners
Valve arrangement	inclined overhead, 4 per cylinder
Valve gear	push rod and rocker arm
Ignition	electronic Bosch Motoplat with variable advance
Carburettor	Dell'Orto PHBH 30 D, PHBH 30 S
Lubrication	lobe pump
Clutch	dry single plate
Gearbox	foot-change 5-speed
Transmission	primary, helical gears; final drive, shaft
Frame	removable tubular duplex cradle
Wheelbase	1470 mm
Front suspension	hydropneumatic fork with pressure equalizer
Rear suspension	s/arm with adjustable hydropneumatic dampers
Wheels	cast light alloy: front MT H2-2.50 × 16"; rear MT H2-2.75 × 18"
Tyres	front, 100/90 V-16"; rear 120/80 H-18"
Brakes	discs: front, d/disc manual-pedal; rear pedal
Weight	187 kgs
Max speed	190 km/h
Normal consumption	(Cuna stds.) 5.6 litres per 100 kms
Fuel tank capacity	17 litres
Lubricant capacity	2.5 litres

The architecture of the *V 75* engine was practically the same as that of the *Lario* engine, but the cylinder (taller, due to the extra stroke) had three more fins.

The *V 75* was a Grand Touring bike with a sober look and a sporting temperament. The finishing and the braking system were both particularly good: the two drilled front discs were 270 mm in diameter, almost as much as the 16" wheel itself. The Guzzi-built hydropneumatic front fork was equipped with a pressure equalizer, while the rear suspension units offered 5-way adjustment.

In response to a request from its French agent, Guzzi prepared a special version of the *750* off-roader for the 1986 Paris-Dakar event. This particular version of the four-valve engine supplied 62 hp at 7100 rpm; the gearbox was still a five-speeder. Particular care was taken with both the "Dakar" style body with the enormous 40-litre tank and the cycle parts: the specially redesigned frame, Marzocchi forks and Olins rear dampers. The tyres were 90/90-21" in front and 140/80-17" behind and the bike could hit 170 km/h.
This interesting experiment unfortunately came to a premature end following a crash in the early stages of the race.

An enduro version of the *750* was also prepared, the *NTX*. All in all, this bike resembled its smaller stablemates pretty closely as far as looks go: a generously proportioned fairing incorporating a 30 litre tank, a fixed bikini fairing and an integral side panels-rear mudguard assembly. Note the streamlined shield sheltering the front disc brake from any stones thrown up by the wheel. The two-valve engine was slightly less compressed (9.7:1) to make it more suitable for enduro conditions. Wheels were spoked with anodized Akront rims shod with tyres measuring 3.00 - 21" in front and 4.00 - 18" at the rear; there were two independent 260 mm discs (the front brake pump was a four-piston type), and Marzocchi suspension. Weight was 180 kgs and top speed 179 km/h.

Along with the *V 65 Baia*, the 1985 Milan Show also featured another avant-garde Guzzi dirt bike, the *V 75 Duna*. It had a 4-valve engine which produced 65 hp at 7200 rpm, electronic ignition with electronically managed spark advance, electric starter and a 5-speed gearbox. Max torque was 6.6 kgm at 5400 rpm. The frame was a square section duplex cradle with detachable bottom rails riding on Double Link rear suspension, which loaded (by means of a special mechanism) a pair of Marzocchi oleo dampers housed under the saddle parallel to the ground; wheel travel was 200 mm. A Marzocchi fork was also mounted at the front end. This bike was also destined to remain at the prototype stage.

The *750 SP*, another novelty from the 1989 Milan Show, is a long-distance grand tourer, favoured by lightweight construction and a more biddable temperament than its 1000 cc stablemates. The weight is in fact less than 185 kgs, while top speed is a more than respectable 170 km/h. The two-valve 743.9 cc (80 × 74 mm) engine develops 46 hp at 6600 rpm running on a 9.7:1 compression ratio; other features include two Dell'Orto PHBH 30 carbs, Motoplat electronic ignition with double pick-up, Guzzi forks, Koni rear suspension units, spoked wheels with 100/90 V-18" and 120/80 V-18" tyres at front and rear respectively and a partial fairing fixed to the frame. Price at launch was 9,798,000 lire without panniers.

The *750 Nevada*, also presented at the 1989 Milan Show, is a new custom model complete with everything that the latest trends demand: note the two chrome-plated tunnels beneath the tank, which house the horns among other things. The engine — like the styling and performance — is practically identical to that of the *750 SP*: the frame has been slightly modified at the front end, as has the trail. The bike also sports Guzzi hydropneumatic forks with pressure equalizer, Ohlins adjustable rear suspension units, spoked wheels shod with 100/90 V-18" and 130/90 V-16" tyres at front and back respectively, and 270 mm floating front discs. Weight is 117 kgs and top speed 170 km/h; the tank holds 17 litres. November 1989 price, 8,556,000 lire.

293

125 C and 125 TT

In 1983 the Guzzi-Benelli group brought out a new 2-stroke 125, which was supposed to replace the obsolescent power unit of the same capacity from a decade before. The new product embodied all the most modern features, like lamellar inlet valves, a separate lubrication system, liquid cooling, and crankgear fitted with an anti-vibration countershaft.

Custom and enduro variants of the new model were also produced and presented at the Milan Show of the same year bearing both Guzzi and Benelli badges.

However the final preparations dragged on for quite some time and two more years passed before the bikes went on sale, with slightly different lines and finishing from the prototypes.

The *125 C* or *Custom* and the *125 TT* (All terrain) are two lightweights aimed principally at sixteen year-olds who (due to age limits) cannot ride bigger bikes but who find the sporty lightweights a fair substitute, at least as far as appearances go.

At time of launch the two bikes cost 3,097,500 and 3,109,300 lire respectively.

At a slightly later date the appearance of the engine was modified when the cylinder finning was eliminated.

Model / year	125 C / 1985-1987
Engine	2-stroke single 56 × 50 mm / 123.15 cc
Compression ratio	11.5:1
Output	16.5 hp at 7000 rpm
Cylinder head	light alloy
Cylinder	light alloy with Nigusil liners
Valve arrangement	lamellar inlet valve
Valve gear	—
Ignition	electronic fixed advance
Carburettor	Dell'Orto PHBL 25 BS
Lubrication	separated, with mechanical mixing pump (1%)
Clutch	wet multiplate type
Gearbox	foot-change 6-speed
Transmission	primary, helical gears; final drive, chain
Frame	trellis type duplex cradle
Wheelbase	1380 mm
Front suspension	teledraulic forks
Rear suspension	s/arm with "Mono System" hydraulic dampers
Wheels	cast light alloy: front 2.15 × 16"; rear 2.15 × 18"
Tyres	front 80/100 - 16"; rear 3.50 H-18"
Brakes	front, manual/disc; rear, pedal/expansion
Weight	110 kgs
Max speed	115 km/h
Normal consumption	(Cuna stds.) 3.5 litres per 100 kms
Fuel tank capacity	11 litres
Lubricant capacity	0.75 litres

The compact engine block of the *125 C*. Although it was liquid cooled, the finning was retained; later models did not possess this feature. The angled cover encloses the oil and cooling pump.

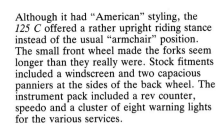

Although it had "American" styling, the *125 C* offered a rather upright riding stance instead of the usual "armchair" position. The small front wheel made the forks seem longer than they really were. Stock fitments included a windscreen and two capacious panniers at the sides of the back wheel. The instrument pack included a rev counter, speedo and a cluster of eight warning lights for the various services.

Put on sale in July 1985, the *125 TT* was quite different from the *C*, both in terms of the body and the mechanical members. The 35 mm offset axle fork stanchions were by Marzocchi and had 200 mm of travel. The wheels were spoked with steel rims and shod with enduro tyres (2.75-21" and 4.10-18" at front and back). The 260 mm front disc sported a Brembo caliper while the rear wheel was fitted with a 125 mm lateral drum. Tank capacity was 11.5 litres, weight 110 kgs, and speed 110 km/h. The drive train was painted black.

GOODS VEHICLES

Motocarri 500 cc

Right from the early days of motor transport, various goods vehicles based on motorcycle components had been proposed, but results had almost always been disappointing, largely because of impractical design. But it was a quite different story as far as the Guzzi "Motocarri" (half bike, half truck) were concerned. Right from their debut in 1928, they stood out for their rationality and simplicity of design. Since then, Guzzi has remained active in the motorcycle truck sector — a market segment which had its heyday during and immediately after the war, but which still has plenty of life in it today — with products which are still appreci-ated for their durability and cheapness. Guzzi motorcycle truck production was traditionally restricted to medium-large capacity vehicles, built over special versions of the 500 cc single in its various guises, from the *Sport* down to the *Astore* and the *Falcone*. But in recent years some smaller "motocarri" have been produced, like the *Ercolino*, powered by a 192 cc engine derived from the *Galletto*, as well as mini motorcycle trucks with 50 cc engines, particularly useful for light delivery work in the cities. The latter were considered mopeds and therefore needed no registration plates; they also fell into an advantageous tax bracket.

Model / year	Sport 14 (type 107) / 1929-1930
Engine	4-stroke flat single 88 × 82 mm / 498.4 cc
Compression ratio	4.5:1
Output	13.2 hp at 3800 rpm
Cylinder head	cast iron
Cylinder	cast iron
Valve arrangement	opposed; inlet at side; exhaust overhead
Valve gear	inlet, tappet; exhaust, push rod - rocker arm
Ignition	Bosch type magneto
Carburettor	Amac
Lubrication	geared pressure pump; vane type scavenge pump
Clutch	wet multiplate type
Gearbox	hand-change 3-speed sliding gears
Transmission	primary, gear driven; final drive, chain
Frame	tubular
Wheelbase	1880 mm / 1250 mm
Front suspension	girder fork with friction dampers
Rear suspension	leaf springs
Wheels	spoked with 19 × 3.00 rims
Tyres	front 3.50-19" , rear 4.00-19"
Brakes	front: manual expansion type; rear, pedal operated strap
Weight/Capacity	322 kgs / 350 kgs
Max speed	60 km/h
Normal consumption	5.5 litres per 100 kms
Fuel tank capacity	11 litres
Lubricant capacity	3 litres

The first civilian motorcycle truck built by Guzzi was called the *Tipo 107* (1928). As can be seen from the above photograph and the diagram on the facing page, the front end was a standard production bike, forks included, which made it possible to convert the truck back into a motorbike in short order. A new series built over *Sport 14* mechanical units followed almost immediately. Cost without the body was 8,150 lire, while the version complete with closed body cost 8,600 lire.

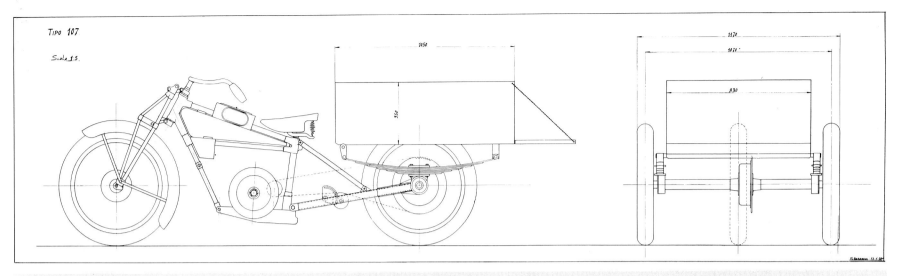

The Motocarro *S* appeared in 1936 with an opposed valve engine, 4-speed gearbox (or three plus reverse), differential rear axle, and a band-type back brake. Carrying capacity was 800 kgs.

299

Model/year	E.R. / 1938-1941
Engine	4-stroke flat single 88 × 82 mm / 498.4 cc
Compression ratio	5.5:1
Output	17.8 hp at 4300 rpm
Cylinder head	cast iron
Cylinder	cast iron
Valve arrangement	inclined overhead
Valve gear	push rod and rocker arm
Ignition	magneto
Carburettor	Dell'Orto 2 MC 25
Lubrication	geared pressure pump; vane type scavenge pump
Clutch	wet multiplate type
Gearbox	hand-change 3-speed and reverse sliding gears
Transmission	primary, helical gear; final drive, chain and differential
Frame	sheet metal
Wheelbase	2300 mm / 1300 mm
Front suspension	girder fork with friction dampers
Rear suspension	swinging arms with leaf springs
Wheels	front: spoked with 19 × 3 rim; rear, 15 × 3 1/2 discs
Tyres	front 3.50-19" , rear 5.50-15" T
Brakes	expansion type; front manual, rear pedal
Weight/Capacity	bodied version 480 kgs / 1,000 kgs
Max speed	60 km/h
Normal consumption	7.1 litres per 100 kms
Fuel tank capacity	16 litres
Lubricant capacity	5.5 litres

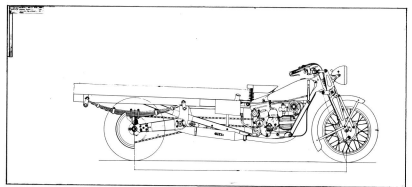

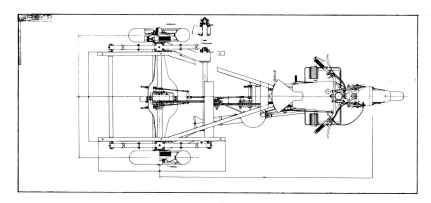

On the facing page, the *E.R.* motorcycle truck from 1938 with the *V*-type overhead valve engine, three-speed gears plus reverse, and three mechanical drum brakes. Carrying capacity was 1,000 kgs. As can been seen, this is qualitatively a far better machine than its immediate predecessors. The chassis cost 9,800 lire and the truck complete with body cost 10,400. Units built until 1941 amounted to 4,319. Right, the *U* model, constructed according to the austerity rules laid down by the government of the day. The main modifications concerned the addition of a fan to boost the forced air cooling system and a reduction gear in the differential housing. This meant a final total of six forward gears plus two reverse gears. Other innovations concerned the sturdier front forks, the front brake bolted onto the wheel and a more rugged chassis in general. Below, a view of the complete engine plus a longitudinal section which clearly shows the layout of the various mechanical units. The engine was mounted with a slightly vertical tilt.

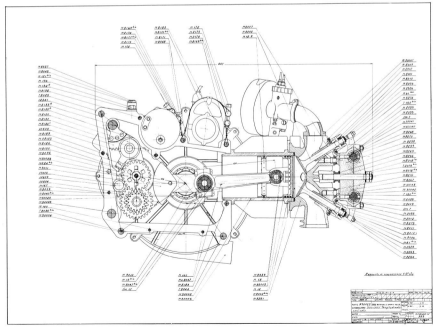

301

Model/year	Ercole / 1946-1949
Engine	4-stroke flat single 88 × 82 mm / 498.4 cc
Compression ratio	5.5:1
Output	17.8 hp at 4300 rpm
Cylinder head	cast iron
Cylinder	cast iron
Valve arrangement	inclined overhead
Valve gear	push rod and rocker arm
Ignition	Marelli type MLA 53 magneto
Carburettor	Dell'Orto MC 26 F
Lubrication	geared pressure pump; vane type scavenge pump
Clutch	wet multiplate type
Gearbox	hand-change 5-speed and reverse constant-mesh
Transmission	primary, gear driven; final drive, cardan shaft
Frame	sheet metal
Wheelbase	2400 mm / 1300 mm
Front suspension	girder fork with friction dampers
Rear suspension	swinging arms with leaf springs
Wheels	front:spoked with 19 × 3 rim; rear, 4.50 E × 16 discs
Tyres	front 4.00-19" , rear 6.50-16" T
Brakes	expansion type; front manual, rear pedal
Weight/Capacity	bodied version 670 kgs / 1500 kgs
Max speed	60 km/h
Normal consumption	(Cuna stds.) 6.7 litres per 100 kms
Fuel tank capacity	16.5 litres
Lubricant capacity	6 litres

Top, the 1946 *Ercole* with the 5-speed plus reverse gearbox mounted at right angles to the engine (from which it received the power via a bevel gear pair) and the shaft drive. Above, the last version of the engine, produced from 1957 onwards with electric starter and coil ignition (the starter motor was in the place previously occupied by the magneto). The aluminium head with the enclosed valve gear was adopted in 1950. On the facing page, top, the last version of the *Ercole*, with hydraulic rear brakes (from 1955) and electric starter.

The *Edile* motorcycle truck from 1946-47 was built with a view to supplanting horse-drawn vehicles. It had an unsprung pressed steel chassis, 7.00-17" tyres in front and 9.75-18" behind, a steering wheel and mechanical drum brakes. The engine was the single-cylinder 500 cc unit with the two overhead valves, which supplied 16 hp at 3700 rpm running on a compression ratio of 5.5:1. The gearbox was an *Ercole*-type 5-speed plus reverse unit. It could carry 3,600 kgs, exceptional in proportion to the 1,350 kg tare. Obviously the gear ratios were extremely close and top speed was barely 25 km/h. When unladen the machine consumed 13.3 litres per 100 kms; the tank contained 53 litres. However it was only a modest commercial success.

Motocarro Ercolino

The first *Ercolino*, a medium capacity motorcycle truck, appeared in 1956. It had a 192 cc engine derived from that of the *Galletto*, with the addition of a forced ventilation fan and a 4-speed gearbox with reverse, laid down longitudinally so as to be coaxial with the final drive shaft.

A bevel gear pair connected the clutch and the gearbox, as in the *Ercole*. This first model had 14" disc wheels in front and 15" at the back with a tested carrying capacity of 350 kgs.

In 1959 smaller 10" wheels were fitted, but with wider section tyres, in order to improve stability and roadholding. The rest of the bike was also improved here and there. Upon request the *Ercolino* could be provided with an electric starter and fitted out to cope with loads of up to 590 kgs, in which case the gearbox was equipped with a two-speed reduction gearbox, operated by an extra pedal mounted on the right.

The *Ercolino* was sold at 389,000 lire, which became 489,000 for the above variant complete with body and cabin. As was the case with the *Ercole*, the frame could be fitted with steps, barrels and a wide variety of special equipment depending on the customer's requirements.

Model / year	Ercolino / 1956-1957
Engine	4-stroke flat single 65 × 58 mm / 192.4 cc
Compression ratio	6.4:1
Output	7.5 hp at 5200 rpm
Cylinder head	light alloy with valve seat inserts
Cylinder	light alloy with pressed-in liner
Valve arrangement	inclined overhead
Valve gear	push rod and rocker arm
Ignition	coil
Carburettor	Dell'Orto MA 19 BS 1
Lubrication	geared pressure pump; vane type scavenge pump
Clutch	wet multiplate type
Gearbox	hand-change 4-speed and reverse constant-mesh
Transmission	primary, helical gear;final drive, shaft
Frame	central spar and sheet metal
Wheelbase	1850 mm / 1130 mm
Front suspension	telescopic forks
Rear suspension	leaf springs
Wheels	discs: front 14 × 2 1/2 rim; rear 15 × 2 3/4
Tyres	front 3.25-14, rear 4.25-15" T
Brakes	expansion type; front and emergency manual, rear pedal
Weight/Capacity	265 kgs / 350 kgs
Max speed	60 km/h
Normal consumption	(Cuna stds.) 4.6 litres per 100 kms
Fuel tank capacity	12 litres
Lubricant capacity	3.7 litres

The *Ercolino* engine without the reduction gear. The illustration shows the cooling fan, the large air filter and the gearbox housing with the coupling for the cardan shaft. On the facing page, top, the 1956 version of the *Ercolino* with the tall wheels. The telescopic fork had no hydraulic dampers. The petrol tank was under the saddle; the oil tank was behind the steering. On the facing page, the 1959 *Ercolino* with the small wheels. This version had the reduction gearbox and could carry 590 kgs. Note the new position occupied by the fuel tank and the other modifications made to the body. The cabin was supplied separately as an optional extra.

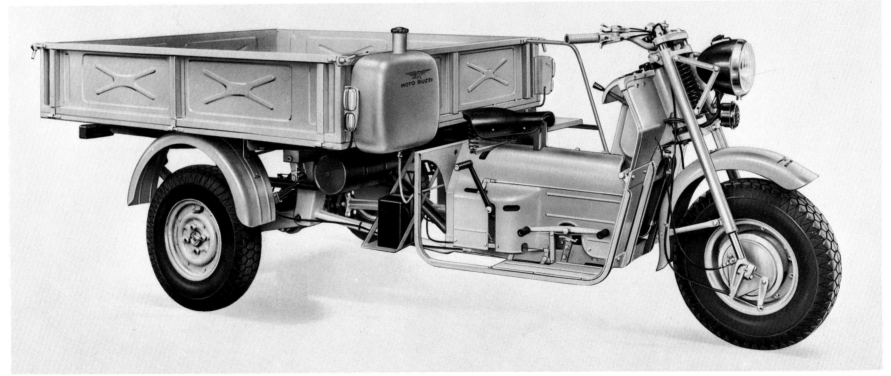

Motocarro Aiace

The *Aiace* was launched in 1962 as a specialist lightweight goods carrier.

It was powered by an engine derived from the *Zigolo 110* power pack with the chrome-lined cylinder mounted close to the rear axle so as to eliminate the final drive.

It had a 3-speed gearbox with reverse gear and hydraulic rear brakes. Instead of the flywheel magneto there was a big belt-driven dynamo; ignition was the coil type. The engine-frame assembly cost 164,000 lire; when sold complete with body and closed cabin the price rose to 243,000 lire.

Model / year	Aiace / 1962-1963
Engine	two stroke flat single 52 × 52 mm / 110.3 cc
Compression ratio	7.5:1
Output	4.2 hp at 5200 rpm
Cylinder head	light alloy
Cylinder	light alloy, chrome bore
Valve arrangement	—
Valve gear	—
Ignition	coil and contact breaker
Carburettor	Dell'Orto MAF 18 B 1
Lubrication	20:1 mixture
Clutch	wet multiplate type
Gearbox	foot-change 3-speed constant-mesh
Transmission	primary and final drive: gear driven
Frame	sheet metal
Wheelbase	1640 mm / 1000 mm
Front suspension	leading link forks and hydraulic dampers
Rear suspension	hydraulic dampers
Wheels	discs with 8 × 2.45 rims
Tyres	4.00-18"
Brakes	expansion type; front and emergency manual, rear pedal
Weight/Capacity	200 kgs / 250 kgs
Max speed	45 km/h
Normal consumption	(Cuna stds.) 3.9 litres per 100 kms
Fuel tank capacity	12.5 litres
Lubricant capacity	—

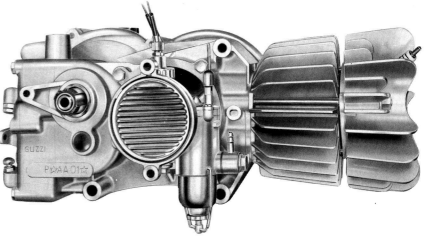

The *Aiace* and its 110 cc engine, which was derived from the *Mk II Zigolo* power unit.

Dingotre

The 1965 *Dingotre* was as cheap and tractable as the *Aiace* but it also offered the additional advantage then possessed by all mopeds, i.e. the driver needed no licence and the vehicle needed no number plate. This little goods carrier powered by the *Dingo*-derived 50 cc engine with the 3-speed gearbox and forced ventilation was therefore the natural alternative to the pedal-powered mini-vans. The power was fed to the wheels by a chain and, in view of the extremely light weight of the vehicle, there was no reverse. The cost swung between 151,500 lire for the engine-frame assembly and 210,500 for the fully equipped version.

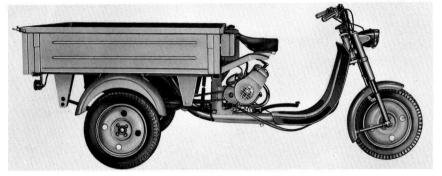

Model / year	Dingotre / 1965-1968
Engine	two stroke single 38.5 × 42 mm / 48.9 cc
Compression ratio	7.5:1
Output	1.47 hp at 5400 rpm
Cylinder head	light alloy
Cylinder	light alloy, chrome bore
Valve arrangement	—
Valve gear	—
Ignition	flywheel magneto
Carburettor	Dell'Orto SHA 14.12
Lubrication	50:1 mixture
Clutch	wet multiplate type
Gearbox	hand-change 3-speed constant-mesh
Transmission	primary, helical gear; final drive, chain
Frame	tubular
Wheelbase	1680 mm / 920 mm
Front suspension	telescopic forks
Rear suspension	leaf springs
Wheels	discs with 12 × 2 1/4 rims
Tyres	3.00-12"
Brakes	expansion type: front manual; rear and emergency, pedal
Weight/Capacity	155 kgs / 200 kgs
Max speed	40 km/h
Normal consumption	2 litres per 100 kms
Fuel tank capacity	5.5 litres
Lubricant capacity	—

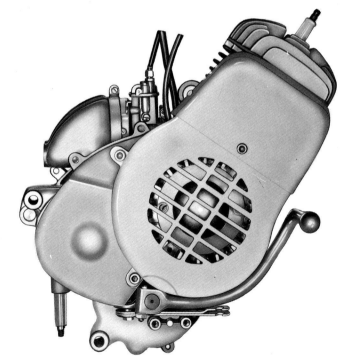

The chain-driven *Dingotre* with the 50 cc, 3-speed *Dingo* engine, equipped with a fan for forced air cooling.

Ciclocarro Furghino

The *Furghino*, which replaced the *Dingotre* in 1968, boasted an important improvement in that it had a shaft instead of the usual chain drive, which was more reliable and required less maintenance. For this reason, the engine — which was still a *Dingo 50* derivative with three speeds and forced ventilation — had been laid cross-wise under the driving seat so that the drive shaft remained axial to the gears. Prices varied from 293,000 lire for the engine-frame assembly to 339,000 for the type with the enclosed body. It went out of production in 1971, leaving a certain gap in the market.

Model/year	Furghino / 1968-1971
Engine	two stroke single 38.5 × 42 mm / 48.9 cc
Compression ratio	9:1
Output	1.5 hp at 6200 rpm
Cylinder head	light alloy
Cylinder	light alloy, chrome bore
Valve arrangement	—
Valve gear	—
Ignition	flywheel magneto
Carburettor	Dell'Orto MB 18 BS
Lubrication	50:1 mixture
Clutch	wet multiplate type
Gearbox	hand-change 3-speed constant-mesh
Transmission	primary, helical gear; final drive, cardan shaft
Frame	single tubular spar
Wheelbase	1520 mm / 890 mm
Front suspension	telescopic forks
Rear suspension	leaf springs
Wheels	discs with 8 × 2.50 c rims
Tyres	3.50-8"
Brakes	expansion type; front and emergency manual, rear pedal
Weight/Capacity	bodied version 155 kgs / 200 kgs
Max speed	40 km/h
Normal consumption	(Cuna stds.) 3.9 litres per 100 kms
Fuel tank capacity	6 litres
Lubricant capacity	—

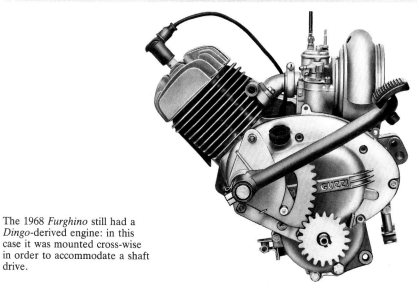

The 1968 *Furghino* still had a *Dingo*-derived engine: in this case it was mounted cross-wise in order to accommodate a shaft drive.

Prototype motorcycle trucks

Apart from the models shown on the previous pages, Guzzi also worked on various other commercial vehicle prototypes, all of which remained at the experimental stage for one reason or another. Worthy of note among these is a light van from 1934-35 with the 232 cc *P*-type engine and chain drive, as well as a medium capacity motocarro created at the end of the Sixties with a single-cylinder engine of about 400 cc which was obtained by "chopping" a *V7* engine. Another very interesting attempt was a two-cylinder diesel unit from around 1960 intended for a heavy-duty vehicle, which was never built.

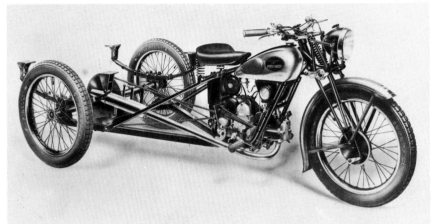

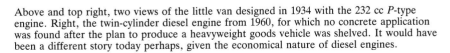
Above and top right, two views of the little van designed in 1934 with the 232 cc *P*-type engine. Right, the twin-cylinder diesel engine from 1960, for which no concrete application was found after the plan to produce a heavyweight goods vehicle was shelved. It would have been a different story today perhaps, given the economical nature of diesel engines.

309

RACING BIKES
AND RECORD BREAKERS

C 2V, 2VT and GT 2VT

The first step in the evolution of the Guzzi engine is represented by the *C 2V* model with parallel overhead valves actuated by push-rods and rocker arms, which was built in 1923 following the Mandello marque's decision to take more interest in racing. It was a very simple design which resulted in considerably improved performance. The frame was also modified by lengthening the wheelbase to 1,410 mm while the sheet metal element under the saddle was replaced by a tube. It was also the first Guzzi to be painted red.
Relieved of its role as a works racer by the *Quattro valvole*, introduced the following year, the *C 2V* was put on sale to the general public, with green paintwork however. Deleted from the catalogue in 1927, it reappeared the next year and remained until 1930, when — fitted with a new *Sport 15*-type chassis and a saddle tank — it was rebaptized the *2VT*. It was to go out of production definitively in 1934. In 1931 the twin overhead valve engine was fitted to a frame with sprung rear suspension, *et voilà* the *GT 2VT*, which was also on sale until 1934. Even as late as 1939 this redoubtable old campaigner of an engine was still being fitted to bikes in preparation for regularity races.

Model / year	C 2V / 1923-1927
Engine	4-stroke flat single 88 × 2 mm / 498.4 cc
Compression ratio	5.25:1
Output	17 hp at 4200 rpm
Cylinder head	cast iron
Cylinder	cast iron
Valve arrangement	parallel overhead
Valve gear	push rod and rocker arm
Ignition	Bosch type magneto
Carburettor	Amac
Lubrication	geared pressure pump; vane type scavenge pump
Clutch	wet multiplate type
Gearbox	hand-change 3-speed sliding gears
Transmission	primary, gear driven; final drive, chain
Frame	tubular duplex cradle
Wheelbase	1410 mm
Front suspension	girder fork with friction dampers
Rear suspension	rigid
Wheels	spoked with 19 × 2 1/2 rims
Tyres	26" × 3
Brakes	single rear expansion brake; manual and pedal control
Weight	130 kgs
Max speed	120 km/h
Normal consumption	4.5 litres per 100 kms
Fuel tank capacity	11 litres
Lubricant capacity	3 litres

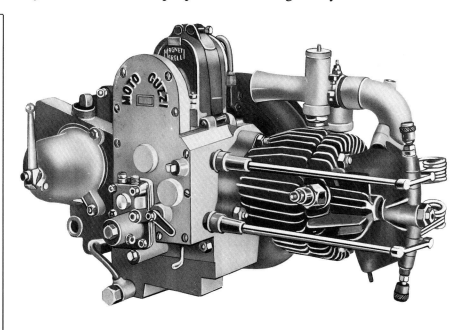

One of the earliest examples of the *C 2V* engine, with dual ignition and racing-type Amac carburettor. The cylinder finning and the gear ratios were also different to those of the *Normale*.

The *C 2V*, the first sporting Guzzi. The model illustrated, which dates from 1925, has dual ignition and two ancillary spiral valve springs which can just be seen between the exposed push-rods. The bike could be fitted with either a Brooks saddle (as shown here) or a Terry, and cost 9,450 lire. Minimum ground clearance was 11 cm. The following version, the *2 VT*, was fitted with a saddle tank and a front brake.

After the introduction of the sprung frame (1928), Guzzi prepared a "springer" for the ohv engine, which was named the *GT 2VT*. This machine weighed about 150 kgs and ran on 26" × 3.50 tyres giving a top speed of 115 km/h. Between 1931 and 1934 167 of these were built. Note the kickstart on the right hand side instead of the left, as was Guzzi's normal practice.

C 4V, 4V TT and 4V SS

First built in 1924, the *Quattro valvole* was the first Grand Prix machine produced by Guzzi and it marked a return to its designer's original engine layout, which had been sidelined as far as mass production was concerned because the overhead valve gear was too expensive. For a while it was one of the fastest "half litre" bikes in the world and it won some major honours, like the first European Championship. Added to the regular catalogue shortly afterwards, it became an excellent racer which enabled some amateur riders to make a good showing in several events, including some important ones. The steady increase in power, which leaped in the space of a few years from 22 to 32 hp, was not matched by an adequate development of the bike as a whole; obsolescent features like the old hand-changed 3-speed gearbox and the unsprung frame were left unaltered and the public gradually fell out of love with the model. Nevertheless it remains an important milestone in motorcycling history, in that it was the first Italian bike to do well in the 500 class, which had been dominated by the bigger, older foreign marques until its appearance. Overall production of the *Quattro valvole* amounted to 486 units, in three successive versions *C 4V*, *4V TT* and *4V SS*.

Model / year	C 4V / 1924-1927
Engine	4-stroke flat single 88 × 82 mm / 498.4 cc
Compression ratio	6:1
Output	22 hp at 5500 rpm
Cylinder head	cast iron
Cylinder	cast iron
Valve arrangement	inclined overhead
Valve gear	overhead camshaft
Ignition	Bosch type magneto
Carburettor	Amac 28.5 mm
Lubrication	geared pressure pump; vane type scavenge pump
Clutch	wet multiplate type
Gearbox	hand-change 3-speed sliding gears
Transmission	primary, spur gear ; final drive, chain
Frame	tubular duplex cradle
Wheelbase	1380 mm
Front suspension	girder fork with friction dampers
Rear suspension	rigid
Wheels	spoked with 21 × 2 1/2 rims
Tyres	27" × 2.75
Brakes	rim brake in front; expansion type at rear
Weight	130 kgs
Max speed	approx. 150 km/h
Normal consumption	—
Fuel tank capacity	10 litres
Lubricant capacity	4 litres

The Guzzi *4V* (4 valves) engine. It was 630 mm long, 370 mm wide and was fitted with a 300 mm flywheel. The camshaft was at an angle because of the offset cylinder. The crankshaft fitted to the *TT* and *SS* types had embodied counterweights, crankpin diameter was 30 mm and the mainshaft measurement was 40 mm. From this model onwards, all Guzzi racing engines were to carry a particular number, preceded by the letter C.

Below, the original *C 4V* from 1924-27, also known as the "European Championship". The model shown above is the one with which Mentasti won the first European Championship in 1924. Top right, the 1928-33 *4V SS*.

This was followed by the *4V TT* (1927-29), a rather more tranquil bike which had the oil tank set forward of the petrol tank. All the *Quattro valvole* were painted red and had Lycett saddles.

250 cc

The sohc racing *250* from 1926 constitutes an important chapter in Guzzi history because its engine — obviously improved and upgraded over the years — stayed at the top of its class for almost three decades, nearly always beating the successive opponents which rival marques lined up against it with arrogant ease. First produced with the 3-speed gearbox and sometimes sold to private individuals in the *TT* and *SS* versions, it later received the 4-speed box and the sprung frame. One version was built with a blower and another with fuel injection; these were the forefathers of the *Albatros* and the *Gambalunghino*. Its engine

was fitted to vetturettes and motor boats for successful record breaking attempts. A good 377 units of the first 3-speed version were made between 1926 and 1933.
For some years after that the 4-speed *250* was reserved for works riders only; it was put on general sale again in 1939, this time known as the *Albatros*.
Among the innumerable successes racked up by this bike there was the outstanding win in the 1935 Isle of Man Tourist Trophy, when the British domination of the toughest road race of them all was finally broken.

Model/year	TT 250 / 1926-1930
Engine	4-stroke flat single 68 × 68 mm / 246.8 cc
Compression ratio	8:1
Output	15 hp at 6000 rpm
Cylinder head	cast iron
Cylinder	cast iron
Valve arrangement	inclined overhead
Valve gear	overhead camshaft
Ignition	Bosch type magneto
Carburettor	Binks 25 mm
Lubrication	geared pressure pump; vane type scavenge pump
Clutch	wet multiplate type
Gearbox	hand-change 3-speed sliding gears
Transmission	primary, spur gear ; final drive, chain
Frame	tubular duplex cradle
Wheelbase	1360 mm
Front suspension	girder fork with friction dampers
Rear suspension	rigid
Wheels	21 × 2 1/2
Tyres	27" × 2.75
Brakes	expansion type; front manual, rear pedal
Weight	105 kgs
Max speed	approx. 125 km/h
Normal consumption	—
Fuel tank capacity	12.5 litres
Lubricant capacity	5 litres

The *SS* version of the Guzzi 250 which was on sale from 1928-33. It had red paintwork and a hand-controlled throttle. Until 1930 the head was in bronze, but cast iron was used thereafter. The initial price of 7,900 lire later fell to 7,250. The model shown, with the left hand side front brake, was one of the first built: the brake was shifted to the right in later models. The *TT* model had a cast iron head and the oil tank mounted in the front end of the petrol tank (which also housed a small metal toolbox). Less powerful, it could touch 118 km/h and cost 7,200 lire, plus another 725 lire for the extra electrics.

From 1934 onwards the *250* was reserved for works riders only. Notable improvements had been made to the engine (4-speed foot-change gearbox) and the frame, the rear end of which had been completely rebuilt (as the photo clearly shows), and fitted with a saddle tank. The front fork is a Brampton, then one of the best around, and useful particularly on long and twisty circuits. Note the plug key fitted to the side of the rear wheel.

The 1930 version of the *250* with the 3-speed box, a type reserved for the factory team. The gearbox was pedal-operated and the forks were Bramptons.
The engine was 550 mm long, 320 wide and weighed 40 kgs; flywheel diameter was 250 mm. Successive versions were quite different as far as the tuning and the design of the rear chassis were concerned.

In 1935 the rear wheel received a spring, making this bike — along with its 500 cc stablemate — the first fully-sprung racer. The rear suspension triangle pivoted near the engine and the springs were contained in two box-like structures alongside the wheel. It was only after the double victory at the Tourist Trophy that the sprung frame concept was accepted by international motorcycle constructors.

In 1938 the 250 engine was fitted with a Cozette blower — then still allowed under racing rules — which pushed the power up to 38 hp at 7800 rpm. Above, the bike tuned up for the endurance records in December (with Tenni), during which it was to exceed 180 km/h. The engine still has the small expansion chamber, later replaced by the large cylinder which can seen in the illustration on the right.

The supercharged engine was mounted in a new frame, used also for the *Albatros* and the *Condor*, which had an aluminium alloy rear chassis. Various experimental fuel injection systems were tried out on the model shown here including Fuscaldo-Caproni electromagnetic equipment as well as some mechanical devices made in Mandello. These experiments were interrupted by the outbreak of war. This prototype, nicknamed "Gerolamo" by the factory design team, came second in the 1939 Milan-Taranto event driven by Raffaele Alberti. Note the curious location chosen for the tube-shaped plug key, which is fitted alongside the rear wheel.

318

After the war the blown *250* was again used for various record attempts in the 350 sidecar class. This is the 1948 version fitted with an articulated sidecar designed by Gino Cavanna (who also rode the bike) which reached a top speed of 172.993 km/h. The engine, which was fed alcohol by a Dell'Orto carburettor, developed 48 hp at 7500 rpm running on a geometric compression ratio of 8.5:1.
The Cozette-type blower (built by Guzzi) rotated at 2,400 rpm. Including the regulation ballast of 60 kgs in the sidecar, the vehicle weighed 205 kgs.

The blown *250* made its last sortie in 1952, in yet another record attempt in the 350 sidecar class. The cycle part was more or less the same, but the streamlining was much improved thanks to the research carried out in the new wind tunnel recently constructed at Mandello. With this ultra-sleek fairing, the bike — still ridden by Gino Cavanna — reached 221.226 km/h, thus establishing records valid also for the 500, 750 and 1200 cc classes.

Quattro cilindri 500 cc

Guzzi's first 4-cylinder bike was this supercharged *Quattro cilindri* from 1930, built at a time when the blower was making headway on all fronts.

An avant-garde machine from many points of view, it also possessed several decidedly dated features, and it was almost never raced as a consequence.

Nevertheless the design was very rational, especially as far as engine layout and the compact dimensions are concerned. Note for example the neat blower assembly and the two magnetos, as well as the architecture of the vertically finned cylinders.

Model / year	Quattro Cilindri / 1930
Engine	4-stroke 4-cylinder transverse 56 × 65 mm / 492.3 cc
Compression ratio	5:1
Output	45 hp at 7800 rpm
Cylinder head	cast iron
Cylinder	cast iron
Valve arrangement	inclined overhead
Valve gear	push rods and rocker arms
Ignition	Bosch type two magnetos
Carburettor	Cozette
Lubrication	double gear-type pressure and scavenge pump
Clutch	wet multiplate type
Gearbox	hand-change 3-speed sliding gears
Transmission	primary, gear driven; final drive, chain
Frame	duplex cradle in tubes and sheet metal
Wheelbase	—
Front suspension	girder fork with friction dampers
Rear suspension	rigid
Wheels	—
Tyres	—
Brakes	expansion type; front manual, rear pedal
Weight	165 kgs
Max speed	approx. 175 km/h
Normal consumption	—
Fuel tank capacity	12 litres
Lubricant capacity	5 litres

Above and on the facing page, two rare pictures of the *Quattro Cilindri*. The other photos highlight the characteristics of the engine: the blower with the transverse expansion chamber, the two magnetos, the oil pump, the hairpin springs for the valves, and the gearbox bolted onto the crankcase. The cradle of the frame was in two parts: the lower and rear elements were made of sheet metal (light alloy).

Bicilindrica 500 cc

One of Carlo Guzzi's most successful brainwaves was the idea of doubling up two cylinders from the unbeatable *250* to produce the *Bicilindrica 500*, a bike with an original 120 degree V-twin engine and unorthodox but strictly functional lines. The *Bicilindrica* enjoyed an almost twenty year-long racing career during which it scored numerous prestigious victories including the 1935 Tourist Trophy. Highly versatile, it could adapt to all kinds of circuit and was the marque's star performer for many years. Both the engine and the other components were subjected to continuous development and improvement during that time. It was the first racing

bike in the world (along with its 250 cc stablemate) to be fitted with sprung rear suspension. Before the war broke out it received aluminium cylinder barrels and head, a new frame and a twin cam front brake, a real novelty at that time. In the post-war period modifications were made to the engine (which was still able to develop 47 hp despite the obligatory requirement to use 72 octane petrol instead of petrol-benzole mixture) and to the frame, which was made more streamlined. It was pensioned off in 1951 (because its "look" was considered a bit dated), when its career was by no means completely over.

Model / year	Bicilindrica / 1933-1935
Engine	4-stroke 120 degree V-twin 68 × 68 mm / 493.6 cc
Compression ratio	8.5:1
Output	44 hp at 7800 rpm
Cylinder head	cast iron
Cylinder	cast iron
Valve arrangement	inclined overhead
Valve gear	overhead camshaft
Ignition	magneto
Carburettor	Dell'Orto 28.5 mm
Lubrication	geared pressure and scavenge pumps
Clutch	wet multiplate type
Gearbox	foot-change 4-speed constant-mesh
Transmission	primary, gear driven; final drive, chain
Frame	duplex cradle in tubes and sheet metal
Wheelbase	1390 mm
Front suspension	girder fork with friction dampers
Rear suspension	rigid
Wheels	spoked
Tyres	front 3.00-21"; rear 3.25-20"
Brakes	expansion type; front manual, rear pedal
Weight	151 kgs
Max speed	180 km/h
Normal consumption	—
Fuel tank capacity	20 litres
Lubricant capacity	7 litres

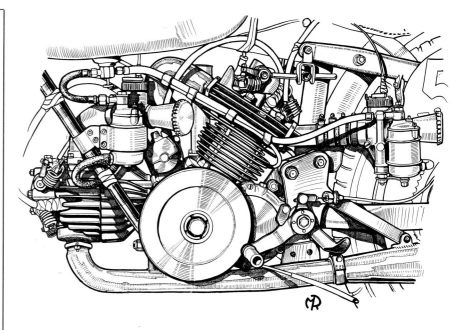

The last version of the *Bicilindrica* engine (1951) in a splendid drawing from *Moto Revue*: the artist's concern for realism extended to showing the little protective caps fitted over the carburettor trumpets to prevent foreign bodies from entering the engine when the bike was not in use.

The original 1933 version of the *Bicilindrica*, with the unsprung frame. The tank was tilted slightly backwards and this helped channel the air over the rear cylinder. The forks were Bramptons. The crankshaft was 306.5 mm long and the distance between the cranks was 74 mm. The shaft ran on two lateral roller bearings and one central needle bearing measuring 36 mm. The two superimposed tanks contained 20 litres of petrol and 7 of oil.

The *Bicilindrica* prepared for the victorious expedition to the 1935 *TT*. It had rear suspension with dampers which could be adjusted when on the move by means of the remote control "cable-car" system fitted under the fuel tank. The springs were housed in horizontal boxes mounted at the sides of the wheels.

The last pre-war version had the new frame with the light alloy rear chassis elements. It was also fitted with a twin-cam 280 mm front brake and modified fuel and oil tanks. In those days alcohol-powered engines were fitted with cast iron cylinder blocks and heads whereas aluminium was used for petrol engines.

323

The post-war development of the *Bicilindrica*. On the previous page, top left, the 1946-47 edition, only slightly different from the pre-war model. Top right, the version with the new frame designed by Antonio Micucci in 1948. Below, the 1949 machine, perhaps the most elegant of them all, with the original centrally-mounted front brake.

This page, left, the strictly functional 1950 model with the anatomically shaped tank; below, the last version from 1951, with the little tail on the saddle and the return of the Hartford-style rear dampers in place of the hydraulic system mounted horizontally under the engine. To compensate for the length of the intake manifolds, the carburettor which fed the rear cylinder found itself in a most unusual position: alongside the wheel. The exceptionally long sporting career enjoyed by the various versions of the *Bicilindrica* make it one of the most enduring monuments to the "Guzzi style": an absolutely functional philosophy, but one which is nonetheless a clear statement of the instrinsic beauty of "good engineering".

Condor 500 cc

In order to encourage amateur riders, practically excluded from the major events by the predominance of the unobtainable supercharged bikes, races were set up for production machines bearing number plates and all the other obligatory roadgoing accessories. After having produced a beefed up version of the standard *G.T.V.* (the *G.T.C.*), Guzzi went on to build a gorgeous production racer that was the fruit of the experience gained with the works machines and which was soon lusted after by many, even though the 11,000 lire price tag put her beyond the reach of most would-be owners. Widespread use of special light alloys was made for the new bike, both for the frame — which resembled the one fitted to the *250 Compressore* — and the engine. It made its first appearance at the *Circuito del Lario* event in 1938 baptized the *Nuova C*, and went on sale some months later as the *G.T.C.L.*, still with the cast iron cylinders and head. The definitive edition was called the *Condor* and it made its debut in 1939. Between then and the war 69 units were built, some of which were sold to the Traffic Police, who used them to patrol the roads and raced them in events reserved for their own officers. The *Condor* had red paintwork with amaranth panels on the tank.

Model / year	Condor / 1938-1940
Engine	4-stroke flat single 88 × 82 mm / 498.4 cc
Compression ratio	7:1
Output	28 hp at 5000 rpm
Cylinder head	light alloy with valve seat inserts
Cylinder	light alloy with pressed-in liners
Valve arrangement	inclined overhead
Valve gear	push rods and rocker arms
Ignition	magneto
Carburettor	Dell'Orto SS 32 M
Lubrication	geared pressure pump; vane type scavenge pump
Clutch	wet multiplate type
Gearbox	foot-change 4-speed constant-mesh
Transmission	primary, spur gear ; final drive, chain
Frame	duplex cradle in tubes and sheet metal
Wheelbase	1470 mm
Front suspension	girder fork with friction dampers
Rear suspension	swinging arm with friction dampers
Wheels	spoked with 21 × 2 1/4 rims
Tyres	front 2.75-21"; rear 3.00-21"
Brakes	expansion type; front manual, rear pedal
Weight	roadgoing version 140 kgs
Max speed	approx. 160 km/h
Normal consumption	—
Fuel tank capacity	18 litres
Lubricant capacity	3.5 litres

The *Condor* engine, much of which was made of special light alloys, was also equipped with a new constant-mesh gearbox.

Homologated for production bike competition, the *Condor* was sold with the complete electrical system, stand, kickstart, toolboxes and silencer. The extensive use of light alloys even for little details like the brake levers brought the weight down to very low levels. The front forks had a single central spring and friction dampers at each side; the rear suspension still had the long *G.T.V.* type "springs in a box" arrangement under the engine while the aluminium dampers had only two friction discs.

A *Condor* for circuit racing and therefore devoid of the electrical system. In this guise the bike weighed less than 130 kgs. The engine was fitted with a sodium-filled exhaust valve and a piston with only two rings and one oil scraper. The con-rod weighed 450 grammes while the flywheel, lightened to 6.600 kgs, had a diameter of 260 mm with a sharply angular rather than rounded edge. The plug key (the only tool always to be carried, even on circuit bikes) can be seen on the front forks.

Albatros 250 cc

The *Albatros* came along in 1939, a result of a joint effort by Carlo Guzzi and an engineer called Giulio Cesare Carcano, whom we shall come across from this moment on in connection with all the most important Guzzi creations. Built for the races reserved for amateur riders on their production bikes, it was simply the works Grand Prix machine minus the blower and plus the electrics and other regulation accessories. After the war, when supercharging was banned, it became the marque's top racer in the 250 class. Guzzi continued to sell the *Albatros* to the general public and it became very popular with amateur riders. Mechanical perform-

ance was virtually on a par with the works machines and this enhanced the importance of the rider's skills as far as competition was concerned. The *Albatros* had red livery with amaranth panels on the tank. In 1939 the price was 12,500 lire, even more than a motorcycle truck. By the end of the Forties devaluation had taken the price up to 870,000 lire, a figure justified by the precision workmanship and the large number of parts which had to be hand finished in the race shop. In 1949 it gave way to the *Gambalunghino*, which was not however on general sale but was reserved for Guzzi works riders only.

Model / year	Albatros / 1939-1949
Engine	4-stroke flat single 68 × 68 mm / 246.8 cc
Compression ratio	8.5:1
Output	20 hp at 7000 rpm
Cylinder head	light alloy with valve seat inserts
Cylinder	light alloy with pressed-in liners
Valve arrangement	inclined overhead
Valve gear	overhead camshaft
Ignition	magneto
Carburettor	Dell'Orto SS 30 M
Lubrication	geared pressure pump; vane type scavenge pump
Clutch	wet multiplate type
Gearbox	foot-change 4-speed constant-mesh
Transmission	primary, helical gear; final drive, chain
Frame	duplex cradle in tubes and sheet metal
Wheelbase	1430 mm
Front suspension	girder fork with friction dampers
Rear suspension	swinging arm with friction dampers
Wheels	spoked with 21 × 2 1/4 rims
Tyres	front 2.75-21"; rear 3.00-21"
Brakes	expansion type; front manual, rear pedal
Weight	roadgoing version 135 kgs
Max speed	approx. 140 km/h
Normal consumption	—
Fuel tank capacity	20 litres
Lubricant capacity	5 litres

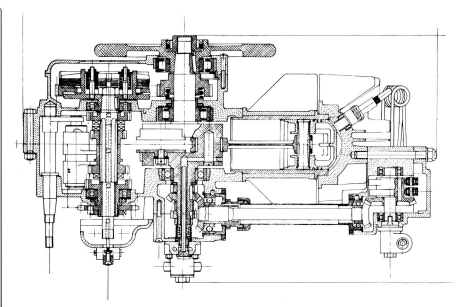

A cross-section of the *Albatros* engine. Note the one-piece crankshaft with the embodied counterweights, the three main bearings, the valve gear (pressure lubricated), the six-spring clutch and the frontally meshing gears. The crankpin (on needle bearings) and main journals measured 30 mm. The valves were set at 80 degrees to each other and the diameters were 33 mm inlet (later uprated to 35 mm) and 31 mm exhaust (sodium). The 30 mm carburettor was later changed for a 32 mm instrument. Straight-cut gears were chosen for the primary drive.

The original version of the *Albatros* sold in 1939 for production bike competition, complete with roadgoing accoutrements. It weighed 135 kgs and developed 20 hp. The frame design, derived from the works version, made extensive use of light alloys, as had been the case with the *Condor*: light alloy was used for the rear part of the cradle, the mudguards, the wheels, the brakes and even the saddle ribs.

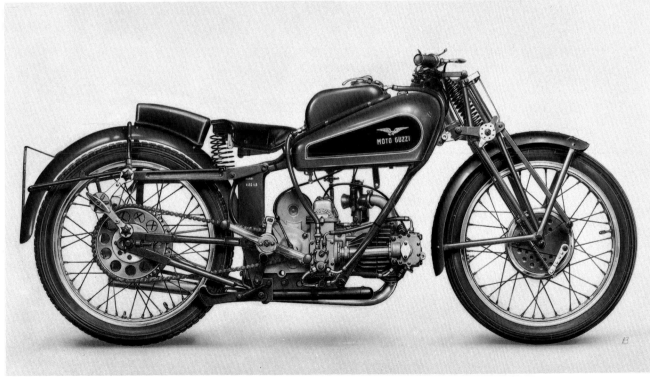

An *Albatros* from the immediate post-war period, devoid of the electrical system and with a new-style tank. A short time after, the redundant appendage for the dynamo drive (which had been originally taken from the blower drive) was eliminated by cutting the crankcase casting which was then covered with a little metal plate.
The long rear suspension box was also made of aluminium.

Tre cilindri 500 cc

Carlo Guzzi designed the blown 3-cylinder *500* in 1939 as his reply to the supercharged multi-cylinder machines then being manufactured by other Italian and foreign marques. Even though he stuck to an engine design which had already been tested at Mandello, this bike is outwith the mainstream Guzzi tradition, not only for the power unit (chain driven dohc, magneto ignition, clutch on the drive shaft) but also for the original frame. Other interesting technical features included the extremely extensive use of modern light alloys like electron and hydronalium, and the 5-speed gearbox. The imminence of the second World War made it impossible to perfect and exploit the qualities of this most original bike, which made a sole appearance at the Lido di Albaro circuit near Genoa in the May of 1940. Guglielmo Sandri was the rider on that occasion. After the war blown engines were banned from competition, partially because of safety considerations and largely because the victorious English wanted to deprive the vanquished Italians (and Germans) of a weapon which had made them demonstrably unbeatable.

The *Tre cilindri* still exists, albeit in a partially dismantled state, in the Guzzi Museum.

Model / year	Tre Cilindri / 1940
Engine	4-stroke three-in-line 59 × 60 mm / 491.8 cc
Compression ratio	8:1
Output	65 hp at 8000 rpm
Cylinder head	light alloy
Cylinder	light alloy with pressed-in liners
Valve arrangement	inclined overhead
Valve gear	double overhead camshaft
Ignition	magneto
Carburettor	Cozette
Lubrication	geared pressure and scavenge pumps
Clutch	dry multiplate type
Gearbox	foot-change 5-speed
Transmission	primary, gear driven; final drive, chain
Frame	tubes and sheet metal
Wheelbase	1470 mm
Front suspension	girder fork with friction dampers
Rear suspension	swinging arm with friction dampers
Wheels	spoked with 21 × 2 1/4 rims
Tyres	front 2.75-21"; rear 3.00-21"
Brakes	expansion type; front manual, rear pedal
Weight	175 kgs
Max speed	approx. 230 km/h
Normal consumption	—
Fuel tank capacity	22 litres
Lubricant capacity	5 litres

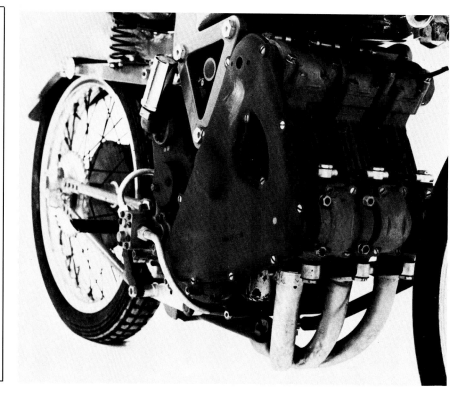

The supercharged *Tre Cilindri* is one of the least known Guzzis. These are probably the only photographs in existence of the complete machine. The architecture of the engine and the frame (with rear pressings made of hydronalium) can clearly be seen, as well as the supercharger and the clutch mounted on the crankshaft. The exhaust was a single pipe, on the left.

The timing chain for the twin camshafts was protected by the large casing visible on the right hand side. The dual oil pump can be seen under the supercharger. Widespread use was made of electron for the engine castings and the same material was also used for the wheel hubs, although aluminium was preferred for the rims. The bike was fitted with Brampton front forks.

Dondolino 500 cc

A direct descendant of the *Condor*, the *Dondolino* appeared in 1946 with improved brakes and rear suspension, as well as retouched styling. The engine had been upgraded obviously; the new 35 mm carburettor plus the modifications made to the timing diagram, valves and compression resulted in an improved output of 33 hp at 5500 rpm. A further update was made in 1948 with the addition of a third main bearing to the "Faenza" version, which took its name from the town where it made its debut. In the immediate post-war period, along with the rival Gilera *Saturno*, it was the most popular half-litre racer around as far as private entrants were concerned and it won stacks of circuit events and hill-climbs, as well as a considerable number of minor championships. But it is especially remembered for its domination of the big races like the Milano-Taranto which, thanks to its robust construction, it won four times in a row between 1950 and '53, a worthy successor to the victorious pre-war *Condor*. Like its stablemate the *Albatros*, the *Dondolino* was built until 1951 (in small batches of 25 or 50 units) by the Guzzi racing department. The devaluation of the lira took the price up to 895,000 lire. The colour scheme was the same as that of the *Condor*.

Model / year	Dondolino / 1946-1951
Engine	4-stroke flat single 88 × 82 mm / 498.4 cc
Compression ratio	8.5:1
Output	33 hp at 5500 rpm
Cylinder head	light alloy with valve seat inserts
Cylinder	light alloy with pressed-in liners
Valve arrangement	inclined overhead
Valve gear	push rods and rocker arms
Ignition	magneto
Carburettor	Dell'Orto SS 35 M
Lubrication	geared pressure pump; vane type scavenge pump
Clutch	wet multiplate type
Gearbox	foot-change 4-speed constant-mesh
Transmission	primary, spur gear ; final drive, chain
Frame	duplex cradle in tubes and sheet metal
Wheelbase	1470 mm
Front suspension	girder fork with friction dampers
Rear suspension	swinging arm with friction dampers
Wheels	spoked with 21 × 2 1/4 rims
Tyres	front 2.75-21"; rear 3.00-21"
Brakes	expansion type; front manual, rear pedal
Weight	128 kgs
Max speed	approx. 170 km/h
Normal consumption	—
Fuel tank capacity	19 litres
Lubricant capacity	3.5 litres

The *Dondolino* engine differed from that of the *Condor* in that it had a new 35 mm carburettor, different valve gear, and from 1948 onwards, a third main bearing housed in the primary drive cover.

When production bike competition was abolished shortly after the war, the *Dondolino* was almost always supplied without the electrical system, which was fitted only for the Milano-Taranto event or if specially requested by those customers who wished to use this racer as a "gran turismo" speedster. The big 260 mm front brake had all its works fitted internally so as to leave the drum as smooth and streamlined as possible.

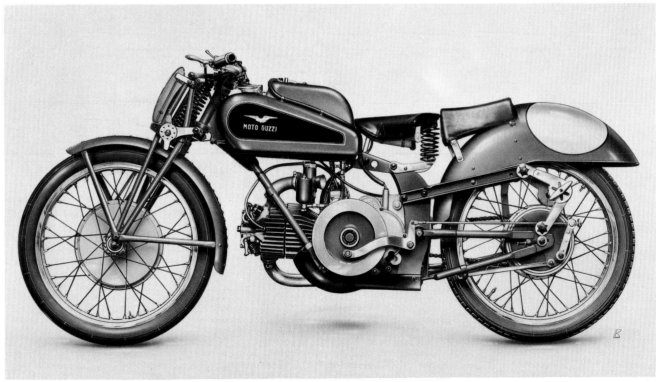

The *Dondolino* frame was practically identical to that of the *Condor*, but the rear suspension had one spring only — with a counteracting spring — in place of the old double pack. This was covered, along with the crankcase, by a small metal fairing. The *Dondolino* was assembled in small batches by the Guzzi race shop, and so small variations in colour and other details may be found between one model and another, as can be seen from the two photographs on this page.

Gambalunga 500 cc

The *Gambalunga*, a *Dondolino* derivative which was created in 1946, is the first "modern" Guzzi racer. The new racer represented a break with a quarter century of stylistic tradition on the one hand and the culmination, at least as far as performance was concerned, of Carlo Guzzi's original single-cylinder design on the other. At first the new "long-stroker" (hence the name, which means "long leg") had the con-rod at less of an angle so as to reduce engine stress, but it was later fitted with a classic 88 × 82 mm "short-stroke" engine. This was better suited to the business of turning out high revs, even though it had a new three-bearing crankshaft, which was also fitted to the *Dondolino* at a slightly later date.

In theory reserved for works riders (but one or two models found their way into the hands of privaters just the same), the *Gambalunga* was raced until 1951, because it was more manageable than the *Bicilindrica* over mixed circuits. Modifications were made to the chassis and the suspension over the years with a view to lowering and streamlining the bike. Carcano's original leading link forks were later adopted in slightly modified form for all Guzzi Grand Prix machines until 1957.

Model / year	Gambalunga / 1946-1948
Engine	4-stroke flat single 84 × 90 mm / 498.5 cc
Compression ratio	8:1
Output	35 hp at 5800 rpm
Cylinder head	light alloy with valve seat inserts
Cylinder	light alloy with pressed-in liners
Valve arrangement	inclined overhead
Valve gear	push rods and rocker arms
Ignition	magneto
Carburettor	Dell'Orto SS 35 M
Lubrication	geared pressure pump; vane type scavenge pump
Clutch	wet multiplate type
Gearbox	foot-change 4-speed constant-mesh
Transmission	primary, spur gear ; final drive, chain
Frame	duplex cradle in tubes and sheet metal
Wheelbase	1470 mm
Front suspension	leading link fork with friction dampers
Rear suspension	swinging arm with friction dampers
Wheels	spoked with 21 × 2 1/4 rims
Tyres	front: ribbed 2.75-21"; rear studded 3.00-21"
Brakes	expansion type; front manual, rear pedal
Weight	125 kgs
Max speed	approx. 180 km/h
Normal consumption	—
Fuel tank capacity	23 litres
Lubricant capacity	3 litres

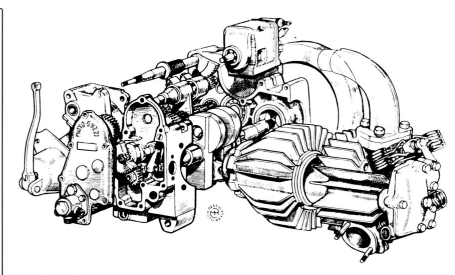

The *Gambalunga* engine broken down into its principal elements, in a drawing originally published in *Moto Revue*. As can be seen, it was plainly inspired by the *Dondolino* and therefore also by the normal *V*-type engines. The variation in the stroke was obtained by increasing the thickness of the flange at the base of the cylinder and obviously by fitting a new crankshaft. As from 1948, with the return to popularity of the "short stroke" design, it was fitted with a third main (roller) bearing, which was housed in the primary drive cover. The three photographs on the following page illustrate the evolution of the *Gambalunga*. Top left, the original version from 1946, with frame and forks from the *Dondolino* and 21" wheels; top right, the 1950 model with modified rear end and 20" wheels. The largest photo is the last version (1951), which had a carb with a detachable float chamber.

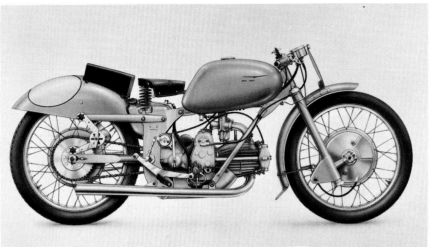

Due cilindri 250 cc

The first completely new competition machine to make its appearance after the war was the dohc *250 bicilindrica* from 1947. Designed by Micucci (the father of the *65*), this was vaguely inspired by the blown *Tre cilindri* from 1939-1940. The principal characteristic of this bike was the widespread use of light alloys and decidedly advanced technology: electron was used for engine and brakes, the frame was in hydronalium, while the combustion chambers were made of aluminium bronze. A blower was also fitted, as its definitive abolition was still uncertain at that time. The lubrication system, so important in an air-cooled engine, was also designed with care; it was composed of a double feed pump and one return pump. Two slightly different versions were prepared, one in 1947 and one in 1948. These were tested on various circuits but the results were well below expectations since the extra horses (compared to the *Albatros*) in no way made up for the increased dimensions and reduced manageability. The *250 bicilindrica* was sidelined in the end, and Guzzi chose to work on perfecting the tried and tested single-cylinder engine. Nevertheless this twin-cylinder model remains a very interesting chapter in the history of racing bikes.

Model / year	Due Cilindri / 1947-1948
Engine	4-stroke inclined twin 54 × 54 mm / 247.2 cc
Compression ratio	10:1
Output	25 hp at 9000 rpm
Cylinder head	light alloy with valve seat inserts
Cylinder	light alloy with pressed-in liners
Valve arrangement	inclined overhead
Valve gear	dohc
Ignition	Bosch type magneto
Carburettors	Dell'Orto
Lubrication	geared pressure and scavenge pumps
Clutch	wet multiplate type
Gearbox	foot-change 4-speed constant-mesh
Transmission	primary, gear driven; final drive, chain
Frame	single spar and sheet metal
Wheelbase	1420 mm
Front suspension	teledraulic fork
Rear suspension	swinging arm with friction dampers
Wheels	spoked with 21 × 2 1/4 rims
Tyres	front 2.75-21"; rear 3.00-21"
Brakes	expansion type; front manual, rear pedal
Weight	125 kgs
Max speed	approx. 170 km/h
Normal consumption	—
Fuel tank capacity	21 litres
Lubricant capacity	4.5 litres

The 1948 version of the *250* twin-cylinder engine.

The first version of the *250* twin (1947), with the oil tank mounted beneath the fuel tank and the cylinder heads fixed to the steering with hydronalium plates. The cylinder finning was very original: partly transverse, partly longitudinal. Under the motor you can see the rear suspension pack with the built-in hydraulic dampers. The offset axle design of the telescopic front forks was ahead of its time and is the "latest thing" today.

The 1948 version of the *250* twin with the modified front frame and new tanks (the oil tank had been shifted to under the saddle). The two overhead camshafts were driven by a train of five gears, one of which was mounted on an eccentric support in order to vary the centre distances in case it were ever necessary to alter the compression ratio by raising or lowering the heads. The valves were actuated by the action of a small steel slider.

Gambalunghino 250 cc

The *Gambalunghino* ("Little long-leg") entered this world almost by chance when Enrico Lorenzetti thought to repair his accident-damaged *Albatros* using *Gambalunga* components. The result was a classic case of hybrid vigour, for the *Gambalunghino* went on to become a Guzzi works machine in 1949, the year in which it brought the 250 class World Championship home to Mandello del Lario for the first time ever. The big-hearted single-cylinder engine, even though it dated from 1926, was still able to beat its closest rivals, but it needed an updated frame. As a result, the *Gambalunghino* chassis was perfected until the final version

was produced in 1952: a masterpiece of functionality, this was the forerunner of the aerodynamic research of the following years which was to enable Guzzi to produce streamlined machines capable of seeing off even those opponents with larger engines. The *Gambalunghino* was reserved for works riders but several private individuals nevertheless managed to get their hands on the parts they needed to convert their old *Albatros*, and so at the end of the day there were more *Gambalunghinos* running around than were actually built! The first versions were painted silver, the last in red.

Model / year	Gambalunghino / 1949
Engine	4-stroke flat single 68 × 68 mm / 246.8 cc
Compression ratio	8.5:1
Output	25 hp at 8000 rpm
Cylinder head	light alloy with valve seat inserts
Cylinder	light alloy with pressed-in liners
Valve arrangement	inclined overhead
Valve gear	overhead camshaft
Ignition	magneto
Carburettor	Dell'Orto SS 35
Lubrication	geared pressure pump; vane type scavenge pump
Clutch	wet multiplate type
Gearbox	foot-change 4-speed constant-mesh
Transmission	primary, spur gear ; final drive, chain
Frame	duplex cradle in tubes and sheet metal
Wheelbase	1420 mm
Front suspension	leading link fork with friction dampers
Rear suspension	swinging arm with friction dampers
Wheels	spoked with 21 × 2 1/4 rims
Tyres	front 2.75-21"; rear 3.00-21"
Brakes	expansion type; front manual, rear pedal
Weight	122 kgs
Max speed	180 km/h
Normal consumption	—
Fuel tank capacity	21 litres
Lubricant capacity	4 litres

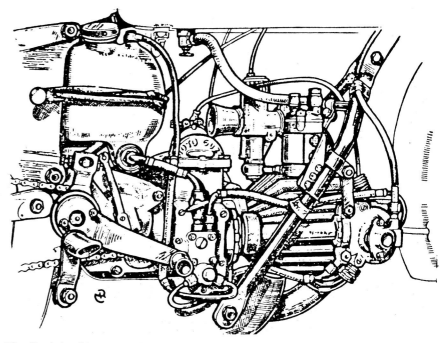

The *Gambalunghino*-type engine, a direct descendant of the *Albatros*, after a drawing published in *Moto Revue*. This is the version prepared for the 1949 Grand Prix of Nations; it had a carburettor with a detachable float chamber and the oil tank was held in place by rubber stays.

The first version of the *Gambalunghino* appeared at the beginning of 1949. The frame and rear suspension were still those of the *Albatros*, and so indeed was the engine. Note the addition of the little stays running between the frame and the timing cover. The wheels were 21".

In the first version of the *Gambalunghino*, directly derived from Lorenzetti's *Albatros* conversion, we still find the single-barrel carburettor. The front brake had been pirated from the *Gambalunga*, while the 200 mm rear brake was left unchanged. In 1949 the *Gambalunghino* was to win the first World Championship, with Bruno Ruffo in the saddle.

The first substantial modifications to the *Gambalunghino* were made in 1950, when the bike received a lower, more streamlined look. The engine was fitted with a new carburettor which fed the mixture to the engine in a straight line. Note too the additional stays running from the bolt on the lower chassis to the head. A five-speed gearbox was tried out in 1951 (in photo).

The last version of the *Gambalunghino* dates from 1952. This strictly functional machine had slightly modified rear suspension (sporadic experimentation had begun the previous year), and a longer fuel tank while the oil was held in the upper spar of the new frame. Thanks to these changes the bike seemed much longer than it really was, an effect which was heightened by the empty space created above the engine. However the lines were sleek and low slung, the first step on the road to integral fairings and the virtually perfect streamlining of the future.

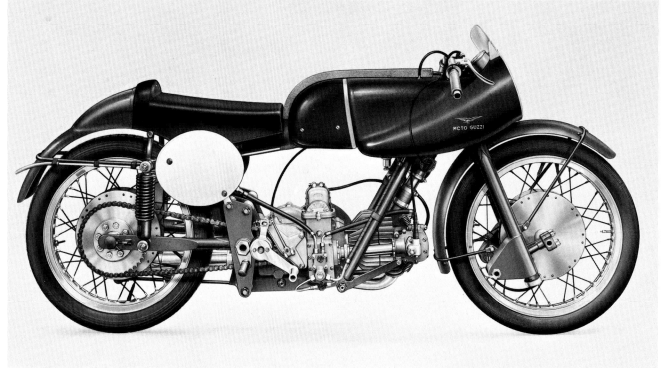

In 1950 and '51 the *Gambalunghino* was also used for some long distance record attempts, still at the Montlhéry autodrome in France, where a speed of 160 km/h was returned for the 2 hours, 144.9 km/h for the 1,000 kms and 139.8 km/h for the Thousand Miles. These averages include the dead times for refuelling and change of riders.

As can be seen, the record breaking *Gambalunghino* (this is the bike used in 1951) was practically identical to the normal racing versions; the only differences being a small fairing over the steering head, a larger capacity tank and the footrests (which had been shifted to a more ergonomic position with a view to easing the strain on the rider over long distances).

Quattro cilindri 500 cc

The four-cylinder half-litre machine which came out in 1952 represented a decisive break with classic Guzzi design schemes: the job of designing it had been handed over to a young Roman engineer called Gianini because it was felt that no-one at Mandello was able to break away from the bonds of traditional Guzzi engineering. The new bike had a longitudinal shaft-driven engine mounted on a trellis-type chassis made of small diameter tubing. A carburettor rather like the one fitted to the pre-war "Gerolamo" engine fed the fuel to the engine. Practically only the front part of the frame with the *Gambalunga*-type forks resembled the other competition Guzzis. It was first raced in 1953 with what can only be described as a "bird-beak" fairing, while later in that same season the frame was radically modified and the bike was fitted with a "dustbin" fairing. Another remarkable feature was the braking system which could apportion the braking force between front and rear, one of Guzzi's first stabs at what was later to become known as "integral braking", a standard feature on modern bikes. Powerful, but hard to ride, this four-cylinder model managed to score only two wins, and it was definitively pensioned off in 1954.

Model / year	Quattro cilindri / 1952-1954
Engine	4-stroke four-in-line 56 × 50 mm / 492.3 cc
Compression ratio	11:1
Output	54 hp at 9000 rpm
Cylinder head	light alloy
Cylinder	light alloy with pressed-in liners
Valve arrangement	inclined overhead
Valve gear	double overhead camshaft
Ignition	magneto
Carburettor	indirect injection
Lubrication	geared pressure pump; vane type scavenge pump
Clutch	wet multiplate type
Gearbox	foot-change 4-speed constant-mesh
Transmission	primary, gear driven; final drive, shaft
Frame	tubular trellis
Wheelbase	1400 mm
Front suspension	leading link fork with friction dampers
Rear suspension	swinging arm with friction dampers
Wheels	spoked: front 19", rear 18"
Tyres	front 3.00-19"; rear 3.25-18"
Brakes	expansion type; front, manual (4 shoes); rear, pedal
Weight	145 kgs
Max speed	230 km/h
Normal consumption	—
Fuel tank capacity	28 litres
Lubricant capacity	4.5 litres

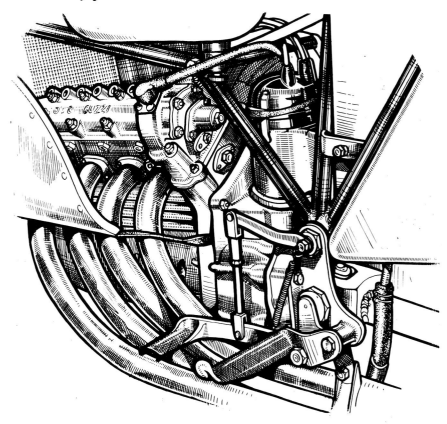

The definitive version of the *Quattro cilindri* which made its competition debut in 1953, equipped with the new "bird beak" fairing. The tank, saddle and rear mudguard were different to the prototype. The carburettor was on the right, while the four exhaust pipes were arranged in an organ pipe pattern on the left. The drive shaft ran in the left hand side tube of the swinging arm, which pivoted on the chassis. The front brakes had twin leading shoes as well as two hangers which connected the fork with the brake shoe carriers on both sides.

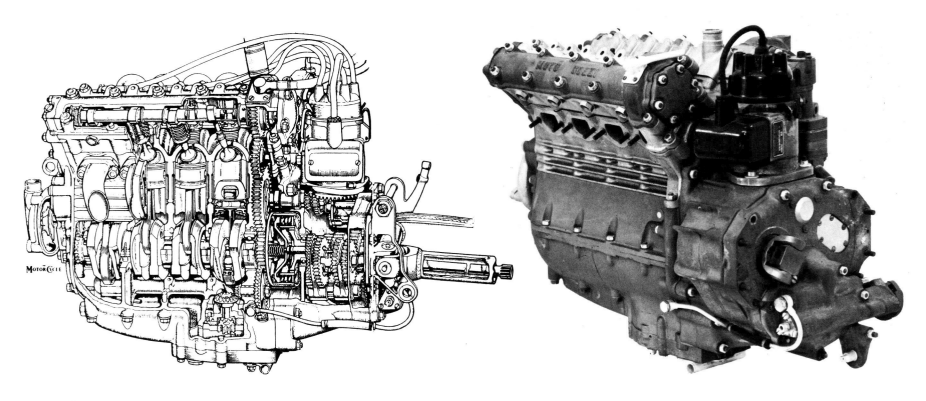

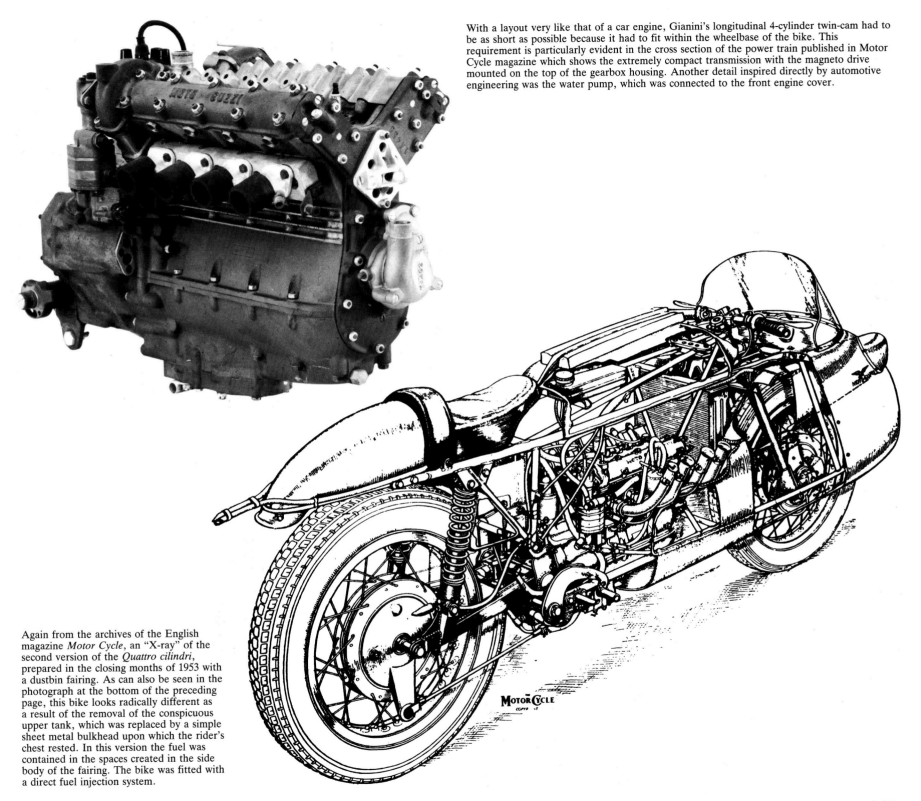

With a layout very like that of a car engine, Gianini's longitudinal 4-cylinder twin-cam had to be as short as possible because it had to fit within the wheelbase of the bike. This requirement is particularly evident in the cross section of the power train published in Motor Cycle magazine which shows the extremely compact transmission with the magneto drive mounted on the top of the gearbox housing. Another detail inspired directly by automotive engineering was the water pump, which was connected to the front engine cover.

Again from the archives of the English magazine *Motor Cycle*, an "X-ray" of the second version of the *Quattro cilindri*, prepared in the closing months of 1953 with a dustbin fairing. As can also be seen in the photograph at the bottom of the preceding page, this bike looks radically different as a result of the removal of the conspicuous upper tank, which was replaced by a simple sheet metal bulkhead upon which the rider's chest rested. In this version the fuel was contained in the spaces created in the side body of the fairing. The bike was fitted with a direct fuel injection system.

MotorCycle

345

250 cc bialbero

Research into the transformation of the *250* single into a twin-cam version began in 1950 with the introduction of a four-valve head which did not however produce satisfactory results. A two-valve version produced in 1953 proved much more successful and the old Guzzi engine was once more on an equal footing with its younger and highly competitive rivals. Effectively speaking, this was the *Gambalunghino* power unit with a new cast electron rocker cover beneath which the two camshafts were connected to the upper bevel gear by a spur gear train. Another important innovation from that year was the sheet elec-

tron fairing which had been created after experimentation in the new wind tunnel recently installed at the Mandello works.
The new streamlining resulted in much higher speeds of around 200 km/h.
The *250 bialbero*, which used *Gambalunghino* cycle parts, apart from the large lowered tank, was raced successfully in 1953 and '54; in 1955 it appeared in minor races only and was pensioned off at the end of that season, Guzzi having decided to sacrifice the quarter litre category in order to concentrate upon competition reserved for the larger bikes.

Model / year	250 bialbero / 1953
Engine	4-stroke flat single 68 × 68.4 mm / 248.2 cc
Compression ratio	9.5:1
Output	28 hp at 8000 rpm
Cylinder head	light alloy with valve seat inserts
Cylinder	light alloy with pressed-in liners
Valve arrangement	inclined overhead
Valve gear	double overhead camshaft
Ignition	magneto
Carburettor	Dell'Orto 40 mm
Lubrication	geared pressure pump; vane type scavenge pump
Clutch	wet multiplate type
Gearbox	foot-change 4 or 5-speed constant-mesh
Transmission	primary, spur gear ; final drive, chain
Frame	tubular main spar and sheet metal
Wheelbase	1420 mm
Front suspension	swinging link fork with friction dampers
Rear suspension	swinging arm with friction dampers
Wheels	spoked: front 19 × 2 1/4, rear 19 × 2 1/2
Tyres	front ribbed 2.75-19"; rear studded 3.00-19"
Brakes	expansion type: front manual (2 shoes); rear, pedal
Weight	122 kgs
Max speed	200 km/h
Normal consumption	—
Fuel tank capacity	21 litres
Lubricant capacity	4 litres

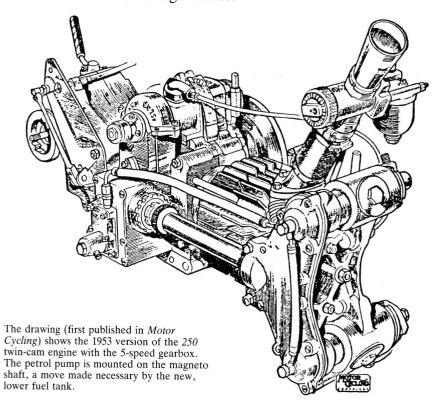

The drawing (first published in *Motor Cycling*) shows the 1953 version of the *250* twin-cam engine with the 5-speed gearbox. The petrol pump is mounted on the magneto shaft, a move made necessary by the new, lower fuel tank.

The dohc *250* from the beginning of 1953 with an original "bird beak" fairing, the fruit of wind tunnel research. Only the lower part of the body contained fuel: the upper part was merely to support the rider's chest. This had the effect of lowering the centre of gravity quite considerably.

At the 1953 Grand Prix of Nations the bike appeared with an improved, even lower fairing which was to be retained for some seasons to come. During this period the bike was often lined up in support of the new model with the dustbin fairing.

350 cc and 500 cc

In 1953 it was decided to compete in the 350 class, which had a big following abroad. At first a sohc *Gambalunghino* engine was uprated as far as possible (to 317 cc) then, following modifications to the crankcase, the displacement was pushed up to 345 cc and finally to 349 cc. The results were exceptional right from the start and the World Constructors' and Riders' Championships were soon winging their way to Mandello. A new single-cylinder engine was prepared for the following year in 250 cc (used only rarely however) 350 and 500 cc versions; the latter being intended as an alternative to the *Otto cilindri* for use on twistier circuits.

The crankcase and heads were of new design. During the years that followed further changes were made: to the cylinder measurements (250 and 350); the ignition system (a coil feeding two plugs and then a magneto); the frame; and finally to the fairing, which was made sleeker than ever. Naturally performance kept pace with these improvements, so much so that — thanks also to minimal weight and excellent streamlining — these machines were able to handle even their most powerful multi-cylinder rivals. This was especially true of the 350, which took its riders to World Championship victory without a break until 1957.

Model / year	350 bialbero / 1954
Engine	4-stroke flat single 80 × 69.5 mm / 349.2 cc
Compression ratio	9.4:1
Output	35 hp at 7800 rpm
Cylinder head	light alloy with valve seat inserts
Cylinder	light alloy with pressed-in liners
Valve arrangement	inclined overhead
Valve gear	double overhead camshaft
Ignition	coil
Carburettor	Dell'Orto
Lubrication	geared pressure pump; vane type scavenge pump
Clutch	wet multiplate type
Gearbox	foot-change 5-speed constant-mesh
Transmission	primary, spur gear ; final drive, chain
Frame	tubular trellis
Wheelbase	1470 mm
Front suspension	leading link fork with friction dampers
Rear suspension	swinging arm with friction dampers
Wheels	spoked with 19 × 2 1/4 rims
Tyres	front 2.75-19"; rear 3.00-19"
Brakes	expansion type: front, manual (4 shoes); rear, pedal
Weight	127 kgs
Max speed	220 km/h
Normal consumption	—
Fuel tank capacity	20 litres
Lubricant capacity	3 litres

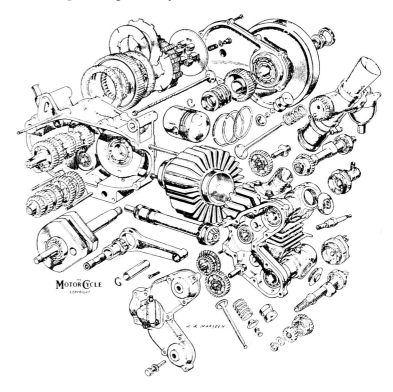

The preceding page shows an exploded view (from *Motor Cycle*) of the monobloc version of the single-cylinder *350* twin-cam. This is the '56-'57 model with attachments for the raised frame. The 500 engine was virtually identical. Left, the first 350 from 1953, with the sohc *Gambalunghino*-derived engine. Capacity was successively uprated from 317 cc (72 × 78 mm) to 345 cc (75 × 78) and finally to 349 cc (75 × 79). Power was increased from 31 to 33 hp at 7500 rpm. Depending on the circuit, the bike was fitted with either a four or a five-speed gearbox. Other details: magneto ignition, a 35 mm carburettor (later increased to 40 mm), a 2.75-19" front tyre and a 3.00-19" tyre at the rear, twin-shoe front brake, 1420 mm wheelbase, weight 122 kgs, 21 litre fuel tank and a top speed of about 210 km/h.

The first single-cylinder bike with a dustbin fairing appeared at the beginning of 1954, with the engine supported by a trellis frame. The fuel was contained in the side body of the fairing. Then the new twin-cam engines with the monobloc head were fitted to the 250 (68 × 68.4 mm and then 70 × 64.8), the 350 (80 × 69.5 mm, 35 hp at 7800 rpm) and the 500 (88 x 82 mm, 42 hp at 7000 rpm). Instead of the classic magneto, there was dual coil ignition with the distributor mounted on top of the crankcase. The gearbox was a 5-speed unit. The 250 cc engine was also fitted to the old frame with the bird-beak fairing. The very first 500 cc engine was a sohc version.

349

In the course of 1954 the fairing was given a more raked line at the front. The new barrel-type tank was first mounted cross-wise, and then integrated with the upper tank thus providing a total capacity of 30 litres. The rear element of the fairing, as shown in the photo, was used practically by Anderson alone, and only on certain circuits at that. The 350 ran on 2.75-19" tyres in front and 3.00-20" behind, weighed 123 kgs and could reach 220-230 km/h depending on the fairing. The vane-type petrol pump can just be seen on the extension of the contact breaker shaft. Note the unusual two-piece gear pedal.

In 1955 the dustbin fairing fitted to the singles was further refined, thanks to new research carried out in the wind tunnel. Moreover, the joint half away along the side wall was eliminated. The model shown is fitted with the double tank, which had an overall capacity of 30 litres. The engines and frames were practically the same as the previous year, but the more favourable drag factor led to even higher speeds.

350

In 1956 further work was done on the fairing (note the new windscreen) and the chassis was remodelled: a large new upper tube doubled as an oil tank and the engine hung from a trellis type structure, which made for easier dismantling. Some work had also been done on the engine: the contact breaker for the dual ignition system was mounted on the side, above the geared oil pump, as can be seen in the photo below.

The petrol pump was fitted to the left hand end of the intake camshaft. In 1957 the designers went back to the magneto with a single spark plug, however this too was mounted on the right hand side instead of its old place above the crankcase (photo above). The front forks and brake were the *Otto cilindri* type. In this version, the *350 GP* engine developed 38 hp at 8000 rpm, with bore and stroke of 75 × 79 mm, 39 mm intake valves and 32 mm exhaust, 10 mm spark plug, 2.50-19" tyres, while the *500* produced 42 hp at 7000 rpm. Speeds were around 230-240 km/h.

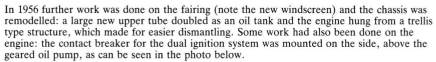

The sohc 350 cc engine was also used for various record attempts, all of which were crowned by success. For example in 1955 a record for the prestigious one hour run was established with an average speed of 210.130 km/h, as well a series of other long distance records up to and including the 1,000 Miles at 173.700 km/h, the 2,000 kms at 164.660 km/h and the 12 hours at 164.570 km/h. The record bids took place at the Montlhéry circuit on two separate occasions, in March and at the end of October with riders Agostini, Anderson, Dale and Kavanagh. Note the handguards added to the fairing; the photo (taken at Mandello) shows the front "beak" which was later removed for the record attempt.

During the second session, which was held at Montlhéry at the end of October 1955, record bids were also made in the 350 sidecar class with Anderson and Lomas. The bike with the sohc engine and the '53 model fairing was fitted with a small, streamlined sidecar carrying the regulation ballast of 60 kgs. The records established went from the 10 km at an average of 196.190 km/h, to the one hour run (without the sidecar) at 210.129 km/h; and from the 50 kms at an average of 163.480 km/h, to the two hour run (with the sidecar) at an average of 155.560 km/h.

352

In the October of 1956 Guzzi beat another two world records in the 350 class : i.e. the standing kilometre, run in 24" 29/100 at 148.109 km/h, and the standing mile in 34" 9, at a speed of 165.911 km/h. These are two hard records to beat because you need lightning acceleration allied to great riding skills on the rider's part. The photo on the left shows the record-breaking bike minus the fairing.

The October 1956 record attempts were staged on the runway of a military airstrip at Montichiari. The ride was given to the experienced Enrico Lorenzetti, who also made an important contribution to the work of tuning the bike, which was fitted with several components pirated from the custom-built special he had had made some little time before. It is worth noting that immediately after the brilliant results achieved at Montichiari, Guzzi went back to magneto ignition, even for its Grand Prix bikes.

Otto cilindri 500 cc

The *V8*, over and beyond the practical results it achieved, is also a vitally important chapter in the history of motorcycling, a technical tour de force which is still in a class of its own despite all the progress made since 1955. Carcano's 500 cc power unit represents the ultimate in multi-cylinder motorcycle engines and is the concrete expression of an idea which no other designer has had the courage to imitate from that day to this. The fruit of research specifically aimed at producing a bike in a class above its rivals, the *V8* was created with incredible speed and the first tests were already underway by 1955. Preparation continued all through 1956, accompanied by all the predictable difficulties that such complex designs bring in their wake, but results were promising. By 1957 the bike was becoming decidedly competitive and some convincing wins did in fact come along as well as some prestigious records, some of which stood for over twenty years.

Probably 1958 would have been the *V8*'s year of grace, but unfortunately the marque's withdrawal from racing brought this fabulous bike's career to a premature end. Two models are on show at the Guzzi Museum in Mandello.

Model / year	Otto cilindri / 1955-1957
Engine	4-stroke 90 degree V8 44 × 41 mm / 498.5 cc
Compression ratio	10:1
Output	68 hp at 12,000 rpm (1955) 72 hp at 12,000 rpm (1957)
Cylinder head	light alloy
Cylinder	light alloy with pressed-in liners
Valve arrangement	inclined overhead
Valve gear	double overhead camshaft
Ignition	coil
Carburettors	8 Dell'Orto 20 mm
Lubrication	geared pressure and scavenge pumps
Clutch	dry multiplate type
Gearbox	foot change 4-speed constant mesh
Transmission	primary, spur gear ; final drive, chain
Frame	tubular duplex cradle
Wheelbase	1420 mm
Front suspension	leading link fork with friction dampers
Rear suspension	swinging arm with friction dampers
Wheels	spoked: front 19 × 2 1/4; rear 20 × 2 1/2
Tyres	front 2.75-19"; rear 3.00-20"
Brakes	expansion type: front, manual (4 shoes); rear, pedal
Weight	150 kgs
Max speed	275 km/h
Normal consumption	—
Fuel tank capacity	34 litres
Lubricant capacity	4 litres

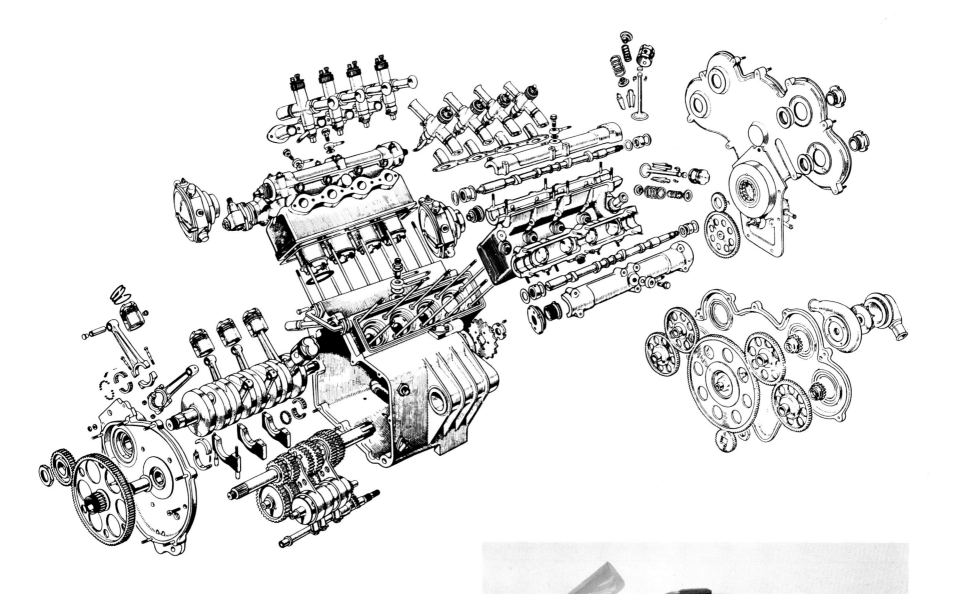

On the facing page, the first version of the V8 engine, seen from the rear. The closely packed rank of Dell'Orto carburettors, specially made to fit into a very restricted space, can be seen along the top of the engine. Above, an exploded view of the V8 engine.
This is also the first version, with the 6-speed gearbox (which was later reduced to five, and then four). Note too the carburettors, which were not equipped with individual float chambers. Other modifications were later made to the valve gear (valve guides and tappets) and the crankshaft. The firing order was 1-8-3-6-4-5-2-7, from right to left and starting from the group in front.
There is also a sturdy attachment point for the rear swinging arm support spindle.
On the right, the first version of the V8 was tested on several circuits during 1955 with the hand beaten dustbin fairing still showing the signs of the panelbeater's hammer.

Another two shots of the *V8*. Here we see an experimental version of the bike fitted out for short circuits (note the small tank and the fairing with no air intakes).
In the photo of the bike minus the fairing much of the front suspension has been removed. The form of the duplex cradle can clearly be seen as can the large upper spar (which doubled as an oil tank) as well as the supporting framework for the fairing. The ignition coils were mounted four on each side of the engine. The front brake had twin leading shoes and two cams.

On the following page, the definitive version of the *V8*, with the two fairings, partial and dustbin type, whose deployment depended on the characteristics of the various circuits. In the photo above (which shows the bike without the fairing), you can see the timing cover and the centrifugal water pump, the complex linkages for the simultaneous control of the eight carburettors and the double oil pump. Note the layout of the exhaust pipes. The radiator was mounted in front, at a slight downwards tilt.

Four-wheeled record breakers

Guzzi competition engines, thanks to a highly favourable weight-power ratio plus their undeniable powers of resistance have always been widely used outside the strictly motorcycling field.

For example, there were many famous nautical applications, especially the work of Gino Alquati who won a great deal of races and set numerous records after the war using an *Albatros* engine as an outboard motor.

Numerous applications were also found for motor cars, particularly for record attempts in the small engine categories. Wor-

thy of note in this regard are the *Nibbio* vetturette which was designed and driven in 1935 by Count Giovanni Lurani, and Piero Taruffi's *Bisiluro* (1948), both of which were powered by the wide-angled 500 V-twin engine. In 1956 and '57 the *Nibbio II* was built. This was a super sleek affair with a Ghia body along the lines of the *Gilda*, a concept car which is still on show at the Ford Museum in Detroit.

The engine in this case was the 350 sohc single. Finally, in 1963 Campanella and Poggio produced the *Colibrì*, powered by the 1954 version of the 250 twin-cam engine.

These two pages show a photographic synthesis of the principal four-wheeled record breakers, powered by specially prepared Guzzi engines. Top left, the second version of the *Nibbio*, designed by Giovanni Lurani with the help of Ulisse Guzzi (Carlo's son). Fitted out with the wide-angled V-twin engine mounted on a tubular chassis with a Fiat 508 front axle, the first *Nibbio* developed 50 hp: on the 5th of November 1935 on the Firenze-Mare road it broke the record for the kilometre and the mile for the under 500 cc vetturette class. The standing start records fell the following day at the hands of Möritz on the DKW and this provoked Guzzi into preparing a second version of the Nibbio, with improved streamlining and Tecnauto independent suspension at the front. In May 1939 Lurani set new records at Dessau-Bitterfeld on a special stretch of the Berlin-Munich autobahn. The top speed had gone from 162 to 174 km/h.

Piero Taruffi smashed several motoring records with the post-war version of the V-twin engine, after installing it in the "Bisiluro Tarf", an original construction with a very low coefficient of drag which he designed and built himself. The basic concept was to house the engine and the driver in a tubular structure which also contained a pair of wheels. With less power at his disposal than Lurani had been blessed with, in 1948 Taruffi managed to obtain a top speed of about 207 km/h. In May 1955 Lurani, along with friends Piero Campanella and Angelo Poggio, instigated the preparation of the *Nibbio II*, which was powered by a sohc single-cylinder 350 cc engine mounted in a Volpini frame. The body was designed by Ghia on the basis of drawings by an engineer called Giovanni Savonuzzi. The career of the *Nibbio II* (preceding page, on the right) was a long one, studded with a series of middle and long distance records, set at the Monza autodrome from March 1956 to 1958. The same vehicle scored some new records in 1960, but on that occasion it was fitted with a 250 cc twin-cam single-cylinder engine. The last four-wheeler from Poggio and Campanella came along in 1963 and was called the *Colibrì* (humming bird — the traditional Guzzi predilection for ornithological names was continued even though the Mandello marque's involvement in these initiatives was strictly unofficial). A 250 cc single-cylinder twin-cam engine with a 5-speed gearbox was mounted on a Stanguellini frame and bodied by the Modena firm of Gransport. Designed for long distance work, the engine developed about 29 hp and gave a top speed of over 165 km/h. Campanella and Poggio broke records for the 50 to 200 kms as well as 50 to 100 miles distance, not forgetting the record for the Hour for the K class. Left, Cavanna's *Cobra* vetturette.

MILITARY AND POLICE MOTORCYCLES

G.T. 17

The *G.T. 17* was Guzzi's first purpose-built military motorcycle, as the *G.T. 16*s with which the army had been previously supplied were merely civilian machines with some minor modifications. A very robust bike, with a 500 cc opposed valve engine, three-speed gearbox and sprung frame, the *G.T. 17* became very popular, especially during the African War of 1935-36, where it was arguably the most efficient motorized vehicle which the Italians possessed. It was built in single and two-seater versions with adjustable suspension and, in order to satisfy the military authorities (who did not have a clear idea of the possible appli-

cations of motorcycles in wartime) it was fitted with light and heavy machine guns.

Other purpose-built variants with different equipment (panniers etc) were also supplied.

The *G.T. 17* was painted dark green or sand. The *Milizia della Strada* (Traffic Police) also took delivery of a goodly number of units. In 1939 this bike was replaced by the 4-speed *G.T. 20*, but many models remained in service until the end of the war. In total 4,810 units were made, an important number for Guzzi, but not enough to equip an army.

Model / year	G.T. 17 / 1932-1939
Engine	4-stroke flat single 88 × 82 mm / 498.4 cc
Compression ratio	4.7:1
Output	13.2 hp at 4000 rpm
Cylinder head	cast iron
Cylinder	cast iron
Valve arrangement	opposed; inlet at side; exhaust overhead
Valve gear	inlet, tappet; exhaust, push rod-rocker arm
Ignition	Marelli MLA 1 type magneto
Carburettor	Dell'Orto MC 26 F
Lubrication	geared pressure pump; vane type scavenge pump
Clutch	wet multiplate type
Gearbox	hand-change 3-speed sliding gears
Transmission	primary, helical gear; final drive, chain
Frame	duplex cradle in tubes and sheet metal
Wheelbase	1500 mm
Front suspension	girder fork with friction dampers
Rear suspension	swinging arm with friction dampers
Wheels	spoked with 19 × 3 rims
Tyres	3.50-19"
Brakes	expansion type: front manual, rear pedal control
Weight	single-seater in running order 196 kgs
Max speed	100 km/h
Normal consumption	4.9 litres per 100 kms
Fuel tank capacity	11.5 litres
Lubricant capacity	2.5 litres

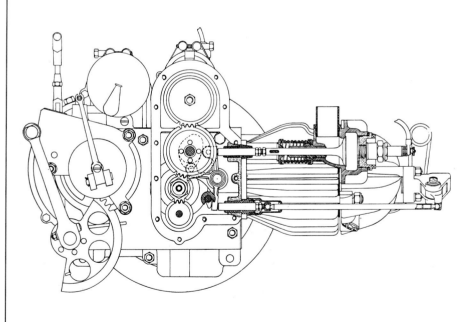

The engine of the *G.T. 17* was practically the one from the *G.T. 16* and the *Sport 15* with a few modifications (kickstart on the right). The electrical system had no battery, and so the dynamo was a special type, with a voltage regulator.

The dispatch rider's single-seater version of the *G.T. 17* without any particular special equipment. The double-barrel exhaust was a typical feature, mounted as a standard fitting. The brakes were the same as those found on civilian models, 177 mm in front and 200 behind.

The two-seater version of the *G.T. 17*, as well as having the adjustable rear springing which was actuated by shifting the RH rear footrest, had a slightly shorter fuel tank with a more pronounced upper arch, due to the fact that the rider's seat had been shifted forwards.

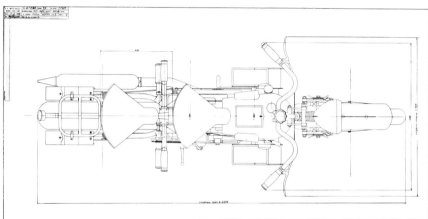

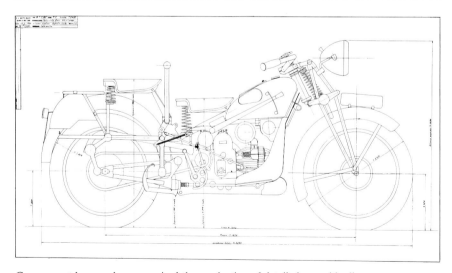

Government buyers always required the production of detailed assembly diagrams.

364

Some particular versions of the *G.T. 17*. On the facing page, a two-seater with metal panniers, and a single-seater converted into a heavy machine gun carrier (Fiat 35 or Breda 37) with a tripod support.

Some *G.T. 17*s were equipped with machine guns which could be detached, or used with the special tripod when the bike was not moving. In this case the saddle was tilted backwards and the rider-machine gunner could keep a lower profile by seating himself on the chassis.

G.T. 20

A new military motorcycle was designed in 1938. This machine obviously had what had become classic Guzzi lines by that time, but it was also the fruit of both the latest technological advances and the experience acquired with the *G.T. 17* during the African War of 1936. The *G.T. 20* had a new engine, derived from the 4-speed *S* type and mounted in a much improved frame offering lots of ground clearance for off-road work. The designers did away with the rear suspension adjuster, while the front forks had detachable sides for easy repair in case of accidents. The wheels were interchangeable, independent of the brake, and the rear wheel was fitted with an anti-slip device (for use on steep gradients) consisting of a pawl which locked on to the sprocket wheel.

In order to raise the engine, the oil tank was mounted on the uppermost part of the frame just under the petrol tank, which ended up by covering it completely.

However, the *G.T. 20* was no more than a transitional model: only 248 units were built before the introduction of the *Alce*, or Elk (the most famous military Guzzi), which went into production in 1939.

Model / year	G.T. 20 / 1938
Engine	4-stroke flat single 88 × 82 mm / 498.4 cc
Compression ratio	4.7:1
Output	13.2 hp at 4000 rpm
Cylinder head	cast iron
Cylinder	cast iron
Valve arrangement	opposed; inlet at side; exhaust overhead
Valve gear	inlet, tappet; exhaust, push rod — rocker arm
Ignition	Marelli MLA 1 type magneto
Carburettor	Dell'Orto MC 26 F
Lubrication	geared pressure pump; vane type scavenge pump
Clutch	wet multiplate type
Gearbox	hand-change 4-speed sliding gears
Transmission	primary, helical gear; final drive, chain
Frame	duplex cradle in tubes and sheet metal
Wheelbase	1440 mm
Front suspension	girder fork with friction dampers
Rear suspension	swinging arm with friction dampers
Wheels	spoked with 19 × 3 rims
Tyres	front and rear 3.50-19"
Brakes	expansion type: front manual, rear pedal
Weight	single-seater in running order 179.5 kgs
Max speed	single-seater version 90.5 km/h
Normal consumption	4 litres per 100 kms
Fuel tank capacity	13.5 litres
Lubricant capacity	2.5 litres

The *1938 G.T. 20* can be considered the immediate forerunner of the *Alce*. The designers of this vehicle raised both engine and frame in order to obtain the maximum ground clearance. Typical features were the upswept exhaust, the flywheel cover (aimed at protecting the rider's legs), and the oil tank, which was now hidden under the main tank. The gearbox was a hand-change 4-speed unit with preselector (as on the *S* type) with a gear indicator (operated by a flexible cable) fitted to the petrol tank.

Alce and Trialce

The *Alce* was very similar to the *G.T. 20* but there were some minor modifications, like the automatic valve on the oil pump in place of the manual stopcock, the legshields, the tool boxes mounted in a different place, the stronger stand, and the exhaust pipe which took a different route. The change of name was really more of a lexical matter than anything else as the "zoological era" had begun at Guzzi with the arrival of the *Condor*, the *Albatros* and the *Airone*. The *Alce*, 6,390 of which were built between 1939 and 1945 (more than 669 were equipped complete with sidecar), was the backbone of the Italian motorcycle corps during the last war and it was employed on all fronts for the delivery of dispatches and orders, reconnaissance work and by some special assault groups. It was highly appreciated by Italian servicemen and enjoyed the respect of the allied forces, who were always very glad to capture reusable models.

The *Alce* came in single and two-seater versions, as well as special models equipped to carry machine guns and other weapons. As we mentioned before, Guzzi also supplied the bike complete with an open pressed steel sidecar which had a sprung third wheel but no brake.

Model / year	Alce / 1939-1945
Engine	4-stroke flat single 88 × 82 mm / 498.4 cc
Compression ratio	4.7:1
Output	13.2 hp at 4000 rpm
Cylinder head	cast iron
Cylinder	cast iron
Valve arrangement	opposed; inlet at side; exhaust overhead
Valve gear	inlet, tappet; exhaust, push rod-rocker arm
Ignition	Marelli MLA 1 type magneto
Carburettor	Dell'Orto MC 26 F
Lubrication	geared pressure pump; vane type scavenge pump
Clutch	wet multiplate type
Gearbox	hand-change 4-speed sliding gears
Transmission	primary, helical gear; final drive, chain
Frame	duplex cradle in tubes and sheet metal
Wheelbase	1455 mm
Front suspension	girder fork with friction dampers
Rear suspension	swinging arm with friction dampers
Wheels	spoked with 19 × 3 rims
Tyres	3.50-19"
Brakes	expansion type; front manual, rear pedal
Weight	single-seater in running order 179 kgs
Max speed	single-seater version 90.5 km/h
Normal consumption	4 litres per 100 kms
Fuel tank capacity	13.5 litres
Lubricant capacity	2.5 litres

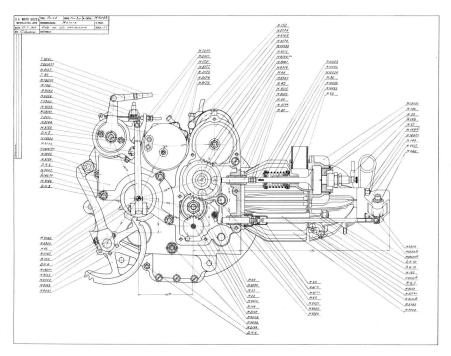

The opposed valve engine of the Guzzi *Alce*, with the 4-speed gearbox plus preselector. It was derived from the *S* type and was the last engine produced by Guzzi with this type of valve gear, for which the military authorities had an anachronistic preference.

A single-seater *Alce* with the toolbox attached to the inside of the legshield. The throttle control was still a little lever; note the hooter with the rubber bulb in addition to the electric horn, mounted on the left. In this version, the final drive ratio was 16/48, which made it possible to squeeze a touch more than 90 km/h out of the engine. The *Alce* was normally painted a dark grey-green, but some versions were camouflaged in various ways. Note the ALCE logo on the tank, instead of the usual Moto Guzzi emblem.

Left, a view of the *Alce* engine. The oil pump had an automatic on-off valve (standard equipment for the first time) instead of the manual control. Above, the *Alce V* with the two inclined overhead valves and 4-speed gearbox. Several experimental versions of this bike were built during the war years and these laid the ground for the *Superalce* which was still to come. Note the better quality finishing, with pinstriping and chromed tank, an indication that these bikes were destined for metropolitan paramilitary bodies like the *Milizia della Strada* (the Fascist name for the present day *Polizia Stradale*, or Traffic Police).

This strange motorcycle was built in 1939 over a *G.T. 20* type frame and fitted with a hybrid engine which included parts of the old *2 VT* (note the heavily finned cylinder-head assembly, typical of that engine). The aim was to obtain a more powerful, snappier bike than was normal with military machines. Handed over to some departments of the *Milizia della Strada* (as can be seen from the registration plate) it was raced in the Six Days event, held in Austria that year and interrupted by the outbreak of war.

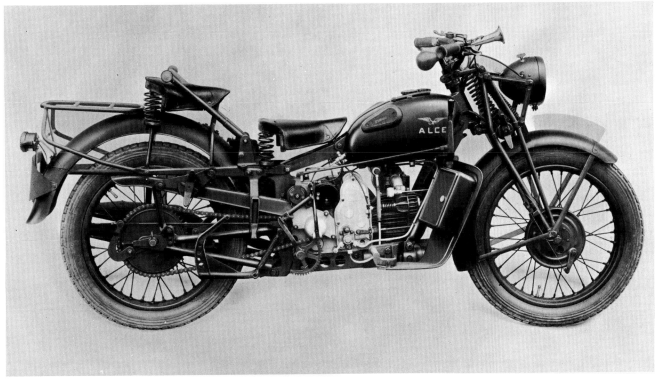

A two-seater version of the *Alce*. The final drive ratio in this case was 15/48, which allowed a top speed of 85 km/h. The *Alce* could also be fitted with a pedal-controlled gearchange, which could be mounted in the hole ahead of the oil pump. This model could climb gradients of up to 91% with a solo rider and up to 66% with a pillion passenger aboard. The pawl which prevented the bike from slipping backwards was actuated by a little lever on the LH handlebar, coaxial with the advance/retard lever.

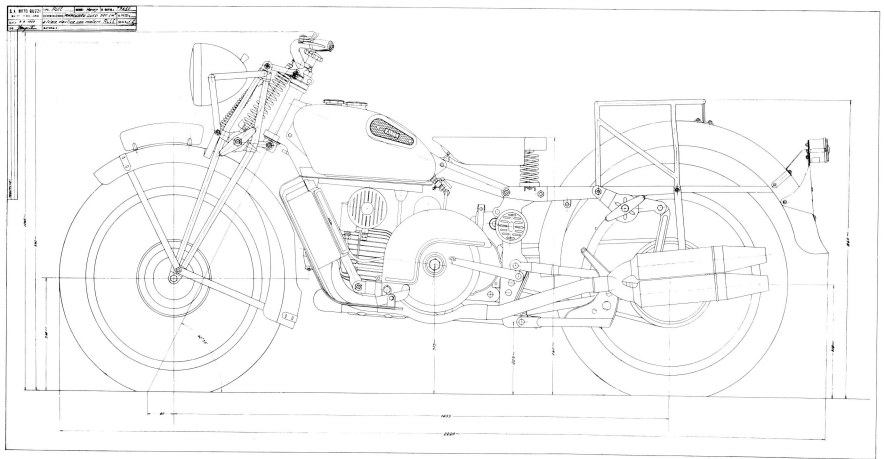

Above, an assembly diagram of the *Alce* showing the principal dimensions. As can be seen, ground clearance is about 21 cm. Assembly diagrams, very detailed and repeated for each version, were part of the specifications required by the military General Staff when orders were negotiated. They were not normally made for civilian motorcycles.

Right, another photo of the *Alce V*, a two seater version this time. The single-silencer exhaust was also chromed, while the nameplate included the MOTO GUZZI logo as well as the name of the model.

Above, two special versions of the *Alce*, with ammunition cases and heavy machine gun. Left, a *Cicogna* (Stork) on skis. Extensive use was made of light alloys in the construction of this ultra-light *Alce*-derived experimental bike, which unfortunately never got beyond the prototype stage. It was also used for various moto-mountaineering exploits. The experiments with the skis were carried out when a possible sale to the Finnish army was in the air. The priority rights over this experimental area, later the subject of Japanese research, are claimed by Moto Guzzi.

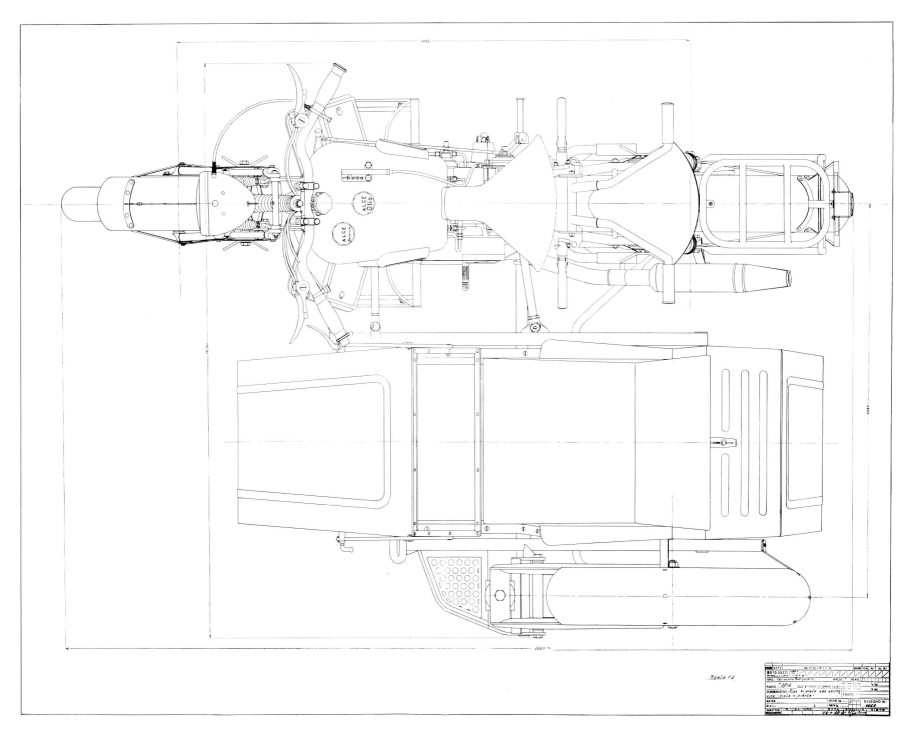

Drawing (plan view) of the *Alce* with sidecar. In this guise the vehicle had a wheelbase of 1.45 m, tracks of 1.09 m, and a dry weight of 250 kgs. In running order, fuelled and with two persons aboard, the weight went up to 416 kgs. The final drive ratio was 14/48 and the bike could do 78 km/h. It could climb gradients of up to 53%, still fully loaded. This drawing was executed at the request of the military General Staff.

Below, two views of the *Trialce* light motocarro, of which a total of 1741 units were built between 1940 and 1943. It had a wheelbase measuring 1880 mm and tracks of 1120 mm while weight was 336 kgs. Top speed was 73 km/h. The second photo shows the collapsible version made for the parachute regiment: a central catch simplified the business of breaking the vehicle down into two parts. This version also had a different type of silencer.

On the right, the *Alce* with sidecar (which was produced on the basis of the diagram on the previous page). Below, on the right hand side of the page, two shots of an experimental vehicle made in 1942-43 and also named the *Trialce*. This was a hybrid consisting of a motorcycle with a *V*-type engine, a 4-speed gearbox with a reduction gear and a triple chain drive, plus a sidecar with a third drive wheel (selectable at will but with no differential and therefore designed for off-road use only). The rapidly deteriorating military situation put an effective halt to research and the machine remained a prototype, which has been preserved.

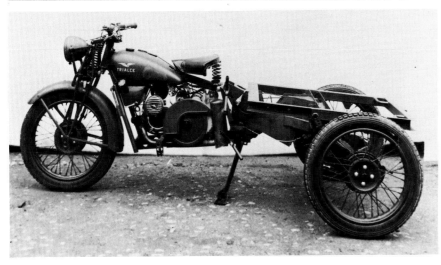

Superalce

The glorious *Alce* was replaced by the *Superalce* in 1946. This new version had an engine derived from the *V* unit with two inclined overhead valves and a 4-speed gearbox. Wartime research had already led to the construction of the *Alce V*, which remained a prototype however. The cycle part of the *Superalce* was practically identical to its predecessor: the most important variation consisted in the reintroduction of the adjustable rear suspension, which was worked by a little wheel set under the engine on the right hand side. The *Superalce*, which obviously offered better performance than the *Alce*, was also available in single and two-seater versions. The model prepared for the army had dark olive-green livery with blued accessories while the model prepared for the Carabinieri was painted light olive green and had chromed accessories. The *Superalce* was also supplied with a sidecar. It remained in production until 1957 with few modifications: a magneto with automatic advance was fitted in 1952 while a cylindrical silencer took the place of the double *Alce*-type silencers in 1955. In 1949 the price was 480,000 lire (490,000 for the two-seater version) but it was never put on direct sale to the general public.

Model / year	Superalce / 1946-1957
Engine	4-stroke flat single 88 × 82 mm / 498.4 cc
Compression ratio	5.5:1
Output	18.5 hp at 4300 rpm
Cylinder head	cast iron
Cylinder	cast iron
Valve arrangement	inclined overhead
Valve gear	push rod and rocker arm
Ignition	magneto
Carburettor	Dell'Orto MD 27 F
Lubrication	geared pressure pump; vane type scavenge pump
Clutch	wet multiplate type
Gearbox	foot-change 4-speed constant mesh
Transmission	primary, helical gear; final drive, chain
Frame	duplex cradle in tubes and sheet metal
Wheelbase	1455 mm
Front suspension	girder fork with friction dampers
Rear suspension	swinging arm with friction dampers
Wheels	spoked with 19 × 3 rims
Tyres	3.50-19"
Brakes	expansion type; front manual, rear pedal
Weight	195 kgs
Max speed	110 km/h
Normal consumption	5.4 litres per 100 kms
Fuel tank capacity	12.5 litres
Lubricant capacity	2.5 litres

The *Superalce*-type engine with two inclined overhead valves and a four-speed gearbox.

The *Superalce* two-seater built for the Army (painted olive green with no chromework) with and without sidecar.

Airone Militare

A military version of the *Airone* was introduced with little fanfare in 1940. The government regulations at that time required that the army use low compression half-litre engines which were not a problem as far as fuel was concerned. Only a very few units of this model were built, and even though it was practically identical to its civilian stablemate, it was used in a very limited fashion, largely for experimental purposes. After the war, times and requirements having changed, the *Airone* was supplied on a regular basis to various branches of the armed forces: the Carabinieri, the Air Force, the Navy etc. These machines had slightly different accessories from their civilian counterparts, like the air filter on the carburettor, the pillion, and lateral crash bars instead of the legshields. The completely military version did not come along until 1952, but it was only marginally different to the civilian *Turismo* type, as is explained in the captions on the following page. The *Airone Militare* was painted in various colours depending upon the branch of the Services to which it was destined: dark olive-green for the Carabinieri, blue for the Air Force and so on. Production ceased in 1957, and no successive model appeared in this capacity class.

Model/year	Airone / 1940
Engine	4-stroke flat single 70 × 64 mm / 246 cc
Compression ratio	6:1
Output	9.5 hp at 4800 rpm
Cylinder head	cast iron
Cylinder	cast iron
Valve arrangement	inclined overhead
Valve gear	push rod and rocker arm
Ignition	Marelli BL 1 type magneto
Carburettor	Cozette SB 22
Lubrication	geared pressure pump; vane type scavenge pump
Clutch	wet multiplate type
Gearbox	foot-change 4-speed constant mesh
Transmission	primary, helical gear; final drive, chain
Frame	tubular cradle
Wheelbase	1370 mm
Front suspension	girder fork with friction dampers
Rear suspension	swinging arm with friction dampers
Wheels	spoked with 19 × 2 1/4 rims
Tyres	3.00-19"
Brakes	expansion type: front manual, rear pedal
Weight	135 kgs
Max speed	approx. 90 km/h
Normal consumption	3.3 litres per 100 kms
Fuel tank capacity	11 litres
Lubricant capacity	2 litres

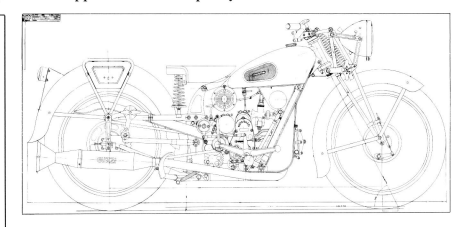

Assembly diagram of the military version of the *Airone*, first planned in 1940. Practically speaking, this was the contemporary civilian model (the early version with the *P.E.*-derived tubular frame) with the various military colour schemes.

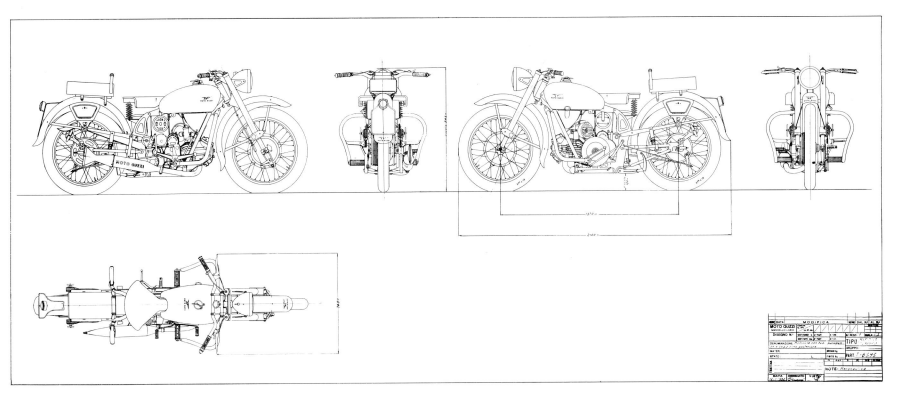

Left, the 1952 *Airone Militare*. The differences with regard to the *Turismo* model from the same period were: standard legshields, 25 mm handlebars instead of 22 mm, 3.25-19" tyres, pillion seat with footrest, Marelli MCR 4-G magneto, final drive ratio of 3.46:1 (teeth 13/45), inverted rear brake linkages, and numberplate holder. Weight was 150 kgs and top speed 92 km/h. The plate showing the five views of the version supplied to the Air Force (which had a different pillion, crash bars in place of the legshields and an air filter over the carburettor), gives an idea of the meticulous documentation demanded by the terms of military contracts.

Falcone Militare

The *Falcone* was supplied in considerable numbers to the Traffic Police, which ended up by absorbing virtually the entire production of this model. The police took both *Turismo* and *Sport* variants, which differed from the standard production machines only in terms of the paintwork (amaranth at first and then grey-green). The *Corazzieri* (Presidential Guard) were supplied with some special models, while the *Guardia di Finanza* (Customs Police) ordered a small batch of specially tuned bikes (in Guzzi red) which were slightly faster than the production version. Production continued until 1967.

Model / year	Falcone / 1953-1967
Engine	4-stroke flat single 88 × 82 mm / 498.4 cc
Compression ratio	5.5:1
Output	18.9 hp at 4300 rpm
Cylinder head	light alloy with valves in oil-bath
Cylinder	light alloy with pressed-in liners
Valve arrangement	inclined overhead
Valve gear	push rod and rocker arm
Ignition	Marelli MCR 4 E type magneto
Carburettor	Dell'Orto MD 27 F
Lubrication	geared pressure pump; vane type scavenge pump
Clutch	wet multiplate type
Gearbox	foot-change 4-speed constant mesh
Transmission	primary, helical gear; final drive, chain
Frame	duplex cradle in tubes and sheet metal
Wheelbase	1500 mm
Front suspension	teledraulic fork
Rear suspension	swinging arm with friction dampers
Wheels	spoked with 19 × 2 1/2 rims
Tyres	3.50-19"
Brakes	expansion type: front manual, rear pedal control
Weight	dry weight 170 kgs
Max speed	approx. 120 km/h
Normal consumption	4.5 litres per 100 kms
Fuel tank capacity	17.5 litres
Lubricant capacity	3 litres

Above, the version of the *Falcone Sport* supplied in various batches to the *Corazzieri* (Presidential Guard) in 1951. It had a blue finish with a white leather saddle and chromed crash bars. Below, the *Turismo* version built for the Traffic Police, with the raised headlamp and the 60 W dynamo.

Above, the special version of the *Falcone Sport* prepared for the *Corazzieri* in 1957. It had a blue finish and an electric starter (with ancillary batteries). below, the 1966 model of the *Falcone Turismo* built for the Traffic Police.

3 × 3 Mountain vehicle

Towards the end of the '50s the Ministry of Defence asked Guzzi to create a three-wheeler with some exceptional features, able to pull a load of 500 kgs over all kinds of terrain, mountainous country in particular. As well as all-wheel drive, it was to have variable track, so that it could handle the narrowest trails and be fitted with tracks (as opposed to wheels).

The original design for the *3 × 3*, the work of General Garbari, was developed by the engineers at Mandello, first by Micucci, then Soldavini and finally by Giulio Cesare Carcano, who fitted the machine with a specially prepared version of his V engine,

which he had been working on for some time. The result was a highly complex but technically very interesting machine, which was assigned to some regiments of mountain troops as a replacement for the mule teams hitherto used to transport heavy field pieces and boxes of shells. In practice however there were persistent problems as far as both dimensions and manoeuverability were concerned. Indeed, the many arduous problems related to transportation in mountainous areas have yet to be resolved. The *3 × 3* was built in two batches of about 200 units, plus a preproduction run of 20 units, from 1960 to 1963.

Model / year	3 × 3 mountain motor vehicle / 1960-1963
Engine	4-stroke 90 degree V-twin 80 × 75 mm / 754 cc
Compression ratio	6.5:1
Output	20 hp at 4000 rpm
Cylinder head	light alloy
Cylinder	light alloy, chrome bore
Valve arrangement	parallel overhead
Valve gear	push rod and rocker arm
Ignition	coil
Carburettor	Weber 26 IMB 1 or 26 IMB 4
Lubrication	geared pressure and scavenge pumps
Clutch	dry single plate type
Gearbox	6-speed and reverse constant mesh
Transmission	primary, gear driven; final drive, cardan shaft
Frame	tubes and sheet metal
Wheelbase	2030 ÷ 2050 mm / 850 ÷ 1300 mm
Front suspension	single telescopic fork
Rear suspension	swinging arms
Wheels	discs with 4 1/2 × 15 K rims
Tyres	with special tread, 6.00-15"
Brakes	expansion: front and emergency, manual; rear, pedal
Weight	1000 kgs / 570 kgs
Max speed	fully loaded 50 km/h
Normal consumption	15 litres per 100 kms
Fuel tank capacity	53 litres
Lubricant capacity	5.4 litres

The power train of the *3 × 3*, with forced air cooling. The photo shows the shielded ignition system, the petrol pump and, below, the starter motor. As can be seen, the details are rather different from the future *V7* engine, even though the general architecture is the same. Above, the gearbox and differential assembly. On the facing page, two side views of the *3 × 3* and, below, the vehicle in action.

V7 Militare and its derivatives

First created as a result of the military connection, the *V7* fits naturally into this section of the catalogue too. It has enjoyed considerable success in Italy and abroad, thanks to its robustness and that air of imposing power which befits escort and ceremonial duties so well.

The early versions with the 703 cc engine and the 4-speed gears were soon superseded by 757 and 850 cc models. The Italian *Polizia Stradale* currently uses the *850 T5* type while the model fitted with the hydraulic torque converter, the *V 1000 I Convert*, has been bought by the police forces of various countries, both in Europe and in other continents, but not Italy.

Model / year	V7 / 1967-1969
Engine	4-stroke 90 degree V-twin 80 × 70 mm / 703.7 cm³
Compression ratio	7.2:1
Output	35 hp at 5000 rpm
Cylinder head	light alloy with valve seat inserts
Cylinder	light alloy, chrome bore
Valve arrangement	inclined overhead
Valve gear	push rod and rocker arm
Ignition	coil
Carburettor	Dell'Orto VHB 29 CD, VHB 29 CS
Lubrication	geared pressure pump
Clutch	dry, dual plate type
Gearbox	foot-change 4-speed constant mesh
Transmission	primary, gear driven; final drive, shaft
Frame	tubular duplex cradle
Wheelbase	1445 mm
Front suspension	teledraulic fork
Rear suspension	swinging arm with friction dampers
Wheels	spoked with 18 × 3 rims
Tyres	studded 4.00-18"
Brakes	expansion: front manual (twin cams); rear, pedal
Weight	250 kgs
Max speed	150 km/h
Normal consumption	(Cuna stds.) 6.5 litres per 100 kms
Fuel tank capacity	20 litres
Lubricant capacity	3 litres

The military *V7* (first series) with the 703 cc engine as supplied to the *Corazzieri* (above) and the Carabinieri (below). On the facing page, a special version of the *V7* prepared for the Californian police. This is the *Ambassador* with the 757 cc engine.

The *V7* as prepared for the Turkish police: it had the 703 cc engine and a Hollandia sidecar.

The second 703 cc version supplied to the *Polizia Stradale* (olive green with black panels).

The second 703 cc version supplied to the Carabinieri (different mudguards and panniers).

The *V 850 GT* supplied to various Italian and foreign metropolitan police forces.

The police version of the *V 1000 I Convert*. This was sold to police forces in the Sudan, the city of Lausanne and various American states.

As from 1985, various public authorities were supplied with special versions of the *850 T5*, in place of the T4. This is the version prepared for the Traffic Police, ever faithful Guzzi clients. The mechanics are virtually identical to those of the civilian *Nuova 850 T5*: compression 9.5:1, power 67 hp at 7000 rpm, torque 7.5 kgm at 8500 rpm, two 30 mm Dell'Orto PHF carbs, coil ignition with two sets of contact breaker points, 5-speed gearbox, and spoked wheels with 110/90-18" tyres all round. The bike was supplied with a wide windscreen linked to the legshields by a flexible connection, lateral crash bars, rear panniers, single-saddle, as well as all the specific accessories (siren, extra lights, radio unit etc). Regulation colours were white and light blue. The rocker box covers were also painted light blue.

In 1986 the outline of the mini fairing-windscreen assembly was slightly altered but the flexible connection remained: this represented efficient protection for the rider against the inclemencies of the weather and was an indispensable fitment in any case given that the mini fairing turned with the steering. Tank capacity was 22 litres. Top speed in running order complete with all accessories was 170 km/h; this could be upped to 190 km/h without the mini fairing and the panniers.

The 1986 version of the *850 T5* prepared for the Carabinieri was very like the model prepared for the Police: apart from the dark blue finish, typical of Carabinieri vehicles, practically the only difference lay in the two flashing blue lamps on the front and rear mudguards. The model shown already had the new electronic two-tone siren as well as the usual electric horns. These new sirens were much more powerful than the traditional type and used less current into the bargain.

The *850 T5 PA NC* made its appearance in 1988; this was a new version of the big twin ordered by the various state organizations (*PA NC* is an Italian acronym which stands for New Fairing Public Administration, would you believe). The most noticeable difference here is in fact the new plastic fairing (four mouldings bolted together) firmly anchored to the frame in place of the old windscreen-legshields assembly. Other specific accessories include lateral crash bars, metal panniers at the rear, radio unit, a blue flashing light on a flexible mounting, and electronic sirens. Tyres are 110/90-18" in front and 120/90-18" behind, fuel tank capacity is 22.5 litres, weight is 260 kgs when fully equipped and top speed is 175 km/h. The version shown is the Traffic Police model, with white and blue livery; the same bike has also been delivered to the Carabinieri (painted dark blue) and all the town councils (usually in black and white).

Nuovo Falcone Militare

Around 1967 research began aimed at producing a new military motorcycle with a 500 cc single-cylinder engine. The intention was to produce a lighter alternative to the heavier *V7* by updating the existing *Falcone*. At first an attempt was made to beef up the old power unit but this was soon abandoned in favour of a completely new engine (still a flat single with classic 88 × 82 mm vital statistics) which was to be housed in a tubular duplex cradle, also completely redesigned. The *Nuovo Falcone* — as the bike was baptized — was introduced for the first time at the Milan Show of 1969 and went into production shortly afterwards.

Customers included the Traffic Police (grey-green finish), the Carabinieri (dark blue), the Army (olive green) as well as numerous municipal police authorities. It was also sold to various foreign governments. A massive, heavy machine (the electric starter with dynamotor was an optional), it was by no means as nimble and manoeuverable as the *Falcone*: it would be more exact to describe it as a descendant of the *Superalce*. A civilian version was also prepared, aimed at those customers who appreciated the robustness of traditional Guzzis. Production was discontinued in 1976.

Model / year	Nuovo Falcone / 1970-1976
Engine	4-stroke flat single 88 × 82 mm / 498.4 cc
Compression ratio	6.8:1
Output	26.2 hp at 4800 rpm
Cylinder head	light alloy with valve seat inserts
Cylinder	light alloy with pressed-in liners
Valve arrangement	inclined overhead
Valve gear	push rod and rocker arm
Ignition	coil
Carburettor	Dell'Orto VHB 29 A
Lubrication	gear pump
Clutch	wet multiplate type
Gearbox	foot-change 4-speed constant mesh
Transmission	primary, helical gear; final drive, chain
Frame	duplex cradle in tubes and sheet metal
Wheelbase	1450 mm
Front suspension	teledraulic forks
Rear suspension	swinging arm with teledraulic dampers
Wheels	spoked with 18 × 3 rims
Tyres	3.50-18"R
Brakes	expansion type: front manual (twin cams), rear pedal
Weight	214 kgs
Max speed	127 km/h
Normal consumption	(Cuna regs) 6.6 litres per 100 kms
Fuel tank capacity	18 litres
Lubricant capacity	3 litres

The military version of the *Nuovo Falcone*. Differences from the civilian model included the tank, single-saddle, double-barrel exhaust and air filter. The version above, with windscreen and grey-green finish, was prepared for the Traffic Police. On the facing page, top left, the version of the *Nuovo Falcone* made for the Yugoslavian police; top right, the dark blue *Carabinieri* model; below, the olive-green two-seater made for the Italian Army.

V 50 PA and its derivatives

The *V 50* was supplied to several public bodies, town councils and the Police right from the start, but these bikes were the same as the models on sale to the general public, with the exception of a single-seater saddle and a few accessories here and there. A particular version known as the *V 50 PA* (the initials stand for *Pubbliche Amministrazioni*) came along in 1983, fitted with special, purpose-built componentry.

Following the evolutionary trail blazed by the civilian models, 350 and 850 cc bikes were also planned in response to the requirements of the various customers. Variations in the specifications followed in due course, as had previously been the case with the *850 T5* series: and so the legshields and the windscreen mounted on the handlebars were supplanted in 1988 by a wide fairing fixed to the frame and a lower spoiler rather like the one which had been fitted to the *Lario*, while the special accessories (sirens, flashing lights, etc.) benefitted from the arrival of more efficient electronic equipment.

For the record, the motorcycles in this latest version bear the initials *PA NC* with NC standing for *Nuova Carenatura*, or "New Fairing".

Model / year	V 50 PA / 1983-...
Engine	4-stroke 90 degree V-twin 74 × 57 mm / 490 cc
Compression ratio	10.4:1
Output	44 hp at 7200 rpm
Cylinder head	light alloy with valve seat inserts
Cylinder	light alloy with Nigusil liners
Valve arrangement	parallel overhead
Valve gear	push rod and rocker arm
Ignition	electronic with magnetic pick-up and variable advance
Carburettor	Dell'Orto PBHB 28 DB, PBHB 28 BS
Lubrication	lobe pump
Clutch	dry single plate
Gearbox	foot-change 5-spead
Transmission	primary, helical gears; final drive, shaft
Frame	tubular duplex cradle
Wheelbase	1420 mm
Front suspension	teledraulic fork
Rear suspension	swinging arm with teledraulic dampers
Wheels	cast light alloy; front WM 2/1.85 × 18", rear WM 3/2.15 × 18"
Tyres	front 90/90 S-18", rear 100/90 S-18"
Brakes	discs: front, d/disc manual-pedal; rear pedal
Weight	215 kgs
Max speed	150 km/h
Normal consumption	(Cuna stds.) 4 litres per 100 kms
Fuel tank capacity	16 litres
Lubricant capacity	2.5 litres

The *V 50 PA* engine is the same as the "civilian" version. It is slightly less compressed though, which makes for greater suppleness.

The 1983 version of the *V 50 PA* with standard trim, including windscreen, legshields (provided with cutaways to expose cylinder heads to the cooling airstream), metal panniers, crash bars and a radio unit attached to the rear mudguard. The windscreen is linked to the legshields by a flexible apron.

There was also a *Pubbliche Amministrazioni* version of the *V 35*, which had the same fitments as the *V 50*. This is the 1987 version: bore and stroke were 66 × 50.6 mm, compression 10.5:1, and power was 35 hp at 8100 rpm. Other data: two 26 mm Dell'Orto VHBZ carbs, electronic ignition, spoked wheels with 90/90 S-18" tyres in front and 100/90 S-18" at the rear, twin 260 mm discs in front with a 235 mm unit behind, and a 16 litre tank. When fully kitted out the bike weighed 215 kgs; top speed was 135 km/h.

The state also took delivery of a specially prepared *V 65* version: this is the 1985 model. Bore and stroke were 80 × 64 mm for 643.4 cc; compression was 10:1 and output was 52 hp at 7000 rpm. Other fitments included two 30 mm Dell'Orto PHBH carbs, electronic ignition, a 5-speed box, teledraulic forks, hydropneumatic rear dampers, twin 260 mm discs in front and a 235 mm unit behind plus a 16 litre tank. Weight was 215 kgs and top speed 170 km/h.

The 1988 *V 65 PA NC* sported a fixed plastic fairing like the one made for the analogous version of the *850 T5*. The outline was slightly different however; note the two blue flashing lights mounted at the sides of the headlamp, and the lower spoiler surrounding the engine cradle. The saddle-mudguard assembly is also different from that of the previous model while the mechanical features are virtually identical; as is the weight. Top speed is approx. 160 km/h.

750 NTX

For some time now the Italian police, the Traffic Police in particular, have been using modern off-road vehicles, which make it possible to operate even under the most difficult conditions (as for example during the winter or in case of natural calamity). This new dimension could not fail to involve the motorcycle industry and so Moto Guzzi began supplying the forces of law and order with a special version of the *750 NTX* which is virtually identical to its civilian stablemate in everything bar a few variations in specifications.

The *750 NTX* is intended for special duties and so it has been as-signed to specially selected officers who are able to exploit the potential of this rather particular bike to the maximum.

Besides, for years now the Italian Home Office sporting club known as the "Fiamme d'Oro" (Gold Flames) has attracted the best off-road riders in the country, both cross and enduro specialists, and therefore the police are not short of people able to make the best of the bike.

And this is not all, the daily use of the *750 NTX* will almost certainly bring new talents to the fore and this will do the sport in Italy no harm at all.

Model / year	750 NTX / 1990-...
Engine	4-stroke 90 degree V-twin 80 × 74 mm / 743.9 cc
Compression ratio	9.7:1
Output	61 hp at 7100 rpm
Cylinder head	light alloy with valve seat inserts
Cylinder	light alloy with nigusil bores
Valve arrangement	parallel overhead, two per cylinder
Valve gear	push rod and rocker arm
Ignition	electronic with variable advance
Carburettor	Dell'Orto PHBH 30D, PHBH 30S
Lubrication	under pressure with lobe pump
Clutch	dry single plate type
Gearbox	foot-change 5-speed
Transmission	primary, helical gears; final drive, shaft
Frame	dismountable tubular cradle
Wheelbase	1470 mm
Front suspension	Marzocchi teledraulic fork
Rear suspension	s/arm with adjustable hydropneumatic dampers
Wheels	spoked 2.5 × 2" rims (front), 3.5 × 18" rear
Tyres	front, 3.00 - 21"; rear, 4.00 - 18"
Brakes	260 mm discs, front manual, rear pedal
Weight	180 kgs
Max speed	180 km/h
Normal consumption	6 litres per 100 kms
Fuel tank capacity	25 litres
Lubricant capacity	2.5 litres

The police specification *750 NTX* with blue finish.

MILITARY MOTORCYCLE TRUCKS, PROTOTYPES AND ARMOURED VEHICLES

Mototriciclo 32

Before and during the last World War, Guzzi also supplied the Army with various motorcycle trucks. Appreciated for their manageability and cheapness, these machines represent an important chapter in the history of the motorized divisions of the Italian armed services, perennially short of vehicles and fuel. The series began with the *Mototriciclo 32*, built between 1933 and 1936 (also sold in a civilian version), and powered by a *Sport 15* engine with a 3-speed gearbox mounted on a chassis with a shorter wheelbase than that of the other goods vehicles which we have dealt with so far, but which it otherwise resembled quite closely. During the following years Guzzi turned out *U* and *E.R.* type motocarros, which were normally used for liaison duties, or by the Fire Brigade and the *U.N.P.A.* (volunteer air-raid wardens), who were supplied with special versions. The same machine was also employed at the front by the crack Bersaglieri regiment, which was equipped with the 1940 *Trialce* type with a machine gun mounted on the body. Production of the *Trialce* amounted to 1,741 units, including a collapsible version for the parachute regiment. The army took delivery of 935 *Mototricicli 32*s, while 143 units (which could accept bulkier loads) went to the general public.

Model / year	Mototriciclo 32 / 1933-1936
Engine	4-stroke flat single 88 × 82 mm / 498.4 cc
Compression ratio	4.7:1
Output	13.2 hp at 4000 rpm
Cylinder head	cast iron
Cylinder	cast iron
Valve arrangement	opposed: inlet at side, exhaust overhead
Valve gear	inlet, tappet; exhaust, push rod — rocker arm
Ignition	Marelli LAN 1 type magneto
Carburettor	Amal
Lubrication	geared pressure pump; vane type scavenge pump
Clutch	wet, multiplate type
Gearbox	hand-change 3-speed sliding gears
Transmission	primary, helical gear; final drive, chain
Frame	tubular
Wheelbase	1815 mm / 1090 mm
Front suspension	girder fork with friction dampers
Rear suspension	leaf spring
Wheels	spoked with 19 × 3 rims
Tyres	3.50-19"
Brakes	front, manual expansion type; rear pedal-operated strap
Weight	in running order 388 kgs / 350 kgs
Max speed	approx. 53 km/h
Normal consumption	6.6 litres per 100 kms
Fuel tank capacity	18 litres
Lubricant capacity	3 litres

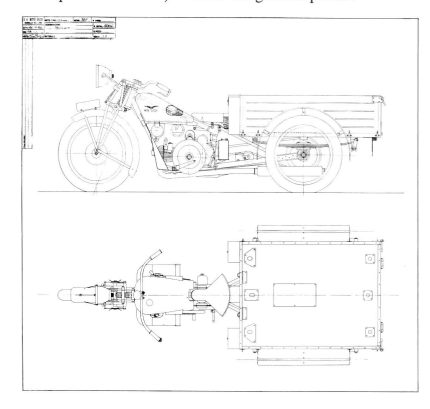

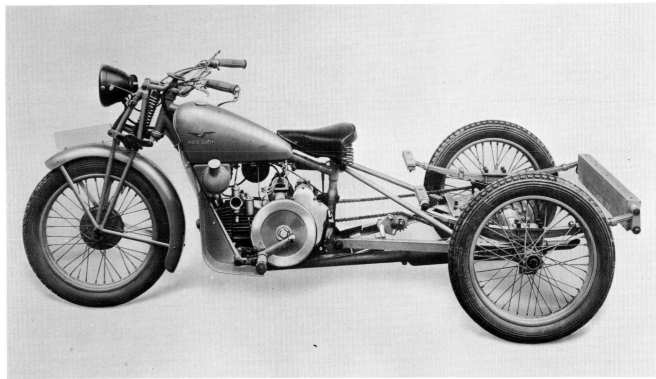

The *Mototriciclo 32*, equipped with a *Sport 15*-type engine, was built like a normal Moto Guzzi motorcycle truck: the front end, practically identical to a regular motorcycle, was attached to a tubular rear frame which bore the body with the aid of two semi-elliptic springs. Both the wheelbase and the track were made rather shorter than those of the civilian model in the interests of improved handling. Speed and carrying capacity were the same.

Experiments and prototypes

As well as those models scheduled to go into production in the normal way, all the R & D divisions of the major factories design and test a large number of engines or complete vehicles which then, for many different reasons, are not developed any further. Most times the results of all this labour are either lost or even destroyed; but at Guzzi much has been preserved and may be admired today in the works Museum at Mandello. The following pages represent a sample of the most interesting prototypes of which at least a photographic record remains. There is no shortage of decidedly heterodox machinery, like the armour plated vehicles from around 1930 — when conveyances of this type were being prepared pretty much all over Europe — and the tractor-type unit with the offset axles or the pre-war cyclecar, all of which were powered by opposed valve and ohv versions of the 500 single engine. In conclusion, it is worth remembering that the opposed valve engine was also transformed into an outboard motor; it even drove industrial electrical generators and hydraulic pumping equipment, which were also sold to the general public even though they never became on important part of Guzzi production.

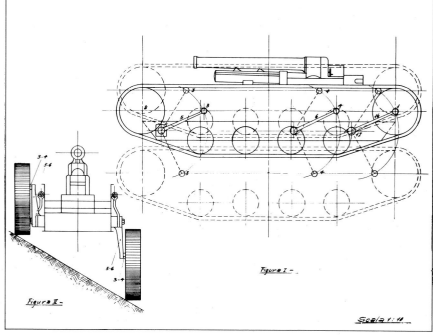

Right, an explanatory diagram showing the vehicle with the offset axles and how they functioned. The machine was designed to carry a light field gun in mountainous areas, but its possible agricultural applications were also investigated. The photo on the left is the only one left which shows this incredible machine in action.

Above, two shots of the experimental three-wheeled armoured motorcycle from around 1930, when research into such vehicles was going on in various countries.
It was equipped with tyres and the rear wheels could be fitted with tracks for increased grip

As the photographs show, the armour plating of the single-seater cockpit could be partially dismantled. Below, a vetturette chassis, with a *V*-type 500 cc engine, developed shortly before the war. The designers swithered between military or civilian applications, but the project was not taken any further.

Apart from the Cozette blower, in 1937-38
experiments were carried out on the 250
engine which was fitted with an original
piston supercharger with valve regulated
induction, the valve being operated in its
turn by a push-rod and rocker arm. In the
end, as we have seen, Guzzi opted for an
assembly including a vane-type supercharger
and an expansion chamber; a simpler
arrangement mechanically speaking, which
guaranteed a steady flow of fuel mixture.
Note the positioning of the contact breaker,
a clue to the clearly experimental nature of
this engine.

Before serious work began on the blown 3-
cylinder 500, an attempt was made in 1939
to beef up the engine of the wide-angled V-
twin. The conversion, the work of Carcano,
was later sidelined to make way for a
completely new propulsion unit. The photo
shows the supercharger attachment points
with the blower drive cover and the clutch
exposed.

400

During the last war various utility vehicles were planned, with a view to preparing for probable demand once peace returned. Among others, there was this handsome 125 cc, 4-stroke light motorcycle with push-rod and rocker arm timing gear and pedal-operated 3-speed gearbox, which was very much an example of mainstream Guzzi styling even though the frame had been simplified somewhat. However production costs would still have been pretty high and so they opted for the simpler and "revolutionary" 65 in the end. Some features, like the rear suspension, were fitted to later models. The wheels were shod with 2.50-19" and 3.00-19" tyres at front and rear respectively.

This 2-stroke, 75 cc engine dates from the Fifties and was originally intended for a low-price vehicle, perhaps even to replace the glorious "Guzzino". Of fairly orthodox construction, it had gears for the primary drive and a triple series of ports. Note the Y-shaped finning of the head, as well as the cable leading to the hand-change gearbox, a typical feature on utility bikes. (400)

In 1953 Guzzi erupted onto the 350 competition scene and promptly walked off with the world title. It seemed logical therefore to exploit this success to the full with the launch of a bike in this capacity class. The research led to this *GT 350* from 1955, which had a blend of new features (*Zigolo*-type forks, faired headlight, racing style bump-stop saddle, faired engine) and traditional styling elements like the tank, the rear suspension with the springs under the engine, and the head. The light alloy wheels had 3.00-19" tyres at front and back and the bike used a 27 mm carburettor. However the projected market share was not considered sufficient and the project was shelved.

This first engine for the *GT 350* dates from 1953. The *Falcone*-type head (which had the casing for the push-rods partially embodied) was fitted over a different, more compact crankcase with the speedo drive mounted on the back. The engine had a coil ignition system and a 4-speed gearbox while the fuel supply was handled by a Grand Prix-type 38 mm Dell'Orto, presumably in an attempt to test the engine's inherent qualities and powers of resistance to the limits. Note also the upper frame lug, which was later eliminated.

This partially faired light motorcycle prototype, which was going to be called the *Zigolo* too, also dates from 1955. The engine was a 2-stroke 125 cc unit with a 3-speed gearbox and 2 1/2-17" tyres. It bore a singular stylistic resemblance to the *254* which was to come along twenty years later, right down to the filler cap, (hidden by a flap) and the positioning of the speedometer. However the body panelling was made of metal rather than plastic.

Military orders have always been an important item of Guzzi production: a fact borne out by the variety of prototypes churned out during the Fifities, which included an *Airone 250* with parallelogram forks and a reduction gear in the hub of the rear wheel, and a *Lodola*. The most interesting new bike from that period was however this *350* from 1957 with a push-rod engine, dry sump lubrication with the tank under the saddle, coil ignition and a 4-speed gearbox. The frame was a tubular duplex cradle while the steel wheels were shod with 3.25-18" tyres and carried lateral drum brakes. It is clearly a *Lodola*-derived unit though, as can be seen by the frontally-mounted dynamo.

This light motorcycle from 1958 (the period which witnessed the first signs of the impending crisis within the motorcycle industry), illustrates the search for maximum simplicity and economy of construction: a single spar frame inspired by that of the *Cardellino*, swinging link forks, no fairings, 110 cc 2-stroke engine and 3-speed gearbox. The tyres were 2.50-16". The bike, rather a miserable creature to be honest, was shelved.

The 1959 *Gallinella* (Hen) was not intended merely to be a companion for the *Galletto* (Cockerel). The bike was intended to be a development of one of Guzzi's pet ideas, the scooter with large wheels and a smaller (and hence cheaper) engine. The engine was taken from the *Zigolo 110*, and the front fork from the "undressed" light motorcycle dealt with earlier; the tyres were 2.50-16". A second version with more extensive bodywork both at front and back was also planned.

The *Ghez* — a Lombard dialect word for the green lizard — emerged from the R & D division to be introduced to the public at the Milan Show in the November of 1969. It was an extraordinary ultra-lightweight motorcycle with a 50 cc 2-stroke twin-cylinder engine and 5-speed gears, but the legal requirement that the bike carry a number plate (its performance took it well over the limits set for mopeds) would have made it uncompetitive price-wise and so the project was abandoned. It was a very interesting piece of engineering just the same: the frame is a raised duplex cradle (derived from the frame of the *Dingo*), which was a very fashionable component on high performance bikes in those days.

The 2-stroke twin formula was also tried out on larger engines, 100 and 125 cc, with results which were very interesting from both a stylistic and technical point of view, but these projects were never brought to a conclusion. The bike on the left, nicknamed the *Bidingo* by the factory staff, has the front fork from the 5-speed *Stornello*. It is a typical research mock-up: the tank and the toolbox are made of wood. Two 18 mm carburettors have been fitted and the tyres are 2.50-17" in front and 3.00-17" behind.

The first experiments with a medium capacity *V* engine, which was later to spawn the *V 50*, *V 35* and all their descendants, dates from 1972. For the road tests the new propulsion units (this is the 350 version) were mounted in a *V7 Sport*, a large flange having been fitted to adapt them to the gearbox. As can be seen, these engines had a vertically split crankcase. The carburettors fitted were 22 mm units while the definitive version received 24 mm instruments.

From the most recent body of research, this is without a doubt one of the most sensational pieces: the arrow engine designed in 1981-82 by Lino Tonti, with a total displacement of 992 cc. The cylinders are set at 65 degress and the valve gear is operated by push-rods and rocker arms with two camshafts in the engine block, alongside the central cylinder. There are also three 30 mm Dell'Ortos. In the research division's records this engine is identified by the code *W 103*. Unfortunately it was decided not to take the project any further.

CHRONOLOGY OF PRODUCTION

Dates and frame numbers

Moto Guzzi engines are made up of two principal families: the quarter and half litre units. The major structural similarities linking the various types of engine from these two basic categories (or perhaps the fact that Carlo Guzzi considered that every bike he built represented the logical development of its predecessor) persuaded the marque to stamp its motorcycle frames and engines with progressive serial numbers composed of only two double numerical sequences, which account for all the 250 and 500 cc models from the origins to 1954. A third double sequence was used for three-wheeled goods vehicles from the same period. The fact that a single numerical progression can cover a variety of different models makes it obviously impossible to effect a year by year identification of the fundamental data which usually enable us to classify the type and the date of manufacture of the various models (according to the criteria usually adopted by car manufacturers). Nor are the initials (used to identify the engine type) preceding the number stamped on the timing cover of any use for this purpose: even the engine numbers are all mixed up. Ascertaining the date of manufacture of a certain model is thus possible only by looking through the factory records. For reasons of convenience and space (there are tens of thousands of numbers in question) we cannot print a complete list. Collectors must therefore apply to the factory when they wish to have their vehicles definitively identified and dated. Nevertheless we thought it would be useful to give at least the most important of these numerical sequences, indicating the models which fall within them and the years within which they were produced.

From 1954 onwards each model has its own sequence of serial numbers. However, since these are formed by a combination of letters and numbers, exact dating is not possible in this case either, and so interested parties are invited once more to apply to the makers.

500 cc frames numbered at random

Normale (1921-1924)
Sport (1923-1928)
C 2V (1923-1930)
4V SS (1928-1933)
G.T. and *G.T. militaire* (1928-1930)
Sport 14 (1929-1930)
Sport 15 (1931-1939)
2 VT (1931-1934)
G.T. 16 (1931-1934)
G.T. 2 VT (1931-1934)
G.T. 17 (1932-1939)
S (1934-1940)
V (1934-1940)
G.T.S. (1934-1940)
G.T.V. (1934-1946)
W (1935-1939)

G.T.W. (1935-1946)
G.T.C. (1937-1939)
Condor (1938-1940)
G.T. 20 (1938)
Alce (1940-1945)
Alce V Milizia della Strada (1940)
Superalce (1946-1954)
Dondolino (1946-1947)
G.T.V. teledraulic (1947-1948)
G.T.W. teledraulic (1947-1948)
Astore (1949-1953)
Falcone (1950-1953)
Falcone Turismo (1953-1954)
Falcone Sport (1953-1954)

All the abovementioned types fall within the progression running from frame 51 (1921) to frame 33864 (1954).

250 cc frames numbered at random

P 175 (1932)
P 250 (1934-1937)
P.E. sprung frame (1934-1939)
P.L. pressed steel frame (1937-1939)
P.L.S. sport version (1937-1939)
P.E.S. sprung sport type (1938-1939)
Albatros (1938-1947)
Ardetta (1939-1940)
Airone tubular frame (1939-1940)
Airone pressed steel frame (1940-1946)
Airone teledraulic (1949-1951)
Airone Sport teledraulic (1949-1951)
Airone Turismo (1952-1954)
Airone Sport (1952-1954)

All the abovementioned types, including the 175

cc P 175, fall within the progression running from frame 1 to frame 29509.

Numbered frames with single progressions*

Motoleggera 65 (1946-1954)
from frame 1 to frame 53021 (1946-1949)
from frame 18110001 to frame 21120035

Galletto 160 cc (1950-1952)
from frame 15110001 to frame 15301000

Galletto 175 cc (1952-1953)
from frame 29110001 to frame 29300500

Galletto 192 cc (1954-1966)
from frame G 00 AA to frame G 99 HZ

Zigolo 98 cc (1953-1957)
from frame 23110001 to frame 23201300

Zigolo 98 cc Turismo and *Lusso (1954-1957)*
from frame 26110001 to frame 27120000
then from frame Z 00 AA to frame Z 99 BZ

Zigolo 98 cc second series (1958-1959)
from frame V 00 AA to frame V 74 QQ

Zigolo 110 cc (1960-1966)
from frame I 00 AA to frame I 99 ZZ

Airone Sport and *Turismo (1954-1958)*
from frame M 00 AA to frame M 50 DS

Falcone Turismo (1954-1968)
from frame R 00 AA to frame F 72 CP

Falcone Sport (1954-1964)
from frame FS 00 AA to frame FS 88 AB

Superalce (1954-1958)
from frame S 00 AA to frame S 79 AR

Cardellino 65 cc (1954-1956)
from frame A 00 AA to frame A 49 GZ

Cardellino 73 cc (1957-1961)
from frame B 00 AA to frame B 24 FF

Cardellino 83 cc (1962-1965)
from frame C 00 AA to frame C 99 CF

Lodola Turismo and *Sport (1956-1959)*
from frame L 00 AA to frame L 99 FL

Lodola 235 cc (1959-1962)
from frame F 00 AA to frame R 99 HV

Lodola 235 cc Regolarità (1959-1963)
from frame K 22 AO to frame K 12 BO

Stornello 125 cc (1960-1968)
from frame N 00 AA to frame N 49 NA

Stornello 125 cc Sport (1961-1968)
from frame T 00 AA to frame T 99 GZ

Stornello 160 cc 4-speed (1968-1970)
from frame SA 00 AA to frame SA 35 AS

Stornello 125 cc 5-speed (1971-1974)
from frame ST 00 AA to frame ST 55 RG

Stornello 160 cc 5-speed (1971-1974)
from frame SM 00 AA to frame SM 94 CN

Stornello Scrambler 125 cc (1971-1974)
from frame SS 11111 to frame SS 11989

Dingo Turismo and *Sport* and *Dingo 3M 49 cc*
from frame CM 00 AA to frame CM 85 ALI

Dingo Super 49 cc (1966-1974)
from frame CMS 00 AA to frame CMS 95 IM

Dingo Cross and *GT 49 cc (1966-1974)*
from frame CMC 00 AA to frame CMC 69 NEI

Dingo 49 M (1969-1973)
from frame IM 00 AA to frame IM 80 TV

Dingo MM 50 cc (1975-1976)
from frame DA 11111 to frame DA 18225

Dingo 3V 50 cc (1975-1976)
from frame DB 11111 to frame DB 20825

Trotter and *Trotter Super 40 (1966-1970)*
from frame CE 00 AA to frame CE 99 AGZ

Trotter Special M 50 cc (1971-1973)
from frame TA 00 AA to frame TA 34 GA

Trotter Special V 50 cc (1971-1973)
from frame TB 00 AA to frame TB 45 GA

Trotter Mark M 50 cc (1971-1973)
from frame TC 00 AA to frame TC 14 CG

Trotter Mark V 50 cc (1971-1973)
from frame TD 00 AA to frame TD 60 CG

Falcone N 500 cc (1969-1976)
from frame NF 00 AA to frame NF 99 GH

Falcone C 500 cc (1971-1974)
from frame CF 11111 to frame CF 13985

V7 700 cc (1967-1976)
from frame VS 00 AA to frame VS 99SS

V7 750 Special (1969-1971)
from frame VM 00 AA to frame VM 25EP

V 750 Sport (1972-1974)
from frame VK 11111 to frame VK 11990

750 S (1974-1975)
from frame VK 1 11111 to frame VK 112170

750 S3 (1975-1976)
from frame YK2 15003 to frame VK2 15930

GT 850 cc (1972-1974)
from frame VP 00 AA to frame Vp 58WH

GT 850 cc California (1972-1974)
from frame VP 11111 to frame VP 16230

850 T (1974-1975)
from frame VC 11111 to frame VC 13793

850 T3 (1975-1985)
from frame VD 11111 to frame VD 26537

850 T3 California (1975-1980)
from frame VD 11478 to frame VD 22640

850 T4 (1980-1984)
from frame VD 21345 to frame VD 26537

850 Le Mans (1976-1978)
from frame VE 11111 to frame VE 13040

850 Le Mans II (1978-1980)
from frame VE 13041 to frame VE 24086

850 Le Mans III (1981-1984)
from frame VF 11111 to frame VF 20700

V 1000 I Convert (1975-1984)
from frame VG 11111 to frame VG 25693

1000 SP (1978-1983)
from frame VG 18781** to frame VG 25693

V 1000 G5 (1978-1985)
from frame VG 18744** to frame VG 25693

1000 California II (1981-1987)
from frame VT 11111 to frame VT 20479

250 TS Drum brake (1974-1975)
from frame AB 11111 to frame AB 15760

250 TS Disc brake (1976-1982)
from frame AB1 15761 to frame AB1 22957

350 GTS Drum brake (1974-1975)
from frame BD 11111 to frame BD 12112

350 GTS Disc brake (1974-1979)
from frame BM 11111 to frame BM 13377

400 GTS Disc brake (1974-1979)
from frame BL 11111 to frame BL 13644

Cross 50 (1975-1976)
from frame GR 11111 to frame GR 16141

Cross 50 cc (1976-1982)
from frame GL 11111 to frame GL 16250

Nibbio 50 cc (1975-1976)
from frame GS 11111 to frame GS 16123

Chiù 50 cc (1974-1976)
from frame CH 11111 to frame CH 20314

Magnum 50 cc (1976-1979)
from frame GH 11111 to frame GH 19075

Tuttoterreno 125 cc (1974-1981)
from frame MC 13363 to frame MC 17057

125 cc Turismo (1974-1981)
from frame MD 11111 to frame MD 14896

254 - 250 cc (1977-1981)
from frame BH 11111 to frame BH 12181

V 35 - 350 cc (1977-1979)
from frame PA 11111 to frame PA 17046

V 35 II - 350 cc (1980-...)
from frame PD 11111 to frame ...

V 35 C - 350 cc (1982-1986)
from frame PL 11111 to frame PL 21090

V 35 Imola - 350 cc (1979-1984)
from frame PC 11111 to frame PC 19261

V 50 - 500 cc (1977-1980)
from frame PB 11111 to frame PB 18454

V 50 III - 500 cc (1980-...)
from frame PF 11111 to frame ...

V 50 C - 500 cc (1982-1986)
from frame PM 11111 to frame PM 12530

V 50 Monza - 500 cc (1980-1984)
from frame PE 11111 to frame PE 15265

125 2C 4T - 125 cc (1979-1981)
from frame BV 11111 to frame BV 12293

V 65 - 650 cc (1981-...)
from frame PG 11111** to frame ...

V 65 SP - 650 cc (1981-...)
from frame PG 11111** to frame ...

125 Custom - 125 cc (1985-1987)
from frame RC 11111 to frame RC 11614

125 TT - 125 cc (1985-1988)
from frame RE 11111 to frame RE 12063

V 35 TT - 350 cc (1984-1986)
from frame PU 11111 to frame PU 12866

V 35 Imola II - 350 cc (1984-...)
from frame PS 11111 to frame ...

V 35 III - 350 cc (1985-...)
from frame PY 11111 to frame ...

V 35 Florida - 350 cc (1985-...)
from frame PK 11111 to frame ...

V 35 NTX - 350 cc (1986-...)
from frame LA 11111 to frame ...

V 35 GT - 350 cc (1988-...)
from frame PY 21111 to frame ...

V 65 Custom - 650 cc (1983-1986)
from frame PN 11111 to frame PN 15390

V 65 Lario - 650 cc (1983-1989)
from frame PT 11111 to frame PT 15032

V 65 TT - 650 cc (1984-1986)
from frame PV 11111 to frame PV 12800

V 65 Florida - 650 cc (1985-...)
from frame PW 11111 to frame ...

V 65 NTX - 650 cc (1986-...)
from frame LB 11111 to frame ...

V 65 GT - 650 cc (1988-...)
from frame PG 11111 to frame ...

V 75 (1985-1986)
from frame PX 11111 to frame PX 12000

750 NTX (1988-...)
from frame LX 11111 to frame ...

750 Targa (1990-...)
from frame LT 11111 to frame ...

850 T5 Front wheel 16", back wheel 16"
(1983-1984)
from frame VR 11111 to frame VR 13115

850 T5 Front wheel 16", back wheel 18"
(1984-1987)
from frame VR 14001 to frame VR 14400

850 T5 P.A. (1986-...)
from frame VR 30001 to frame ...

Le Mans 1000 (1984-...)
from frame VV 11111 to frame ...

1000 SP II (1984-1987)
from frame VH 11111 to frame VH 12229

1000 California III (1987-...)
from frame VW 11111 to frame ...

1000 SP III (1988-...)
from frame VN 11111 to frame ...

1000 California III I.E. (1990-...)
from frame VY 11111 to frame ...

1000 S (1990-...)
from frame VV 50001 to frame ...

* Between 1954 and 1972 a new set of criteria was used to identify frames: in place of the numerical progression using Arabic numerals the makers began using a code formed by one or two letters, two numbers and two letters. The first letter or group of letters identifies the vehicle type and, especially at the beginning of the series, this was often an abbreviation for the commercial name of the motorcycle. For example, L = Lodola, FS = Falcone Sport. The combination of the numbers and the letters of the second and third group form the serial number of the unit in question.

** Models bearing a serial number with the same prefix differ only as far as trim is concerned and belong to the same homologation batch.

Any inconsistencies between the dates shown in this list and those quoted in the text are due to the time lapses between the manufacture and the actual launch of the various models.